How to Defend a Bridge Hand

♣   ♢   ♡   ♠   ♣   ♢   ♡   ♠

by William S. Root

Introduction by Alan Truscott

Richard Pavlicek, Technical Consultant

Phillip Alder, Editor

CROWN PUBLISHERS, INC., New York

OTHER BOOKS BY WILLIAM S. ROOT

MODERN BRIDGE CONVENTIONS
(coauthored with Richard Pavlicek)
COMMONSENSE BIDDING
HOW TO PLAY A BRIDGE HAND

Published by Crown Publishers, Inc., 201 East 50th Street, New York, NY 10022. Member of the Crown Publishing Group.

Random House, Inc. New York, Toronto, London, Sydney, Auckland

CROWN is a trademark of Crown Publishers, Inc.

Type-set by Phillip Alder

Manufactured in the United States of America

Library of Congress Cataloging-in-Publication Data
Root, William S.
    How to Play a Bridge Hand / by William S. Root : introduction by
Alan Truscott ; Phillip Alder, editor.
        p.   cm.
        1. Contract bridge—Defensive play.   I. Title.
GV1282.42.R66   1994
795.41'53—dc20   93-39169
                                                                     CIP

ISBN: 0-517-59160-X

10 9 8 7 6 5 4 3 2 1

First Edition

Contents

Introduction by Alan Truscott

Introduction

♣ ♢ ♡ ♠ ♣ ♢ ♡ ♠

It is certain that Bill Root has taught bridge to more people than anyone else in the world. The number may well be in six figures: In more than three decades of teaching large groups in the New York area and in Florida, he has helped them take the vital step from bad player to good player. And they keep coming back for more.

This has only been possible because he is an expert player of the highest class. He has won twelve of the major national team titles that are coveted by every tournament enthusiast.

He has distilled all this knowledge and experience, as a teacher and player, into a series of excellent books, of which this is the latest. It deals with the crucial subject of defense, at which many who can bid sensibly and play the dummy adequately fail abysmally.

This is, as far as I know, the first book in the 68-year history of the game to deal comprehensively in an organized way with every aspect of this vital area. There is a wealth of illustrative deals and quizzes, and as one would expect from a teacher, the deals are on exactly the right level, between beginning simplicity and advanced complexity. The reader is taken from leads, opening and subsequent, through second- and third-hand play to a variety of trump maneuvers, discarding problems and deceptions, ending with a wide variety of signals, both traditional and modern.

This book is a major contribution to the literature of the game.

Alan Truscott

1

Opening Leads

The opening lead is the most challenging defensive play because it is the only one that is made before the dummy is exposed. The clues to guide the opening leader come from *the nature of his hand* (some suit combinations are more attractive to lead from than others) and *the bidding*. What would you lead from the following hand?

#1	West	West	North	East	South
	♠ Q				1♠
	♡ Q 7 3 2	Pass	2♠	Pass	4♠
	◇ Q 8 6 5	Pass	Pass	Pass	
	♣ Q 7 4 3				

No lead is attractive, but you must lead something. Although one lead may work out better that the others, there are no clues in this case and even an expert would be baffled. The point I am making is that the choice of an opening lead is sometimes a pure guess.

The following pages show how to use whatever information is available to help you make an intelligent decision. First you must decide *which suit* to lead. Then you must decide *which card* of the chosen suit to lead. We will begin with "Which Card to Lead." This is the easier part because there is a "standard formula" to guide you.[1] Since there is a sizable difference in the strategy for choosing which suit to lead between notrump contracts and trump contracts, they will be treated separately in the following pages: "Which Suit to Lead Versus Notrump Contracts," and then "Which Suit to Lead Versus Trump Contracts."

Which Card to Lead

The bidding sometimes indicates that the best opening lead is from a suit combination that normally would not be chosen. Depending on the auction, it might be right to lead from distasteful holdings such as A Q x, K J x, K x, etc. The following recommendations assume that you have made up your mind to lead the given suit; the only concern here is *which card* should you lead. If the choice depends on whether the contract is played in notrump or a suit, two answers are given.

A Doubleton

From a two-card suit (A K, A Q, K 10, Q 9, J 10, J 3, 8 5, etc.), *lead the higher card*.

Three-Card Sequences

When the suit you intend to lead has a three-card sequence headed by the king, queen, jack or ten (K Q J, Q J 10, J 10 9, 10 9 8), *lead the top of the sequence* regardless of the length of the suit. It is also best to lead top of the sequence from K Q 10, Q J 9, J 10 8 or 10 9 7, regardless of the length of the suit. In other words, if you are missing the third card

---

1. The "standard formula" simply means the methods used by a vast majority of players, but there are a few debatable points that will be revealed in this chapter. Modern conventions for "Which Card to Lead," used by partnership agreement in advance and practiced mostly in expert circles, are described in *Conventional Leads and Signals* on page 382.

of the sequence but have the fourth, treat these holdings as if they are three-card sequences. This applies in both notrump and suit contracts, and these leads are usually good choices. (Note that it is occasionally right to lead fourth-highest from a three-card sequence if dummy or declarer is known to have four cards in the suit. See #22, page 11.)

Two-Card Sequences

If you have a three-card suit, lead the top of a two-card sequence headed by the king, queen, jack or ten against both notrump and suit contracts: *Lead the king* from K Q x, *the queen* from Q J x, *the jack* from J 10 x and *the ten* from 10 9 x.

With four or more cards in the suit, *lead fourth-highest against notrump contracts: Lead the five* from K Q 9 5 2, Q J 7 5 4, J 10 7 5 4 or 10 9 6 5. Exception: *If partner has bid the suit, lead the top of any two-card sequence*, regardless of length.

If leading from a two-card sequence in a four-card or longer suit versus a trump contract, the choice to lead the top card of the sequence or fourth-highest is debatable. Most authorities would recommend you *lead the king* from K Q x x, but *lead fourth-highest* from J 10 x x or 10 9 x x. Whether to lead the queen or fourth-highest from Q J x x is the toughest decision and you will have to use your judgment. However, if you decide to lead from Q J x x in a suit that has been bid by the dummy, *lead fourth-highest*.

Ace-King Combinations Versus Notrump Contracts

If your opponents reach a partscore or game in notrump, the right lead might be the king, fourth-highest or, in rare cases, the ace, depending on the length of the suit and whether or not the suit contains other honors. *The king* is routine from A K Q x, A K J x, A K 10 x or A K x, but *lead fourth-highest* from A K x x x, especially if you have no reentry cards.

The choice from some holdings is debatable: Most authorities recommend leading *fourth-highest* from A K x x, but this is a close call and the king could work out better; so listen to the bidding and use your judgment. *Leading the king* from A K Q x x, A K J x x will work out best most of the time, but again it is a close call: *fourth-highest* would be the winning choice if partner had J x or Q x and declarer has 10 x x x; or in cases like the following deal.

#2

```
                            ♠ 6 2
                            ♡ K 5 4
                            ◊ Q J 9 7 3
                            ♣ K Q 10
        ♠ A K J 5 3                             ♠ 9 4
        ♡ 8 7                                   ♡ J 10 6 3 2
        ◊ 4 2                                   ◊ A 8 5
        ♣ 9 6 5 3                               ♣ 8 7 4
                            ♠ Q 10 8 7
                            ♡ A Q 9
                            ◊ K 10 6
                            ♣ A J 2
```

West	North	East	South
			1NT
Pass	3NT	All Pass	

Note that *the five-of-spades lead*—fourth-highest—will beat the contract: East will return a spade when he gets the lead with the ace of diamonds and you win four spade tricks. If you led the king of spades, only three spade tricks are possible, so the contract is unbeatable.

The ace is the normal lead versus a notrump contract when you hold four honor cards, or three top honor cards and a six-card or longer suit (A K Q 10, A K J 10 x, A K J x x x or conceivably from A Q J 10 x if you have a side entry). In the old days, the lead of the ace versus a notrump contract commanded partner to play his highest card in the suit. An improvement on this convention (which is not construed as standard) is the ace lead commands partner to play his highest card if it is the king, queen or jack. If not, he should play his *highest card from any even number of cards*, or *his lowest card from any odd number of cards*. Illustration #12 on page 246 show how this "count signal" can help the opening leader.

Ace-King Combinations Versus Suit Contracts

The king is the normal lead from any ace-king combination, except *lead the ace from a doubleton ace-king*.[2]

Inside Sequences

If you are defending against a notrump contract and decide to lead a suit that contains an "inside sequence" (also called an "interior sequence"), the standard procedure is to lead the *top card of the sequence if it is an honor card,* regardless of the length of the suit. For example, lead the *queen* from A Q J x x; the *jack* from A J 10 9 8 or K J 10 x; the *ten* from A 10 9, K 10 9 x or Q 10 9 x x.[3] If your sequence is not headed by an honor card, lead *fourth-highest*: Lead the *seven* from K 9 8 7 6.

Also, if you suspect that the dummy or declarer has four cards in the suit, it is probably better to lead fourth-highest from a *two-card* inside sequence (from K 10 9 4 or Q 10 9 4 2, lead the four; but from K 10 9 8 or Q 10 9 8 4, lead the ten); it is not always an easy choice. Suppose this is the layout:

#3

	North	
	J 4 2	
West		East
K 10 9 3		Q 6 5
	South	
	A 8 7	

Note that if West leads the three, declarer can win two tricks by playing low from dummy: If East plays low, he can win with the eight; if East plays the queen, he can win with the ace and eventually win a second trick with the jack.

Assuming West leads the ten: If declarer plays low from dummy, East plays low. If declarer plays the jack from dummy, East covers with the queen. In either case, declarer is limited to one trick.

Now suppose the cards are changed so that dummy has J 2 and declarer A 8 7 4: If West leads the ten, declarer can win two tricks; but if he leads fourth-highest, declarer can win only one trick.

---

2. A modern idea that is gaining popularity with most experienced players is to lead the *ace* from ace-king combinations versus trump contracts, so partner can distinguish whether the lead is from ace-king or king-queen. This procedure has merit and is explained in *Conventional Leads and Signals, page 382. Until then, the king will be considered the normal card to lead from ace-king.*

3. A popular variation is to lead the *second-highest card* of the sequence. In other words, lead the *nine* from K 10 9 x or Q 10 9 8. See "Zero or Two Higher" in *Conventional Leads and Signals*, page 385.

If you are defending a trump contract, you should lead the same card as against a notrump contract except *do not underlead an ace against a trump contract*. If you decide to lead from A Q J x x, A J 10 9 or A 10 9 (rarely good choices), *lead the ace*.

With Suits Headed by One or More Honor Cards Not in Sequence

With a four-card or longer suit headed by the king, queen, jack or ten, *lead fourth-highest*.
Lead the four from K J 6 4 3 2, Q 9 8 4 2, J 7 5 4, 10 8 5 4. When the suit is headed by the ace (such as A Q 10 4 3) *lead fourth-highest* versus a notrump contract, but *lead the ace* versus a trump contract. Please note that this recommendation applies to non-trump suits: It is sometimes okay to underlead the ace of trumps (i.e., *lead the two* from A 7 2).

From a three-card holding headed by the king, queen, jack or ten, lead the *lowest*: Lead the *three* from K 6 3, Q 9 3, J 6 3 or 10 7 3. If the three-card suit is headed by the ace (as A 8 2), lead the *lowest* versus notrump, but lead the *ace* versus a trump contract.

By now you should realize that it is *my recommendation that you do not underlead aces versus trump contracts*. It is true that underleading an ace against a trump contract may gain a trick, or fool the declarer and cause him to misguess how to play the hand; but it is more likely to cost a trick, or fool your partner into making the wrong defensive play.

Leading from a three-card holding with two honor cards not in sequence (such as A Q 2, A J 2, K J 2) is usually frowned upon, but there are auctions where it is the right choice. There is no standard formula for which card to lead versus a notrump contract; but it is usually better to lead an *honor card* so you do not block the suit. If it is a trump contract, lead the *ace* from A Q 2 or A J 3, but lead the *two* from K J 2. Here is one example where leading the jack from A J 3 versus a notrump contract pays off.

#4

```
                        ♠ A 10 9 8
                        ♡ J 4
                        ◇ 7 6
                        ♣ A Q J 10 2
        ♠ K J 5                              ♠ 7 4 3
        ♡ 9 8 5 2                            ♡ A 6 3
        ◇ A J 3                              ◇ Q 9 8 5 2
        ♣ 7 6 4                              ♣ 9 5
                        ♠ Q 6 2
                        ♡ K Q 10 7
                        ◇ K 10 4
                        ♣ K 8 3
```

West	North	East	South
	1♣	Pass	1♡
Pass	1♠	Pass	2NT
Pass	3NT	All Pass	

Leading a diamond is reasonable because it is the only unbid suit. If you work up your courage to make this brave lead, the right card to lead is the *jack* (although in this case the ace works out equally well). In this layout the declarer has only seven winners after taking his one diamond trick. He must eventually play hearts and your partner can win with the ace and run four diamond tricks to set the contract. The diamond suit would block if you led the three-spot; you must lead the ace or jack to beat the contract.

With Suits Containing No Honor Cards
Versus Notrump Contracts

With a three-card suit containing no honor cards (such as 9 7 4), lead the *highest*; to inform your partner that you have led from a worthless suit. Also, it is sometimes right to lead the highest card, or the second-highest card, from a worthless four-card suit. Note the following three illustrations.

#5	West		West	North	East	South
	♠ 8 7 5 2					1NT
	♡ 4 3		Pass	3NT	All Pass	
	◇ A Q J 9					
	♣ J 8 7					

If you decide to lead a spade, *lead the eight* to tell partner you have nothing in spades and do not want him to return that suit. If he should get the lead, the diamond weakness in dummy should make it apparent that he should return a diamond.

#6	West		West	North	East	South
	♠ 8 7 5 2					1NT
	♡ Q 4 3		Pass	3NT	All Pass	
	◇ 9 7 6					
	♣ J 8 7					

Lead the two of spades. Since you have no strong suit that you wish partner to lead, you might as well lead your fourth-highest spade; although some good players would lead a high spade to discourage partner from returning the suit.

#7	West		West	North	East	South
	♠ 9 7 5 4					1NT
	♡ 4 3		Pass	3NT	All Pass	
	◇ A Q J 9					
	♣ J 8 7					

The nine may be an important card, so *lead the seven of spades*. Partner should read the seven to be a high card (as opposed to fourth-highest) and, if he gets the lead, not return a spade. The nine is the wrong card to lead because there are suit combinations where leading it would give the declarer an extra trick. For example:

```
                        North
                        A 10
         West                          East
         9 7 5 4                       J 6 3
                        South
                        K Q 8 2
```

If you lead the nine, declarer can win a fourth trick with the eight. When you wish to discourage your partner from returning your suit, and leading the highest card might waste a trick, *lead the second-highest card*.

The usual lead is *fourth-highest* from an honorless five-card or longer suit if you have one or more entry cards. For example:

#8	West	*West*	*North*	*East*	*South*
	♠ 9 8 7 6 3				1NT
	♡ 6 5 2	Pass	3NT	All Pass	
	◇ A Q				
	♣ 10 5 4				

Lead the six of spades (fourth-highest), to encourage partner to return the suit if he should get the lead. Although declarer may have two or three spade stoppers, developing long cards in the spade suit offers the best chance to beat the contract.

Note that leading the top card of a sequence does not apply here because the sequence is not headed by an honor, but, if you had a strong holding in another suit (such as A Q J x), the nine from 9 8 7 6 3 would be a good lead; to tell partner that you do not want him to return that suit.

With Suits Containing No Honor Cards
Versus Trump Contracts

With a worthless four-card or longer suit, *lead your fourth-highest: Lead the three* from 9 7 6 3 or 8 7 5 3 2. You should also lead fourth-best from a suit headed by the king, queen, jack or ten, but *a low spot-card opening lead does not promise an honor.*

With a worthless three-card suit (such as 7 4 2), the choice of which card to lead is debatable: some lead the top, some lead the middle, but most good players *lead the lowest.*

The lead of the top card is old-fashioned (hardly any good players play this way today), but if you decide to lead the top card you should follow with the middle card: From 7 4 2, *lead the seven, then play the four next*; if you play the seven followed by the two, it confirms a doubleton.

The lead of the middle card is a convention called "MUD," which is named for the rotation in which you intend to play the cards: middle, up, down. From 7 4 2, you would *lead the four, planning to play the seven next and the two last*. Very few good players play this convention, however more detailed information about MUD can be found in *Conventional Leads and Signals*, page 392.

Since a vast majority of the good players *lead low* from three spot cards versus trump contracts (they would lead the *two* from 7 4 2), shouldn't you play this way too? Then if you lead a spot card and follow with a lower spot card, your partner has an easier time determining when you have a doubleton. Since this is a controversial area, be sure to come to an agreement with your regular partners.

There are two exception to leading low from three spot cards:

(1) If at some point in the bidding you have raised your partner's bid suit, *lead the top* from three low; he already knows you have at least three cards in the suit. So leading your lowest card should show an honor or a four-card suit.

(2) If you decide to lead a trump, lead your lowest card from an even number—two or four—and lead the highest card you can spare from an odd number (three or five). This procedure is practiced by a limited number of good partnerships and may be out of place in this chapter on "standard opening leads." But it is an exception to leading low from three low cards. For further information see Chapter 7, page 249, "The Trump Echo."

In Conclusion

Although not considered as such in bridge terminology, the card you lead is a "signal" to tell your partner something about your length and/or your strength in the suit. The card you lead also reveals this information to the declarer, so you may be wondering why you shouldn't violate the guidelines in the preceding pages and make a lead that may fool the declarer? The answer is obvious: *An undisciplined lead is more apt to fool partner than declarer.* Experts almost always adhere to their partnership agreements, so you should do the same.

In *Conventional Leads and Signals*, starting on page 382, you will find new ideas about Which Card To Lead that conflict with what you have read in this chapter. These modern methods are in most cases better than standard methods, but only in the hands of a seasoned partnership. So stick to the standard procedures recommended in this chapter unless you have an experienced partnership and have discussed any variations. I recommend that the first convention you should adopt is "Ace From Ace-King" versus trump contracts, which is becoming very popular; it was a difficult choice deciding not to include it as standard procedure in this chapter.

Which Suit to Lead Versus Notrump Contracts

When nothing in the bidding has suggested otherwise, the general rule for opening leads against notrump contracts is to lead your longest and strongest suit. For example:

#9

```
                        ♠ J 5
                        ♡ Q J 10
                        ◇ K J 10 9 2
                        ♣ 7 6 2

    ♠ Q 10 7 6 3                        ♠ K 9 2
    ♡ 9 5                               ♡ 7 4 3 2
    ◇ A 8                               ◇ 6 5 3
    ♣ Q J 10 5                          ♣ K 8 4

                        ♠ A 8 4
                        ♡ A K 8 6
                        ◇ Q 7 4
                        ♣ A 9 3
```

West	North	East	South
			1NT
Pass	2NT	Pass	3NT
Pass	Pass	Pass	

The recommended lead with the West hand is the *six of spades* (fourth-highest), and in this case it takes a spade lead to beat the contract. If the declarer holds up his ace, the defenders will continue to lead spades until the ace is driven out (although a club shift is okay too). Declarer has no chance to make his contract without developing diamond tricks, so West will regain the lead with the ace of diamonds and cash the rest of his spades.

Note that the queen of club is a tempting choice for the opening lead. But even though partner has the king of clubs, you can establish only three club tricks to win when you regain the lead with the ace of diamonds. It is usually better to lead from a five-card suit rather than from a four-card suit, unless the five-card suit is very weak and the four-card suit contains an honor sequence. For example, change the spades in the hand above to 10 x x x x and the queen-of-clubs lead becomes a more attractive choice.

Leading a suit with one or more honor cards not in sequence versus a notrump contract is common practice if you have a five-card or longer suit. It may also be the winning lead from a four-card suit, but it is a doubtful choice. Leads from suits such as A Q x x, A J x x, A x x x, K J x x, etc., are questionable because declarer may win a trick he is not entitled to, and your chances of developing enough long cards to beat the contract are slim. It is sometimes better to lead a weaker, or a shorter, suit. For example:

#10

```
                                    ♠ A 6 5
                                    ♡ 8 7 2
                                    ◇ K Q J
                                    ♣ J 10 7 3
        ♠ 9 7 2                                              ♠ J 10 8 3
        ♡ A 10 4 3                                           ♡ Q J 9 5
        ◇ 7 4 3                                              ◇ 9 6 2
        ♣ 8 6 5                                              ♣ A 4
                                    ♠ K Q 4
                                    ♡ K 6
                                    ◇ A 10 8 5
                                    ♣ K Q 9 2
```

West	North	East	South
			1NT
Pass	3NT	All Pass	

Note that if you lead the three of hearts, declarer will win the first trick with the king of hearts and make his contract. When partner gets the lead with the ace of clubs, you can collect only three heart tricks. Suppose you *lead the nine of spades*, although any lead but a heart will beat the contract. When partner gets the lead with the ace of clubs, he will switch to the queen of hearts; you told him by leading the nine that you have nothing in spades.

Suppose the auction had gone like this:

West	North	East	South
	1♣	Pass	1◇
Pass	3♣	Pass	3NT
Pass	Pass	Pass	

Now, because the bidding has indicated that the declarer or the dummy has a long and strong suit, it is usually best to lead from strength; *lead the three of hearts* from the West hand above. These passive leads—such as the nine of spades here—are more apt to be successful when the bidding has suggested that declarer will not be able to win five or six tricks in one long suit.

#11 West
```
     ♠ 8 5
     ♡ K 5 2
     ◇ A 8 5 3
     ♣ Q 7 6 4
```

West	North	East	South
			1♡
Pass	1♠	Pass	1NT
Pass	3NT	All Pass	

When the choice is between two four-card suits, one headed by an ace and the other headed by a king or queen, it is usually better to lead the suit *without* the ace. The recommended lead here is the *four of clubs*.

#12 West
```
     ♠ 10 8 6 3
     ♡ J 2
     ◇ A Q 10 8
     ♣ 9 5 4
```

West	North	East	South
			1NT
Pass	3NT	All Pass	

The experts would not lead a diamond from this four-card holding, but they would if it were a five-card suit ($\Diamond$ A Q 10 8 x). The popular choice would be the *eight of spades*, breaking the rule that you lead low from four to an honor, because you do not want partner to return a spade. (Note that leading the ten is wrong as it might waste a spade trick.) Partner will be able to read that the eight is not your fourth-highest and therefore know that you do not want a spade returned. When partner does get the lead, the expected weak diamond holding in dummy should make it clear that he ought to switch to that suit; but if you led the three of spades, he would be more likely to return a spade.

#13	West	West	North	East	South
	♠ Q 9 5 3				1NT
	♡ 6 4	Pass	3NT	All Pass	
	◇ Q 9 7 6				
	♣ K 10 8				

Lead the three of spades. With a close choice of suits to lead, prefer a major suit rather than a minor suit. Raising one notrump to three notrump is common practice with length in the minor suits, but rare with a four-card or longer major suit. So the dummy is more likely to have length and strength in diamonds than spades.

#14	West	West	North	East	South
	♠ 10 9 7				1♣
	♡ Q 5 2	Pass	1♡	Pass	1NT
	◇ 10 9 5	Pass	2NT	Pass	3NT
	♣ 8 6 4 3	Pass	Pass	Pass	

Lead the ten of diamonds. This lead contradicts the theory in the last hand—with two relatively equal suits, lead the major rather than the minor—but consider what was learned from the bidding. In view of your weak hand and the opponents' sluggish bidding, partner must have a pretty good hand: about 12 or 13 high-card points. Why didn't he bid over one heart? With a reasonably good spade suit he probably would have bid one spade. But you need a better hand to overcall at the two-level, so he is more likely to have passed with good diamonds than with good spades.

#15	West	West	North	East	South
	♠ 7 2				1NT
	♡ J 10	Pass	2NT	Pass	3NT
	◇ 9 8 6 4 3	Pass	Pass	Pass	
	♣ 10 8 7 5				

Lead the jack of hearts. Leading your own long suit seems hopeless because you have no reentry cards. So your short-suit lead is a stab at finding partner's long suit. The jack-ten makes hearts a better choice than spades. If you had a couple of high cards so that you could regain the lead, then the four of diamonds would be the best choice.

#16	West	West	North	East	South
	♠ Q 9 8 2		1♣	Pass	1♡
	♡ K 10 3	Pass	1♠	Pass	1NT
	◇ J 7	Pass	Pass	Pass	
	♣ K 10 6 5				

Lead the jack of diamonds. Granted, an ugly choice, but it is the least of evils. Leading a suit bid by the opponents from any of your honor holdings is even less attractive.

#17	West	*West*	*North*	*East*	*South*
	♠ Q J 10 2		1♣	Pass	1♡
	♡ A 5 4	Pass	1♠	Pass	1NT
	◇ J 10 9	Pass	Pass	Pass	
	♣ J 8 6				

Lead the *jack of diamonds*. Although a spade lead could work out well if partner has an honor (or the nine-spot), it is risky to lead from Q J 10 x when dummy has bid the suit. If the suit divides dummy ♠ K 9 8 x and declarer ♠ A x, the queen-of-spades lead gives declarer a third spade trick; and there are other combinations where the same would be true. If you did not have a good alternative—to lead the jack form ◇ J 10 9—the queen of spades would be a reasonable choice, even though it risks giving declarer an extra spade trick.

#18	West	*West*	*North*	*East*	*South*
	♠ Q J 9 3				1NT
	♡ 7 4 2	Pass	2♣	Pass	2♡
	◇ Q J 7 2	Pass	3NT	All Pass	
	♣ A 8				

Lead the two of diamonds. Dummy's two-club bid was Stayman, which when followed by three notrump shows at least one four-card major suit. Since he did not raise hearts, he must have four spades. Hence the decision to lead a diamond instead of a spade.

#19	West	*West*	*North*	*East*	*South*
	♠ 8 5				1NT
	♡ Q 10 7 6 3	Pass	2♣	Pass	2♡
	◇ A 9 2	Pass	3NT	All Pass	
	♣ K 7 4				

Lead the six of hearts, in spite of the fact that declarer has bid the suit. Dummy bid three notrump after his partner bid hearts, so he might have a singleton. The best chance to beat the contract is to find partner with a good heart holding—such as ♡ J 9 x.

#20	West	*West*	*North*	*East*	*South*
	♠ 7 6				1♣
	♡ 8 7 2	Pass	1♠	Pass	2NT
	◇ A 5 4	Pass	3NT	All Pass	
	♣ K J 9 6 3				

Lead the six of clubs. This is a gambling lead since South bid clubs, but it is not uncommon to bid one club with a weak three- or four-card suit. If you are lucky, partner will have the ace or queen of clubs. Since a club lead is apt to give declarer an overtrick, it is a doubtful choice at duplicate bridge; but I would lead a club anyway.

#21	West	*West*	*North*	*East*	*South*
	♠ 7 6				1♡
	♡ K J 9 6 3	Pass	1♠	Pass	1NT
	◇ A 5 4	Pass	3NT	All Pass	
	♣ 8 7 2				

This is the same hand as #20 but with the heart and club suits switched. Opening bids of one of a major suit are rarely made without a substantial suit, so it is inadvisable to lead from K J 9 6 3 this time. *Lead the eight of clubs,* although the four of diamonds or the seven of spades are conceivable choices.

#22	West	West	North	East	South
	♠ 7 6				1♣
	♡ A 9 5	Pass	1♡	Pass	1NT
	♢ 9 8 2	Pass	3NT	All Pass	
	♣ Q J 10 4 3				

Here again a club lead is indicated even though South bid the suit. Since South did not raise hearts or bid one spade over one heart, he should have at least seven minor-suit cards and is a favorite to have precisely four clubs. The best chance to beat the contract is to *lead the four of clubs* and find partner with the ace or king of clubs (or maybe the nine). Suppose this is the full deal:

```
                    ♠ A Q 8 2
                    ♡ K J 10 7
                    ♢ K 6 3
                    ♣ 6 5
     ♠ 7 6                          ♠ 10 9 4 3
     ♡ A 9 5                        ♡ 8 4 2
     ♢ 9 8 2                        ♢ Q J 10 5
     ♣ Q J 10 4 3                   ♣ K 7
                    ♠ K J 5
                    ♡ Q 6 3
                    ♢ A 7 4
                    ♣ A 9 8 2
```

Note that the four-of-clubs lead beats the contract: By leading clubs until the ace is driven out, the defenders will be able to win four club tricks and the ace of hearts before declarer can develop nine tricks. If you lead the queen of clubs, the suit blocks and declarer will make his contract. As stated earlier: It may be right to lead fourth-highest from a three-card sequence if dummy or declarer is known to have four cards in the suit.

When to Lead Your Partner's Bid Suit

When your partner has been in the bidding, it is generally right to lead his suit. Do not be discouraged when one or both opponents bid notrump after his bid. For example:

#23	West	West	North	East	South
	♠ 8 6 3 2		1♢	1♡	2NT
	♡ Q 7 4	Pass	3NT	All Pass	
	♢ 10 3				
	♣ J 9 8 2				

Lead the four of hearts. If you decide to lead from three to an honor, the normal card to lead is the lowest; whether your partner has bid the suit or not. The old rule from the dark ages—"Always lead the highest card of your partner's bid suit"—has no merit whatsoever. In a vast majority of cases, you should lead the same card that you would lead if partner has not bid the suit. Suppose these are the four hands:

♠ A Q J
♡ 9 3
♢ K Q J 6
♣ 7 5 4 3

♠ 8 6 3 2   ♠ 10 9 5
♡ Q 7 4   ♡ A 10 8 6 2
♢ 10 3   ♢ 7 5 4
♣ J 9 8 2   ♣ A K

♠ K 7 4
♡ K J 5
♢ A 9 8 2
♣ Q 10 6

Note that leading the four of hearts beats the contract. Partner will win the first trick with the ace and return a heart; trapping the jack and limiting declarer to one heart trick. If you lead the queen of hearts, declarer will win two heart tricks and make his contract.

#24	West	West	North	East	South
	♠ Q J 10 7 2		1♡	2♣	2NT
	♡ 9 5	Pass	3NT	All Pass	
	♢ 10 9 8 4				
	♣ 8 3				

Lead the eight of clubs. When your partner overcalls at the two-level, he advertises a good suit and wants you to lead it. If you lead a club and the opponents make their contract, your partner will still love you. However, if you do *not* lead his suit and as a result the opponents make their contract, your partner may say, or at least be thinking: Howcoulda-greatplayerlikeyoumakesuchadumblead???

#25	West	West	North	East	South
	♠ J 10 9 7 5	Pass	Pass	1♣	1NT
	♡ K 8 2	Pass	2NT	Pass	3NT
	♢ 9 6 3	Pass	Pass	Pass	
	♣ 7 4				

This time your partner opened the bidding with one club, so he may have a weak and/or short club suit. The *jack of spades* is a more attractive lead than a club; especially since you have a probable reentry card—the king of hearts.

When an Opponent Bids Three Notrump over his Partner's Preemptive Bid

Lead from strength, rather than length. For example:

#26	West	West	North	East	South
	♠ Q J 10 9 3		3♣	Pass	3NT
	♡ 8 4 2	Pass	Pass	Pass	
	♢ A K 6				
	♣ 7 5				

Without the preemptive bid, the queen of spades would be the normal lead. But when there is a chance that declarer will win seven tricks in one suit if he gets the lead, it is better to lead from strength. So *lead the king of diamonds* to get a look at the dummy and a signal from your partner. If partner gives a discouraging signal, you can lead a spade next. It is unlikely that an original spade lead has any better chance of beating the contract than a spade lead at trick two. Suppose these are the four hands:

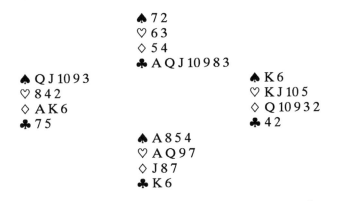

                    ♠ 7 2
                    ♡ 6 3
                    ◇ 5 4
                    ♣ A Q J 10 9 8 3

    ♠ Q J 10 9 3   ♠ K 6
    ♡ 8 4 2   ♡ K J 10 5
    ◇ A K 6   ◇ Q 10 9 3 2
    ♣ 7 5   ♣ 4 2

                    ♠ A 8 5 4
                    ♡ A Q 9 7
                    ◇ J 8 7
                    ♣ K 6

Your partner will play the ten of diamonds to encourage you to continue leading the suit, so you will set the hand by winning the first five diamond tricks. If you do not lead a diamond, declarer can win at least nine tricks.

#27	West	West	North	East	South
	♠ A Q 5				3NT
	♡ J 10 9 7 2	Pass	Pass	Pass	
	◇ 5				
	♣ Q 6 4 3				

If the three-notrump opening bid shows a very strong balanced hand—the *jack of hearts* is the normal choice for an opening lead.

But suppose you are informed that it is a "gambling" three-notrump opening, showing a long solid minor suit with little or no strength on the side (this convention is popular with experienced players, especially in duplicate bridge games). Then you should *lead the ace of spades*. It is not unlikely that declarer will be able to win nine tricks when he gets the lead. So you must make every effort to win the first five tricks. Leading an ace is your best bet; so you can see the dummy and get a signal from partner before committing yourself. Suppose these are the four hands:

                    ♠ 10 7 2
                    ♡ A 8 4 3
                    ◇ 9 4
                    ♣ A K 8 7

    ♠ A Q 5   ♠ K 9 8 6 4
    ♡ J 10 9 7 2   ♡ K 6 5
    ◇ 5   ◇ 10 8 2
    ♣ Q 6 4 3   ♣ J 9

                    ♠ J 3
                    ♡ Q
                    ◇ A K Q J 7 6 3
                    ♣ 10 5 2

You can win the first five spade tricks, but without a spade lead, declarer runs ten tricks.

Leads Versus Notrump Slams

When your opponents bid six or seven notrump, the strategy is to choose the safest lead, the one least likely to give away a trick. For example:

#28	West	*West*	*North*	*East*	*South*
	♠ K 9 8 7 3				2NT
	♡ 10 4	Pass	6NT	All Pass	
	◇ 10 7 5				
	♣ J 10 2				

Since the opponents did not bid any suits, you have nothing to guide you except the nature of your hand. *Do not lead a spade.* The seven of spades would be the normal lead against a lower notrump contract because you are trying to establish several tricks to set the hand; but you need only two tricks to beat a small slam. When on lead against a notrump slam, your primary concern is that your lead does not cost your side a trick: Avoid leading away from an unguarded honor—the king, queen or jack.

The next question is what should you lead? A club lead appears to be the safest choice, and the jack is the normal lead from J 10 x. But another possibility is the *ten of clubs*. Deceptive opening leads versus lower contracts are not recommended because they are more apt to fool your partner than declarer. But versus slams, when partner is known to have a very weak hand, the odds are better. This is when an expert is most likely to try to deceive the declarer by making an unorthodox opening lead. Suppose you lead the ten of clubs and this turns out to be the full deal:

```
                         ♠ 10 5
                         ♡ A J 8
                         ◇ Q 6 3 2
                         ♣ K Q 7 6
      ♠ K 9 8 7 3                        ♠ J 6 2
      ♡ 10 4                             ♡ Q 9 6 3 2
      ◇ 10 7 5                           ◇ 9 4
      ♣ J 10 2                           ♣ 8 5 4
                         ♠ A Q 4
                         ♡ K 7 5
                         ◇ A K J 8
                         ♣ A 9 3
```

Declarer may believe the ten-of-clubs lead and play your partner to have four to the jack: He may win the first trick with dummy's queen and then finesse the nine. A good declarer is unlikely to fall into this trap (he would reason that leading the ten from 10 x is not a normal lead), but even if declarer does win his four club tricks, he still has only eleven winners. He will try the two finesses, but with the king of spades and queen of hearts both offside, he will be set. If West leads a spade, the contract is easily made.

#29	West	*West*	*North*	*East*	*South*
	♠ A 10 5 2				1NT
	♡ 10 8 3	Pass	6NT	All Pass	
	◇ 6 5 4				
	♣ 8 7 6				

Lead any diamond or any club; do not lay down the ace of spades. Aces were meant to capture kings and queens, and it is usually wrong to lead an ace against a notrump slam: *unless you have two of them or the contract is seven.* You may be wondering, why not lead a heart? Leading from a ten is more likely to give away a trick than leading from a worthless suit. For example:

```
                      ♠ Q 6 3
                      ♡ K J 9
                      ♢ K Q 2
                      ♣ A Q 10 9
        ♠ A 10 5 2                    ♠ J 7 4
        ♡ 10 8 3                      ♡ Q 6 5 4
        ♢ 6 5 4                       ♢ 8 7 3
        ♣ 8 7 6                       ♣ 5 3 2
                      ♠ K 9 8
                      ♡ A 7 2
                      ♢ A J 10 9
                      ♣ K J 4
```

Declarer has eight tricks in the minor suits and must win four in the majors to make his slam. If you lead the ace of spades, he will win two spades and two hearts. If you lead a heart, declarer will play the nine from dummy. This gives him a third heart trick, and he can always win one spade.

If you lead a club or a diamond, declarer must break the heart suit himself. He can win the three heart tricks he needs to make his contract if he leads the jack of hearts and take a "backward finesse." But this is against the odds, so he will more than likely lead a heart toward the king-jack and take a losing finesse.

Lead-Directing Doubles

Sometimes your partner can help you make the winning opening lead by a "lead-directing double." This topic is more appropriate in bidding books, but here are three illustrations showing what you should lead when your partner has made a lead-directing double in a notrump contract.

#30	West	*West*	*North*	*East*	*South*
	♠ 7 6 4				1NT
	♡ Q J 10 9	Pass	2♣	Double	2♢
	♢ 8 4 3	Pass	3NT	All Pass	
	♣ 9 5 2				

North's two-club bid was artificial—the Stayman Convention. Your partner's double indicated he has length and strength in the club suit and wants you to lead that suit. Your correct lead is the *nine of clubs*. Here is a possible layout where it takes a club lead to beat the contract:

```
                        ♠ A Q 8 3
                        ♡ K 8 7 2
                        ◇ 10 5
                        ♣ J 6 4
      ♠ 7 6 4                              ♠ J 5 2
      ♡ Q J 10 9                           ♡ 5 4
      ◇ 8 4 3                              ◇ A 9 6
      ♣ 9 5 2                              ♣ A Q 10 8 3
                        ♠ K 10 9
                        ♡ A 6 3
                        ◇ K Q J 7 2
                        ♣ K 7
```

Declarer should be allowed to win the first trick with the king of clubs. When East gets the lead with the ace of diamonds, he can run four club tricks and beat the contract. Note that without partner's double, your normal lead would be the ineffective queen of hearts.

The double of any artificial bid is a lead-directing double. This applies in trump contracts as well as in notrump contracts; see #65, #66 and #67 on pages 32 and 33.

#31	West	West	North	East	South
	♠ Q 10 7 4 2				1◇
	♡ 7	Pass	1♡	Pass	1NT
	◇ J 10 9 6	Pass	2NT	Pass	3NT
	♣ 7 5 3	Pass	Pass	Double	All Pass

When you and your partner have never bid, the double of any notrump contract—from one notrump through seven notrump—calls for the lead of the first suit bid by the dummy. So here you must *lead the seven of hearts.* Suppose this is the full deal:

```
                        ♠ K 5 3
                        ♡ A J 8 5 4
                        ◇ K 2
                        ♣ 9 8 6
      ♠ Q 10 7 4 2                        ♠ 8 6
      ♡ 7                                 ♡ K Q 10 9 2
      ◇ J 10 9 6                          ◇ 7 5 3
      ♣ 7 5 3                             ♣ A K 4
                        ♠ A J 9
                        ♡ 6 3
                        ◇ A Q 8 4
                        ♣ Q J 10 2
```

The heart lead is the killer. With careful defense, the contract cannot be made. Note that without the double the normal lead is the four of spades. This gives declarer an extra spade trick and the timing he needs to develop his nine tricks.

#32	West	West	North	East	South
	♠ J 10 9 7 5	Pass	Pass	1♣	1NT
	♡ K 8 2	Pass	2NT	Pass	3NT
	◇ 9 6 3	Pass	3NT	Double	All Pass
	♣ 7 4				
```
```

This is a repeat of hand #25, page 12, with which I recommended that you lead the jack of spades. The bidding here is the same except your partner doubles the final contract. If you have never entered the auction and your partner doubles a notrump contract after he has bid a suit, it is a command for you to lead his suit. *Lead the seven of clubs*. These might be the four hands:

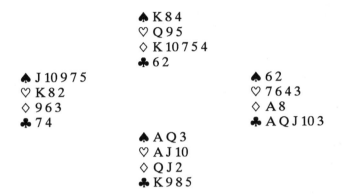

♠ K 8 4
♡ Q 9 5
◇ K 10 7 5 4
♣ 6 2

♠ J 10 9 7 5
♡ K 8 2
◇ 9 6 3
♣ 7 4

♠ 6 2
♡ 7 6 4 3
◇ A 8
♣ A Q J 10 3

♠ A Q 3
♡ A J 10
◇ Q J 2
♣ K 9 8 5

As you can see, it takes a club lead to set the contract.

Note that if your partner doubles a notrump contract after *you (the opening leader)* have bid a suit, he wants *your suit* led; this applies even if your partner or dummy have bid a suit.

Which Suit to Lead Versus Trump Contracts

Leading a long suit in an effort to establish "long cards" is normal procedure at notrump contracts, but not at trump contracts. After a suit has been led once, twice or occasionally three times, the declarer can ruff; so defenders must depend on high cards and trumps to win their tricks.

Leads from suit combinations such as A K x, K Q J and Q J 10 9 are attractive choices because they are safe and may win or promote tricks quickly, but that does not mean that you should rush into leading from such holdings without thinking. First analyze the bidding carefully and consider all four suits; it may be better to lead a trump, a short-suit (singleton or doubleton) or even a suit combination that would normally not be a good choice.

While considering which of the four suits to lead, your primary thought should be to make a "passive lead" when you judge there is no urgency to win tricks; or an "aggressive lead" if you think declarer will be able to dispose of his losers if you don't take them quickly.

A passive lead is one in which your primary aim is not to give away a trick because of your lead; you would be just as happy if you did not have the lead. Choose the safest lead you can find: Lead the top of a sequence, a worthless suit or possibly even a trump from holdings that are unlikely to jeopardize a trick; do not lead a suit which may give declarer a trick he could not win if he led the suit himself. In other words, do not do declarer's work for him; sit back and wait for your tricks.

An aggressive lead is one from strength; you must get your tricks quickly or you will not get them. This tactic is indicated when you are suspicious that the dummy or declarer has a long and strong side suit; in which case he will be able to discard his losers if you give him time. A very good lead is from a sequence headed by the ace, king or queen. If you do not have an aggressive lead that is safe, lead away from a king or a queen, or lead an ace: Do *not* lead a worthless suit or a trump.

Other kinds of leads which call for decisive action early are: leading a trump, to cut down declarer's ruffing power; leading a short suit, in the hope of getting a ruff; leading a long suit, to give your partner a ruff; or leading a long suit when you have length in the enemy trump suit, to force declarer to ruff so he will be unable to draw trumps and maintain control of the trump suit.

The various types of passive and aggressive opening leads are described in the following pages. The analysis that follows explains how to read the clues and select an opening lead. You can challenge yourself as you go along by studying the hand and the bidding, and then choosing your opening lead before reading the analysis.

Passive Leads

In the next five deals you are looking for the safest possible lead.

#33	West	West	North	East	South
	♠ Q 6 3				1♠
	♡ Q J 7	Pass	3♠	Pass	4♠
	◇ K 9 5 2	Pass	Pass	Pass	
	♣ J 10 9				

The *jack of clubs* is the best opening lead because it is the least likely to give away a trick.

The queen of hearts is a tempting choice, but dangerous. For example, dummy may have ♡ K 10 x and declarer ♡ A x x, in which case declarer can win a third heart trick by winning the first trick with the ace and then finessing the ten. If you had ♡ Q J 10, the queen of hearts would be the indicated lead.

#34	West	West	North	East	South
	♠ A J 6 3				1♡
	♡ Q 9 5	Pass	2♡	All Pass	
	◇ Q 8 4				
	♣ J 6 2				

This time each suit has an unguarded honor card; there is no good lead. A trump lead from Q x x, or a spade from A J x x, should be ruled out, so the unenviable choice is between clubs and diamonds. *Lead the four of diamonds, or the two of clubs.*

#35	West	West	North	East	South
	♠ 10 9 8				1♠
	♡ Q 8 4	Pass	2♠	All Pass	
	◇ A 7 5 2				
	♣ K 7 3				

Here again a passive lead is indicated, and a trump appears to be the safest choice. *Lead the ten of spades.*

#36	West	West	North	East	South
	♠ 7				1♣
	♡ Q J 10 9	Pass	1♡	Pass	1♠
	◇ A 7 5 2	Pass	3♠	Pass	4♠
	♣ J 6 4 3	Pass	Pass	Pass	

Lead the queen of hearts. Although you generally choose a lead from among the suits that your opponents did not bid, it is okay to lead their suit if you have a four-card sequence, especially when there is no good alternative.

While we're at it, let me point out that a singleton trump is usually a poor choice for an opening lead; it will finesse your partner out of a potential trick from a variety of holdings.

#37	West	West	North	East	South
	♠ J 6		1♣	Pass	1♢
	♡ Q J 7 4	Pass	1♡	Pass	1♠
	♢ A J 10 8	Pass	3♠	Pass	3NT
	♣ Q 9 2	Pass	4♠	All Pass	

In this case, you wish you did not have to make an opening lead. A passive lead is indicated, but the opponents have bid all four suits and every lead looks like it might blow a trick. It is usually better to lead from a suit bid by dummy, rather than a suit bid by declarer, and leading from the queen-jack of hearts looks better than leading from the queen of clubs. Whether you should lead the queen or fourth-highest from Q J x x is debatable, but when dummy has bid the suit you should lead fourth-highest. So, *lead the four of hearts*. Suppose these are the four hands:

```
                        ♠ Q 9 8 2
                        ♡ A K 10 5
                        ♢ 9 3
                        ♣ K 7 4
      ♠ J 6                                ♠ K 10 5
      ♡ Q J 7 4                            ♡ 9 8 2
      ♢ A J 10 8                           ♢ 7 6 4
      ♣ Q 9 2                              ♣ 10 8 6 3
                        ♠ A 7 4 3
                        ♡ 6 3
                        ♢ K Q 5 2
                        ♣ A J 5
```

Declarer has four possible losers (two spades, one diamond and one club) and can make his contract no matter what you lead, but the low-heart lead is more likely than any other to cause declarer to choose a losing line of play. If you lead the queen of hearts, declarer, assuming you have led from the queen-jack, will eventually finesse the ten so he can discard his losing club. True, he could finesse the ten of hearts at trick one, but that is a ridiculous play when he has so many better chances. Declarer will win the first trick with the ace or king of hearts; after which there is a good chance he will be set.

Aggressive Leads

The next five deals illustrate cases where decisive action must be taken early:

#38	West	West	North	East	South
	♠ 7 3				1♠
	♡ A 9 5 3	Pass	2♢	Pass	2♠
	♢ 10 9 8	Pass	3♠	Pass	4♠
	♣ K 10 6 2	Pass	Pass	Pass	

Lead the two of clubs. The bidding indicated that the dummy is likely to have a long and strong diamond suit. When declarer gets the lead, his predictable line of play is to draw trumps and discard his losers on the long diamond suit. So, when you suspect that dummy has a long and strong suit you must lead from strength; get your tricks in the side suits before the declarer can discard them. Suppose these are the four hands:

```
                        ♠ K 10
                        ♡ 8 7 4
                        ◇ A Q 6 4 3 2
                        ♣ 9 4
        ♠ 7 3                               ♠ 8 5 4
        ♡ A 9 5 3                           ♡ Q J 10 2
        ◇ 10 9 8                            ◇ J 5
        ♣ K 10 6 2                          ♣ A J 7 5
                        ♠ A Q J 9 6 2
                        ♡ K 6
                        ◇ K 7
                        ♣ Q 8 3
```

The only lead to beat the contract is a club, If partner wins with the ace of clubs and switches to the queen of hearts, you can win the first four tricks. Note that if you lead a spade or a diamond, declarer can win the first twelve tricks. The ace of hearts would also be an aggressive lead, but in this case will not beat the contract; it is usually better to lead from a king or queen, rather than to lead (or underlead) an ace.

#39	West	West	North	East	South
	♠ A 7		1♣	Pass	1♠
	♡ J 5 4	Pass	2♠	Pass	3♣
	◇ J 10 9 2	Pass	4♠	All Pass	
	♣ A 8 6 3				

Another way to beat a contract is to give your partner one or more ruffs. This bidding suggests that the opponents have eight clubs and eight spades between them; in which case your partner has a singleton club and three spades. If this is true, you can give your partner two club ruffs and beat the contract by *leading the ace and another club*. Suppose this is the full deal.

```
                        ♠ K J 10 3
                        ♡ A Q 8 2
                        ◇ 7 5
                        ♣ K J 9
        ♠ A 7                               ♠ 6 4 2
        ♡ J 5 4                             ♡ K 10 9 6
        ◇ J 10 9 2                          ◇ Q 8 4 3
        ♣ A 8 6 3                           ♣ 7 5
                        ♠ Q 9 8 5
                        ♡ 7 3
                        ◇ A K 6
                        ♣ Q 10 4 2
```

It is disappointing to find the dummy with only three clubs and partner with a doubleton, but you can still give him one ruff by leading a third round of clubs after you win the first spade lead. Since partner has a natural heart trick, the contract will be set anyway. Note that if declarer plays correctly, the contract cannot be set without a club lead.

#40	West	*West*	*North*	*East*	*South*
	♠ A 4 3 2				1♠
	♡ K J 9 7 6	Pass	2♠	Pass	4♠
	◇ 8 3	Pass	Pass	Pass	
	♣ J 8				

Lead the seven of hearts. Here is another kind of aggressive lead: When you have length in the enemy trump suit (four cards or more) and a long side suit, it is often right to lead your long suit. You goal is to shorten declarer's trumps by forcing him to ruff. See "Forcing Declarer to Ruff," Chapter 8, page 303.

#41	West	*West*	*North*	*East*	*South*
	♠ 7 4 3				1◇
	♡ A Q 5 2	Pass	2♣	Pass	3◇
	◇ 6 5	Pass	3♠	Pass	5◇
	♣ J 10 9 8	Pass	Pass	Pass	

Lead the ace of hearts. Leading an ace is rarely right, especially from ace-queen, but here it is the only unbid suit and declarer may discard one or more heart losers if you do not lead the suit. Note that it is unlikely declarer has the guarded king of hearts; since he did not bid three notrump over three spades.

#42	West	*West*	*North*	*East*	*South*
	♠ Q 8 5				1◇
	♡ 5 4 2	Pass	1♠	Pass	2♡
	◇ Q 8 6	Pass	2♠	Pass	3♡
	♣ A Q J 3	Pass	4◇	Pass	5◇
		Pass	Pass	Pass	

Lead the ace of clubs. South's bidding has shown five-six distribution in the red suits, so he has only two black cards. If you do not lead the ace of clubs, you may lose a club trick. These might be the four hands:

```
                    ♠ A J 10 7 3 2
                    ♡ 9
                    ◇ J 5 2
                    ♣ 10 8 4
  ♠ Q 8 5                              ♠ K 9 6 4
  ♡ 5 3 2                              ♡ Q 7 6 4
  ◇ Q 8 6                              ◇ 4
  ♣ A Q J 3                            ♣ K 9 7 5
                    ♠ —
                    ♡ A K J 10 8
                    ◇ A K 10 9 7 3
                    ♣ 6 2
```

You must take the first two club tricks, or the declarer will make his contract by discarding one of his losers on the ace of spades.

When to Lead a Trump

A trump lead may be the way to beat the contract. For example:

#43	West	West	North	East	South
	♠ K J 9 8				1♠
	♡ A 5 4	Pass	1NT	Pass	3♡
	◇ 7 5 2	Pass	4♡	All Pass	
	♣ J 10 9				

Lead the four of hearts (or the ace and another heart). Predictably, declarer is planning to ruff spades in dummy. With your powerful spade holding, you should lead a heart to eliminate some of dummy's trumps. In the following layout, it takes three heart leads to beat the contract.

```
                        ♠ 6 2
                        ♡ 9 8 3
                        ◇ 10 9 8 4 3
                        ♣ A K 5
        ♠ K J 9 8                          ♠ 4 3
        ♡ A 5 4                            ♡ 7 2
        ◇ 7 5 2                            ◇ K Q J 6
        ♣ J 10 9                           ♣ Q 7 4 3 2
                        ♠ A Q 10 7 5
                        ♡ K Q J 10 6
                        ◇ A
                        ♣ 8 6
```

Declarer must give up a spade trick before he can ruff any spades in dummy. When you regain the lead, you will continue with the ace and another heart. Since the dummy will have no more hearts, declarer must lose two more spade tricks.

When declarer has a two-suited hand and you have a long and strong holding in his side suit, the best opening lead is usually a trump.

#44	West	West	North	East	South
	♠ 8 4 3				1♠
	♡ J 10	Pass	2♠	Pass	3NT
	◇ A J 9 5	Pass	4♠	All Pass	
	♣ K 10 7 2				

Lead a trump. North would have passed three notrump unless he had a short suit, so a trump lead is indicated to cut down dummy's ruffing power. This might be the layout:

```
                        ♠ K J 7
                        ♡ K 8 5 4
                        ◇ 2
                        ♣ 9 6 5 4 3
        ♠ 8 4 3                            ♠ 6 5
        ♡ J 10                             ♡ Q 9 7 2
        ◇ A J 9 5                          ◇ Q 10 8 4 3
        ♣ K 10 7 2                         ♣ Q 8
                        ♠ A Q 10 9 2
                        ♡ A 6 3
                        ◇ K 7 6
                        ♣ A J
```

Note that declarer must ruff two diamonds in dummy to make his contract. The opening trump lead, followed by another trump lead when declarer concedes a diamond trick, leaves dummy with only one trump—so he will be able to ruff only one diamond. Without a trump lead, the contract cannot be defeated.

In the next deal, your side is vulnerable and the opponents are not.

#45	West	West	North	East	South
	♠ A 6 2			1♡	2♠
	♡ J 10 6	3♣	3♠	4♢	Pass
	◇ A J	4♡	4♠	Pass	Pass
	♣ Q J 10 9 8	Double	Pass	Pass	Pass

South's two-spade bid was a weak jump overcall. North bid four spades as a "sacrifice," reasoning that if he is doubled, it will be less expensive than allowing the opponents to make a vulnerable game; or maybe they will bid to the five-level and be set. You elect to double four spades and have the opening lead. The opponents have far fewer high cards than your side and their main source of tricks will be the trump suit, so *lead the ace of spades* to cut down on the number of trump tricks they can win. Suppose these are the four hands:

```
                    North
                    ♠ K J 9
                    ♡ 7
                    ◇ 8 5 4 2
                    ♣ A 7 4 3 2
    West                            East
    ♠ A 6 2                         ♠ 3
    ♡ J 10 6                        ♡ K Q 9 5 4
    ◇ A J                           ◇ K Q 10 9 3
    ♣ Q J 10 9 8                    ♣ K 6
                    South
                    ♠ Q 10 8 7 5 4
                    ♡ A 8 3 2
                    ◇ 7 6
                    ♣ 5
```

Upon seeing the dummy, you should of course follow up with another trump lead at trick two. Declarer can still ruff one heart in dummy, but will be limited to eight tricks; setting the contract two tricks is the best you can do. If you allow the declarer to get the lead before you play any trumps, he will be able to ruff all three of his hearts in dummy and actually make his contract.

Note that a five-heart contract would be set, so doubling four spades was the winning decision. However, if North bid four spades at his first turn, as he should, a bid of five hearts would be more tempting.

#46	West	West	North	East	South
	♠ A Q 10 7				1♣
	♡ K Q 9 5	Double	Pass	Pass	Pass
	◇ Q 10 8 2				
	♣ 6				

Lead the six of clubs. This is a rare auction, but it calls for a trump lead. You made a takeout double and your partner passed; something he should never do unless he has a powerful five-card or longer club holding (such as ♣ K Q J 10 x). The trump lead is to help your partner draw trumps; to prevent the declarer from scoring tricks by ruffing with low trumps.

Short-Suit Leads

Leading a singleton is often a good choice because you may gain a trick by ruffing. But singleton leads are not always good; they sometimes expose your partner's holding in the suit and help declarer. The best time to lead a singleton is when you have the right trump holding and there is a good chance that your partner will be able to get the lead and give you the ruff. The next three illustrations show times when it is inadvisable to lead a singleton.

#47	West	West	North	East	South
	♠ 7				1♡
	♡ K Q 10	Pass	3♡	Pass	4♡
	◇ 10 9 8 5	Pass	Pass	Pass	
	♣ 9 6 4 3 2				

Lead the ten of diamonds. You should not lead the singleton spade because you have natural trump tricks. The seven-of-spades lead would be attractive lead if your heart holding were A x x, K x x, x x x or other trump holdings where you would gain a trick by ruffing.

#48	West	West	North	East	South
	♠ J 10 9 5				1♡
	♡ A 7 2	Pass	3♡	Pass	4♡
	◇ 8	Pass	Pass	Pass	
	♣ A Q 7 4 3				

Lead the *jack of spades*. Do not lead the singleton diamond, even though you have the ideal trump holding. One important thing to remember about leading a short suit: *You will not get a ruff unless your partner can get the lead*; the declarer certainly is not going to lead the suit for you. In view of the opponents' strong bidding and your array of high cards, it is unlikely that your partner has an entry card. Since the singleton lead may help declarer (by exposing your partner's diamond holding), and it is unlikely that you will be able to get your partner on lead, the jack of spades is the attractive lead.

#49	West	West	North	East	South
	♠ 8 5 2				1♠
	♡ K	Pass	2♣	Pass	4♠
	◇ Q 9 7 4	Pass	Pass	Pass	
	♣ K 10 6 4 3				

Leading a singleton king (or queen) sometimes works out well, but it is more likely to cost a trick than to gain one. In this case a passive lead looks best, so *lead the five of spades (or any spade)*.

#50	West	West	North	East	South
	♠ J 10 9 5				1♡
	♡ A 7 2	Pass	3♡	Pass	4♡
	◇ 8	Pass	Pass	Pass	
	♣ 10 8 7 4 3				

Lead the eight of diamonds. Finally, the right hand to lead a singleton for three good reasons:

(1) You have the perfect trump holding; if declarer wins the first trick, you will regain the lead with the ace of hearts before he can draw your trumps and will get a second chance to put partner on lead and obtain your ruff.

(2) Your hand is not too strong and there is a likelihood that partner will have a quick entry card.

(3) Your singleton is not the king or queen.

#51	West	West	North	East	South
	♠ K 4				1♡
	♡ 10 2	Pass	3♡	Pass	4♡
	◇ 10 9 5 2	Pass	Pass	Pass	
	♣ J 8 7 6 4				

Lead the king of spades. Although not as promising as leading a singleton, leading a doubleton king, doubleton ace, or even a worthless doubleton may enable you to get a ruff. In this case you have a very weak hand and the opponents' bidding was very strong; it seems unlikely that the contract can be set with passive defense.

Aside from getting a ruff, partner may have other good spade holdings that will gain a trick if you lead the king of spades; but it is still a risky choice and more likely to cost a trick that to gain a trick. Leading the king of spades is a good gamble because the extra trick declarer may gain figures to be an overtrick—rather than the one he needs to make his contract—while the trick you gain may be the one that beats the contract.

Finally, note that the king-of-spades lead is a doubtful choice at duplicate bridge, where overtricks are much more important.

#52	West	West	North	East	South
	♠ 7 4 3				1NT
	♡ K J 5 2	Pass	2♣	Pass	2♠
	◇ 8 4	Pass	4♠	All Pass	
	♣ Q 10 9 6				

With three low trumps and a relatively weak hand, the *eight of diamonds* appears to be a good lead. In the following layout, it is the only lead to beat the contract.

```
                    ♠ J 9 8 5
                    ♡ 7 4
                    ◇ A J 10 3
                    ♣ K 8 2
     ♠ 7 4 3                        ♠ A 6
     ♡ K J 5 2                      ♡ Q 10 8 3
     ◇ 8 4                          ◇ K 7 6 5
     ♣ Q 10 9 6                     ♣ 7 5 3
                    ♠ K Q 10 2
                    ♡ A 9 6
                    ◇ Q 9 2
                    ♣ A J 4
```

Declarer cannot prevent you from getting a diamond ruff. Probably partner will be allowed to win the first trick with the king of diamonds, and he will return a diamond. When he regains the lead with the ace of spades, he will lead a third diamond for you to ruff. Declarer must still lose a heart trick and will go down one. Without the diamond lead the contract cannot be set.

Leading from a doubleton worked out well in this case, but it was lucky. Change the East and South cards slightly and it becomes the only lead to give away the contract:

```
                          ♠ J 9 8 5
                          ♡ 7 4
                          ◇ A J 6 3
                          ♣ K 8 2
         ♠ 7 4 3                              ♠ 6 2
         ♡ K J 5 2                            ♡ A Q 10 8
         ◇ 8 4                                ◇ Q 10 7 5
         ♣ Q 10 9 6                           ♣ J 5 3
                          ♠ A K Q 10
                          ♡ 9 6 3
                          ◇ K 9 2
                          ♣ A 7 4
```

The declarer has four losing tricks (two hearts, one diamond and one club) and will lose them all *unless you lead a diamond*. With a diamond lead, declarer will play low in dummy and capture East's ten with his king. After drawing three rounds of trumps, he will lead the nine of diamonds to knock out East's queen. Dummy is left with the ace and jack of diamonds, so he can make his contract by discarding his club loser on dummy's fourth diamond.

With a different lead, declarer has to break the diamond suit himself and will be set unless he plays in peculiar fashion—leads a low diamond from dummy and finesses the nine. If the opening lead were anything but a diamond, the best way to play the diamond suit (after drawing three rounds of trumps) is to *cash the ace and king of diamonds—in that order—and then lead the nine of diamonds*. This line succeeds unless East has four or more diamonds including the queen and ten.

Is the eight of diamonds a bad lead? Nobody knows. Some experts would lead a diamond, but I suspect a majority would prefer a trump lead. In either case it is a shot in the dark; sometimes the appealing lead turns out to be the wrong lead. The purpose of showing you these hands is to make you aware that leading a doubleton (or a singleton) reveals to the declarer how the suit will divide and may help him to make his contract. So following the advice given in the preceding page about when to lead and when not to lead a short suit will not always guide you to the winning decision, but it should improve your batting average. Good luck!

When to Lead Partner's Suit

Here are four deals on the subject.

#53	West		West	North	East	South
	♠ 8 6 5					1♡
	♡ 9 7 3		Pass	2♡	2♠	4♡
	◇ 7 5 4 2		Pass	Pass	Pass	
	♣ A Q 9					

Lead the five of spades. In a great majority of cases, the best defense is to lead your partner's bid suit.

The lead of the five assumes you and your partner have agreed to lead low from three spot cards. Here is the full deal where leading the lowest card from three spot cards can guide your partner to the winning defense.

```
                        ♠ Q 10 2
                        ♡ J 8 6
                        ◇ A J 10 9 3
                        ♣ 7 4
        ♠ 8 6 5                          ♠ A K J 9 3
        ♡ 9 7 3                          ♡ 4 2
        ◇ 7 5 4 2                        ◇ 8 6
        ♣ A Q 9                          ♣ J 10 6 5
                        ♠ 7 4
                        ♡ A K Q 10 5
                        ◇ K Q
                        ♣ K 8 3 2
```

Suppose your partner wins the first trick with the jack of spades and then leads the king of spades. When you play the six of spades, he will know that declarer began with a doubleton. Since he knows he cannot win any more spade tricks, he should automatically switch to a club; the only defense to beat the contract.

In this case, leading the middle card (MUD, see page 392 in *Conventional Leads and Signals*) works out okay because your partner sees you play the six and then the eight before he has to make a decision. But if your partnership agreement is to lead the top of three low cards, you would lead the eight of spades and follow with the six; not being sure whether you or declarer has the missing five-spot, he may try to cash a third spade winner and declarer will make his contract.

In the next deal, the winning defense is to cash the third high spade.

```
#54                     ♠ Q 10 2
                        ♡ J 8 6
                        ◇ A J 10 9 3
                        ♣ 7 4
        ♠ 8 6                            ♠ A K J 9 3
        ♡ 9 7 3                          ♡ 4 2
        ◇ 7 5 4 2                        ◇ 8 6
        ♣ A 9 8 2                        ♣ J 10 6 5
                        ♠ 7 5 4
                        ♡ A K Q 10 5
                        ◇ K Q
                        ♣ K Q 3
```

West	North	East	South
			1♡
Pass	2♡	2♠	4♡
Pass	Pass	Pass	

This time you have a doubleton spade, so you should lead the *eight*. When your partner cashes his second spade and you follow with the six, he will know that you started with a doubleton; that is if your agreement is to lead low from three spot cards. Aware that declarer has another spade, partner will beat the contract by cashing his third spade and switching to a club when you discard the nine of clubs as a signal.

#55	West		*West*	*North*	*East*	*South*
	♠ 8 6 3 2			1NT	2♡	3♠
	♡ Q 7 4		Pass	4♠	All Pass	
	◇ J 9 8 2					
	♣ 10 3					

Lead the queen of hearts. The normal lead from three to an honor in your partner's suit is low (see #23, page 11), but here is a rare exception to the rule. The bidding tipped you off that North is likely to have any missing heart honors, and he might have the king. In the following layout, the queen of hearts is the only lead to beat the contract.

```
                      ♠ K Q 5
                      ♡ K 9 3
                      ◇ A K 10 5
                      ♣ J 8 7
      ♠ 8 6 3 2                        ♠ 7
      ♡ Q 7 4                          ♡ A J 10 8 2
      ◇ J 9 8 2                        ◇ Q 6 4 3
      ♣ 10 3                           ♣ A 9 5
                      ♠ A J 10 9 4
                      ♡ 6 5
                      ◇ 7
                      ♣ K Q 6 4 2
```

Whether declarer covers the queen of hearts with the king or not, three rounds of hearts will be led and he will be forced to ruff the third round. Declarer will then lead two rounds of trumps. When your partner shows out on the second lead, declarer cannot make his contract with good defense. If he plays his last two trumps, partner can cash his hearts when he gets the lead with the ace of clubs. If he leads clubs, you will play high-low and your partner should duck the first round, win the second and lead a third round of clubs, which you will ruff.

There are times when it is better not to lead your partner's suit. For example:

#56	West		*West*	*North*	*East*	*South*
	♠ 7 5 2				1♠	2♡
	♡ 9 6		2♠	3♡	Pass	4♡
	◇ J 10 7 3		Pass	Pass	Pass	
	♣ K Q J 4					

Lead the king of clubs. When your partner has bid a suit, you should lead it unless you have a very good alternative; such as this club holding.

#57	West		*West*	*North*	*East*	*South*
	♠ 10 9 8				1♠	2♡
	♡ 7 6 2		Pass	4♡	All Pass	
	◇ Q 9 8 5 4 3					
	♣ 7					

Lead the seven of clubs. It is unlikely that you can beat the contract unless you can get one or two club ruffs, so here is another type of hand where *not* leading your partner's suit is a good idea.

Leads Versus Slams

The opening leader must analyze the bidding and decide whether to make an aggressive lead or a passive lead against a slam. Here are seven illustrations:

#58	West	West	North	East	South
	♠ 7 3 2				1♠
	♡ 10 8 7 2	Pass	2♢	Pass	3♠
	♢ 6 4 3	Pass	4♠	Pass	4NT
	♣ K Q 5	Pass	5♢	Pass	6♠
		Pass	Pass	Pass	

Lead the king of clubs. This bidding calls for an attacking lead: It sounds as though the dummy will come down with a long and strong diamond suit, and your diamond holding—three low—suggests that declarer will have no trouble establishing the suit for discards. Declarer's predictable line of play is to draw trumps and discard his losers on the long diamonds. It is your hope that partner can win a trick in spades or diamonds in time to cash a club trick.

#59	West	West	North	East	South
	♠ 7 3 2				1♠
	♡ 10 8 7 2	Pass	2♢	Pass	3♠
	♢ 6 4 3	Pass	4♠	Pass	4NT
	♣ K 5 4	Pass	5♢	Pass	6♠
		Pass	Pass	Pass	

Lead the four of clubs. A club lead is more likely to establish a trick than a heart lead. You must hope that partner has the queen of clubs (or conceivably the ace) and declarer and dummy both have two or more clubs. Then if your partner can get the lead before declarer can draws trumps and discard his losers on the diamond suit, you will be able to cash a club trick. Suppose this is the full deal:

```
                  ♠ Q 5
                  ♡ A 9 3
                  ♢ K Q J 10 8
                  ♣ 7 6 2
  ♠ 7 3 2                        ♠ 10 6
  ♡ 10 8 7 2                     ♡ J 5 4
  ♢ 6 4 3                        ♢ A 9 5 2
  ♣ K 5 4                        ♣ J 9 8 3
                  ♠ A K J 9 8 4
                  ♡ K Q 6
                  ♢ 7
                  ♣ A Q 10
```

Alas, declarer has the ace and queen of clubs, so the contract cannot be set. But note that declarer will make this contract no matter what you lead; your club lead cost nothing.

Now suppose you change the club holding so declarer has ♣ A J 10 and your partner has the queen. A club lead is the only way to beat the contract: When partner gets the lead with the ace of diamonds, a club trick can be cashed; but with any other lead, declarer will have time to discard his losing clubs on the diamond suit.

Note that the club lead was an easy choice when you had the king-queen, but to lead away from a king against a slam, wow!

When is it right and when is it wrong to lead an ace against a slam? Here are three examples:

#60	West	West	North	East	South
	♠ J 7 4				1♡
	♡ 6 5 2	Pass	3♡	Pass	4NT
	◇ A 10 9 3	Pass	5♡	Pass	6♡
	♣ 10 9 8	Pass	Pass	Pass	

Lead the ten of clubs. There is no indication from the bidding that declarer will be able to discard losing diamonds on another suit, so choose the safest possible lead; do not lead your ace. It is tricks within the diamond suit itself you should be concerned about: If declarer is forced to break the diamond suit, your ace may capture the king or queen and deprive him of a trick; if you lead the ace, you will probably capture two spot cards.

You should lead an ace if you have another trick, and if you are reasonably sure your ace will not be ruffed. For example:

#61	West	West	North	East	South
	♠ J 7 4				1♡
	♡ Q J 2	Pass	3♡	Pass	4NT
	◇ A 6 5 3	Pass	5♡	Pass	6♡
	♣ 10 9 8	Pass	Pass	Pass	

The bidding indicates that declarer does not have a void diamond suit (he should not use Blackwood with a void suit) and you have a heart trick, so you definitely should *lead the ace of diamonds*.

It gets more interesting if you hold ♡ Q x x: If the dummy has the ace or king of hearts, declarer can avoid a heart loser by finessing through you for the queen. Since a good defender is more likely to lead an ace when he thinks he has a second trick, a good declarer is more likely to play you for the queen of hearts if you lead the ace of diamonds than if you do not. Suppose, with the same bidding as above, you lead the ace of diamonds and this turns out to be the full deal:

#62

```
                    ♠ A 6 5
                    ♡ K 10 8 4
                    ◇ 9 7
                    ♣ A J 3 2
    ♠ J 7 4                         ♠ Q 10 9 3 2
    ♡ Q 7 2                         ♡ 5
    ◇ A 6 5 3                       ◇ J 10 8
    ♣ 10 9 8                        ♣ 7 6 5 4
                    ♠ K 8
                    ♡ A J 9 6 3
                    ◇ K Q 4 2
                    ♣ K Q
```

With nine hearts, declarer's normal play is to cash the ace or king and if both opponents follow suit, to cash the other high honor and hope the queen drops. But the odds whether to finesse or play for the drop are very close. Declarer may decide to finesse you for the queen of hearts because you led the ace of diamonds; something you would be unlikely to do unless you thought you could win another trick.

Since the bidding suggested that you will not lose your ace of diamonds if you do not lead it—and as you can see you will not—leading the ace when you hold ♡ Q x x is a mistake; especially against a sharp declarer.

#63

```
                          North
                          ♠ A Q J 2
                          ♡ K 10 3
                          ◇ A Q
                          ♣ K 7 6 3

                          South
                          ♠ K 10 9 7 4 3
                          ♡ J 8 6 5
                          ◇ —
                          ♣ A Q J
```

West	North	East	South
	1♣	Pass	1♠
Pass	4♠	Pass	6♠
Pass	Pass	Pass	

Declarer must hold his heart losers to one. He can discard two hearts on dummy's ace of diamonds and fourth club, but that leaves him with two hearts in his hand and the fate of the contract depends on finding West with the ace or queen of hearts and guessing which. *West leads the four of hearts!* Since players rarely underlead aces against suit contracts, especially slams, the sensible thing for declarer to do is to play a low heart and hope West has led from the queen. Alas, the four hands:

```
                          ♠ A Q J 2
                          ♡ K 10 3
                          ◇ A Q
                          ♣ K 7 6 3
    ♠ 8 5                                      ♠ 6
    ♡ A 7 4                                    ♡ Q 9 2
    ◇ 10 8 6 4 3 2                             ◇ K J 9 7 5
    ♣ 9 4                                      ♣ 10 8 5 2
                          ♠ K 10 9 7 4 3
                          ♡ J 8 6 5
                          ◇ —
                          ♣ A Q J
```

West did underlead his ace. His spectacular lead would fool most declarers; they would play a low heart from dummy and the contract can be set. But as was mentioned earlier, underleading aces versus suit contracts is more likely to fool your partner than the declarer, and this partner was no exception. When declarer played a low heart from dummy, *East played the nine* (which would be the right play if his partner had the jack instead of the ace. So declarer won the first trick with the jack and made his contract. Who should be blamed, East or West? Answer: Consult your analyst.

If underleading an ace against a trump contract is ever right, it is when the dummy has done the strong bidding and is a big favorite to have the king—which was the case here. But even then it is more apt to cost a trick than to gain a trick. Underleading an ace versus a trump contract is a losing proposition in the long run. The following deal is a rare exception; although a gambling lead, it cannot mislead your partner.

#64	West	West	North	East	South
	♠ —				1♠
	♡ 8 6 3	2◇	3♣	Pass	3♡
	◇ A K Q 4 3 2	Pass	4♡	Pass	4NT
	♣ 9 7 6 5	Pass	5◇	Pass	6♡
		Pass	Pass	Pass	

Lead the four of diamonds; yes, underlead the ace-king-queen. Declarer's bidding indicates that he has a singleton diamond (he would not use Blackwood with a void suit, and he would not bid a slam with two losing diamonds). So unless partner has a trick (very doubtful), you need a spade ruff to beat the contract. Now do you see the merit of the lead? If partner has the jack of diamonds, you can beat the slam. Here is the actual deal; it really happened:

```
                      ♠ K J
                      ♡ K 7 5
                      ◇ J 9 8
                      ♣ A 10 8 4 3
    ♠ —                                 ♠ 9 8 6 4 3 2
    ♡ 8 6 3                             ♡ 10 2
    ◇ A K Q 4 3 2                       ◇ 10 7 5
    ♣ 9 7 6 5                           ♣ Q J
                      ♠ A Q 10 7 5
                      ♡ A Q J 9 4
                      ◇ 6
                      ♣ K 2
```

No luck! East did not have the jack of diamonds, but declarer was lazy; *he did not play the jack of diamonds from dummy*. East won the first trick with the ten of diamonds and realized that his partner's spectacular lead was a desperate attempt to get him on lead; something he would not do unless he had a void suit. South had opened one spade, yet East could see eight spades between his hand and the dummy. Confident that his partner was void in the suit, East led a spade and beat the slam. This hand made the newspapers, and deservedly so, but the declarer was a well-known expert and his name was never mentioned.

Lead-Directing Doubles of Artificial Bids

The double of any artificial bid calls for that suit to be led; it does not matter whether the eventual contract is played in notrump or in a suit. The most common artificial bids are: a Stayman response to an opening notrump bid (see illustration #30, page 15), a response to Blackwood or Gerber, a control-showing bid or a transfer bid. Here are three examples:

#65	West	West	North	East	South
	♠ J 10 2				1♡
	♡ 7 4 3	Pass	3♡	Pass	4NT
	◇ J 8 6	Pass	5◇	Double	6♡
	♣ Q J 9 5	Pass	Pass	Pass	

Lead the six of diamonds. The five-diamond response to Blackwood is an artificial bid, so partner's double asks for a diamond lead.

#66	West	West	North	East	South
	♠ 9 7 3				1♠
	♡ 10 9 6 5	Pass	3♠	Pass	4♣
	◇ Q 8	Pass	4◇	Double	4♠
	♣ 10 7 4 3	Pass	Pass	Pass	

Lead the queen of diamonds. North's four-diamond bid is a control-showing bid, so partner's double calls for a diamond lead.

#67	West	West	North	East	South
	♠ Q 10 4				1NT
	♡ 7 2	Pass	2♡ (a)	Double	2♠
	◇ Q 9 6 3	Pass	3NT	Pass	4♠
	♣ J 10 8 7	Pass	Pass	Pass	

(a) A transfer bid showing five or more spades

Lead the seven of hearts. North's two-heart bid is artificial, so partner's double calls for a heart lead.

Lead-Directing Doubles of Slams Bid in a Suit

If your opponents arrive at a slam in a trump contract and your partner has the opening lead, a double calls for an "unusual lead." For example:

#68	West	West	North	East	South
	♠ 7 4				1♠
	♡ Q 8 7 4 3 2	Pass	2NT	Pass	3♡
	◇ J 10 9	Pass	3♠	Pass	6♠
	♣ 9 6	Pass	Pass	Double	All Pass

Lead the four of hearts. When you and your partner have never bid, an unusual lead is defined as a suit bid by the enemy. The doubler is usually void in the suit he wants led; in this case, you can expect him to ruff your heart lead. These lead-directing doubles of suit slams are called "Lightner Doubles," named after Theodore Lightner, who had the original idea in 1929.

#69	West	West	North	East	South
	♠ 5 3 2				1♠
	♡ 6 3	Pass	2♣	3◇	3♡
	◇ J 10 7	Pass	4♡	Pass	4NT
	♣ 9 8 7 6 4	Pass	5♡	Pass	6♡
		Pass	Pass	Double	All Pass

Lead the six of clubs. Partner's double said: "Don't lead my suit." So the other two suits (whether the opponents bid both of them or not) are in the category of *unusual*. Partner wants you to lead a club or a spade. In most cases the doubler has a void suit and wants to ruff the opening lead. Since you have five clubs and only three spades, it is much more likely that partner is void in clubs. Partner's double would be appropriate with the following East hand:

#70

                        ♠ A 6
                        ♡ Q 10 7
                        ◇ Q 4
                        ♣ A Q 10 5 3 2

♠ 5 3 2   ♠ 10 9 8
♡ 6 3   ♡ 8 4 2
◇ J 10 7   ◇ A K 9 8 6 5 3
♣ 9 8 7 6 4   ♣ —

                        ♠ K Q J 7 4
                        ♡ A K J 9 5
                        ◇ 2
                        ♣ K J

Note that only a club lead will beat the contract. Also note that the opponents cannot escape to another slam contract which is makable; another consideration when you are making a lead-directing double.

Quiz for Chapter One

Studying the bidding carefully and then choose your opening lead for each of the following hands.

1.	West	West	North	East	South
	♠ 10 9 8 4				1NT
	♡ 10 6 5 4 2	Pass	3NT	All Pass	
	◇ A 3				
	♣ K 3				

2.	West	West	North	East	South
	♠ Q J 10 7		1♠	Pass	2NT
	♡ Q 6 3	Pass	6NT	All Pass	
	◇ J 4				
	♣ 9 8 4 2				

3.	West	West	North	East	South
	♠ K J 2		1♣	Pass	1♡
	♡ 7 6	Pass	3♣	Pass	3♡
	◇ 9 8 5 3 2	Pass	4♡	All Pass	
	♣ J 10 9				

4.	West	West	North	East	South
	♠ A 3				1♠
	♡ J 10 9 8	Pass	2◇	Pass	3◇
	◇ 7 6 4 2	Pass	3♠	Pass	4♠
	♣ A 8 5	Pass	Pass	Pass	

5.	West	West	North	East	South
	♠ J 5 2				1♠
	♡ A Q 10 8	Pass	2♣	Pass	2♡
	◇ Q J 10 9	Pass	2♠	Pass	3♡
	♣ 6 3	Pass	4♠	All Pass	

6.	West	West	North	East	South
	♠ 10 8 6 3		1♣	Pass	2NT
	♡ J 2	Pass	3NT	All Pass	
	◇ A Q 9 8				
	♣ 9 5 4				

7.	West	West	North	East	South
	♠ Q J 10 3		1◇	Pass	1♡
	♡ 6	Pass	3♡	Pass	4NT
	◇ J 7 6 4	Pass	5♡	Pass	6♡
	♣ Q 10 9 8	Pass	Pass	Double	All Pass

8.	West	West	North	East	South
	♠ K 7 4		1♣	Pass	1♡
	♡ 5 4	Pass	3♣	Pass	3♡
	◇ 10 9 8 7 3	Pass	4♡	Pass	4NT
	♣ A 6 2	Pass	5◇	Pass	6♡
		Pass	Pass	Pass	

Quiz Answers for Chapter One

1.

	North	
	♠ K 3 2	
	♡ K J	
	◇ 8 6 5 4	
	♣ Q J 7 2	
West		**East**
♠ 10 9 8 4		♠ J 7 6
♡ 10 6 5 4 2		♡ 9 7 3
◇ A 3		◇ J 10 9
♣ K 3		♣ A 8 5 4
	South	
	♠ A Q 5	
	♡ A Q 8	
	◇ K Q 7 2	
	♣ 10 9 6	

West	North	East	South
			1NT
Pass	3NT	All Pass	

Lead the four of hearts. The declarer must drive out the ace of diamonds and the ace and king of clubs before he can win nine tricks, so, even though he has three heart stoppers, you can establish two long cards in hearts and beat the contract if you and your partner lead hearts at every turn. The four of hearts—the fourth highest—is the correct card to lead: This indicates that you are trying to establish long heart tricks, and would like your partner to return the suit when he gets the lead.

If you chose a spade lead, you would not beat the contract because only one long card could be established. Leading a five-card suit is preferable to leading a four-card suit versus a three- notrump contract, unless the five-card suit is very weak and the four-card suit is very strong.

2.

	North	
	♠ A 9 8 6 3	
	♡ K 7 2	
	◇ A 5	
	♣ A K J	
West		**East**
♠ Q J 10 7		♠ 4 2
♡ Q 6 3		♡ J 8 5 4
◇ J 4		◇ Q 10 7 6 2
♣ 9 8 4 2		♣ 5 3
	South	
	♠ K 5	
	♡ A 10 9	
	◇ K 9 8 3	
	♣ Q 10 7 6	

West	North	East	South
	1♠	Pass	2NT
Pass	6NT	All Pass	

Lead the two of clubs (or any club). Declarer has ten top tricks. Since the spade suit offers the only chance for two extra tricks, he will be set because the suit does not divide favorably.

The queen-of-spades lead would be desirable if spades were an unbid suit, but it is very dangerous when dummy has bid the suit. In this case declarer can maneuver to win four spade tricks if you lead a spade.

Note that an opening lead of a heart or a diamond would give declarer one extra trick; not enough to make his bid *this time;* but leading from these combinations should be ruled out. Against notrump slams, the best opening lead is the one least likely to give declarer an unearned trick; in this case, it is a club.

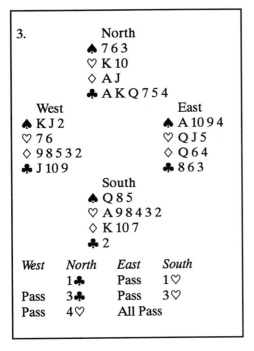

3.　　　　North
　　　　♠ 7 6 3
　　　　♡ K 10
　　　　♢ A J
　　　　♣ A K Q 7 5 4
West　　　　　　　East
♠ K J 2　　　　　♠ A 10 9 4
♡ 7 6　　　　　　♡ Q J 5
♢ 9 8 5 3 2　　　♢ Q 6 4
♣ J 10 9　　　　　♣ 8 6 3
　　　　South
　　　　♠ Q 8 5
　　　　♡ A 9 8 4 3 2
　　　　♢ K 10 7
　　　　♣ 2

West	North	East	South
	1♣	Pass	1♡
Pass	3♣	Pass	3♡
Pass	4♡	All Pass	

Lead the two of spades. The bidding tells you that dummy has a powerful club suit, and, given time, the declarer is going to discard some of his losers. This is clearly a time to attack—lead from strength. Granted, it is lucky to be able to win the first three spade tricks, but, whether you lead the suit or not, it is very unlikely that you will ever win any spade tricks unless your partner has the ace or queen. Note that the spade lead beats the contract, while declarer can win twelve tricks with any other lead.

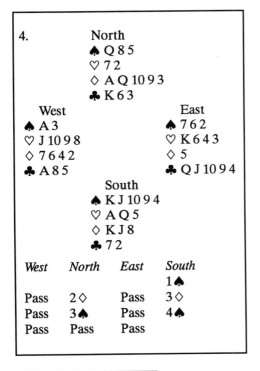

4.　　　　North
　　　　♠ Q 8 5
　　　　♡ 7 2
　　　　♢ A Q 10 9 3
　　　　♣ K 6 3
West　　　　　　　East
♠ A 3　　　　　　♠ 7 6 2
♡ J 10 9 8　　　♡ K 6 4 3
♢ 7 6 4 2　　　　♢ 5
♣ A 8 5　　　　　♣ Q J 10 9 4
　　　　South
　　　　♠ K J 10 9 4
　　　　♡ A Q 5
　　　　♢ K J 8
　　　　♣ 7 2

West	North	East	South
			1♠
Pass	2♢	Pass	3♢
Pass	3♠	Pass	4♠
Pass	Pass	Pass	

Lead the two of diamonds. North and South both bid diamonds, so your partner figures to have at most one. Since you have the ace of trumps and can regain the lead before declarer can draw trumps, there is an excellent chance to give partner one or two diamond ruffs. Assume declarer wins the first diamond trick and leads a trump. You should win with your ace and *lead the four of diamonds,*[1] which your partner will ruff. If partner returns a club, you will win with the ace and give him a second diamond ruff. Note that declarer would make his contract with an overtrick if your opening lead were a heart.

---

1. Leading your lowest diamond (in this case the four-spot) is a "suit-preference signal," asking partner to return the lower-ranking suit, clubs (for a full explanation, see Chapter 7).

5.   North
                  ♠ A 10 8
                  ♡ 7 3
                  ◇ 7 6 2
                  ♣ A K 9 5 4
West   East
♠ J 5 2   ♠ 6 3
♡ A Q 10 8   ♡ 9 4
◇ Q J 10 9   ◇ K 8 5 4
♣ 6 3   ♣ Q J 10 7 2
                  South
                  ♠ K Q 9 7 4
                  ♡ K J 6 5 2
                  ◇ A 3
                  ♣ 8

West	North	East	South
			1♠
Pass	2♣	Pass	2♡
Pass	2♠	Pass	3♡
Pass	4♠	All Pass	

Lead the five (or two) of spades. With length and strength in declarer's side suit—hearts—the obvious choice is a trump lead to cut down on dummy's ruffing power. Note that declarer must give up two heart tricks before the dummy is void in hearts. If you lead a spade each time you get the lead, the dummy will have no more trumps. As a result, declarer will be unable to ruff any hearts and you will win four heart tricks. Without a trump lead, the declarer could always ruff at least one heart in dummy and make his contract.

6.   North
                  ♠ K 9 4
                  ♡ K Q 8
                  ◇ 6 5 2
                  ♣ K Q 10 3
West   East
♠ 10 8 6 3   ♠ Q 5 2
♡ J 2   ♡ 9 7 6 5 3
◇ A Q 9 8   ◇ J 10 3
♣ 9 5 4   ♣ A 7
                  South
                  ♠ A J 7
                  ♡ A 10 4
                  ◇ K 7 4
                  ♣ J 8 6 2

West	North	East	South
	1♣	Pass	2NT
Pass	3NT	All Pass	

Lead the eight of spades. The fourth best diamond would be the appropriate choice if you had a fifth diamond, but those in the know frown upon leading from four-card holdings such as A Q 9 8. Note that the only lead permitting declarer to make his bid is a diamond. The reason for leading the *eight* of spades is to discourage your partner from returning the suit; he can see that the eight is not your fourth best, and therefore should assume you are leading the top card of a worthless suit. (Note that it would be wrong to lead the ten, because there are many combinations where it would give declarer an extra spade trick.)

Your partner will eventually get the lead with the ace of clubs. Remembering that you led the eight of spades, and seeing the weak diamonds in dummy, he should switch to the jack of diamonds.

7.

        North
        ♠ K 6 5
        ♡ A J 3 2
        ◇ A Q 10 9 8
        ♣ 4

West   East
♠ Q J 10 3   ♠ A 8 7 4 2
♡ 6   ♡ 9 8 5
◇ J 7 6 4   ◇ —
♣ Q 10 9 8   ♣ J 7 6 5 3

        South
        ♠ 9
        ♡ K Q 10 7 4
        ◇ K 5 3 2
        ♣ A K 2

West	North	East	South
	1◇	Pass	1♡
Pass	3♡	Pass	4NT
Pass	5♡	Pass	6♡
Pass	Pass	Double	All Pass

Lead a diamond. Partner has made a "lead-directing double," calling for an unusual lead. Leading an unbid suit would be a normal choice, and the double never calls for a trump lead. So, the only unusual lead is the suit bid by dummy—diamonds. Partner will ruff the diamond lead and cash the ace of spades to set the contract.

Note that the opponents cannot safely escape to six notrump because South would be declarer. Six notrump can be made if played by North. Also, six diamonds can be made, but they cannot bid it over six hearts.

8.

        North
        ♠ 10 5
        ♡ A 6
        ◇ K Q J
        ♣ K Q J 10 9 4

West   East
♠ K 7 4   ♠ Q 8 6 3 2
♡ 5 4   ♡ 9 8 2
◇ 10 9 8 7 3   ◇ 5 4
♣ A 6 2   ♣ 7 5 3

        South
        ♠ A J 9
        ♡ K Q J 10 7 3
        ◇ A 6 2
        ♣ 8

West	North	East	South
	1♣	Pass	1♡
Pass	3♣	Pass	3♡
Pass	4♡	Pass	4NT
Pass	5◇	Pass	6♡
Pass	Pass	Pass	

Lead the four of spades. The bidding indicates a long and strong club suit will show up in dummy, so this is a time to attack: lead from strength. If declarer has any losers in the side suits, he will discard them on dummy's clubs *if you give him time.* You must try to establish a trick to cash when you win the lead with the ace of clubs, and the best hope is to find your partner with the queen of spades.

Another reason to rule out a diamond lead is that partner did not double the artificial five-diamond bid.

2
Third-Hand Play

"Third hand high,"—is it a good rule? It usually is if your partner has led a low card, the dummy has no high cards and you are trying to win or promote a trick for your side. For example:

Dummy
7 5 4

Partner   You
leads the 2   K 10 3

By all means, play the *king*. You cannot lose and will gain a trick if declarer has Q x x, A J x, etc.

When you have a suit headed by a sequence—two or more cards of equal value—*play the low card* of the sequence. For example, if you change your holding in the above illustration: Play the *jack* from Q J 9, the *ten* from Q J 10, the *nine* from 10 9 4, etc. This procedure is extremely important, as you shall see in later chapters.

When there is a high card in dummy that you have "surrounded," play the lowest card that will effectively win or promote a trick. For example, your partner leads a low card and the three is played from a dummy holding of Q 7 3: Play the *jack* from K J 8, the *ten* from K J 10, the *nine* from K 10 9, etc. Another case for "trapping" dummy's honor card is when partner leads an honor card: For example, partner leads the ten and dummy has J 7 3; *do not play your honor* from Q 6 5 or K 6 5 unless the jack is played.

If your partner or dummy has already played a card higher than any in your hand, your play cannot win or promote a trick. Therefore, *the card you play sends a signal to your partner.* "Defensive Signals" will be covered thoroughly in Chapters Six and Seven. Although a high percentage of signals are given by third hand, the topic is ignored in this chapter, except in the Table of Fundamentals that follows.

Table of Fundamentals

There are many situations where the winning third-hand play is not obvious, but before getting into the more intricate decisions, here is a Table of Fundamentals for you to mull over. All of these recommended plays are not 100 percent correct all of the time; but the exceptions are rare and you would be wise to abide by them unless you have figured a good reason to do otherwise. The underlined card is the one played from dummy.

	Lead	Dummy	You	
1.	3	9 5 **4**	J 10 6	Play the ten. If you play the jack, you deny the ten.
2.	2	9 7 **4**	J 10 8	Play the eight. If you play the ten, you deny the eight.
3.	4	Q 6 **5**	A J 2	Play the jack.
4.	2	K 6 **4**	Q J 10	Play the ten.

	Lead	Dummy	You	
5.	2	K 6 4	Q J 10	Play the queen, a signal to tell partner that you have the jack and probably the ten.
6.	3	K 6 4	A 10 2	Play the ten.
7.	3	J 6 4	K 9 2	Play the nine.
8.	3	A Q 9	K 10 6	Play the ten; partner may have the jack.
9.	8	A Q 9	K 10 6	Play the king. Partner would not lead the eight if he had the jack.
10.	10	A 6 5	Q 7 2	Play the queen. Partner may have led the ten from K 10 9 x.
11.	10	A 6 5	K Q 2	Play the queen.
12.	Q	6 5 4	K 2	Play the king, to unblock.
13.	Q	10 4 3	K 2	Play the two. If you play the king, declarer will be able to win a trick with the ten.
14.	Q	6 5 4	K 8 2	Play the eight—an attitude signal—assuming you wish to encourage partner to continue leading the suit.
15.	Q	8 7 3	10 6 2	Play the six. A come-on signal is usually right if partner leads the queen and you hold the ten.
16.	K	8 6 3	Q J 2	Play the queen, a signal telling partner that you have the jack.
17.	K	8 6 3	Q 2	Play the two, even in a trump contract. If you play the queen, partner will think you have the jack and may underlead his ace.
18.	K	9 5 2	7 4	Play the seven versus a trump contract if you wish partner to continue leading the suit so you can ruff the third round. (It is unlucky if declarer holds up with A J x.) But play the four versus a notrump contract.

Third-Hand Play is a huge topic and many of the deals coming up would be appropriate in other chapters, and vice versa. So, there is much more to be learned about Third-Hand Play later in the book. However, this chapter does contain many interesting deals showing the task of third hand. The opening lead is a major source of information and should be analyzed carefully. We will begin with "The Rule of Eleven."

The Rule of Eleven

When partner makes a lead of his fourth-highest card in a suit (versus trump contracts as well as notrump contracts), the Rule of Eleven sometimes gives third hand useful information about declarer's holding in the suit led.

Here is how it works: If the ace, king, queen and jack had numbers, the cards in a suit would be numbered from two to fourteen. So, if you subtract any card from fourteen, you learn how many higher cards are in that suit. When a player leads his fourth-highest card, he holds exactly three cards higher than the one he led; the other three hands have the rest. Since you see your hand and the dummy, it is simple to figure out how many higher cards are held by the declarer. Suppose your partner leads the six (his fourth-highest card): six from fourteen leaves eight higher. Your partner has three of them, so the three remaining hands have five cards higher than the six. Now for the simplification: Subtract six from eleven to get the same number, five.

So, assuming partner has led fourth-highest, subtract the card he led from eleven to learn how many higher cards are held by the dummy, the declarer and you. That is all there is to the Rule of Eleven. Here are three examples of how this information can be useful.

#1

North
♠ A K Q J 9
♡ K 5 3
♢ A 10 3
♣ K 6

East
♠ 10 7 2
♡ A J 9 2
♢ 8 5 4
♣ A 10 3

West	North	East	South
	1♠	Pass	1NT
Pass	3NT	All Pass	

Partner leads the seven of hearts and dummy plays the three. Before reading further, which heart would you play?

Here is the full deal:

♠ A K Q J 9
♡ K 5 3
♢ A 10 3
♣ K 6

♠ 6 4 3
♡ Q 10 8 7
♢ 9 7 6 2
♣ J 5

♠ 10 7 2
♡ A J 9 2
♢ 8 5 4
♣ A 10 3

♠ 8 5
♡ 6 4
♢ K Q J
♣ Q 9 8 7 4 2

The only way to beat the contract is to play the *two of hearts*, so partner can win the trick with the seven and lead a second heart through the king. It is likely that partner has led his fourth-highest heart, and seven from eleven is four. The four cards higher than the seven are all in sight, so declarer cannot beat the seven.

#2

North
♠ Q 10 9 8 7
♡ K 9 3
◇ K J 2
♣ A 5

East
♠ 6 3 2
♡ A J 7
◇ 6 5 4
♣ 10 9 8 7

West	North	East	South
	1♠	Pass	2NT
Pass	3NT	All Pass	

Partner leads the five of hearts and the three is played from dummy. You should *play the seven*. Five from eleven is six and you can see five of the cards higher than the five in your hand and dummy. So declarer has one higher and it is likely to be the queen; his two-notrump bid said he had stoppers in the unbid suits. The four hands:

♠ Q 10 9 8 7
♡ K 9 3
◇ K J 2
♣ A 5

♠ A K 4
♡ 10 8 6 5
◇ 9 7 3
♣ Q 4 2

♠ 6 3 2
♡ A J 7
◇ 6 5 4
♣ 10 9 8 7

♠ J 5
♡ Q 4 2
◇ A Q 10 8
♣ K J 6 3

As you can see, the seven of hearts will drive out the queen. Declarer's only chance to make his contract is to drive out the ace and king of spades and hope you cannot win enough heart tricks to beat him.

When partner gets the lead with the king of spades at trick two, he will lead another heart. After you cash your two heart tricks it does not matter what you lead; declarer must give your partner the lead again with the ace of spades, and he will set the contract by cashing his thirteenth heart.

Actually, declarer's correct technical play is the *nine* of hearts at trick one; in which case you would play the jack without problem. But when he plays the three, you should insert the seven to avoid giving him a second heart stopper.

The declarer also can use the Rule of Eleven to learn something about third hand: In the diagram above, he sees his hand and dummy; with three cards higher than the five in sight, he knows that East has three cards higher. Also note that declarer can see all of the cards lower than the five, so he knows that West has a four-card suit. This time the information is valueless to the declarer; another time it will help declarer and be valueless to third hand. So why should you lead fourth-highest? Obviously, because the information is more often useful to the defense.

In the next deal the Rule of Eleven enables third hand to eliminate a problem for his partner:

#3   North
                                            ♠ A 8 5 2
                                            ♡ 10 6 4
                                            ◇ J 10 7 3
                                            ♣ Q 9
                                                              East
                                                              ♠ Q J 10 7
                                                              ♡ J 9 8 3
                                                              ◇ 6 5 4
                                                              ♣ J 2

West	North	East	South
			1◇
Pass	1♠	Pass	2NT
Pass	3NT	All Pass	

Partner leads the seven of clubs and the queen is played from dummy. Seven from eleven is four, so declarer has one card higher which figures to be the ace or king, so you should *play the jack* under the queen. Here are the four hands to show you how this helps your partner:

                                            ♠ A 8 5 2
                                            ♡ 10 6 4
                                            ◇ J 10 7 3
                                            ♣ Q 9
        ♠ 9 6 3   ♠ Q J 10 7
        ♡ 7 5 2   ♡ J 9 8 3
        ◇ A Q   ◇ 6 5 4
        ♣ K 10 8 7 4   ♣ J 2
                                            ♠ K 4
                                            ♡ A K Q
                                            ◇ K 9 8 2
                                            ♣ A 6 5 3

After winning the first trick with the queen of clubs, declarer leads the jack of diamonds and lets it ride around to your partner's queen. With the queen and jack gone, partner knows it is safe to lead another club from ♣ K 10 8 4 and drive out declarer's ace. When he regains the lead with the ace of diamonds, he has enough club tricks to set the contract.

Granted, the contract can be defeated if you play the two of clubs, but this requires partner to make an unusual play: When he gains the lead in diamonds, not only must he return a club unsure who has the jack, but he must also lead the *king* (else the suit blocks). Playing the jack of clubs at trick one solves both of these problems for your partner.

The Rule of Eleven is more likely to help when an intermediate spot card is led—such as a four, five, six, seven or eight—but it can be used even when the two or three is led. Suppose partner leads the two. You and the dummy have five cards in the suit between you. Two from eleven is nine, so the declarer has four cards higher than the two. Of course, you do not know which ones they are, but the knowledge that he has a four-card suit can sometimes be helpful.

If your partner has led fourth-highest and your goal is to find out his *length* in the suit (rather than declarer's high-card holding), *look for the cards lower than the one partner has led*; the Rule of Eleven is not needed. For example, partner leads the four, dummy has 7 2 and you have A 10 3. There are eight cards missing and you can tell that partner has four because the two and three are in sight; consequently, the declarer has four. If partner leads the four, dummy has 7 5 and you have A 10 3, the two is missing and you cannot tell whether partner has led from four or five; but if you keep your eyes peeled, you will eventually know when the two appears.

Third Hand High?

Now for some full deals, where the decision whether or not to play third hand high requires some thought.

#4

```
                    North
                    ♠ 10 7 2
                    ♡ K 8
                    ◇ A K Q J 9 6
                    ♣ A K
                                        East
                                        ♠ A 9 6 4
                                        ♡ A 7 5
                                        ◇ 8 4 3
                                        ♣ 8 3 2
```

West	North	East	South
	1◇	Pass	1NT
Pass	3NT	All Pass	

Your partner leads the jack of hearts and declarer plays low from dummy. With a different dummy more times than not it would be correct to play low and let declarer win with his queen; you save the ace to capture the king and limit declarer to one heart trick. But in this case declarer has nine tricks if you let him win the first trick with the queen of hearts. So the only play that offers a chance to beat the contract is to *win the first trick with the ace of hearts and lead the four of spades*, hoping that partner has ♠ K J x or better. The four hands:

```
                    ♠ 10 7 2
                    ♡ K 8
                    ◇ A K Q J 9 6
                    ♣ A K
        ♠ K J 8                         ♠ A 9 6 4
        ♡ J 10 9 3 2                    ♡ A 7 5
        ◇ 7 5                           ◇ 8 4 3
        ♣ 10 5 4                        ♣ 8 3 2
                    ♠ Q 5 3
                    ♡ Q 6 4
                    ◇ 10 2
                    ♣ Q J 9 7 6
```

Partner has one of the spade holdings you were hoping for, so by winning the first trick with the ace of hearts and leading the four of spades you can take the first five tricks. Note that if you let declarer win the first heart trick, he can win twelve tricks (one heart, six diamonds and five clubs).

#5
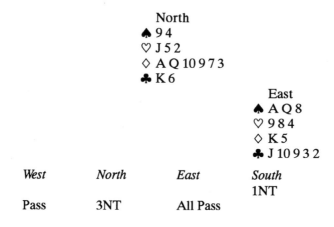

North
♠ 9 4
♡ J 5 2
◇ A Q 10 9 7 3
♣ K 6

East
♠ A Q 8
♡ 9 8 4
◇ K 5
♣ J 10 9 3 2

West	North	East	South
			1NT
Pass	3NT	All Pass	

Your partner leads the six of spades and you should play the *queen*. Declarer has one card higher than the six, probably the king, and you cannot prevent him from winning that trick. Here is the full deal to show why it is wrong to win the first trick with the ace.

♠ 9 4
♡ J 5 2
◇ A Q 10 9 7 3
♣ K 6

♠ J 10 7 6 3
♡ K 7 6 3
◇ 4 2
♣ 8 5

♠ A Q 8
♡ 9 8 4
◇ K 5
♣ J 10 9 3 2

♠ K 5 2
♡ A Q 10
◇ J 8 6
♣ A Q 7 4

Note that if you win the first trick with the ace of spades and return the queen, declarer will hold up until the third round; when you regain the lead with the king of diamonds, you will have no more spades to lead. It is true that declarer can make his contract even if your first play is the queen of spades—by holding up his king—but he is unlikely to do so for fear that your partner has the ace; in which case he would lose the first five spade tricks and be set even if the king of diamonds were onside.

#6

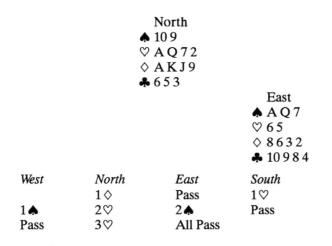

West	North	East	South
	1♢	Pass	1♡
1♠	2♡	2♠	Pass
Pass	3♡	All Pass	

Your partner leads the six of spades. Which spade do you play? Why?

The six of spades is obviously partner's fourth-highest, so declarer has no card higher than the six (six from eleven is five, and you see five cards higher than the six between your hand and dummy). So you can win the first trick with the queen or the ace. The better play is the *queen*, as it eliminates a defensive problem for your partner. Suppose you win the first trick with the queen of spades and lead the ten of clubs. The four hands:

♠ 10 9
♡ A Q 7 2
♢ A K J 9
♣ 6 5 3

♠ K J 8 6 2	♠ A Q 7
♡ K 4	♡ 6 5
♢ 10 5 4	♢ 8 6 3 2
♣ A Q 7	♣ 10 9 8 4

♠ 5 4 3
♡ J 10 9 8 3
♢ Q 7
♣ K J 2

Note that the only way to beat the contract is to win the first five tricks (three clubs and two spades), which means you must lead clubs through declarer twice. When your partner captures declarer's jack of clubs with his queen (or king with his ace), he will routinely return a second spade so you can win with the ace and lead another club.

If you won the first trick with the ace of spades, partner would not know whether you or declarer had the queen. He would have to underlead his king of spades so that you could win with the queen and lead another club. Although your partner might do so, it is a tough play. If you win the first trick with the queen, he cannot go wrong.

#7   North
                                          ♠ K Q J 10
                                          ♡ 9 8 3
                                          ◇ 6 5 4
                                          ♣ K J 7

                                                              East
                                                              ♠ A 6 5 4 3
                                                              ♡ K J 4
                                                              ◇ J 9 8 7
                                                              ♣ 2

West	North	East	South
			1♣
Pass	1♠	Pass	3♣
Pass	4♣	Pass	5♣
Pass	Pass	Pass	

Partner lead the two of hearts and you should play the *jack*; to find out who has the queen. Partner's lead indicates a maximum of four hearts, so declarer has ♡ A x x or ♡ A Q x (presumably your partner is not underleading the ace against a trump contract). Declarer's predictable line of play is to win the first trick, draw two rounds of trumps and lead a spade. You win with your ace and, since declarer will discard his losers on the spade suit when he regains the lead, the only chance to beat him is to win the next two tricks. If declarer captured your jack of hearts with the ace, partner must have the queen and you can cash two heart tricks; if declarer won the first trick with the queen of hearts, the only chance is to lead a diamond; hoping partner has the ace and queen.

Here is a possible layout, where the diamond switch is the winning defense:

                                          ♠ K Q J 10
                                          ♡ 9 8 3
                                          ◇ 6 5 4
                                          ♣ K J 7
        ♠ 9 8 2   ♠ A 6 5 4 3
        ♡ 10 7 6 2   ♡ K J 4
        ◇ A Q 10 3   ◇ J 9 8 7
        ♣ 5 4   ♣ 2
                                          ♠ 7
                                          ♡ A Q 5
                                          ◇ K 2
                                          ♣ A Q 10 9 8 6 3

Take note that if your first play were the king of hearts and declarer won with his ace, you would not know who had the queen of hearts. Also note that the *king* would be the right third-hand play versus a notrump contract because partner may have underled the ace.

#8   North
                                      ♠ K Q 3 2
                                      ♡ 10 7
                                      ◊ 6 5 2
                                      ♣ J 10 6 3
                                                                    East
                                                                    ♠ 8 6 5 4
                                                                    ♡ Q 9 4
                                                                    ◊ Q J 7
                                                                    ♣ A 8 2

West	North	East	South
			2NT
Pass	3♣	Pass	3◊
Pass	3NT	All Pass	

Partner leads the three of hearts and the seven is played from dummy. Declarer denied a four-card major suit in the bidding, so partner obviously has led from a five-card suit. The queen would be the winning third-hand play if partner has underled the ace and king, but that would leave declarer with only 18 high-card points—not enough for his two-notrump bid. So the *nine* is the correct choice because it gains a trick if declarer has K J x, and breaks even against other holdings.

In the following layout, you must play the nine to beat the contract.

                              ♠ K Q 3 2
                              ♡ 10 7
                              ◊ 6 5 2
                              ♣ J 10 6 3
        ♠ 9 7   ♠ 8 6 5 4
        ♡ A 8 6 3 2   ♡ Q 9 4
        ◊ 10 8 4 3   ◊ Q J 7
        ♣ 7 4   ♣ A 8 2
                              ♠ A J 10
                              ♡ K J 5
                              ◊ A K 9
                              ♣ K Q 9 5

Assuming the declarer wins the first trick with the jack of hearts (he cannot gain by ducking), you can win four heart tricks and set the contract by leading the queen of hearts when you get the lead with the ace of clubs.

#9   North
                                                                  ♠ Q 9 7
                                                                  ♡ J 10 6
                                                                  ♢ A 10 9 5 2
                                                                  ♣ 6 3

                                                                                East
                                                                                ♠ 8 5 4 2
                                                                                ♡ Q 9 5 3
                                                                                ♢ K 7
                                                                                ♣ A 5 4

West	*North*	*East*	*South*
			1♣
Pass	1♢	Pass	2NT
Pass	3NT	All Pass	

Partner leads the two of hearts and dummy plays the jack. Clearly partner has led from A x x x, K x x x or x x x x (declarer showed about nineteen high-card points, so partner cannot have the ace and king). Playing the queen breaks even opposite K x x x, but loses opposite A x x x or x x x x. The right play is clearly *not to play the queen*. The four hands:

                                      ♠ Q 9 7
                                      ♡ J 10 6
                                      ♢ A 10 9 5 2
                                      ♣ 6 3
          ♠ 10 6   ♠ 8 5 4 2
          ♡ A 8 4 2   ♡ Q 9 5 3
          ♢ 6 4 3   ♢ K 7
          ♣ J 9 7 2   ♣ A 5 4
                                      ♠ A K J 3
                                      ♡ K 7
                                      ♢ Q J 8
                                      ♣ K Q 10 8

If you play third hand low, you hold declarer to one heart trick and beat the contract. You win one diamond, one club and *three* heart tricks before declarer can establish nine tricks.

#10   North
                                                                  ♠ Q 6 2
                                                                  ♡ Q 6
                                                                  ♢ A 9 8
                                                                  ♣ K 10 7 4 3

                                                                                East
                                                                                ♠ A J 7 5
                                                                                ♡ K 10 8 3
                                                                                ♢ 5 4
                                                                                ♣ 9 5 2

West	*North*	*East*	*South*
			1NT
Pass	3NT	All Pass	

Partner leads the five of hearts and dummy plays the *six*. Partner has obviously led his fourth-highest heart, so the Rule of Eleven tells you that declarer has exactly one card higher than the five. If it were the ace, *declarer would have played the queen from dummy*. So your partner is marked with the ace of hearts and the correct third-hand play is the *king*.

The four hands might be:

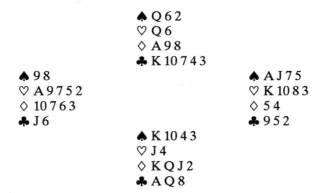

The only holdings the declarer might have where not playing the queen from dummy would make sense, are J x or J x x. To guard against losing a trick to the doubleton jack, you must play the king of hearts on the first trick; if declarer has J x x, he can win one heart trick no matter which heart you play.

#11

North
♠ K Q J 4
♡ A 10 4
◇ 7 6 2
♣ Q J 10

East
♠ 8 5 2
♡ J 5 3
◇ A J 9 4
♣ 8 7 6

West	North	East	South
	1♣	Pass	1♠
Pass	2♠	Pass	4♠
Pass	Pass	Pass	

Your partner leads the two of hearts and dummy plays the four. Which heart would you play? Why?

If partner held the king and queen, he would not lead the two versus a trump contract. So declarer has K Q x, K x x or Q x x. In the first two cases, he can win three tricks no matter which heart you play; but if he has Q x x, you save a trick by playing *low*. Here is the full deal:

```
                            ♠ K Q J 4
                            ♡ A 10 4
                            ◇ 7 6 2
                            ♣ Q J 10
        ♠ 3                                      ♠ 8 5 2
        ♡ K 7 6 2                                ♡ J 5 3
        ◇ K 10 8 5                               ◇ A J 9 4
        ♣ K 9 4 3                                ♣ 8 7 6
                            ♠ A 10 9 7 6
                            ♡ Q 9 8
                            ◇ Q 3
                            ♣ A 5 2
```

Note that if you play the jack of hearts, declarer can win three heart tricks by capturing the jack with the queen and eventually finessing the ten. Your partner made an unfortunate opening lead, but he had a tough decision. However, you can save the day if you play a low heart at trick one; declarer will be limited to two heart tricks as long as you or your partner do not lead the suit again. (Actually, your partner must shift to a diamond after winning with the king of clubs, else declarer can succeed in the end-position by leading all of his trumps.)

Unblocking

One of the common ways to beat a notrump contract is to win a number of tricks in a long suit. Third hand must be careful not to block the suit. For example:

#12   North
                                           ♠ A Q 8
                                           ♡ A 2
                                           ◇ Q J 10 4 3
                                           ♣ 7 6 5
                                                              East
                                                              ♠ J 10 4 3
                                                              ♡ K Q 7
                                                              ◇ A 8 2
                                                              ♣ J 10 9

West	North	East	South
			1♣
Pass	1◇	Pass	1NT
Pass	3NT	All Pass	

Partner leads the six of hearts and declarer plays a low heart from dummy. Which heart would you play?

The *queen*—the low card of your sequence—is right; and then you should lead the *king of hearts*. This is an unblocking situation: You must save your seven of hearts to play when you regain the lead with the ace of diamonds; then partner will be able to win the third heart trick and run the rest of the suit.

When you are defending against a notrump contract and your partner is hoping to win tricks by running a long suit, you should be alert to unblock by saving a low card in the suit to play last. You may be thinking that leading the king of hearts would waste a trick if declarer held ♡ J x x, but with the help of the Rule of Eleven you can figure out that partner has the jack. Before explaining further, here are the four hands:

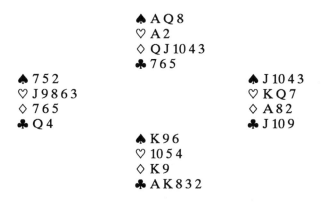

Subtracting partner's six from eleven leaves five; since you and dummy have four hearts higher than the six, declarer has only one. If it were the jack, partner's three higher cards would be the 10 9 8; in which case he would have led the ten, not fourth-highest. Since partner would lead the jack from J 10 9 and J 10 8, he is marked with J 9 8 and declarer's one higher card is the ten. (Note that even if the opening lead were the four or five of hearts—in which case you could not be sure whether partner or declarer had the jack—you should still lead the king of hearts at trick two because it looks like the only chance to beat the contract.)

One last thought before leaving this deal. If declarer plays the ace of hearts on the first trick, your first two heart plays should be the king and then the queen.

#13

North
♠ Q 2
♡ 9 6 5
◇ K J 4
♣ K Q 10 8 3

West
♠ J 9 6 5
♡ K 8 4
◇ 8 6 5 2
♣ A 7

West	North	East	South
			1NT
Pass	3NT	All Pass	

This time you are West. You lead the five of spades, the two is played from dummy, partner wins with the ace and declarer follows with the ten. At trick two, partner leads the four of spades and declarer puts on the king. Which spade do you play? Why?

Here are the four hands:

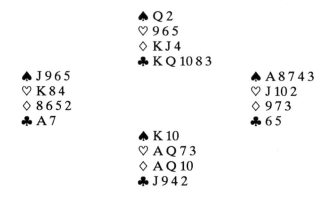

                                    ♠ Q 2
                                    ♡ 9 6 5
                                    ◇ K J 4
                                    ♣ K Q 10 8 3
        ♠ J 9 6 5   ♠ A 8 7 4 3
        ♡ K 8 4   ♡ J 10 2
        ◇ 8 6 5 2   ◇ 9 7 3
        ♣ A 7   ♣ 6 5
                                    ♠ K 10
                                    ♡ A Q 7 3
                                    ◇ A Q 10
                                    ♣ J 9 4 2

Declarer would not have played the king of spades on the second trick unless he had a doubleton. So your partner is known to have five spades and *you must unblock by playing the jack (or the nine) on the second trick.* When you get the lead with the ace of clubs, you can cash the nine of spades (or the jack) and lead the six of spades. This way partner can win the fourth spade trick and beat the contract by cashing the fifth.

#14   North
                                             ♠ K 8 6 3
                                             ♡ 6 5 4
                                             ◇ A K J
                                             ♣ Q 10 2
                                                            East
                                                            ♠ J 10 7
                                                            ♡ A 8 3
                                                            ◇ 6 5 4 2
                                                            ♣ 9 8 3

        West   North   East   South
                                                        1♣
        Pass   1♠   Pass   1NT
        Pass   3NT   All Pass

Your partner leads the king of hearts, you signal with the eight and declarer plays the two. Then your partner leads the queen of hearts. Would you play the ace to unblock the suit or follow with the three?

The correct play is the *three of hearts.* The full deal might be:

                                    ♠ K 8 6 3
                                    ♡ 6 5 4
                                    ◇ A K J
                                    ♣ Q 10 2
        ♠ A 9 2   ♠ J 10 7
        ♡ K Q 9   ♡ A 8 3
        ◇ 8 7 3   ◇ 6 5 4 2
        ♣ 7 6 5 4   ♣ 9 8 3
                                    ♠ Q 5 4
                                    ♡ J 10 7 2
                                    ◇ Q 10 9
                                    ♣ A K J

Note that it is a disaster if you play the ace of hearts. Declarer then can win two heart tricks and make his contract without difficulty. You may question your partner's opening lead, but the two unbid suits are hearts and diamonds, and hearts is surely the logical choice. His decision to lead a second heart was influenced by your encouraging signal; and he led the queen to unblock in case you had four hearts to the ace.

Now you might be thinking, suppose my partner did want me to unblock: play the ace? *Then his second lead should not be the queen.* If he has a three- or four-card sequence, his second lead should be the *low card of his sequence.* For example:

```
                  ♠ K 8 6 3
                  ♡ 6 5 4
                  ◇ A K J
                  ♣ Q 10 2
  ♠ 9 4 2                        ♠ A 10 7
  ♡ K Q J 9                      ♡ A 8 3
  ◇ 8 7 3                        ◇ 6 5 4 2
  ♣ 7 6 5                        ♣ 9 8 3
                  ♠ Q J 5
                  ♡ 10 7 2
                  ◇ Q 10 9
                  ♣ A K J 4
```

With this heart holding, your partner's second lead should be the *jack*. This lead makes it safe for you to unblock by playing the ace, because you know your partner has the queen. With K Q J 10, his second lead should be the *ten*; with K Q 10 x, he should lead the low card.

Many players habitually lead the highest of a sequence and follow with the second-highest from three- and four-card sequences. Most of the time it does not matter. But, when you suspect that your partner has a higher card in the suit and you want him to unblock, your second play should be the low card of your sequence.

There are other combinations that should be handled this way. For example:

```
                  North
                  9 5 4
  West                           East
  Q J 10 7                       K 8 3
                  South
                  A 6 2
```

Suppose West leads the queen, East plays the eight and declarer the two. West should lead the *ten* at trick two and East should unblock by playing his king. If West leads the queen from Q J x and decides to lead the suit again, his second lead should be the jack.

#15

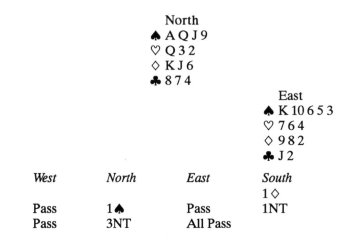

West	*North*	*East*	*South*
			1 ◇
Pass	1 ♠	Pass	1NT
Pass	3NT	All Pass	

The opening lead is the king of clubs and you should play the *jack*. Your partner may be leading from K Q 10 and the declarer probably will allow him to win the first trick. If you play the two, partner will think declarer is holding up with the ace-jack; he will not (and should not) lead the suit again. Suppose these are the four hands:

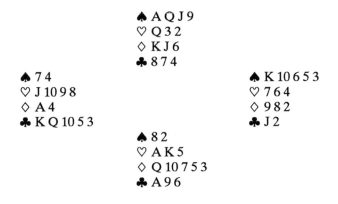

Note how playing the jack clears the picture for your partner. He will continue leading clubs until the ace is driven out, and will beat the contract by cashing the rest of his clubs when he regains the lead with the ace of diamonds. If you played the two of clubs on the first trick, he should switch to the jack of hearts; in which case declarer has an easy road to nine tricks. Holding ♣ J x x, you can give an encouraging signal by playing your middle club; but with a doubleton you cannot and therefore should throw the jack.

If you are thinking that partner may have led the king from an ace-king combination (not K Q 10), that's true; but playing the jack will not mislead partner or cost a trick; it may even help partner. For example:

North
7 6 3

West   East
A K 10 5 4   J 2

South
Q 9 8

Let's assume the contract is three notrump and your partner leads the king. If you play the jack, partner should reason that you most likely have a doubleton jack (conceivably a singleton); if you held queen-jack, you would play the queen; and if you held J x x, you most likely would have signaled with the middle card. Hence your partner should usually switch suits and hope that you can gain the lead to play through declarer's queen.

However, note that it is not always right to play the jack from J x versus trump contracts, as partner may be leading the king from K Q x x or K Q x x x; he does not promise the ten. Playing the jack from J x to show a doubleton might guide your partner to the winning defense, but it could also cost your side a trick if the declarer has A 10 9, or he holds up with A 10 x and your partner leads the suit again.

In the next deal, partner leads the queen and the ten becomes an important card.

#16

                                    North
                                    ♠ K 8 4 3
                                    ♡ A 7 2
                                    ◇ J 10 6 3
                                    ♣ A J
                                                          East
                                                          ♠ Q J 10 9
                                                          ♡ 10 4
                                                          ◇ 8 5 2
                                                          ♣ 10 7 6 4

West	North	East	South
	1◇	Pass	2NT
Pass	3NT	All Pass	

Your partner leads the queen of hearts, dummy wins with the ace and you should *play the ten*. Partner should have at least five hearts headed by Q J 9 (declarer presumably would have bid one heart with four, and partner would have led fourth-highest without the nine); if you play the ten he will know it is safe to continue leading the suit. The four hands:

                                    ♠ K 8 4 3
                                    ♡ A 7 2
                                    ◇ J 10 6 3
                                    ♣ A J
           ♠ 7 6   ♠ Q J 10 9
           ♡ Q J 9 8 3   ♡ 10 4
           ◇ A Q   ◇ 8 5 2
           ♣ 9 8 5 2   ♣ 10 7 6 4
                                    ♠ A 5 2
                                    ♡ K 6 5
                                    ◇ K 9 7 4
                                    ♣ K Q 3

Declarer must establish the diamond suit before he can win nine tricks. His obvious line of play is to take a diamond finesse at trick two. Your partner will win with the queen and drive out the king of hearts. When he regains the lead with the ace of diamonds, he has enough heart tricks to set the contract.

If you play the four of hearts on the first trick, your partner should assume that the declarer has ♡ K 10; he should not lead the suit a second time.

Overtaking

Overtaking a high card (a winner) played by your partner is another important way of solving communication problems. For example:

#17   North
                                       ♠ 9 3
                                       ♡ K 2
                                       ◇ A Q J 10 9 7
                                       ♣ A Q 8
                                                            East
                                                            ♠ A J 10 8 5 2
                                                            ♡ Q J 4
                                                            ◇ K 2
                                                            ♣ 6 5

West	North	East	South
	1◇	1♠	1NT
Pass	3NT	All Pass	

Your partner leads the king of spades, predictably from king singleton or doubleton; declarer must have Q x x x or Q x x for his notrump bid. With your good spade spots, you can afford to *overtake the king with your ace* to make sure spades are led until the queen is driven out. Declarer will get exactly one spade trick whether you overtake or not. Here is a likely layout of the four hands:

                                       ♠ 9 3
                                       ♡ K 2
                                       ◇ A Q J 10 9 7
                                       ♣ A Q 8
            ♠ K   ♠ A J 10 8 5 2
            ♡ 10 8 7 5 3   ♡ Q J 4
            ◇ 6 3   ◇ K 4
            ♣ 10 9 7 4 2   ♣ 6 5
                                       ♠ Q 7 6 4
                                       ♡ A 9 6
                                       ◇ 8 5 2
                                       ♣ K J 3

Partner would be unable to lead another spade if you did not overtake, so declarer would make his contract with an overtrick. By overtaking and establishing the spade suit, you can set the contract by two tricks when you regain the lead with the king of diamonds.

#18   North
                                                  ♠ A K J
                                                  ♡ A Q 7
                                                  ◇ K Q 10 8 4
                                                  ♣ 10 8
                 West
                 ♠ 8 6
                 ♡ J 9 6 3
                 ◇ A 3
                 ♣ K 9 7 3 2

West	*North*	*East*	*South*
	1 ◇	Pass	1NT
Pass	3NT	All Pass	

You are West and lead the three of clubs. Partner wins with the ace and declarer plays the four. Next, partner leads the queen of clubs and declarer plays the five. Are you watching the spot cards? Are you counting the tricks? Which club would you play on the second trick?

Most emphatically, you should play the *king of clubs* because that will surely beat the contract one trick. The four hands:

                                        ♠ A K J
                                        ♡ A Q 7
                                        ◇ K Q 10 8 4
                                        ♣ 10 8
            ♠ 8 6   ♠ 10 7 4 3 2
            ♡ J 9 6 3   ♡ 8 4 2
            ◇ A 3   ◇ 9 5 2
            ♣ K 9 7 3 2   ♣ A Q
                                        ♠ Q 9 5
                                        ♡ K 10 5
                                        ◇ J 7 6
                                        ♣ J 6 5 4

After two rounds of clubs have been played, you are left with 9 7 2 and the declarer with J 6. By leading the nine and driving out the ace, you will be able to win two more club tricks when you get the lead with the ace of diamonds; setting declarer by one trick. If you allow partner to win the second trick with his queen of clubs, he cannot lead the suit again and there is no longer a way to beat the contract. It's true that you could run five club tricks if partner had a third club and you did not overtake (although a good player might play the queen of clubs on the first trick from ♣ A Q x). But the goal in defense is to beat the contract by one trick and that requires only four club tricks. Furthermore, the bidding indicated that declarer has four clubs: He bid one notrump over one diamond—something he is not suppose to do with a four-card or longer major suit—so his long suit figures to be clubs.

#19   North
                                             ♠ A Q 7 5
                                             ♡ 8 4
                                             ◊ K Q J 6 3
                                             ♣ K 9
                                                                        East
                                                                        ♠ J 8 4
                                                                        ♡ A K Q 6
                                                                        ◊ A
                                                                        ♣ Q 10 7 3 2

West	North	East	South
	1◊	Double	1♠
Pass	3♠	Pass	4♠
Pass	Pass	Pass	

Your partner leads the jack of hearts, which is almost surely from a jack-ten combination: The only time it is right to lead the jack without the ten is when you have a singleton or a doubleton, and that is very unlikely because then declarer would have five or six hearts. Assuming partner has the ten of hearts, there is an easy road to beating this contract. Can you see it?

Overtake the jack of hearts with the queen, cash the ace of diamonds and underlead your ace-king of hearts. When partner gets the lead with the ten, he will lead a diamond for you to ruff. The explanation is completed, but here are the four hands anyway:

                                          ♠ A Q 7 5
                                          ♡ 8 4
                                          ◊ K Q J 6 3
                                          ♣ K 9
        ♠ 3   ♠ J 8 4
        ♡ J 10 9 5   ♡ A K Q 6
        ◊ 8 7 4 2   ◊ A
        ♣ 8 6 5 4   ♣ Q 10 7 3 2
                                          ♠ K 10 9 6 2
                                          ♡ 7 3 2
                                          ◊ 10 9 5
                                          ♣ A J

Here's another deal in which you must overtake to help out your partner.

#20

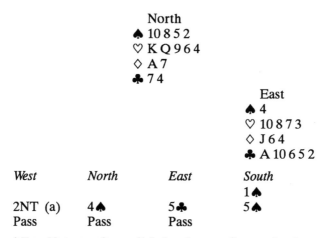

North
♠ 10 8 5 2
♡ K Q 9 6 4
◇ A 7
♣ 7 4

East
♠ 4
♡ 10 8 7 3
◇ J 6 4
♣ A 10 6 5 2

West	North	East	South
			1♠
2NT (a)	4♠	5♣	5♠
Pass	Pass	Pass	

(a) The "Unusual Two-Notrump Overcall," showing two five-card or longer minor suits

Partner leads the king of clubs. You know partner has a five-card club suit, so you cannot win more than one club trick. This means you cannot beat the contract unless partner has the ace of hearts or a spade trick and you can win a diamond trick before declarer has a chance to discard on dummy's heart suit. A diamond lead at trick two is mandatory, and you should lead it in case declarer has the ◇ Q x. So, *overtake partner's king of clubs with your ace and lead a low diamond.* In the following layout, this defense gets the money.

```
            ♠ 10 8 5 2
            ♡ K Q 9 6 4
            ◇ A 7
            ♣ 7 4
♠ K 7                      ♠ 4
♡ 5                        ♡ 10 8 7 3
◇ K 10 9 8 2               ◇ J 6 4
♣ K Q J 9 3               ♣ A 10 6 5 2
            ♠ A Q J 9 6 3
            ♡ A J 2
            ◇ Q 5 3
            ♣ 8
```

Note that your diamond lead at trick two traps the queen. When partner gets the lead with the king of spades, he will be able to win a diamond trick and set the contract. Without a diamond lead from your side at trick two, five spades is unbeatable.

Another play to gain the lead, which is similar to overtaking your partner's good trick, is to *ruff your partner's good trick.* For example:

#21

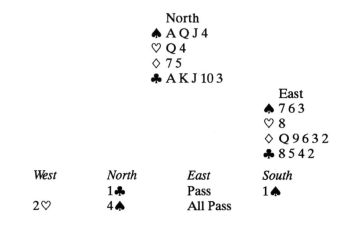

North
♠ A Q J 4
♡ Q 4
◇ 7 5
♣ A K J 10 3

East
♠ 7 6 3
♡ 8
◇ Q 9 6 3 2
♣ 8 5 4 2

West	North	East	South
	1♣	Pass	1♠
2♡	4♠	All Pass	

Your partner leads the king of hearts and follows with the ace of hearts. It should be obvious that the best chance to beat this contract is to win two diamond tricks right away; if declarer gets the lead, he will be able to discard any losing diamonds on the club suit. Since your three little spades are of no value and the diamond lead should come from your side, you must *trump your partner's ace* and lead a diamond. Here is what you are hoping for:

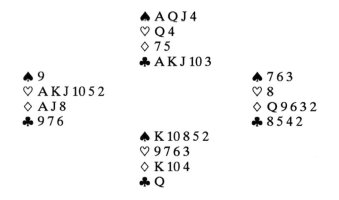

♠ A Q J 4
♡ Q 4
◇ 7 5
♣ A K J 10 3

♠ 9
♡ A K J 10 5 2
◇ A J 8
♣ 9 7 6

♠ 7 6 3
♡ 8
◇ Q 9 6 3 2
♣ 8 5 4 2

♠ K 10 8 5 2
♡ 9 7 6 3
◇ K 10 4
♣ Q

Since partner has the ace and jack of diamonds, you can beat the contract by leading a diamond at trick three. Note that you may also beat the contract if South has the king and jack of diamonds: He must guess whether you are underleading the queen or the ace. If you do not trump your partner's ace of hearts, declarer will succeed easily, and your partner will have to cash the ace of diamonds to prevent an overtrick.

Ducking

Playing a low card to a trick that you could win is sometimes necessary to maintain communication with your partner. Here are several examples:

#22

                North
                ♠ J 5 4
                ♡ A 10 2
                ◇ Q 10 2
                ♣ A K 8 3
                                        East
                                        ♠ A K 8 7 6
                                        ♡ J 7 4
                                        ◇ 5 3
                                        ♣ Q 9 4

West	North	East	South
	1♣	1♠	2◇
Pass	3◇	Pass	3NT
Pass	Pass	Pass	

Your partner leads the nine of spades, which is predictably from a two-card suit. (He might have a singleton, but then declarer has two spade stoppers and there is little hope to beat the contract, so you must assume a doubleton.) The bidding suggests that declarer has at least five diamonds, so the contract is unbeatable if he has the ace and king of diamonds. The only good chance to defeat the contract is to find partner with the ace or king of diamonds and a doubleton spade. The key play is to *duck the first spade lead but to signal encouragement with the eight*.

Here are the four hands:

                ♠ J 5 4
                ♡ A 10 2
                ◇ Q 10 2
                ♣ A K 8 3
    ♠ 9 3   ♠ A K 8 7 6
    ♡ 9 8 5 3   ♡ J 7 4
    ◇ K 6   ◇ 5 3
    ♣ 10 7 6 5 2   ♣ Q 9 4
                ♠ Q 10 2
                ♡ K Q 6
                ◇ A J 9 8 7 4
                ♣ J

Partner does have the king of diamonds and a doubleton spade. When he gets the lead with his king, he will lead his three of spades and you will cash four spade tricks.

#23   North
                                               ♠ A Q 5 3
                                               ♡ Q J 5 2
                                               ◊ Q J 10
                                               ♣ 8 5
                                                                        East
                                                                        ♠ 9 7 2
                                                                        ♡ 4 3
                                                                        ◊ A 8 5 2
                                                                        ♣ 10 9 7 6

West	North	East	South
			1NT
Pass	2♣	Pass	2♡
Pass	4♡	All Pass	

The opening lead is the nine of diamonds, apparently from a short suit. If partner has a singleton diamond, you should win the first trick and give him a ruff. But if he has a doubleton, you should play the eight of diamonds, encouraging a second diamond lead if he can win the lead before declarer draws the trumps. So you must decide whether partner has led a singleton or a doubleton, and the clue to the right decision is in the bidding. If your partner has a singleton diamond, South has five; it is unlikely that he would open the bidding with one notrump with five diamonds and four hearts: an unbalanced hand. Therefore, you should assume that partner has two diamonds and *play the encouraging eight of diamonds* on the first trick. Here are the four hands:

                                               ♠ A Q 5 3
                                               ♡ Q J 5 2
                                               ◊ Q J 10
                                               ♣ 8 5
        ♠ 10 8 4   ♠ 9 7 2
        ♡ K 7 6   ♡ 4 3
        ◊ 9 3   ◊ A 8 5 2
        ♣ A J 4 3 2   ♣ 10 9 7 6
                                               ♠ K J 6
                                               ♡ A 10 9 8
                                               ◊ K 7 6 4
                                               ♣ K Q

Suppose declarer wins the first trick with the ten of diamonds and tries the heart finesse (no other play is any better). Your partner will win with the king of hearts, lead another diamond to your ace and ruff the third diamond when you return it. The ace of clubs is then the setting trick. Note that the diamond ruff is necessary to beat the contract, and if you do not duck the first diamond, you cannot regain the lead to give your partner the ruff.

#24

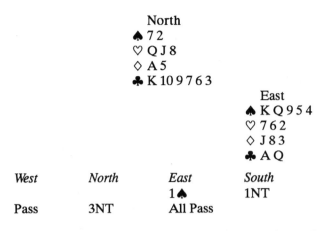

North
♠ 7 2
♡ Q J 8
◇ A 5
♣ K 10 9 7 6 3

East
♠ K Q 9 5 4
♡ 7 6 2
◇ J 8 3
♣ A Q

West	North	East	South
		1♠	1NT
Pass	3NT	All Pass	

Your partner leads the ten of spades. Which spade would you play on the first trick?

You must duck; *play the five of spades.* Partner apparently has a doubleton spade—he would lead low from 10 x x—so declarer must have A J x x. To guard against declarer's having ♠ A J 8 x, you must save the ♠ K Q 9 to limit him to two spade tricks. This time you have two entry cards—the ace and queen of clubs—and are not concerned with communicating with your partner; you duck to preserve an extra trick in your suit.

Suppose this is the full deal:

```
                ♠ 7 2
                ♡ Q J 8
                ◇ A 5
                ♣ K 10 9 7 6 3
♠ 10 6                          ♠ K Q 9 5 4
♡ 9 5 4 3                       ♡ 7 6 2
◇ Q 10 9 7 6                    ◇ J 8 3
♣ 8 2                           ♣ A Q
                ♠ A J 8 3
                ♡ A K 10
                ◇ K 4 2
                ♣ J 5 4
```

Declarer must develop club tricks to make his contract, and you will get the lead twice with the ace and queen. After your partner's ten drives out the jack of spades (declarer cannot gain by ducking), declarer will try the club finesse and lose to your queen. Since you still have ♠ K Q 9 5 and declarer has ♠ A 8 3, you can drive out his ace and establish three spade tricks, which you will win when you regain the lead with the ace of clubs. Note that if you do not play a low spade on the first trick, declarer will have *three* spade stoppers and make his contract.

#25   North
                                         ♠ A 2
                                         ♡ K 5
                                         ◊ K J 10 7 4 3
                                         ♣ 9 8 3
                                                         East
                                                         ♠ K 8 5
                                                         ♡ 9 7 6 3 2
                                                         ◊ A Q
                                                         ♣ Q J 10

West	*North*	*East*	*South*
			1NT
Pass	3NT	All Pass	

Your partner leads the jack of spades and the two is played from dummy. Partner cannot have any other high cards (you can see 23 HCPs, so only seventeen are missing and declarer should have at least sixteen for his opening bid), and yet there is a chance to beat the contract if partner has a five-card spade suit and you can put him on lead to run it. This can be done if you *duck the first spade trick* and declarer wins with his queen.

The four hands:

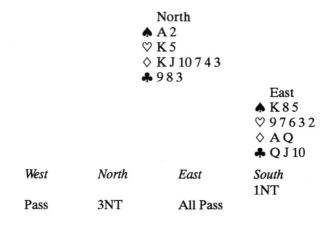

                        ♠ A 2
                        ♡ K 5
                        ◊ K J 10 7 4 3
                        ♣ 9 8 3
    ♠ J 10 9 4 3   ♠ K 8 5
    ♡ 10 8 4   ♡ 9 7 6 3 2
    ◊ 6 2   ◊ A Q
    ♣ 7 6 5   ♣ Q J 10
                        ♠ Q 7 6
                        ♡ A Q J
                        ◊ 9 8 5
                        ♣ A K 4 2

Assume declarer wins the first trick with his queen and plays a diamond. (He can block the spade suit and make his contract if he ducks, but that would be an illogical play.) You win the second trick and *lead the king of spades* to drive out dummy's ace. When you regain the lead with your second high diamond and play your low spade, partner will cash three tricks.

If you win the first trick with the king of spades, declarer will win the second with the ace and the third with the queen. There is no way to put partner on lead, so declarer will make his contract.

In the next two deals, the purpose of ducking is to block the declarer's communication with his dummy.

#26

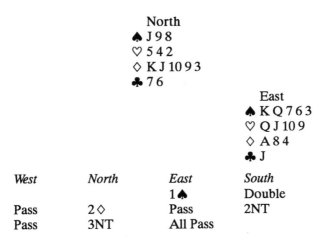

North
♠ J 9 8
♡ 5 4 2
◇ K J 10 9 3
♣ 7 6

East
♠ K Q 7 6 3
♡ Q J 10 9
◇ A 8 4
♣ J

West	North	East	South
		1♠	Double
Pass	2◇	Pass	2NT
Pass	3NT	All Pass	

Partner leads the ten of spades, dummy plays the jack and *you must duck*. Partner's most probable spade holding is 10 x—in which case declarer has ♠ A x x—so declarer will win two spade tricks whether you cover the jack or not. The reason for ducking is to eliminate an entry to dummy. Suppose these are the four hands:

```
              ♠ J 9 8
              ♡ 5 4 2
              ◇ K J 10 9 3
              ♣ 7 6
♠ 10 2                      ♠ K Q 7 6 3
♡ 8 7 6                     ♡ Q J 10 9
◇ 5 2                       ◇ A 8 4
♣ Q 10 9 5 4 3             ♣ J
              ♠ A 5 4
              ♡ A K 3
              ◇ Q 7 6
              ♣ A K 8 2
```

Declarer can win two spades, two hearts and two clubs, so he needs three diamond tricks to make his contract. When he eventually leads diamonds, you can limit him to two diamond tricks by holding up your ace until the third round; provided you did not cover the jack if spades at trick one. Note that if you play the king or queen of spades on the first trick and declarer takes his ace, he is left with ♠ 9 8 in dummy and ♠ 5 4 in his hand; after knocking out your other high spade, he can get to dummy to score two more diamond tricks.

#27   North
                                                 ♠ 3
                                                 ♡ 6 5
                                                 ◇ A K 9 7 4 2
                                                 ♣ K Q 10 8
                                                                              East
                                                                              ♠ J 9 8 4 2
                                                                              ♡ 8 3
                                                                              ◇ Q J 6
                                                                              ♣ A J 5

West	North	East	South
	1◇	Pass	1♡
Pass	2♣	Pass	3♡
Pass	4♡	Pass	4NT
Pass	5◇	Pass	6♡
Pass	Pass	Pass	

Your partner leads the nine of clubs and the king is played from dummy. How many clubs does partner have? Which club do you play on the first trick? Why?

Let's look at the four hands while the questions are being answered:

```
                              ♠ 3
                              ♡ 6 5
                              ◇ A K 9 7 4 2
                              ♣ K Q 10 8
        ♠ K 10 7 6 5                                ♠ J 9 8 4 2
        ♡ 9 7 4                                     ♡ 8 3
        ◇ 10 8 3                                    ◇ Q J 6
        ♣ 9 2                                       ♣ A J 5
                              ♠ A Q
                              ♡ A K Q J 10 2
                              ◇ 5
                              ♣ 7 6 4 3
```

The correct card to lead from 9 x x x is the *lowest*, and most good players lead low from 9 x x, so it is reasonable to assume that your partner has at most two clubs; you will not lose your ace if you *duck the first club lead*. The purpose of ducking is to deprive declarer of an entry to dummy. If you play the ace of clubs, declarer will be able to establish the diamond suit and then go to dummy with the queen of clubs to discard his losers. If you duck there is no way for him to escape losing two tricks.

Quiz for Chapter Two

As East, what is your third-hand play on each of the following hands?

1.
North
♠ J 9 6
♡ 7 3
◇ A Q 6 2
♣ 9 5 4 2

East
♠ Q 7 4
♡ 9 6 2
◇ K 8 7 4 3
♣ K 8

West	North	East	South
			1♠
Pass	2♠	Pass	4♠
Pass	Pass	Pass	

Your partner leads the three of spades and dummy plays the jack.

2.
North
♠ A Q J 9
♡ 5
◇ A K Q 10 2
♣ 7 4 3

East
♠ 3 2
♡ A 9 7 4
◇ 8 6 5 4
♣ Q 9 6

West	North	East	South
	1◇	Pass	1♠
2♡	3♠	4♡	4♠
Pass	Pass	Pass	

Your partner leads the king of hearts.

3.
North
♠ A Q
♡ 5 4 3 2
◇ K J 10 9 7
♣ K 6

East
♠ 7 6 3
♡ K 10 9 8 7
◇ A Q
♣ Q 8 2

West	North	East	South
	1◇	1♡	2NT
Pass	3NT	All Pass	

Your partner leads the queen of hearts.

4.
North
♠ 6 5 2
♡ K 2
◇ A K Q
♣ J 10 8 4 2

East
♠ K Q 9 8 7
♡ 7 4
◇ J 5 2
♣ A 7 6

West	North	East	South
	1♣	1♠	2NT
Pass	3NT	All Pass	

Your partner leads the ten of spades.

5.   North
                  ♠ A 2
                  ♡ K J
                  ◇ Q J 10 9 8 4
                  ♣ A K 3
                                   East
                                   ♠ K 8 7 6 4 3
                                   ♡ Q 10 9
                                   ◇ A 3
                                   ♣ 5 2

West	North	East	South
	1◇	1♠	1NT
Pass	3NT	All Pass	

Your partner leads the nine of spades and dummy plays the two.

6.   North
                  ♠ 6 5
                  ♡ A 8
                  ◇ K 10 7 4 3
                  ♣ Q J 10 2
                                   East
                                   ♠ J 10 9 7 3
                                   ♡ J 4
                                   ◇ A 8 5
                                   ♣ 9 6 3

West	North	East	South
			1NT
Pass	3NT	All Pass	

Your partner leads the seven of hearts and dummy plays the ace.

7.   North
                  ♠ K J 9
                  ♡ J 9 5 3
                  ◇ 10 6 2
                  ♣ A Q 7
                                   East
                                   ♠ 7 4 2
                                   ♡ 6 2
                                   ◇ A 8 5 4 3
                                   ♣ 9 5 3

West	North	East	South
			1♠
Double	Redouble	2◇	Pass
3◇	3♠	Pass	4♠
Pass	Pass	Pass	

Your partner leads the king of diamonds.

8.   North
                  ♠ Q J
                  ♡ 9 6 5
                  ◇ K J 9 8 5 4
                  ♣ K 10
                                   East
                                   ♠ K 10 8 7 3
                                   ♡ Q 8
                                   ◇ A 3 2
                                   ♣ A 5 2

West	North	East	South
		1♠	1NT
Pass	3NT	All Pass	

Your partner leads the nine of spades.

Quiz Answers for Chapter Two

1.

```
              North
              ♠ J 9 6
              ♡ 7 3
              ◇ A Q 6 2
              ♣ 9 5 4 2
West                        East
♠ 5 3                       ♠ Q 7 4
♡ Q 10 8 4                  ♡ 9 6 2
◇ J 9 5                     ◇ K 8 7 4 3
♣ A J 10 7                  ♣ K 8
              South
              ♠ A K 10 8 2
              ♡ A K J 5
              ◇ 10
              ♣ Q 6 3
```

West	North	East	South
			1♠
Pass	2♠	Pass	4♠
Pass	Pass	Pass	

Your partner leads the three of spades and dummy plays the jack.

From the bidding, partner's lead and declarer's play of the jack, you know that declarer has the ace, king and ten of spades, so your queen is trapped and it may seem to make no difference whether you cover the jack with the queen or not. But there is some hope of saving a trick if you do not cover, so *play a low spade on the first trick*. In the diagram, declarer has three losing clubs and two losing hearts. If you cover the jack of spades with the queen, he can make his contract by ruffing the third round of hearts with the six of spades and the fourth round with the nine. By not playing the queen of spades on the first trick, you can set the contract by overruffing the fourth round of hearts with the queen of spades.

2.

```
              North
              ♠ A Q J 9
              ♡ 5
              ◇ A K Q 10 2
              ♣ 7 4 3
West                        East
♠ 7 5                       ♠ 3 2
♡ K Q J 10 8 3              ♡ A 9 7 4
◇ J 7                       ◇ 8 6 5 4
♣ A J 10                    ♣ Q 9 6
              South
              ♠ K 10 8 6 4
              ♡ 6 2
              ◇ 9 3
              ♣ K 8 5 2
```

West	North	East	South
	1◇	Pass	1♠
2♡	3♠	4♡	4♠
Pass	Pass	Pass	

Your partner leads the king of hearts.

It is clear that declarer has no losers in spades or diamonds and only one in hearts. To beat this contract, you must win three club tricks before declarer has a chance to draw trumps and discard his club losers on the diamond suit. This requires finding partner with the ace-king or ace-jack-ten of clubs. Catering to the latter holding, it is imperative that you lead clubs at trick two, so, *overtake the king of hearts with the ace and lead the queen of clubs*.

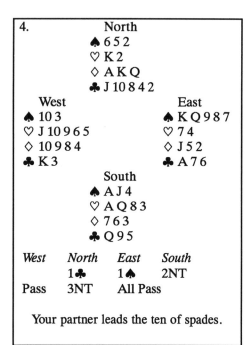

3.   North
           ♠ A Q
           ♡ 5 4 3 2
           ◇ K J 10 9 7
           ♣ K 6

West   East
♠ 10 9 8 5 2   ♠ 7 6 3
♡ Q   ♡ K 10 9 8 7
◇ 8 6 3   ◇ A Q
♣ J 7 5 4   ♣ Q 8 2

              South
           ♠ K J 4
           ♡ A J 6
           ◇ 5 4 2
           ♣ A 10 9 3

West	North	East	South
	1◇	1♡	2NT
Pass	3NT	All Pass	

Your partner leads the queen of hearts.

It is unlikely that declarer can win nine tricks without establishing the diamond suit. If so, you can insure beating the contract *by overtaking partner's queen of hearts with the king*. If declarer ducks, you can continue leading the suit and win three heart tricks before declarer can establish the diamonds. If you do not overtake and partner has a singleton, declarer can make his contract by ducking; your partner cannot lead another heart.

It is true that overtaking with your king would cost a trick if partner had ♡ Q x and declarer ♡ A J, but this is unlikely in view of the bidding, and overtaking with the king would still beat the contract by one trick.

4.   North
           ♠ 6 5 2
           ♡ K 2
           ◇ A K Q
           ♣ J 10 8 4 2

West   East
♠ 10 3   ♠ K Q 9 8 7
♡ J 10 9 6 5   ♡ 7 4
◇ 10 9 8 4   ◇ J 5 2
♣ K 3   ♣ A 7 6

              South
           ♠ A J 4
           ♡ A Q 8 3
           ◇ 7 6 3
           ♣ Q 9 5

West	North	East	South
	1♣	1♠	2NT
Pass	3NT	All Pass	

Your partner leads the ten of spades.

The ten-of-spades lead marks partner with at most a doubleton (he would lead low from 10 x x), so declarer holds ♠ A J x or ♠ A J x x. If declarer has the king and queen of clubs, or seven red-suit winners, he cannot be set: the only chance to beat the contract is to find partner with a doubleton spade and the king of clubs (or with the queen of clubs if declarer has only five red-suit winners). The key play is to *duck the ten-of-spades lead; but play the nine as an encouraging signal*.

With the cards as shown, declarer will win the first trick with the jack of spades and lead a club. Your partner should win with the king and lead a second spade to drive out declarer's ace. This establishes three spade trick for you to win when you get the lead with the ace of clubs.

Note that if you play the king or queen of spades on the first trick, declarer can make his contract by ducking and winning the second spade lead; then partner will be unable to play a spade when he wins a trick with his king of clubs.

5.
```
              North
            ♠ A 2
            ♡ K J
            ◇ Q J 10 9 8 4
            ♣ A K 3
West                        East
♠ 9 5                       ♠ K 8 7 6 4 3
♡ 8 7 6 4 2                 ♡ Q 10 9
◇ K 7                       ◇ A 3
♣ J 10 8 6                  ♣ 5 2
              South
            ♠ Q J 10
            ♡ A 5 3
            ◇ 6 5 2
            ♣ Q 9 7 4
```

West	North	East	South
	1◇	1♠	1NT
Pass	3NT	All Pass	

Your partner leads the nine of spades and dummy plays the two.

The nine-of-spades lead is partner's highest, so the declarer must have the queen, jack, and ten of spades. Unless declarer can run nine tricks without using the diamond suit, you can set the contract if partner has the king of diamonds and a doubleton spade by *ducking the first spade lead; but play the eight as an encouraging signal.* With the cards as shown in the diagram, declarer cannot win nine tricks without establishing the diamond suit. When diamonds are led, your partner will win with the king and lead another spade to clear the suit. This leaves you with four good spade tricks to run when you get the lead with the ace of diamonds.

6.
```
              North
            ♠ 6 5
            ♡ A 8
            ◇ K 10 7 4 3
            ♣ Q J 10 2
West                        East
♠ K 8 4 2                   ♠ J 10 9 7 3
♡ K Q 9 7 3                 ♡ J 4
◇ 6 2                       ◇ A 8 5
♣ 7 5                       ♣ 9 6 3
              South
            ♠ A Q
            ♡ 10 6 5 2
            ◇ Q J 9
            ♣ A K 8 4
```

West	North	East	South
			1NT
Pass	3NT	All Pass	

Your partner leads the seven of hearts and dummy plays the ace.

Play the jack of hearts on the first trick, to unblock. Assuming partner is leading fourth-highest, declarer has only one card higher than the seven; playing the jack cannot cost a trick no matter which higher card he holds. But you can deduce that declarer's one higher card is the *ten.* Partner might lead the seven from K Q 9 7, but would definitely lead the king from K Q 10 7, and the ten from K 10 9 7 or Q 10 9 7. When declarer leads a diamond you win with the ace and play the four of hearts, partner can win four heart tricks; something he could not do if you still had the jack.

Note in the diagram that declarer can make his contract if he plays a low heart at trick one and you return a heart at trick two. But this line of play would fail if your partner has the ace of diamonds, or with the cards as shown if you return a spade at trick two. So winning the first trick with the ace of hearts and hoping the suit will block is a logical play.

7. **North**
    ♠ K J 9
    ♡ J 9 5 3
    ◇ 10 6 2
    ♣ A Q 7

West
♠ 5
♡ A Q 7 4
◇ K Q J 9
♣ J 10 8 6

East
♠ 7 4 2
♡ 6 2
◇ A 8 5 4 3
♣ 9 5 3

South
♠ A Q 10 8 6 3
♡ K 10 8
◇ 7
♣ K 4 2

West	North	East	South
			1♠
Double	Redouble	2◇	Pass
3◇	3♠	Pass	4♠
Pass	Pass	Pass	

Your partner leads the king of diamonds.

It is very unlikely that partner raised diamonds with fewer than four, so you cannot win more than one diamond trick. The best chance to beat the contract is for you to lead a heart at trick two. So, *overtake partner's king of diamonds with your ace and lead the six of hearts.* Fortunately, partner has the perfect heart holding; after winning two heart tricks with the queen and ace, he will lead a third heart for you to ruff.

8. **North**
    ♠ Q J
    ♡ 9 6 5
    ◇ K J 9 8 5 4
    ♣ K 10

West
♠ 9 5 2
♡ J 10 7 2
◇ 6
♣ 8 7 6 4 3

East
♠ K 10 8 7 3
♡ Q 8
◇ A 3 2
♣ A 5 2

South
♠ A 6 4
♡ A K 4 3
◇ Q 10 7
♣ Q J 9

West	North	East	South
		1♠	1NT
Pass	3NT	All Pass	

Your partner leads the nine of spades.

Declarer will win exactly two spade tricks whether you play the king on the first trick or not, but this is the crucial play. *You must play a low spade to deprive declarer of an entry to dummy.* If you then hold up your ace of diamonds until the third round and follow by leading the king of spades to drive out the ace, you will win five tricks before declarer can get to dummy to run the diamond suit.

Note how easy declarer's task is if you play the king of spades on the first trick. He wins with the ace, leads diamonds until the ace is driven out, and has the high spade in dummy as an entry to the diamond suit.

3

Leads After Trick One

In this chapter, we look at leads that occur at trick two and later; starting with:

Returning Partner's Suit

If you lead a suit that your partner led originally, the card you play can help him determine your length in the suit. Here's how it works. If your partner leads a suit in which you hold three cards, lead back the higher of the remaining two: For example, with A 8 2, play the ace and *return the eight*. Holding four cards or more, lead back your original fourth-highest: For example, from A 8 5 2, play the ace and *return the two*; from A 8 6 5 2, play the ace and *return the five*. Here are seven illustrations showing the usefulness of these guidelines.

#1

```
                        North
                        ♠ A Q J 4 2
                        ♡ 9
                        ◇ K Q 10 5
                        ♣ 8 7 6
         West
         ♠ 9 6
         ♡ A J 7 4 3
         ◇ 7 3 2
         ♣ J 5 2
```

West	North	East	South
	1♠	Pass	2NT
Pass	3◇	Pass	3NT
Pass	Pass	Pass	

You lead the four of hearts, partner plays the king and declarer the five. Partner returns the eight of hearts and declarer plays the ten. In order to find out how many hearts your partner and declarer have, you must pay close attention to the spot cards as they are played; as of now the six and two are the only ones missing. Partner denied the queen when he played the king, so his possible heart holdings are A 8 6 2, A 8 6, A 8 2 or A 8. Partner would not return the eight from A 8 6 2, and A 8 should be ruled out because declarer would not have bid two notrump with a five-card heart suit. Partner must have begun with A 8 6 or A 8 2. This means the declarer began with Q 10 6 5 or Q 10 5 2 and, after you win the second trick with your jack, you are left with A 7 3 over declarer's Q 6 or Q 2. *So do not lead another heart.* Sit back and wait for your heart tricks. The next heart lead must come from your partner. Here is a possible layout:

♠ A Q J 4 2
♡ 9
◇ K Q 10 5
♣ 8 7 6

♠ 9 6   ♠ 10 8 7 3
♡ A J 7 4 3   ♡ K 8 2
◇ 7 3 2   ◇ A 6
♣ J 5 2   ♣ Q 10 9 4

♠ K 5
♡ Q 10 6 5
◇ J 9 8 4
♣ A K 3

Fortunately partner has the ace of diamonds and will get the lead to play a heart through declarer and you will win three more heart tricks.

Although any card you lead at trick three except a heart will beat this contract, the best lead is a club. Declarer has nine tricks if he holds the king of spades and the ace of diamonds, so it takes a club lead to set him if partner's one high card happens to be the ace of clubs.

Now let's change the hands so your partner has four hearts and the declarer just three:

♠ A Q J 4 2
♡ 9
◇ K Q 10 5
♣ 8 7 6

♠ 9 6   ♠ 10 8 7 3
♡ A J 7 4 3   ♡ K 8 6 2
◇ 7 3 2   ◇ 9 6
♣ J 5 2   ♣ K Q 4

♠ K 5
♡ Q 10 5
◇ A J 8 4
♣ A 10 9 3

Partner again wins the first trick with the king of hearts and declarer follows with the five, but this time partner returns *the two of hearts*—to show that he started with four—and declarer plays the ten. It is apparent that the declarer started with Q 10 5 and at this point has the lone queen, you should win the second trick with the jack of hearts and *cash the ace*. This way you will win the first five heart tricks *if your partner cooperates and plays the eight under your ace* so the suit will not be blocked. Note that your partner does not have an entry card this time; the only way to set the contract is to win the first five heart tricks.

In the next deal the heart spots have been changed to give the declarer a sure stopper. But the contract can be set with good defense.

#2

<table>
<tr><td></td><td></td><td>North</td><td></td></tr>
<tr><td></td><td></td><td>♠ A Q J 4 2</td><td></td></tr>
<tr><td></td><td></td><td>♡ 9</td><td></td></tr>
<tr><td></td><td></td><td>◇ K Q 10 5</td><td></td></tr>
<tr><td></td><td></td><td>♣ 8 7 6</td><td></td></tr>
</table>

West
♠ 9 6
♡ A J 4 3 2
◇ 7 3 2
♣ J 5 2

West	North	East	South
	1♠	Pass	2NT
Pass	3◇	Pass	3NT
Pass	Pass	Pass	

You lead the three of hearts, partner plays the king and declarer the six. Then partner leads the eight of hearts and declarer plays the ten. The missing spot cards are the seven and five. Since partner would not return the eight from ♡ 8 7 5, he must have ♡ 8 5 or ♡ 8 7. So declarer started with ♡ Q 10 7 6 or ♡ Q 10 6 5 and, if you win the second trick with the jack, it is impossible to win more than three heart tricks—declarer will be left with a stopper (Q 7 or Q 5) and you with A 4 2 and no reentry. However, if partner can get the lead before declarer can run nine tricks, you can win the four heart tricks you need to set the contract by *ducking the second heart lead*. Suppose these are the four hands:

<table>
<tr><td></td><td>♠ A Q J 4 2</td><td></td></tr>
<tr><td></td><td>♡ 9</td><td></td></tr>
<tr><td></td><td>◇ K Q 10 5</td><td></td></tr>
<tr><td></td><td>♣ 8 7 6</td><td></td></tr>
<tr><td>♠ 9 6</td><td></td><td>♠ 10 8 7 3</td></tr>
<tr><td>♡ A J 4 3 2</td><td></td><td>♡ K 8 5</td></tr>
<tr><td>◇ 7 3 2</td><td></td><td>◇ A 6</td></tr>
<tr><td>♣ J 5 2</td><td></td><td>♣ Q 10 9 4</td></tr>
<tr><td></td><td>♠ K 5</td><td></td></tr>
<tr><td></td><td>♡ Q 10 7 6</td><td></td></tr>
<tr><td></td><td>◇ J 9 8 4</td><td></td></tr>
<tr><td></td><td>♣ A K 3</td><td></td></tr>
</table>

After allowing declarer to win the second trick with the ten of hearts, you are left with ♡ A J 4 behind his ♡ Q 7. When partner gets the lead with the ace of diamonds, he will lead the five of hearts through declarer so you can win three more heart tricks.

#3
                                                      North
                                                      ♠ 9
                                                      ♡ A 10 9
                                                      ◇ K Q 10 9 8 3
                                                      ♣ 9 8 2

West
♠ K 8 7 5 2
♡ 8 5 4 3
◇ 6 2
♣ J 10

West	North	East	South
			1NT
Pass	3 ◇	Pass	3NT
Pass	Pass	Pass	

This time you lead the five of spades, partner plays the ace and declarer the three. Partner leads back the jack of spades and declarer plays the queen. Do you win with the king or duck? With the cards as follows, the winning play is to duck:

                                          ♠ 9
                                          ♡ A 10 9
                                          ◇ K Q 10 9 8 3
                                          ♣ 9 8 2
        ♠ K 8 7 5 2   ♠ A J 4
        ♡ 8 5 4 3   ♡ 7 6 2
        ◇ 6 2   ◇ A 4
        ♣ J 10   ♣ Q 7 5 4 3
                                          ♠ Q 10 6 3
                                          ♡ K Q J
                                          ◇ J 7 5
                                          ♣ A K 6

After ducking the second spade, you are left with ♠ K 8 7 and declarer with ♠ 10 6. Since partner has the ace of diamonds and another spade to lead through declarer, ducking the second spade lead is the only way to beat the contract. But suppose this is the layout:

                                          ♠ 9
                                          ♡ A 10 9
                                          ◇ K Q 10 9 8 3
                                          ♣ 9 8 2
        ♠ K 8 7 5 2   ♠ A J 10 4
        ♡ 8 5 4 3   ♡ 7 6 2
        ◇ 6 2   ◇ 5 4
        ♣ J 10   ♣ K Q 5 3
                                          ♠ Q 6 3
                                          ♡ K Q J
                                          ◇ A J 7
                                          ♣ A 7 6 4

Now declarer can run eleven tricks if you let him win the second trick with the queen, while, if you win with the king, you can win the first five tricks! You might think your partner misled you because he did not return his lowest card from a four-card holding. But if he led the four-spot here, the suit blocks—it is impossible to win more than four spade tricks. So the right card to return from A J x and A J 10 x is the jack. How can you tell which? There is no sure answer. Declarer's bidding suggests he is more likely to continue with three notrump over three diamonds with ♠ Q 10 x x than ♠ Q x x, but if you duck he may have nine running tricks. Maybe it is better to win the second trick with the king and hope declarer has ♠ Q x x?

Another thought: If declarer had Q 10 x x and thinks your partner (East) may get the lead before he can run nine tricks, he can *duck the jack of spades* to block the suit; this would limit the defense to three spade tricks unless you (West) have a reentry. Of course, he will not duck the jack of spades with Q 10 x x if he has nine (or more) running tricks, which he does have in this deal.

A good rule for defenders: If you are trying to establish and run a long suit versus a notrump contract when your partner has greater length in the suit than you, *save a low card to play last*. In other words, if you have four cards in a suit and believe that your partner has five, he should be allowed to win the fourth trick so he can cash the fifth. Of course, if you are sure partner has an entry card in another suit, there will be no need to unblock. There is not always an easy solution, but the defender with the long suit should be aware that partner may lead back a card other than his lowest from a four-card holding to avoid blocking the suit.

#4

                                North
                                ♠ 6 4
                                ♡ K J 5
                                ◇ K 9 7 2
                                ♣ K 8 6 3

            West
            ♠ Q 10 8 5
            ♡ 10 7 4
            ◇ A 6 3
            ♣ J 5 2

West	North	East	South
			1NT
Pass	3NT	All Pass	

You lead the five of spades and partner's king drives out the ace. Declarer leads the jack of diamonds and lets it ride to partner's queen. Partner leads the seven of spades, declarer plays the nine and you win this trick with the ten. Where are the remaining spades? The missing spades are the J, 3 and 2. If partner began with K J 7 3, K J 7 2 or K 7 3 2, he would not have returned the seven. So partner is leading from K 7 x. Therefore, declarer began with A J 9 x (or conceivably A J 9 x x). This means declarer still has J x and *you must not lead another spade*. With the cards as follows, any lead but a spade will beat the contract; but leading the ace and another diamond is the logical choice, as a heart or club lead might help declarer.

Here are the four hands:

```
                        ♠ 6 4
                        ♡ K J 5
                        ◇ K 9 7 2
                        ♣ K 8 6 3
      ♠ Q 10 8 5                        ♠ K 7 2
      ♡ 10 7 4                          ♡ 8 6 3 2
      ◇ A 6 3                           ◇ Q 5
      ♣ J 5 2                           ♣ Q 10 9 4
                        ♠ A J 9 3
                        ♡ A Q 9
                        ◇ J 10 8 4
                        ♣ A 7
```

Declarer can win eight tricks (one spade, three hearts, two clubs and two diamonds). But there is no way for him to score a ninth trick unless you lead a spade and allow him to win a trick with the jack.

There are times when you should not return your lowest card from a four-card holding—even though there is no fear of blocking the suit—because it may pose an unnecessary problem for your partner; this is especially true when one of your remaining cards is a high honor. For example:

#5   North
                                ♠ 9 5
                                ♡ 7 6 4
                                ◇ K J 9 8 3
                                ♣ A Q 10
                                              East
                                              ♠ A Q 7 2
                                              ♡ Q J 10 9
                                              ◇ 6 4 2
                                              ♣ J 8

West	North	East	South
			1NT
Pass	3NT	All Pass	

Partner leads the four of spades, you win with the ace and declarer plays the eight. The best lead at trick two is the queen of spades. The four hands:

```
                        ♠ 9 5
                        ♡ 7 6 4
                        ◇ K J 9 8 3
                        ♣ A Q 10
      ♠ K 10 6 4 3                     ♠ A Q 7 2
      ♡ 8 5 3                          ♡ Q J 10 9
      ◇ 10 7                           ◇ 6 4 2
      ♣ 9 5 2                          ♣ J 8
                        ♠ J 8
                        ♡ A K 2
                        ◇ A Q 5
                        ♣ K 7 6 4 3
```

If you play the ace, queen and another spade, partner has no problems and you will win the first five spade tricks. Now suppose you lead the two of spades at trick two. Your partner cannot tell whether you started with ♠ A 2 or ♠ A Q 7 2; he may decide not to lead a spade at trick three from ♠ 10 6 3 because it would give declarer an extra trick if he has ♠ Q 7. Although he probably should lead the spade because it is the best chance to beat the contract, returning the two instead of the queen gives him an unnecessary problem; he may do the wrong thing.

These guidelines for returning partner's suit are useful in trump contracts, as well as in notrump contracts, and since the goal is not to run a long suit, you needn't worry about unblocking. Here are two examples:

#6

```
                          North
                          ♠ K J 5 4
                          ♡ 10 7 2
                          ◇ K J 8 3
                          ♣ K Q

        West
        ♠ 3 2
        ♡ J 8 5 3
        ◇ A 7 5 4
        ♣ A 9 5
```

West	North	East	South
	1 ◇	Pass	1 ♠
Pass	2 ♠	Pass	4 ♠
Pass	Pass	Pass	

You lead the three of hearts to partner's ace and declarer's four. Partner returns the queen of hearts and declarer wins with the king. After drawing a couple of rounds of trumps, declarer leads the two of diamonds. Declarer must have another heart, as partner would lead back his lowest if he began with four. So you can beat the contract by going up with the ace of diamonds and cashing the jack of hearts and ace of clubs. The four hands:

```
                          ♠ K J 5 4
                          ♡ 10 7 2
                          ◇ K J 8 3
                          ♣ K Q
        ♠ 3 2                              ♠ 8
        ♡ J 8 6 3                          ♡ A Q 9
        ◇ A 7 5 4                          ◇ Q 10 9 6
        ♣ A 9 5                            ♣ 8 7 6 4 2
                          ♠ A Q 10 9 7 6
                          ♡ K 5 4
                          ◇ 2
                          ♣ J 10 3
```

Note that if you duck the two-of-diamonds lead, declarer will go up with dummy's king and make his contract. But suppose this were the layout:

                                ♠ K J 5 4
                                ♡ 10 7 2
                                ◇ K J 8 3
                                ♣ K Q
        ♠ 3 2   ♠ 8
        ♡ J 8 6 3   ♡ A Q 9 5
        ◇ A 7 5 4   ◇ Q 9 6
        ♣ A 9 5   ♣ 8 7 6 4 2
                                ♠ A Q 10 9 7 6
                                ♡ K 4
                                ◇ 10 2
                                ♣ J 10 3

Here partner would return the five of hearts at trick two, so declarer began with ♡ K 4 or ♡ K Q 9 4; in neither case can you win another heart trick. So two diamond tricks are needed to set the contract. When South leads the two of diamonds, you must duck smoothly and make him guess whether to play you for the ace or queen.

#7   North
                                                ♠ A K 7
                                                ♡ K Q J 3
                                                ◇ 9 6 5
                                                ♣ Q J 8
                West
                ♠ 4
                ♡ A 9 6 5
                ◇ Q J 10 8 2
                ♣ A K 7

West	*North*	*East*	*South*
	1NT	Pass	4♠
Pass	Pass	Pass	

You win the first trick with the king of clubs and switch to the queen of diamonds, partner playing the ace and declarer the four. Partner leads back the *three* of diamonds to declarer's king. The declarer then leads a heart which you win with the ace. What do you lead now? If declarer has a club or diamond in his hand, you must cash that trick now or he will discard his loser on dummy's hearts. How can you tell? Did you watch the spot cards in diamonds? Partner has played the ace-three and declarer the king-four, so the only diamond missing is the seven. If partner had ◇ A 7 3, he would not have returned the three. So declarer must have the seven of diamonds and the way to set the contract is to cash the jack of diamonds. The four hands:

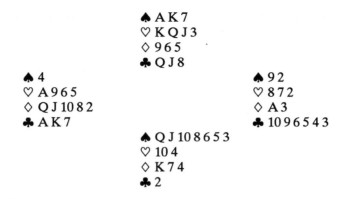

♠ A K 7
♡ K Q J 3
◇ 9 6 5
♣ Q J 8

♠ 4   ♠ 9 2
♡ A 9 6 5   ♡ 8 7 2
◇ Q J 10 8 2   ◇ A 3
♣ A K 7   ♣ 10 9 6 5 4 3

♠ Q J 10 8 6 5 3
♡ 10 4
◇ K 7 4
♣ 2

Leading a New Suit

In Chapter 1 you read that there is a disciplined formula for the opening leader to choose which card to lead. But here we are concerned with leads made after the opening lead (trick two and later), and there are no firm regulations for choosing which card to lead; it might be right to lead a card that would be considered ludicrous as an opening lead.

In most cases it is right to lead fourth-highest, or your lowest card from three, provided you have an honor in the suit: Lead the three from Q 9 5 3 or J 7 3, just as you would on opening lead, but there are exceptions, as you shall see before this chapter ends.

From a worthless three-card or longer suit, it is often right to lead the highest spot card you can spare. The lead of a low spot card implies that you have some strength in the suit and a willingness for partner to return it. To the contrary, a high spot-card lead implies you have no honor cards in the suit: You are not indicating anything about your length (you might lead the eight from 8 6 4, 8 6 5 4 or 8 6 5 4 2), it is simply to discourage partner from returning your suit. Of course, if partner already knows you have nothing in the suit, you can revert to leading as you would on opening lead: For example, if the dummy has great strength in the suit (A Q J x, K Q 10, etc.), lead the four from 8 6 4, 8 6 5 4 or 8 6 5 4 2.

There are also suit combinations with two or three honor cards where you should lead a particular honor card to trap a high card held by declarer or dummy. These are sometimes called "Surrounding Plays." To get started, here are several illustrations showing the merits of leading "low from strength" and "top of nothing."

#8   North
                 ♠ A K 3
                 ♡ K Q J 8
                 ◇ Q J 8 4
                 ♣ K 10

                               East
                               ♠ 9
                               ♡ A 10 4 3
                               ◇ 9 7 5 2
                               ♣ A Q 7 6

West	North	East	South
	1◇	Pass	1♠
Pass	2NT	Pass	4♠
Pass	Pass	Pass	

Your partner leads the two of hearts and you cover dummy's jack with your ace. You would like to get partner on lead to play a club, and a diamond lead is necessary to do this. You should *lead the nine of diamonds* to discourage a diamond return. Here is the full deal:

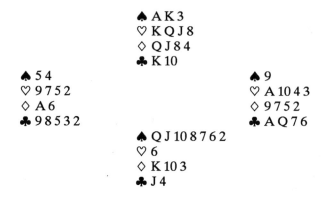

Partner knows you would not lead the nine of diamonds if you had the king, so he should take his ace of diamonds and switch to a club; the only way to beat the contract. It is interesting to note that the opening leader led the two from 9 7 5 2, while you led the nine from the same holding. Both were correct. Now suppose you held the king of diamonds:

#9   North
                                      ♠ A K 3
                                      ♡ K Q J 8
                                      ◇ Q J 8 4
                                      ♣ K 10
                                                            East
                                                            ♠ 9
                                                            ♡ A 10 4 3
                                                            ◇ K 9 7 2
                                                            ♣ Q 7 6 4

        West   *North*   *East*   *South*
                                                         3♠
        Pass   4♠   All Pass

Again partner leads the two of hearts and you win with the ace, but this time you do not want to discourage partner from returning a diamond if he has the ace. So *lead the two of diamonds*. This is a possible layout:

                    ♠ A K 3
                    ♡ K Q J 8
                    ◇ Q J 8 4
                    ♣ K 10
        ♠ 5 4   ♠ 9
        ♡ 9 7 5 2   ♡ A 10 4 3
        ◇ A 6   ◇ K 9 7 2
        ♣ 9 8 5 3 2   ♣ Q 7 6 4
                    ♠ Q J 10 8 7 6 2
                    ♡ 6
                    ◇ 10 5 3
                    ♣ A J

Partner knows you have the king of diamonds, or else you would not have led the two. So he wins with the ace, returns a diamond to your king and you lead a third round of diamonds to give him a ruff; the setting trick.

#10

<pre>
                          North
                          ♠ K 8 6
                          ♡ A Q 3
                          ◇ A Q J
                          ♣ 8 7 4 2
                                              East
                                              ♠ J 10 4
                                              ♡ 5 4
                                              ◇ K 9 7 2
                                              ♣ K Q 9 3
</pre>

West	North	East	South
	1NT	Pass	3♡
Pass	4♡	All Pass	

Partner leads the two of spades, the six is played from dummy, you put in the ten and declarer wins with the queen. After drawing three rounds of trumps (partner follows suit and you discard a diamond), declarer leads a diamond to dummy's jack and you win with the king. The only high cards still missing are the ace of spades and the ace of clubs. Assuming partner does not underlead aces on opening lead versus trump contracts, the only high card he might have is the ace of clubs. What should you lead? Before answering, here are the four hands.

<pre>
                          ♠ K 8 6
                          ♡ A Q 3
                          ◇ A Q J
                          ♣ 8 7 4 2
        ♠ 9 7 5 2   ♠ J 10 4
        ♡ 7 6 2   ♡ 5 4
        ◇ 8 5 4 3   ◇ K 9 7 2
        ♣ A 6   ♣ K Q 9 3
                          ♠ A Q 3
                          ♡ K J 10 9 8
                          ◇ 10 6
                          ♣ J 10 5
</pre>

Unless you win the next three tricks, declarer can make his bid by discarding one of his losing clubs on the third round of diamonds. If the clubs do not divide as shown—declarer has three and partner the doubleton ace—the contract cannot be set. So after winning the fourth trick with the king of diamonds, you should *lead the three of clubs*; if you make the normal play and lead the king, the suit blocks and you can win only two club tricks. Yes, three notrump is a better contract, but they didn't bid it! Also, the ace-of-clubs opening lead will beat the four-heart contract, but not if the cards are distributed as they are in the next deal:

#11   North
                                           ♠ K 8 6
                                           ♡ A Q 3
                                           ◇ A Q J
                                           ♣ 8 7 4 2

                                                              East
                                                              ♠ A J 10
                                                              ♡ 5 4
                                                              ◇ K 9 7 2
                                                              ♣ Q 9 5 3

West	North	East	South
	1NT	Pass	3♡
Pass	4♡	All Pass	

Again partner leads the two of spades, you play the ten and declarer the queen. Partner's lead of the two of spades indicates a four-card suit (or possibly three), so you know that the declarer has at least two more spades in his hand. As in the last deal, declarer proceeds to draw three rounds of trumps and then to take the diamond finesse. When you win the trick with the king of diamonds, what club holding must your partner have to beat the contract? What do you want him to play if he gets the lead? Which club should you lead? The three answers are: the ace or king of clubs, a spade and the *nine of clubs*. Here are the four hands with partner holding the ace of clubs:

                                    ♠ K 8 6
                                    ♡ A Q 3
                                    ◇ A Q J
                                    ♣ 8 7 4 2
        ♠ 9 7 5 2   ♠ A J 10
        ♡ 7 6 2   ♡ 5 4
        ◇ 8 5 4 3   ◇ K 9 7 2
        ♣ A 6   ♣ Q 9 5 3
                                    ♠ Q 4 3
                                    ♡ K J 10 9 8
                                    ◇ 10 6
                                    ♣ K J 10

When you lead the nine of clubs, declarer will play the ten and your partner the ace. He should recognize the nine to be a high club—hence you are not interested in a club return—so his only sensible lead is a spade. This allows you to cash two spade tricks and beat the contract one trick. Without the spade lead, declarer can make his bid by discarding one of his losing spades on a high diamond.

Note that your partner (West) and dummy have the same hands in #10 and #11, and the only thing to guide your partner into the winning defensive play is the size of the club you lead after winning the fifth trick with the king of diamonds.

In the next two deals you are on the other side of the table. The challenge is to read your partner's lead:

#12

```
                              North
                              ♠ K J 4
                              ♡ A K 2
                              ◇ A Q J 9 7
                              ♣ 10 5
         West
         ♠ 9 5 3
         ♡ J 10 9 4
         ◇ 8 4
         ♣ K J 9 3
```

West	North	East	South
	1 ◇	Pass	1NT
Pass	2NT	Pass	3NT
Pass	Pass	Pass	

You lead the jack of hearts, declarer wins in his hand with the queen and leads the ten of diamonds. Partner ducks the first diamond lead and wins the second diamond finesse with the king. He then *leads the two of clubs*, declarer plays the four and you the jack. The lead of the two tells you that partner has the ace or queen, so you *return the three of clubs*. Here are the four hands:

```
                              ♠ K J 4
                              ♡ A K 2
                              ◇ A Q J 9 7
                              ♣ 10 5
         ♠ 9 5 3                              ♠ 8 7 6 2
         ♡ J 10 9 4                           ♡ 8 5 3
         ◇ 8 4                                ◇ K 6 3
         ♣ K J 9 3                            ♣ A 6 2
                              ♠ A Q 10
                              ♡ Q 7 6
                              ◇ 10 5 2
                              ♣ Q 8 7 4
```

It turns out that partner has three clubs to the ace and you can run four club tricks. Note that if partner's first club play were the ace, you could win only three club tricks and declarer would make his contract.

If partner did not have a club honor, he would not have led the two. For example:

```
                              ♠ K J 4
                              ♡ A K 2
                              ◇ A Q J 9 7
                              ♣ 10 5
         ♠ 9 5 3                              ♠ A Q 7 2
         ♡ J 10 9 4                           ♡ 8 5 3
         ◇ 8 4                                ◇ K 6 3
         ♣ K J 9 3                            ♣ 8 6 2
                              ♠ 10 8 6
                              ♡ Q 7 6
                              ◇ 10 5 2
                              ♣ A Q 7 4
```

Again the jack-of-hearts lead is won by declarer with the queen, and he takes the diamond finesse. When partner wins with the king of diamonds, he should lead the *eight of clubs*. Suppose declarer plays the four of clubs and you win with the jack. Partner would not lead the eight of clubs if he held the ace or queen, so declarer has those cards and you should *switch to the nine of spades*. With proper defense, you can win five tricks (one diamond, two clubs and two spades) before declarer can score a ninth trick.

#13   North
                                                ♠ 4 2
                                                ♡ 9 6 5
                                                ◊ Q J 10 7 3
                                                ♣ A K Q
                                                                      East
                                                                      ♠ K 9 5
                                                                      ♡ A 4 3
                                                                      ◊ 6 2
                                                                      ♣ 9 8 7 5 2

West	*North*	*East*	*South*
			1 ◊
Pass	3 ◊	Pass	3NT
Pass	Pass	Pass	

Partner leads the six of spades, you play the king and declarer wins with the ace. At tricks two and three, declarer leads a club to dummy's queen and takes a diamond finesse, which your partner wins with the king. Then partner leads the two of hearts. When you win with the ace, what do you lead back—a spade or a heart? You should lead a heart *because partner led the two of hearts*; if he wanted a spade led back, he would have led a higher heart. These might be the four hands:

                              ♠ 4 2
                              ♡ 9 6 5
                              ◊ Q J 10 7 3
                              ♣ A K Q
        ♠ J 10 7 6 3   ♠ K 9 5
        ♡ K J 8 2   ♡ A 4 3
        ◊ K 4   ◊ 6 2
        ♣ 4 3   ♣ 9 8 7 5 2
                              ♠ A Q 8
                              ♡ Q 10 7
                              ◊ A 9 8 5
                              ♣ J 10 6

Your partner made a good play when he switched to the two of hearts. He knew declarer had the queen of spades (because you played the king) and that he could win nine tricks if he regained the lead. The only hope to beat the contract was to find you with ♡ A x x or better so you could run the next four tricks.

Now let's change the cards so the winning defense is to lead a spade back:

                    ♠ 4 2
                    ♡ 9 6 5
                    ◊ Q J 10 7 3
                    ♣ A K Q

    ♠ Q 10 7 6 3   ♠ K 9 5
    ♡ Q 8 7 2   ♡ A 4 3
    ◊ K 4   ◊ 6 2
    ♣ 4 3   ♣ 9 8 7 5 2

                    ♠ A J 8
                    ♡ K J 10
                    ◊ A 9 8 5
                    ♣ J 10 6

The early plays go as above, up to the point where your partner wins with the king of diamonds. He reasons that if declarer has the ace of hearts and the guarded jack of spades, the contract cannot be set. So he assumes this is not the case and therefore has two options: Continue spades and hope the suit runs, or shift to a heart and hope you have the ace. The choice is not clear-cut, but let's assume he guesses right and leads a heart. To discourage you from returning a heart, he leads the *eight*. You win with the ace and, since partner would not lead the eight from K Q 8 x, K J 8 x or K J 10 8, you should *return the nine of spades*.

#14   North
                                ♠ 6 3
                                ♡ A Q 9 5
                                ◊ A Q J 10
                                ♣ 10 5 4
                                            East
                                            ♠ A 8 5 4
                                            ♡ 8 3
                                            ◊ 9 6 2
                                            ♣ A 7 3 2

    West   *North*   *East*   *South*
                1◊   Pass   1♡
    Pass   2♡   Pass   3NT
    Pass   4♡   All Pass

The opening lead is the queen of spades and you win the first trick with your ace. You cannot win any more spade tricks—partner's lead marks declarer with the king—and the strong hearts and diamonds in dummy suggest you will not win any tricks in those suits. So the only realistic chance to beat the contract is if you can win three club tricks right now! It can be done if partner has ♣ K J x, or ♣ K x if you underlead your ace. So the best lead is the *two of clubs*. Here are the four hands:

```
                    ♠ 6 3
                    ♡ A Q 9 5
                    ◇ A Q J 10
                    ♣ 10 5 4
    ♠ Q J 10 7                          ♠ A 8 5 4
    ♡ 7 6 2                             ♡ 8 3
    ◇ 8 5 4 3                           ◇ 9 6 2
    ♣ Q 8                               ♣ A 7 3 2
                    ♠ K 9 2
                    ♡ K J 10 4
                    ◇ K 7
                    ♣ K J 9 6
```

Partner does not have ♣ K J x or ♣ K x, but you may beat the contract anyway. When you lead the two of clubs, declarer must guess whether you are underleading the ace or the queen. He can make his contract by going up with the king, but if he misguesses, you set him by winning the next three tricks with the queen of clubs, ace of clubs and a club ruff.

Sometimes it is right to lead an honor card without a sequence. For example:

#15   North
                                       ♠ 10 3
                                       ♡ A Q 9
                                       ◇ 8 6
                                       ♣ A K Q J 7 4
                                                        East
                                                        ♠ J 7 2
                                                        ♡ 8 6 5 2
                                                        ◇ A 9 5 4
                                                        ♣ 10 3

West	North	East	South
	1♣	Pass	1♡
1♠	3♣	Pass	3NT
Pass	Pass	Pass	

Your partner leads the queen of diamonds and you win the first trick with the ace. What do you lead at trick two? Declarer is marked with the king of diamonds and will make his bid with overtricks if he gets the lead. The only chance to beat the contract is to win the next four (or more) spade tricks, so *lead the jack of spades*. The four hands:

```
                    ♠ 10 3
                    ♡ A Q 9
                    ◇ 8 6
                    ♣ A K Q J 7 4
    ♠ A Q 9 6 5                          ♠ J 7 2
    ♡ 7 4                                ♡ 8 6 5 2
    ◇ Q J 10 3                           ◇ A 9 5 4
    ♣ 8 2                                ♣ 10 3
                    ♠ K 8 4
                    ♡ K J 10 3
                    ◇ K 7 2
                    ♣ 9 6 5
```

The normal lead from J 7 2 is the two, but if you lead the two, declarer will play low from his hand and the defense can win only two spade tricks. If you lead the jack, your side can run the next five spade tricks. It is lucky to find partner with the ace, queen and nine, but if declarer has ♠ K 9 x or better the contract cannot be set.

In the next four deals, the winning defense is to lead an honor card from a holding of two or three honor cards not in sequence.

#16

<table>
<tr><td></td><td>North</td></tr>
<tr><td></td><td>♠ K Q J 9</td></tr>
<tr><td></td><td>♡ Q 6 3</td></tr>
<tr><td></td><td>◇ A K Q J 2</td></tr>
<tr><td></td><td>♣ 8</td></tr>
</table>

West
♠ A 2
♡ K J 9 4
◇ 8 6
♣ Q 7 6 4 3

West	North	East	South
	1 ◇	Pass	1 ♠
Pass	4 ♠	All Pass	

You lead the four of clubs, partner plays the king and declarer the ace. A spade is led and you take your ace. The only reasonable chance to win any more tricks is if partner has the ace of hearts. So it is clear that you must lead a heart, but which one?

If partner has ♡ A 10 x, you can win three heart tricks no matter which heart you lead. But if he has ♡ A x x, *you must lead the jack to nullify declarer's ten*. For example:

```
              ♠ K Q J 9
              ♡ Q 6 3
              ◇ A K Q J 2
              ♣ 8
♠ A 2                        ♠ 5 3
♡ K J 9 4                    ♡ A 8 7
◇ 8 6                        ◇ 10 7 5
♣ Q 7 6 4 3                  ♣ K 10 9 5 2
              ♠ 10 8 7 6 4
              ♡ 10 5 2
              ◇ 9 4 3
              ♣ A J
```

If you lead the jack of hearts and declarer plays low from dummy, you will win that trick with the jack, and two more with the ace and king. If declarer covers the jack with dummy's queen, your partner will win with the ace and return a heart; note that the ten of hearts is surrounded by your king-nine. In either case you will win three heart tricks. If you lead any heart but the jack, declarer can hold his heart losers to two.

#17   North
                                               ♠ A 9 4
                                               ♡ J 10
                                               ◇ Q 5
                                               ♣ Q J 10 8 7 3

                    West
                    ♠ 8 6 2
                    ♡ Q 9 7 5 3
                    ◇ K J 9 2
                    ♣ A

West	*North*	*East*	*South*
			1NT
Pass	3NT	All Pass	

You lead the five of hearts and dummy wins the first trick with the ten. Then a club is led to declarer's king and your ace. The fact that the ten of hearts won the first trick marks the declarer with the ace and king of hearts, so you know he can win at least nine tricks when he regains the lead (one spade, three hearts and five clubs). The only chance to beat the contract is to win four diamond tricks now! Which diamond would you lead? Before answering, here are the four hands:

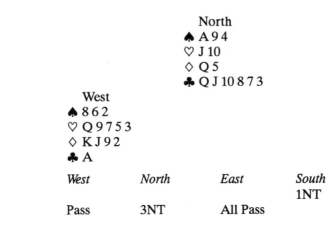

                    ♠ A 9 4
                    ♡ J 10
                    ◇ Q 5
                    ♣ Q J 10 8 7 3

♠ 8 6 2   ♠ 10 7 5 3
♡ Q 9 7 5 3   ♡ 8 4 2
◇ K J 9 2   ◇ A 6 4
♣ A   ♣ 9 6 5

                    ♠ K Q J
                    ♡ A K 6
                    ◇ 10 8 7 3
                    ♣ K 4 2

The right lead is the *king*, because it is the only lead that allows you to win four diamond tricks if declarer has ◇ 10 x x x. Partner will win the second diamond trick with the ace and play a third through declarer so you can score two more tricks with your J 9.

If declarer had only three diamonds, or four diamonds without the ten, you could win four tricks if your first lead were the two; but in the actual layout you would have to lead the third round from J 9 into declarer's 10 8. The king is clearly a better lead, losing only when East has the ace-ten doubleton.

#18

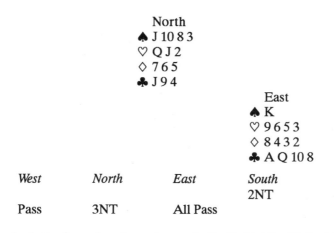

```
North
♠ J 10 8 3
♡ Q J 2
◇ 7 6 5
♣ J 9 4

                              East
                              ♠ K
                              ♡ 9 6 5 3
                              ◇ 8 4 3 2
                              ♣ A Q 10 8
```

West	North	East	South
			2NT
Pass	3NT	All Pass	

Your partner leads the four of spades and you win the first trick with the king, so partner is marked with the ace. Declarer's two-notrump bid shows 21 or 22 high-card points, so partner cannot have any other significant high card. It is likely that declarer will need one or two spade tricks to make his bid, so the only chance to beat the contract is to win three club tricks before declarer can drive out the ace of spades and regain the lead. The right play is to *lead the queen of clubs* at trick two. This is the full deal:

```
                    ♠ J 10 8 3
                    ♡ Q J 2
                    ◇ 7 6 5
                    ♣ J 9 4
♠ A 9 6 4 2                          ♠ K
♡ 10 8 4                             ♡ 9 6 5 3
◇ 10 9                               ◇ 8 4 3 2
♣ 7 5 2                              ♣ A Q 10 8
                    ♠ Q 7 5
                    ♡ A K 7
                    ◇ A K Q J
                    ♣ K 6 3
```

Suppose the declarer covers your queen-of-clubs lead with the king and plays a spade. He needs only one spade trick to make his bid, so your partner must fly in with his ace and return a club. Note that you have the ♣ A 10 8 surrounding dummy's ♣ J 9, so the contract will be set one trick.

You may be thinking that declarer should not cover the queen of clubs with his king. But you can cope with that by leading a low club at trick three; so West will have a club left to lead when he wins a trick with the ace of spades. If West had only two clubs, declarer would succeed by ducking the queen.

#19   North
                                        ♠ 9 5 4
                                        ♡ K Q 8 2
                                        ◇ K J 10 9
                                        ♣ A 9

                                                        East
                                                        ♠ Q 10 8 2
                                                        ♡ 5 4
                                                        ◇ A Q 7
                                                        ♣ 8 6 3 2

West	North	East	South
			1♡
Pass	3♡	Pass	4♡
Pass	Pass	Pass	

Partner leads the two of diamonds, the nine is played from dummy and you win with the queen. The two-of-diamonds lead is predictably from a four-card suit, so declarer has two and will lose two diamond tricks. But you must also be aware that after you play your ace there will be two good diamonds left in dummy; if your side is going to win any spade tricks, you must get them before declarer has a chance to discard on the good diamonds. So, a spade lead at trick two is imperative. In the following layout, the only lead to beat the contract is the *ten of spades*.

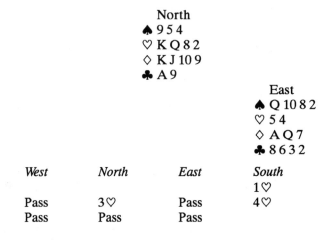

                            ♠ 9 5 4
                            ♡ K Q 8 2
                            ◇ K J 10 9
                            ♣ A 9
        ♠ K 6 3   ♠ Q 10 8 2
        ♡ 10 7   ♡ 5 4
        ◇ 8 6 5 2   ◇ A Q 7
        ♣ Q 10 7 4   ♣ 8 6 3 2
                            ♠ A J 7
                            ♡ A J 9 6 3
                            ◇ 4 3
                            ♣ K J 5

If declarer covers your ten-of-spades lead with the jack, your partner will win with the king and return a spade (note that your queen-eight surrounds dummy's nine). You will be able to win a second spade trick when you regain the lead with the ace of diamonds. If you lead any spade but the ten, declarer can maneuver to lose only one spade trick and make his contract.

The Waiting Game

There are many deals where there is no hurry to get your tricks; you learn from the bidding and the appearance of the dummy that declarer cannot discard any losers on another suit. If you decide the waiting game is best, you should avoid leading from suit combinations that may give the declarer an extra trick, or may eliminate a guessing situation. Force declarer to break his own suits. Let him do his own work. However, there are times when no lead is safe. For example:

#20

```
                              North
                              ♠ 10 9 4
                              ♡ A 9 7
                              ◇ Q 7 6 2
                              ♣ Q 8 5

        West
        ♠ Q 6 3
        ♡ K Q 10 4
        ◇ A 9 5
        ♣ J 3 2
```

West	North	East	South
			1♠
Pass	2♠	All Pass	

You lead the king of hearts, declarer plays low from dummy and partner plays the two. What do you lead next? There might be a lead that will not cost a trick, but there is no way to tell which; every lead is dangerous. Suppose these are the four hands:

```
                    ♠ 10 9 4
                    ♡ A 9 7
                    ◇ Q 7 6 2
                    ♣ Q 8 5
    ♠ Q 6 3                         ♠ 7 5
    ♡ K Q 10 4                      ♡ 8 5 2
    ◇ A 9 5                         ◇ K 10 8 3
    ♣ J 3 2                         ♣ A 9 7 4
                    ♠ A K J 8 2
                    ♡ J 6 3
                    ◇ J 4
                    ♣ K 10 6
```

No matter what you lead, you will probably give declarer a trick. The cards in the South and East hands could be rearranged so that you would not lose a trick no matter which suit you lead. But leading from any of these suit combinations is risky, so you must choose the lead least likely to cost a trick. If you lead a club (probably best), this hands over a club trick; however, this gives declarer a seventh trick and the contract can still be defeated with normal defense.

There is usually at least one suit that can be led without jeopardizing a trick, but you must be able to recognize which leads are safe and which are not. In the next ten illustrations you will be given the chance to challenge yourself:

#21   North
                                                 ♠ Q J 4
                                                 ♡ J 7 4 2
                                                 ◇ 8 6 4
                                                 ♣ A 10 3

                West
                ♠ 9 6 2
                ♡ K 8 5
                ◇ A K 10 3
                ♣ J 8 7

West	North	East	South
			1♠
Pass	2♠	All Pass	

You elect not to bid over two spades and lead the king of diamonds, partner plays the two and declarer the seven. What do you lead now?

A *trump* is of course the right answer; any other lead may cost a trick. Suppose these are the four hands:

                                        ♠ Q J 4
                                        ♡ J 7 4 2
                                        ◇ 8 6 4
                                        ♣ A 10 3
        ♠ 9 6 2   ♠ 7 3
        ♡ K 8 5   ♡ A 10 9 6
        ◇ A K 10 3   ◇ J 5 2
        ♣ J 8 7   ♣ Q 6 5 2
                                        ♠ A K 10 8 5
                                        ♡ Q 3
                                        ◇ Q 9 7
                                        ♣ K 9 4

Declarer has six losers (two hearts, three diamonds and one club), and will lose them all if you lead a spade at trick two and the defense does not slip later. But if you lead a heart, he can establish the jack to discard his club loser; if you lead a diamond, the queen will take a trick; if you lead a club, he will eventually win a third club trick with the ten or nine by finessing.

#22   West   West   North   East   South
           ♠ Q 10 8   2♣
           ♡ 10 9 7   Pass   2◇   Pass   2NT
           ◇ Q 8 3   Pass   Pass   Pass
           ♣ K J 5 2

As you learned in Chapter 1, a passive defense sometimes begins with the opening lead. Here is a case where you use this strategy against a notrump contract. What would you lead?

Right, the *ten of hearts*. Suppose this is the layout:

```
                        ♠ 9 7 4 2
                        ♡ 6 5 4 3
                        ◊ J 10 4
                        ♣ 10 6
        ♠ Q 10 8                        ♠ 6 5 3
        ♡ 10 9 7                        ♡ Q J 8
        ◊ Q 8 3                         ◊ K 9 6 2
        ♣ K J 5 2                       ♣ Q 7 3
                        ♠ A K J
                        ♡ A K 2
                        ◊ A 7 5
                        ♣ A 9 8 4
```

Any lead but a heart would give declarer an extra trick. This strategy must be continued throughout the deal. Your partner should play the jack of hearts on the first trick: a good play so that he can shift to a spade if declarer ducks. But declarer wins the first two tricks with the ace and king of hearts and leads a third heart; breaking a new suit is unattractive, so this is his best play. Your partner wins the third trick with the queen of hearts and leads a spade—his only safe play. If declarer finesses the jack and you are allowed to win the trick with the queen, your safest play is to return a spade; avoid breaking a new suit.

If, when partner led a spade at trick four, declarer played the ace, king and jack of spades to your queen, you are left with the unattractive choice of leading a diamond or a club. The better lead is a low club, which in this layout will enable declarer to win a second club trick; but that is only his seventh trick and he will still be set. If you mistakenly lead a diamond, he can eventually get to dummy with the jack or ten and win two more tricks with the fourth heart and fourth spade—he will wind up with nine tricks.

#23

```
                        North
                        ♠ K 10 4
                        ♡ Q 5 4
                        ◊ A K J 10
                        ♣ J 8 2
                                        East
                                        ♠ J 8 5 2
                                        ♡ A K J
                                        ◊ 9 7 3
                                        ♣ K 10 5
```

West	North	East	South
	1 ◊	Pass	1NT
Pass	Pass	Pass	

Now let's move to the other side of the table. Your partner leads the ten of hearts and you win the first three tricks with your top hearts as all follow suit. Now what?

You could easily give away a trick if you lead a club or a spade, so choose the only safe lead—*a diamond* (any diamond will do, but the nine is normal). This is the full deal:

                              ♠ K 10 4
                              ♡ Q 5 4
                              ◇ A K J 10
                              ♣ J 8 2
         ♠ Q 7 3   ♠ J 8 5 2
         ♡ 10 9 8 7   ♡ A K J
         ◇ 8 6 4   ◇ 9 7 3
         ♣ A 9 3   ♣ K 10 5
                              ♠ A 9 6
                              ♡ 6 3 2
                              ◇ Q 5 2
                              ♣ Q 7 6 4

Declarer can win four diamonds and two spades, but that is all if the defense is accurate. If you lead a club or a spade at trick four, you give declarer the extra trick he needs to make his contract.

#24   North
                                       ♠ Q J 9 3
                                       ♡ K 7 5 2
                                       ◇ Q 6
                                       ♣ K 10 5

         West
         ♠ A 4
         ♡ J 9 8
         ◇ 10 9 8 5
         ♣ Q 7 6 2

West	North	East	South
			1NT
Pass	2♣	Pass	2♠
Pass	4♠	All Pass	

You lead the ten of diamonds. Declarer wins the first two tricks with the ace and king of diamonds. Then he leads the two of spades. Do you play the ace or duck?

By all means, *play the ace*. Look at the four hands to see why:

                              ♠ Q J 9 3
                              ♡ K 7 5 2
                              ◇ Q 6
                              ♣ K 10 5
         ♠ A 4   ♠ 8 6 5
         ♡ J 9 8   ♡ A 6 3
         ◇ 10 9 8 5   ◇ J 7 4 3 2
         ♣ Q 7 6 2   ♣ J 4
                              ♠ K 10 7 2
                              ♡ Q 10 4
                              ◇ A K
                              ♣ A 9 8 3

If you duck declarer's spade lead, he will win the trick in dummy and play another spade. Now you are back on lead and whether you lead a heart, a diamond or a club, it will give declarer a trick (and his contract). You should be suspicious when declarer cashed the second high diamond before leading a spade. Clearly he has a doubleton diamond and is hoping for an "endplay." Winning the first spade trick with the ace is important because you still have the four of spades as a safe exit card. Although declarer can still succeed if he finds the right line of play, at least you will not have helped him.

#25

```
                        North
                        ♠ 10 4 3
                        ♡ K 9 8 7 3
                        ◇ 6 2
                        ♣ K J 5
                                           East
                                           ♠ K 7 6 2
                                           ♡ 4
                                           ◇ A K Q J 4
                                           ♣ Q 8 6
```

West	North	East	South
			1♡
Pass	2♡	Double	4♡
Pass	Pass	Pass	

Partner leads the ten of diamonds and you elect to overtake and cash the first two diamond tricks. What do you lead now?

A diamond lead may give declarer a ruff-and-discard, and a spade lead is not safe with the ten in dummy. So, the best lead is the *four of hearts*. A singleton trump is often a bad lead because it might finesse partner out of a possible trump trick, but it is safe this time because partner is marked with at most two trumps. Here are the four hands:

```
                  ♠ 10 4 3
                  ♡ K 9 8 7 3
                  ◇ 6 2
                  ♣ K J 5
  ♠ Q 9 8                        ♠ K 7 6 2
  ♡ 6                            ♡ 4
  ◇ 10 9 8 5                     ◇ A K Q J 4
  ♣ 10 7 4 3 2                   ♣ Q 8 6
                  ♠ A J 5
                  ♡ A Q J 10 5 2
                  ◇ 7 3
                  ♣ A 9
```

Note that if you lead a spade, diamond or club, declarer will make his bid. But with the trump lead declarer will lose two more tricks if the defense makes no mistakes.

#26   North
                                             ♠ A J 10 8
                                             ♡ Q 3
                                             ◇ K 7 5 4
                                             ♣ K J 6
               West
               ♠ 4
               ♡ J 10 8 5
               ◇ A J 9 3
               ♣ 10 4 3 2

West	North	East	South
	1◇	Pass	1♠
Pass	2♠	Pass	4♠
Pass	Pass	Pass	

You lead the jack of hearts, dummy plays the queen, partner the king and declarer wins with the ace. A spade is led to dummy's jack and partner's king. At trick three partner leads the two of hearts, declarer plays the seven and you win with the eight. What do you lead now?

Partner's lead of the two shows that he started with a four-card heart suit (a doubleton is possible though unlikely), so declarer has another heart in his hand and you will not give him a ruff-and-discard if you lead a third heart. So, rather than leading a dangerous club or diamond, *return the ten of hearts* and let declarer ruff it in dummy. Suppose these are the four hands:

                                             ♠ A J 10 8
                                             ♡ Q 3
                                             ◇ K 7 5 4
                                             ♣ K J 6
               ♠ 4   ♠ K 9 2
               ♡ J 10 8 5   ♡ K 6 4 2
               ◇ A J 9 3   ◇ 10 6
               ♣ 10 4 3 2   ♣ Q 8 7 5
                                             ♠ Q 7 6 5 3
                                             ♡ A 9 7
                                             ◇ Q 8 2
                                             ♣ A 9

As long as you do not lead a club or a diamond when you win the second heart trick, declarer must lose two more tricks in the minor suits and will be set.

#27

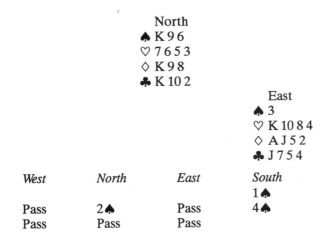

West	North	East	South
			1♠
Pass	2♠	Pass	4♠
Pass	Pass	Pass	

Partner leads the six of diamonds and you win the first trick with the jack. What do you lead at trick two?

Lead the *four of hearts*. Since the dummy has no heart honors, leading that suit is safe. For example:

        ♠ K 9 6
        ♡ 7 6 5 3
        ◇ K 9 8
        ♣ K 10 2

♠ Q 10 2   ♠ 3
♡ J 9   ♡ K 10 8 4
◇ Q 10 7 6 4   ◇ A J 5 2
♣ Q 8 3   ♣ J 7 5 4

        ♠ A J 8 7 5 4
        ♡ A Q 2
        ◇ 3
        ♣ A 9 6

Declarer can always take the heart finesse himself. Once you lead the heart, declarer must lose one trick in each suit if the defense is accurate. Note that a spade lead is safe as the cards lie, but if partner did not have the ten it would trap his queen. A club or diamond lead loses a trick outright.

#28   North
                                       ♠ K 10 7 3
                                       ♡ 6 5
                                       ◇ Q J 10 9 2
                                       ♣ J 8

                West
                ♠ 6 2
                ♡ A K 8 4 3
                ◇ K 7 5
                ♣ A 10 4

West	North	East	South
			1♠
2♡	2♠	4♡	4♠
Pass	Pass	Pass	

You win the first trick with the king of hearts and follow with the ace of hearts, which declarer ruffs. After cashing the ace and king of spades (to which partner follows suit), declarer leads the queen of diamonds and you win with the king. What do you lead now?

It seems that declarer will make his contract by discarding clubs on the long diamonds, and the only hope is to lead a club and find partner with the king. Not so! The correct play is to *return a diamond*. This is the full deal:

                                ♠ K 10 7 3
                                ♡ 6 5
                                ◇ Q J 10 9 2
                                ♣ J 8
        ♠ 6 2   ♠ 8 4
        ♡ A K 8 4 3   ♡ Q J 10 9 7
        ◇ K 7 5   ◇ 4 3
        ♣ A 10 4   ♣ Q 9 6 5
                                ♠ A Q J 9 5
                                ♡ 2
                                ◇ A 8 6
                                ♣ K 7 3 2

With knowledge that declarer was dealt five spades and one heart, you know he has seven minor-suit cards. No matter how his clubs and diamonds are divided, after five rounds of diamonds he will be left with two clubs. So you must not panic and switch to a club when you are on lead with the king of diamonds; you cannot lose by returning a diamond. With the cards as shown, you will eventually get two club tricks and beat the contract if you force declarer to break the club suit.

#29   North
                                           ♠ K 10 6 5
                                           ♡ K 9 7 2
                                           ◇ A 6 4
                                           ♣ K 8

         West
         ♠ Q J 2
         ♡ Q 3
         ◇ 8 7 3
         ♣ J 10 9 6 5

West	North	East	South
			1♠
Pass	3♠	Pass	4NT
Pass	5◇	Pass	6♠
Pass	Pass	Pass	

You lead the jack of clubs, which declarer wins with the ace. He cashes the ace of spades and plays a spade to dummy's king; partner follows once and then discards a club. Next, declarer cashes dummy's king of clubs and drops the queen from his hand. He plays a diamond to his king, a diamond to dummy's ace and ruffs dummy's third diamond in hand, making it apparent that he has no more clubs or diamonds in either hand. Now he throws you on lead with the queen of spades and you must play a club (which gives declarer a ruff-and-discard) or a heart. Which would you choose?

Lead a club because a ruff-and-discard will not help him. The four hands:

                                           ♠ K 10 6 5
                                           ♡ K 9 7 2
                                           ◇ A 6 4
                                           ♣ K 8
         ♠ Q J 2   ♠ 4
         ♡ Q 3   ♡ 8 6 5
         ◇ 8 7 3   ◇ Q J 10 9 5
         ♣ J 10 9 6 5   ♣ 7 4 3 2
                                           ♠ A 9 8 7 3
                                           ♡ A J 10 4
                                           ◇ K 2
                                           ♣ A Q

Declarer has shown up with five spades, two diamonds and two clubs. Therefore, he has four hearts. The dummy has four hearts also, so if you lead a club and give him a ruff-and-discard, he will still have to guess who has the queen of hearts to make his slam. (Note that partner might have ♡ J x x, in which case declarer has no chance to make his slam unless you lead a heart.) However, declarer played the hand well. If you fall into his trap and lead a heart, his troubles are over.

Quiz for Chapter Three

1.

	North		
	♠ 8 6 5		
	♡ A J 9 8		
	◊ A J 3		
	♣ A 10 4		

West
♠ A K J 7 2
♡ 3
◊ 10 6 4 2
♣ Q 8 5

West	North	East	South
	1♣	Pass	1♡
1♠	2♡	Pass	4♡
Pass	Pass	Pass	

You lead the king of spades, partner plays the three, and declarer the four. What do you lead at trick two?

2.

	North		
	♠ K Q J 10 5		
	♡ A J 10		
	◊ A K		
	♣ 9 6 4		

East
♠ A 4 3
♡ K 6
◊ 8 5 3 2
♣ K 10 8 7

West	North	East	South
	1♠	Pass	1NT
Pass	3NT	All Pass	

Your partner leads the three of hearts, the ten is played from dummy, and you win the first trick with the king. What do you lead at trick two?

3.

	North		
	♠ A K Q 10 3 2		
	♡ 5 4		
	◊ A J 9 6		
	♣ 8		

East
♠ —
♡ Q 9 7 2
◊ 5 3 2
♣ A K J 10 5 4

West	North	East	South
	1♠	2♣	2◊
5♣	5◊	All Pass	

Your partner leads the two of clubs and you win the first trick with the king. What do you lead at trick two?

4.

	North		
	♠ 10 9		
	♡ A 6 3 2		
	◊ Q J 10 9 5		
	♣ K 2		

West
♠ K J 4 3 2
♡ 8 4
◊ 4 3
♣ Q 10 9 5

West	North	East	South
			1NT
Pass	2♣	Pass	2◊
Pass	3NT	All Pass	

You lead the three of spades, partner plays the queen, and declarer the ace. At trick two declarer leads the king of diamonds and your partner wins with the ace. Partner then leads the five of spades, declarer plays the eight, and you win with the jack. What do you lead at trick four?

5.
North
♠ 5 2
♡ A K
◇ A K Q 10 9 6
♣ 7 4 3

East
♠ A 9 4
♡ 8 7 6 5
◇ 8 3
♣ K Q J 2

West	North	East	South
	1◇	Pass	1NT
Pass	3NT	All Pass	

Your partner leads the queen of spades and you win the first trick with the ace. What do you lead at trick two?

6.
North
♠ K Q J 10
♡ K 9 2
◇ J 7 4
♣ K 8 3

East
♠ 7 5 4 3
♡ 8 6 5
◇ A Q 10
♣ A Q 2

West	North	East	South
			Pass
Pass	1♠	Pass	2♡
Pass	Pass	Pass	

Your partner leads the jack of clubs and is allowed to win the first trick. He leads another club and you win the next two tricks with the ace and queen of clubs as all follow suit. What do you lead at trick four?

7.
North
♠ 10 9 6
♡ Q 7 3 2
◇ A 10 5
♣ K 8 6

East
♠ Q 5 3
♡ K 6 4
◇ Q 8 7
♣ A Q 10 9

West	North	East	South
			1♠
Pass	2♠	Pass	4♠
Pass	Pass	Pass	

Your partner leads the three of clubs, dummy plays the six, you the queen and declarer the jack. What do you lead at trick two?

8.
North
♠ 10 4 3
♡ 7 4
◇ Q 9 8 6
♣ K J 6 3

East
♠ 9 8 7 6
♡ A 9 3
◇ A K J
♣ 7 5 2

West	North	East	South
			1NT
Pass	Pass	Pass	

Your partner leads the five of hearts and you win with the ace as declarer follows with the two. What do you lead at trick two?

Quiz Answers for Chapter Three

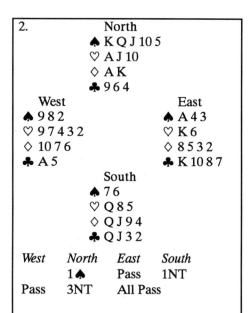

1.

```
              North
            ♠ 8 6 5
            ♡ A J 9 8
            ◇ A J 3
            ♣ A 10 4
West                        East
♠ A K J 7 2                 ♠ 10 9 3
♡ 3                         ♡ Q 5 4
◇ 10 6 4 2                  ◇ Q 8 7
♣ Q 8 5                     ♣ 9 7 6 2
              South
            ♠ Q 4
            ♡ K 10 7 6 2
            ◇ K 9 5
            ♣ K J 3
```

West	North	East	South
	1♣	Pass	1♡
1♠	2♡	Pass	4♡
Pass	Pass	Pass	

You lead the king of spades, partner plays the three, and declarer the four. What do you lead at trick two?

This is a case for passive defense, and the lead least likely to give away a trick is the *ace of spades*. Partner's play of his lowest spade means he probably has three low spades. He could have ♠ Q x or a singleton. In any event, continuing with the ace of spades should not hurt the defense. Note that declarer can succeed if he guesses correctly even if you lead spades at tricks two and three, but if you lead anything else, there is an ironclad way to make his contract without any guesswork.

2.

```
              North
            ♠ K Q J 10 5
            ♡ A J 10
            ◇ A K
            ♣ 9 6 4
West                        East
♠ 9 8 2                     ♠ A 4 3
♡ 9 7 4 3 2                 ♡ K 6
◇ 10 7 6                    ◇ 8 5 3 2
♣ A 5                       ♣ K 10 8 7
              South
            ♠ 7 6
            ♡ Q 8 5
            ◇ Q J 9 4
            ♣ Q J 3 2
```

West	North	East	South
	1♠	Pass	1NT
Pass	3NT	All Pass	

Your partner leads the three of hearts and you win the first trick with the king. What do you lead at trick two?

The only chance to beat three notrump is to win three club tricks before declarer can run the spade suit. The correct lead is the *ten of clubs*, keeping dummy's nine surrounded by your K 8. Suppose declarer plays the jack on your ten. Partner wins with the ace and returns a club. You have the ♣ K 8 7 sitting over the dummy's ♣ 9 6, while declarer is left with the ♣ Q 3 2. You cannot be prevented from establishing two more club tricks.

If you mistakenly lead the seven or eight of clubs at trick two, declarer can prevent you from winning a third club trick by playing a low club from his hand.

Finally, note that the ten of clubs is the only lead to beat the contract if declarer has ♣ A J x.

3. **North**
    ♠ A K Q 10 3 2
    ♡ 5 4
    ◇ A J 9 6
    ♣ 8

    West
    ♠ 8 7 6 5 4
    ♡ A 8 6 3
    ◇ —
    ♣ Q 9 3 2

    East
    ♠ —
    ♡ Q 9 7 2
    ◇ 5 3 2
    ♣ A K J 10 5 4

    South
    ♠ J 9
    ♡ K J 10
    ◇ K Q 10 8 7 4
    ♣ 7 6

West	*North*	*East*	*South*
	1♠	2♣	2◇
5♣	5◇	All Pass	

Your partner leads the two of clubs and you win the first trick with the king. What do you lead at trick two?

It is clear that you should lead a heart, but which one? If declarer has the ace of hearts, he probably has the rest of the tricks, so you should assume that partner has that card. What do you want him to lead back if he gets the lead with the ace of hearts? The answer is, of course, a spade so you can ruff. The right heart to lead at trick two is the *nine*, implying that you have no heart honors and discouraging him from returning a heart. Suppose declarer guesses right and plays the jack of hearts and partner wins with his ace. Knowing that you would not lead the nine of hearts if you wanted a heart returned, your partner should realize that the only hope to beat the contract is to lead a spade and find you with a void suit; something not too unlikely, with eleven spades in sight.

4. **North**
    ♠ 10 9
    ♡ A 6 3 2
    ◇ Q J 10 9 5
    ♣ K 2

    West
    ♠ K J 4 3 2
    ♡ 8 4
    ◇ 4 3
    ♣ Q 10 9 5

    East
    ♠ Q 7 6 5
    ♡ J 9 7 5
    ◇ A 6
    ♣ 8 6 4

    South
    ♠ A 8
    ♡ K Q 10
    ◇ K 8 7 2
    ♣ A J 7 3

West	*North*	*East*	*South*
			1NT
Pass	2♣	Pass	2◇
Pass	3NT	All Pass	

You lead the three of spades, partner plays the queen, and declarer the ace. At trick two declarer leads the king of diamonds and your partner wins with the ace. Partner then leads the five of spades, declarer plays the eight, and you win with the jack. What do you lead at trick four?

If you watched the spade spots as they were played, you would know that only the six and seven are missing. Since declarer denied a four-card major in the bidding, and partner would not have led back the five if he began with Q 7 5 or Q 6 5, partner must have begun with Q 7 6 5; he still has the six and seven. You must *lead a low spade* from your ♠ K 4 2 at trick four; so partner can with the third round and you the fourth and fifth. If you do not take your four spade tricks before declarer regains the lead, you cannot set him.

5.   North
                        ♠ 5 2
                        ♡ A K
                        ◇ A K Q 10 9 6
                        ♣ 7 4 3

West   East
♠ Q J 10 8 7   ♠ A 9 4
♡ 9 4 3 2   ♡ 8 7 6 5
◇ 5 4   ◇ 8 3
♣ A 6   ♣ K Q J 2

                        South
                        ♠ K 6 3
                        ♡ Q J 10
                        ◇ J 7 2
                        ♣ 10 9 8 5

West	North	East	South
	1◇	Pass	1NT
Pass	3NT	All Pass	

Your partner leads the queen of spades and you win the first trick with the ace. What do you lead at trick two?

Partner's queen-of-spades lead marks declarer with the king, and there are eight winning tricks in dummy; if you return a spade, declarer has nine tricks. The only chance to win four more tricks and beat the contract is if partner has the ace of clubs; so you must assume he has that card. To guard against partner's having a doubleton club, *lead the two of clubs.* Partner also can see that declarer has nine tricks if he gets the lead, so he should win with the ace and return a club; you will win the next three tricks with the ♣ K Q J. If you make the mistake of leading the king of clubs, the best your partner can do is overtake with the ace and return a club; but that limits you to three club tricks and declarer will make his bid.

So which is the correct card to lead from K Q J 2? Why the two of course, at least one time in ten thousand.

6.   North
                        ♠ K Q J 10
                        ♡ K 9 2
                        ◇ J 7 4
                        ♣ K 8 3

West   East
♠ A 8 2   ♠ 7 5 4 3
♡ 7 4   ♡ 8 6 5
◇ 9 6 5 3   ◇ A Q 10
♣ J 10 9 6   ♣ A Q 2

                        South
                        ♠ 9 6
                        ♡ A Q J 10 3
                        ◇ K 8 2
                        ♣ 7 5 4

West	North	East	South
			Pass
Pass	1♠	Pass	2♡
Pass	Pass	Pass	

Your partner leads the jack of clubs and is allowed to win the first trick. He leads another club and you win the next two tricks with the ace and queen of clubs as all follow suit. What do you lead at trick four?

Lead the queen of diamonds. A diamond lead is mandatory and the queen offers the only chance to win two diamond tricks if declarer has ◇ K x x. Assume declarer wins with the king and leads a spade. Your partner should go up with his ace and return a diamond. Since you have the ◇ A 10 surrounding dummy's ◇ J 7, you will win the two diamond tricks needed to set the contract. Note that if your first diamond play is the ace or ten, you cannot win more than one diamond trick.

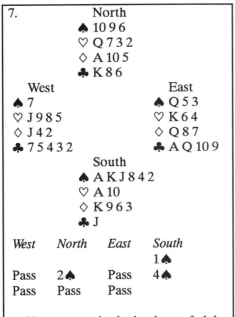

7.

North
♠ 10 9 6
♡ Q 7 3 2
◇ A 10 5
♣ K 8 6

West
♠ 7
♡ J 9 8 5
◇ J 4 2
♣ 7 5 4 3 2

East
♠ Q 5 3
♡ K 6 4
◇ Q 8 7
♣ A Q 10 9

South
♠ A K J 8 4 2
♡ A 10
◇ K 9 6 3
♣ J

West	North	East	South
			1♠
Pass	2♠	Pass	4♠
Pass	Pass	Pass	

Your partner leads the three of clubs, dummy plays the six, you the queen and declarer the jack. What do you lead at trick two?

The jack-of-clubs play is obviously a singleton, so it seems that any lead is dangerous. But there is one lead that is safe regardless of how the cards divide: *a low spade*. You would readily lead a spade without the queen, so your spade lead does not expose your holding and should not affect the way declarer will play the suit—he can finesse for the queen whether you lead the suit or not. Since he has nine trumps, he will probably play the ace and king, hoping the queen drops. But a skillful declarer would survive anyway by leading a third round of spades to put you back on lead—now there is no escape. Declarer can win a tenth trick no matter what you lead.

8.

North
♠ 10 4 3
♡ 7 4
◇ Q 9 8 6
♣ K J 6 3

West
♠ J 5 2
♡ K J 8 5
◇ 10 4 2
♣ 10 8 4

East
♠ 9 8 7 6
♡ A 9 3
◇ A K J
♣ 7 5 2

South
♠ A K Q
♡ Q 10 6 2
◇ 7 5 3
♣ A Q 9

West	North	East	South
			1NT
Pass	Pass	Pass	

Your partner leads the five of hearts and you win with the ace as declarer follows with the two. What do you lead at trick two?

When you get around to returning your partner's suit the right lead is the nine of hearts, but the right play at trick two is the *king of diamonds*. Suppose you did return the nine of hearts at trick two; declarer plays the ten and your partner the jack. He might switch to a spade and declarer would run the next seven tricks. But if you play the king of diamonds before you return a heart, partner knows you have the ace (and probably the jack); he will return a diamond and your side will win the first seven tricks: four hearts and three diamonds.

4

Other Defensive Tactics

In this chapter you will find yourself in situations where you must do some good work in the early going to get your tricks or you won't get them—"The Waiting Game" will lead to disaster.

There are eight categories, beginning with:

Leading from precarious suit combinations

When you see a long and strong suit in the dummy and it is apparent that declarer will be able to discard his losers, you must take the available tricks in the side suits before he can discard those losers. The usual procedure is to lead from strength. This is an easy task from suit combinations such as A K Q, K Q J, etc., but in some cases it is necessary to lead from holdings that you would choose not to lead if there were no hurry to get your tricks, such as A Q x, A J 10, K J x and K x x. Here are six illustrations:

#1

```
                        North
                        ♠ 7 5 2
                        ♡ 10 8
                        ◇ A K Q 10 3
                        ♣ 10 5 4
        West
        ♠ Q J 10 8 6
        ♡ A 5 2
        ◇ J 7
        ♣ K J 3
```

West	North	East	South
			1♡
1♠	2◇	Pass	3♡
Pass	4♡	All Pass	

You lead the queen of spades, partner plays the three and declarer wins with the ace. The next two tricks are a heart, which is won in dummy with the ten, and a heart return to declarer's king and your ace; partner follows suit with the six and nine. It should be clear that declarer started with ♡ K Q J x x x and the ace-king of spades—partner would not have played his lowest spade if he had the king. Your only potential source of tricks is in clubs and, if declarer has any losing clubs, you had better get those tricks now, or South will discard his losers on dummy's diamond winners. You must *lead the three of clubs,* which will beat the contract if declarer has at least three clubs and partner holds the ace. The four hands:

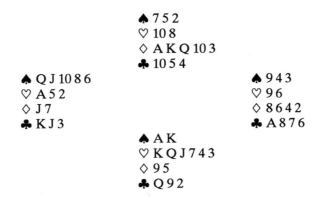

```
              ♠ 7 5 2
              ♡ 10 8
              ◇ A K Q 10 3
              ♣ 10 5 4
♠ Q J 10 8 6                    ♠ 9 4 3
♡ A 5 2                         ♡ 9 6
◇ J 7                          ◇ 8 6 4 2
♣ K J 3                        ♣ A 8 7 6
              ♠ A K
              ♡ K Q J 7 4 3
              ◇ 9 5
              ♣ Q 9 2
```

Partner will win your club lead with his ace and return a club to set the contract one trick. Note that with any lead but a club, declarer will win twelve tricks. You may think it is lucky to find partner with the ace of clubs, but it was predictable because declarer probably would have tried for a slam if he had that card in addition to the ♠ A K and ♡ K Q J x x x. Also note that leading a club would not cost a trick even if declarer had the ace and queen; he could discard any losing clubs on the diamond suit whether you led a club or not. With the actual layout, your bold club switch will undoubtedly make declarer regret that he did not bid three notrump.

#2

```
                        North
                        ♠ A J 5
                        ♡ A 5 4
                        ◇ K Q J
                        ♣ Q J 10 3
                                         East
                                         ♠ K 9 7 2
                                         ♡ 8 6
                                         ◇ 9 6 4 3
                                         ♣ A 7 5
```

West	North	East	South
			3♡
Pass	4♡	All Pass	

Partner leads the two of clubs, dummy plays the queen and you win with the ace. Then you do your detective work: Declarer predictably has seven hearts for his bid and at least two clubs—partner's two-of-clubs lead shows a maximum of four—so declarer has four cards between spades and diamonds and will discard any spade losers on clubs or diamonds if you give him time. The only hope to beat the contract is to find declarer with two or three spades and partner with the king of clubs, the ace of diamonds *and the queen of spades*. So, *lead a spade at trick two*. Here is a hand with the desired spade distribution:

```
                        ♠ A J 5
                        ♡ A 5 4
                        ◇ K Q J
                        ♣ Q J 10 3
    ♠ Q 10 4 3                             ♠ K 9 7 2
    ♡ 2                                     ♡ 8 6
    ◇ A 8 7 5                               ◇ 9 6 4 3
    ♣ K 9 6 2                               ♣ A 7 5
                        ♠ 8 6
                        ♡ K Q J 10 9 7 3
                        ◇ 10 2
                        ♣ 8 4
```

It does not matter which spade you lead, but the two is normal and partner will play the queen to drive out the ace. Now declarer cannot escape losing three more tricks. Note that the spade lead would not cost a trick if declarer had the queen because, if you did not lead the suit, he would establish dummy's clubs or diamonds to discard any spade losers.

#3   **North**
                                    ♠ A Q J 8
                                    ♡ 5
                                    ◇ K Q J 10 9
                                    ♣ K Q 3
                                                        East
                                                        ♠ 6 5
                                                        ♡ A K 8 7 4 2
                                                        ◇ 8 3
                                                        ♣ A J 10

West	*North*	*East*	*South*
	1◇	1♡	1♠
Pass	4♠	All Pass	

The opening lead is the ten of hearts and you win the first trick with the king. If declarer has the ace of diamonds, you cannot beat this contract. If partner has it, you must be able to win two club tricks when he takes his ace; else declarer will discard his losing clubs on the good diamonds. To defeat four spades, declarer must have at least three clubs in his hand, and you must *lead the jack (or ten) of clubs* at trick two. This good defense pays off with the cards as follows:

```
                        ♠ A Q J 8
                        ♡ 5
                        ◇ K Q J 10 9
                        ♣ K Q 3
    ♠ 7 3                                   ♠ 6 5
    ♡ 10 9 6                                 ♡ A K 8 7 4 2
    ◇ A 6 5 4 2                              ◇ 8 3
    ♣ 8 7 5                                  ♣ A J 10
                        ♠ K 10 9 4 2
                        ♡ Q J 3
                        ◇ 7
                        ♣ 9 6 4 2
```

Declarer will win the jack-of-clubs lead with the king or queen, draw trumps and eventually lead a diamond. Your partner will take his ace and return a club to beat the contract one trick.

#4

North
♠ K 6 5
♡ A Q 7 4
◇ 8
♣ K Q J 10 2

East
♠ A Q 3
♡ 8 2
◇ A K 7 6 5 4
♣ A 9

West	North	East	South
	1♣	Double	1♡
Pass	3♡	4◇	4♡
Pass	Pass	Pass	

The opening lead is the ten of diamonds and you win the first trick with the king. After getting over your disappointment that partner did not lead a spade, you realize that you need two spade tricks to beat the contract. Since declarer's obvious line of play will be to dislodge your ace of clubs and discard his spade losers on the established clubs when he regains the lead, you must *lead a spade at trick two*; the best choice is the *three of spades*. This defense will beat the contract if declarer has at least three spades and partner has the jack, as is the case in the following layout:

♠ K 6 5
♡ A Q 7 4
◇ 8
♣ K Q J 10 2

♠ J 8 7 2
♡ 9 5
◇ 10 9 3
♣ 8 6 4 3

♠ A Q 3
♡ 8 2
◇ A K 7 6 5 4
♣ A 9

♠ 10 9 4
♡ K J 10 6 3
◇ Q J 2
♣ 7 5

The second trick will be won in dummy with the king of spades, but when you regain the lead with the ace of clubs, you can cash two spade tricks. Note that here any spade lead at trick two will beat the contract, but the three is best because declarer may have ♠ J 9 x and will have to guess whether to play the jack or the nine.

Leading away from tenace positions and unguarded honor cards is not unusual against notrump contracts, but the following hand is appropriate here because of its similarity to the last few hands, and the unusual defensive play that is required to beat the contract.

#5   North
                                          ♠ K J 10 2
                                          ♡ 9 7
                                          ◇ J 10 9 8
                                          ♣ K 10 5

                                                          East
                                                          ♠ 8 5 4 3
                                                          ♡ J 10 4 3
                                                          ◇ K
                                                          ♣ A Q J 2

West	North	East	South
			1NT
Pass	2♣	Pass	2◇
Pass	2NT	Pass	3NT
Pass	Pass	Pass	

The opening lead is the five of diamonds and you win the first trick with the king—so partner obviously has the ace of diamonds. You can see nineteen high-card points and, assuming the opening one notrump bid showed 16-18; declarer must have the ace-queen of spades, the ace-king-queen of hearts and the queen of diamonds for his bid. That gives him seven winners (four spades and three hearts), and he can develop two more in diamonds by driving out partner's ace. So, the only chance to beat the contract is to win three club tricks when partner gets the lead with the ace of diamonds. A club lead is mandatory. Which club would you lead?

A look at the four hands makes it obvious that you should *lead the two of clubs*.

                                          ♠ K J 10 2
                                          ♡ 9 7
                                          ◇ J 10 9 8
                                          ♣ K 10 5
        ♠ 9 6   ♠ 8 5 4 3
        ♡ 8 6 5 2   ♡ J 10 4 3
        ◇ A 7 6 5 3   ◇ K
        ♣ 4 3   ♣ A Q J 2
                                          ♠ A Q 7
                                          ♡ A K Q
                                          ◇ Q 4 2
                                          ♣ 9 8 7 6

Your club lead gives declarer his eighth trick, so your partner must win the first diamond lead and return a club to beat the contract. You may have thought of leading the queen of clubs rather than the two; but then you cannot win three club tricks when declarer has four clubs—and declarer is a favorite to hold four clubs since he denied a four-card major in the bidding. The two-of-clubs lead will fail only if declarer has five clubs, but in that event there is no way to beat the contract.

#6

North
♠ K Q 9 3
♡ 7 6 2
◇ Q
♣ A Q J 10 8

West
♠ 6 5
♡ A J 8 3
◇ A K J 9 4
♣ 7 5

West	North	East	South
1◇	2♣	Pass	2♠
Pass	4♠	All Pass	

You lead the king of diamonds, partner plays the six and declarer the five. It is apparent that declarer is planning to get discards on the club suit. To defeat the contract you will need to win three heart tricks, or two heart tricks together with the king of clubs (or remotely the ace of spades). The best chance is to find partner with ♡ K x x, or ♡ 10 x x and the king of clubs, so *lead the three of hearts at trick two.* Suppose these are the four hands:

♠ K Q 9 3
♡ 7 6 2
◇ Q
♣ A Q J 10 8

♠ 6 5   ♠ 8 2
♡ A J 8 3   ♡ 10 5 4
◇ A K J 9 4   ◇ 10 8 7 6
♣ 7 5   ♣ K 6 4 3

♠ A J 10 7 4
♡ K Q 9
◇ 5 3 2
♣ 9 2

Declarer's only logical line of play is to capture partner's ten of hearts with the king or queen, draw trumps and take the club finesse. Partner will win with the king and return a heart, setting the contract one trick.

Note that if declarer held ♡ K Q 10, your lead of the three of hearts would allow him to win a trick with the ten, but in that case you could never win more than one heart trick. However, your heart lead would give away the contract if declarer held ♡ K x and partner had an entry card.

Leading a Trump

In Chapter 1 you read that the opening lead of a trump is desirable when there is a need to cut down declarer's ruffing power, or when you opt for a passive defense and choose a trump as the safest lead. Here are two examples of where a trump should be led *after* the opening lead:

#7
                          North
                          ♠ K J
                          ♡ 9 8 6 3
                          ♦ 7
                          ♣ A Q 10 7 4 2

                                              East
                                              ♠ 6 2
                                              ♡ J 7 4
                                              ♦ A J 9 8
                                              ♣ K J 9 5

West	North	East	South
			1♠
Pass	2♣	Pass	3♠
Pass	4♠	All Pass	

The opening lead is the king of diamonds. This time you have strong clubs and declarer will not be able to establish dummy's long suit for discards. If he has any losing heart tricks, he can do nothing about it. But he can do something about diamond losers by ruffing in dummy. The obvious defense is to lead a trump at trick two, but note that it might not be obvious to your partner since he does not know that you have the club suit locked up. So you should overtake your partner's king-of-diamonds lead with your ace and *lead a trump*. Here are the four hands:

                          ♠ K J
                          ♡ 9 8 6 3
                          ♦ 7
                          ♣ A Q 10 7 4 2
        ♠ 9 7 5   ♠ 6 2
        ♡ K 10 5 2   ♡ J 7 4
        ♦ K Q 10 4   ♦ A J 9 8
        ♣ 8 3   ♣ K J 9 5
                          ♠ A Q 10 8 4 3
                          ♡ A Q
                          ♦ 6 5 3 2
                          ♣ 6

After your spade lead, there is only one trump left in the dummy. Declarer will be able to ruff one diamond, but that leaves him with four losers (three diamonds and one heart). Note that if you allowed your partner to win the first trick, he might lead a heart; he does not know that the club suit will not run and may try to grab any possible winners before declarer can discard on the club suit.

#8

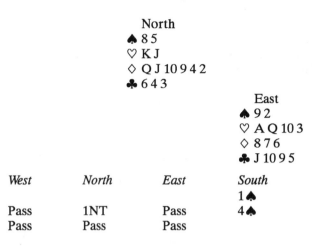

North
♠ 8 5
♡ K J
♢ Q J 10 9 4 2
♣ 6 4 3

East
♠ 9 2
♡ A Q 10 3
♢ 8 7 6
♣ J 10 9 5

West	*North*	*East*	*South*
			1♠
Pass	1NT	Pass	4♠
Pass	Pass	Pass	

The opening lead is the two of hearts, the jack is played in dummy and you win with the queen. The two-of-hearts lead implies that partner has four hearts, so declarer has three and will lose three heart tricks unless he can ruff one in dummy. To thwart that possibility, you must *lead a trump* at trick two. The four hands:

```
                        ♠ 8 5
                        ♡ K J
                        ♢ Q J 10 9 4 2
                        ♣ 6 4 3
        ♠ K 6                           ♠ 9 2
        ♡ 9 7 5 2                       ♡ A Q 10 3
        ♢ K 5 3                         ♢ 8 7 6
        ♣ Q 8 7 2                       ♣ J 10 9 5
                        ♠ A Q J 10 7 4 3
                        ♡ 8 6 4
                        ♢ A
                        ♣ A K
```

Not that it makes any difference, but let's say that declarer finesses the queen of spades at trick two. Your partner wins with the king and leads another spade. All you have to do is sit back and wait. Declarer will eventually give you two more heart tricks with your ace and ten.

Note that if you cash a second heart before leading a trump, or lead anything else, you cannot prevent declarer from ruffing the third round of hearts in dummy.

Attacking Dummy's Entry Cards

Another way to beat a contract is to block the declarer's communication with dummy by eliminating his entry cards. Here are three examples:

#9   North
                                            ♠ Q 3
                                            ♡ A 7 2
                                            ◇ A J 6 5 3
                                            ♣ 10 9 2
                                                                        East
                                                                        ♠ 8 6 4
                                                                        ♡ Q 10 9
                                                                        ◇ K Q 10
                                                                        ♣ A K J 3

West	North	East	South
			1♠
Pass	2◇	Pass	2♠
Pass	3♠	Pass	4♠
Pass	Pass	Pass	

Partner leads the four of clubs to your king and declarer's six. You cash the ace of clubs, declarer plays the queen and partner the five. You need two more tricks to beat the contract. If declarer has a heart loser, there is a danger that he can establish the diamond suit for a discard. Therefore, the best play is to attack dummy's entries. Since declarer cannot discard on diamonds until the trumps have been drawn, the entry that must be removed from dummy is the ace of hearts. If dummy's only remaining entry is the queen of spades, he cannot get to dummy after drawing three rounds of trumps. So, *lead the ten of hearts*. Note that a heart lead cannot cost a trick no matter what declarer has in the suit. The four hands:

                                            ♠ Q 3
                                            ♡ A 7 2
                                            ◇ A J 6 5 3
                                            ♣ 10 9 2
            ♠ 7 5   ♠ 8 6 4
            ♡ J 8 4 3   ♡ Q 10 9
            ◇ 9 7 2   ◇ K Q 10
            ♣ 8 7 5 4   ♣ A K J 3
                                            ♠ A K J 10 9 2
                                            ♡ K 6 5
                                            ◇ 8 4
                                            ♣ Q 6

Suppose declarer wins your heart switch with the king and leads a diamond to the jack and your queen. You then lead a second heart to force out the ace. The diamond suit is now useless, so declarer must lose a heart trick.

If you did not lead a heart at trick three, the contract can be made. Suppose you lead a third club and declarer ruffs. His best play is to lead a diamond to the jack; you win it and lead a heart (it is too late, but no other lead will help), which he wins with his king. Now he leads a diamond to the ace and ruffs a third round of diamonds in his hand. Since dummy's diamonds are now good, he draw trumps, leads a heart to dummy's ace and discards his losing heart on a good diamond.

Note that if you do not lead a heart at trick three, the contract can be made even if diamonds divide four-two. After ruffing the third round of diamonds, declarer leads a spade to dummy's queen and ruffs a fourth diamond. He then draws trumps, goes to dummy with the ace of hearts and discards his loser on the fifth diamond.

#10

```
                        North
                        ♠ A
                        ♡ Q J 9
                        ◇ A 6 4
                        ♣ A 8 7 5 4 2
                                        East
                                        ♠ Q 4 2
                                        ♡ A K 10 7
                                        ◇ J 10 9
                                        ♣ K J 10
```

West	North	East	South
			3♠
Pass	4♠	All Pass	

Partner leads the two of hearts, the jack is played from dummy and you win with the king. You can be sure declarer has another heart because partner led the two. With three tricks in sight (two hearts and one spade), you can beat the contract if you can win a trick in clubs or diamonds. If declarer has a club loser, you will beat the hand with routine defense. The danger is that declarer has a *singleton* club, in which case he may be able to establish the suit for discards. To do this he will need two entries to dummy *after he uses the ace of clubs* and you can prevent this by *leading a trump at trick two*. Suppose these are the four hands:

```
                        ♠ A
                        ♡ Q J 9
                        ◇ A 6 4
                        ♣ A 8 7 5 4 2
        ♠ 9 6                               ♠ Q 4 2
        ♡ 8 5 3 2                           ♡ A K 10 7
        ◇ Q 8 7 3                           ◇ J 10 9
        ♣ Q 9 6                             ♣ K J 10
                        ♠ K J 10 8 7 5 3
                        ♡ 6 4
                        ◇ K 5 2
                        ♣ 3
```

With the ace of spades gone, declarer can play the ace of clubs and ruff a club, lead a diamond to the ace and ruff another club, but he has no more dummy entries and cannot discard on the good clubs. So he must lose four tricks.

Without a spade lead at trick two, the contract is easily made. Suppose the jack of diamonds is led. Declarer wins with his king, leads a club to dummy's ace, ruffs a club, plays a spade to dummy's ace and ruffs another club. The club suit is now established and the ace of diamonds is still in the dummy, so the declarer will cash the king of spades and later be able to discard a loser.

Note that partner made a questionable opening lead (it is usually better to lead from strength on this bidding), but here if he leads a club or a diamond, the contract cannot be set.

#11   North
                                        ♠ A Q J 10 4 2
                                        ♡ 8 7 2
                                        ◇ 9 3
                                        ♣ 9 3

                                                            East
                                                            ♠ K 9 5
                                                            ♡ J 5 4 3
                                                            ◇ 10 4
                                                            ♣ A 8 7 6

West	*North*	*East*	*South*
			2♡
Pass	2♠	Pass	3◇
Pass	3♠	Pass	4◇
Pass	4♡	Pass	4NT
Pass	5◇	Pass	6♡
Pass	Pass	Pass	

After the old-fashioned strong two-heart opening bid, the opponents reach six hearts. Your partner leads the queen of clubs, you win with the ace and declarer plays the two. Now what?

South's probable distribution is 1-5-5-2: By bidding hearts, then bidding and rebidding diamonds, he showed at least five-five in the red suits; he must have the king of clubs because your partner led the queen, and he more than likely has one spade because it is generally wrong to use Blackwood with a void suit. If declarer has a losing diamond trick, the contract will always be set, so you must assume he does not and go to work on how to win a trick with your jack of hearts. Suppose declarer's hearts are A K Q 10 x. His normal play is to cash the ace and king, hoping for a three-two break. But partner has a singleton and will show out on the second heart lead, so declarer will go to dummy and finesse you out of your jack—*if he has an entry to dummy*. Now let's get back to trick two. What do you lead? Why a *spade* of course, to take away dummy's entry. Suppose these are the four hands:

                                        ♠ A Q J 10 4 2
                                        ♡ 8 7 2
                                        ◇ 9 3
                                        ♣ 9 3
        ♠ 8 7 3   ♠ K 9 5
        ♡ 9   ♡ J 5 4 3
        ◇ 8 7 5 2   ◇ 10 4
        ♣ Q J 10 5 4   ♣ A 8 7 6
                                        ♠ 6
                                        ♡ A K Q 10 6
                                        ◇ A K Q J 6
                                        ♣ K 2

After your spade lead at trick two, declarer will not be able to return to dummy after he finds out about the bad trump break. If you did not lead a spade, he could go to dummy with the ace of spades and take a heart finesse. It is true that declarer can make his bid if he leads a heart from dummy at trick three and finesses the ten, but this is a poor percentage play; cashing the top hearts and hoping the jack will fall is much better. Anyway, if he decides to finesse, there is nothing you can do about it.

The Hold-Up Play

In the next four deals, it is a hold-up play that should be considered to block declarer's communication.

#12

```
                    North
                    ♠ 10 5
                    ♡ A 5 2
                    ◇ J 6 3
                    ♣ K 10 9 8 4
                                        East
                                        ♠ Q J 9 8
                                        ♡ 7 6
                                        ◇ 10 5 2
                                        ♣ A Q 3 2
```

West	North	East	South
			1NT
Pass	2NT	Pass	3NT
Pass	Pass	Pass	

Partner leads the jack of hearts and the first trick is won by declarer with the king. He then leads the jack of clubs, partner plays the seven and you must *duck the first club lead*. Declarer continues with the five of clubs, partner plays the six, dummy the eight and this time you should win with your queen.

The four hands:

```
                    ♠ 10 5
                    ♡ A 5 2
                    ◇ J 6 3
                    ♣ K 10 9 8 4
    ♠ 6 3 2                              ♠ Q J 9 8
    ♡ J 10 9 8 4                         ♡ 7 6
    ◇ K Q 8                              ◇ 10 5 2
    ♣ 7 6                                ♣ A Q 3 2
                    ♠ A K 7 4
                    ♡ K Q 3
                    ◇ A 9 7 4
                    ♣ J 5
```

By allowing declarer to win the first club trick and then winning the second when it is led, declarer is limited to one club trick and the contract cannot be made.

If you win the first club trick, declarer can make his contract by winning whatever you return in his hand and leading his second club to knock out your ace and establish the suit. With the ace of hearts still in dummy, there is no way to stop him from winning the three club tricks he needs to make his contract.

#13   North
                                                 ♠ 10 6 3
                                                 ♡ 7 6 2
                                                 ◇ A Q J 10 4
                                                 ♣ 8 5
                                                                                    East
                                                                                    ♠ Q J 9 7
                                                                                    ♡ 10 8
                                                                                    ◇ K 8 7 2
                                                                                    ♣ J 10 6

West	North	East	South
			1♣
Pass	1◇	Pass	2NT
Pass	3NT	All Pass	

Partner leads the four of hearts, you play the ten and declarer the king. The nine of diamonds is led, partner plays the six and dummy the four. You should *duck*. Declarer leads another diamond to dummy's ten and partner discards the three of hearts. You should *duck again*. The four hands:

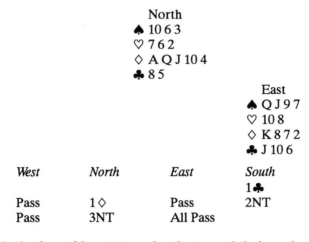

                                                 ♠ 10 6 3
                                                 ♡ 7 6 2
                                                 ◇ A Q J 10 4
                                                 ♣ 8 5
         ♠ 8 5 2   ♠ Q J 9 7
         ♡ J 9 5 4 3   ♡ 10 8
         ◇ 6   ◇ K 8 7 2
         ♣ A Q 7 3   ♣ J 10 6
                                                 ♠ A K 4
                                                 ♡ A K Q
                                                 ◇ 9 5 3
                                                 ♣ K 9 4 2

By ducking the first two diamond leads you limit declarer to three diamond tricks, and with the cards as shown he needs four diamond tricks to make his contract. You of course did not know that he needed four diamond tricks, but winning the second diamond lead will defeat the contract only if the defense can win the *next four tricks*; and this is unlikely as partner would not have discarded a heart on the second diamond if he had strong hearts (such as ♡ A J x x x). If you are thinking you can run four club tricks if declarer has ♣ K x x x and partner ♣ A Q 9 x, or four spade tricks if declarer has ♠ K x and partner ♠ A x x x, it is true; but if you duck the second round of diamonds and declarer has either of those holdings, it is unlikely that he can win more than eight tricks, so you are a big favorite to beat the contract anyway.

The next deal is to caution you that it is not always right to hold up.

#14

                                                North
                                                ♠ 7 3 2
                                                ♡ A K Q
                                                ◇ K 5 3
                                                ♣ K Q J 10

                                                                        East
                                                                        ♠ K J 10 9 5
                                                                        ♡ J 9 6
                                                                        ◇ A 8
                                                                        ♣ A 7 4

West	North	East	South
		1♠	Pass
Pass	Double	Pass	1NT
Pass	2NT	Pass	3NT
Pass	Pass	Pass	

Because you bid the suit, partner dutifully leads the eight of spades. You play the nine and declarer wins with the queen. The two of clubs is led, partner plays the five and dummy the ten. *Win this trick with your ace of clubs; do not hold up.* If you win with the ace and lead another spade, declarer has only eight tricks (two spades, three hearts and three clubs). You will have enough spade tricks to set the contract when you regain the lead with the ace of diamonds. Here are the four hands, to show you what will happen if you duck the club lead:

                            ♠ 7 3 2
                            ♡ A K Q
                            ◇ K 5 3
                            ♣ K Q J 10
        ♠ 8 4   ♠ K J 10 9 5
        ♡ 8 7 3 2   ♡ J 9 6
        ◇ 9 6 4 2   ◇ A 8
        ♣ 9 8 5   ♣ A 7 4
                            ♠ A Q 6
                            ♡ 10 5 4
                            ◇ Q J 10 7
                            ♣ 6 3 2

Declarer has five tricks in the majors, and therefore needs four in the minors to make his contract. If you duck the club lead at trick two, he will switch to diamonds; you cannot stop him from winning three diamonds and one club. Refusing to win a trick is sometimes a good play. Sometimes it is not. So don't do so with reckless abandon; if you don't have a good reason to hold up, win the trick.

In the next deal, you must make a hold-up play *and* drive out an entry card in dummy to beat the contract.

#15   **North**
                                                       ♠ A 6
                                                       ♡ 8 7 4 2
                                                       ◇ 9
                                                       ♣ K J 10 7 5 3

                                                                       East
                                                                       ♠ K 9 5 4
                                                                       ♡ 6 3
                                                                       ◇ J 10 8 6
                                                                       ♣ A Q 2

West	*North*	*East*	*South*
			1NT
Pass	2♣	Pass	2◇
Pass	3♣	Pass	3NT
Pass	Pass	Pass	

Partner leads the queen of hearts and declarer wins with the ace. The nine of clubs is led, partner follows with the four and you play the two. Declarer leads another club, partner discards a low spade and you win with the queen. If partner followed suit to the second lead, declarer would have only two clubs; then the club suit would be useless with only one entry to dummy. But declarer has three clubs and plans to lead his third club to drive out your ace when he regains the lead; then he will be able to win three more club tricks *if the ace of spades is still in dummy*. To prevent this, you must *lead the king of spades* to force out the ace. With the cards as follows, the only defense to beat the contract is to duck the first (or second) club trick and lead the king of spades at your first opportunity.

                                                       ♠ A 6
                                                       ♡ 8 7 4 2
                                                       ◇ 9
                                                       ♣ K J 10 7 5 3
      ♠ 10 7 3 2   ♠ K 9 5 4
      ♡ Q J 10 9   ♡ 6 3
      ◇ Q 5 4 3   ◇ J 10 8 6
      ♣ 4   ♣ A Q 2
                                                       ♠ Q J 8
                                                       ♡ A K 5
                                                       ◇ A K 7 2
                                                       ♣ 9 8 6

Your lead of the king of spades gives declarer an extra spade trick, but deprives him of three club tricks. He can win only eight tricks (three spades, two hearts, two diamonds and one club). The play of the spade king is called a Merrimac Coup.

Although most hold-up plays are to block declarer's communications, it is sometimes a good tactic for other reasons: to allow your partner a chance to give you a signal, to control the trump suit or to prevent a squeeze. Here is one example of each:

#16

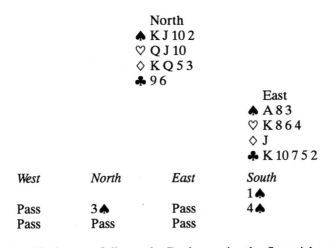

North
♠ K J 10 2
♡ Q J 10
◇ K Q 5 3
♣ 9 6

East
♠ A 8 3
♡ K 8 6 4
◇ J
♣ K 10 7 5 2

West	North	East	South
			1♠
Pass	3♠	Pass	4♠
Pass	Pass	Pass	

The opening lead is the ten of diamonds. Declarer wins the first trick with the ace and leads a spade, partner playing the five and dummy the king. Suppose you win this trick with your ace. What will you lead at trick three? If partner has an ace, you can put him on lead and get a diamond ruff, but you don't know whether to lead a heart or a club! How can you tell? Solution: *Duck the first spade trick.* The bidding makes it clear that partner has a singleton spade, so wait and win the second spade when partner will be able to give you a signal. Here are the four hands:

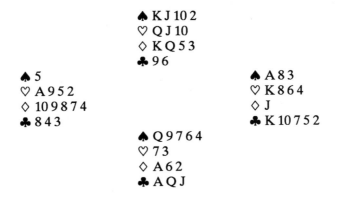

♠ K J 10 2
♡ Q J 10
◇ K Q 5 3
♣ 9 6

♠ 5
♡ A 9 5 2
◇ 10 9 8 7 4
♣ 8 4 3

♠ A 8 3
♡ K 8 6 4
◇ J
♣ K 10 7 5 2

♠ Q 9 7 6 4
♡ 7 3
◇ A 6 2
♣ A Q J

When declarer leads the second round of spades and you win with your ace, partner will encourage a heart lead, probably by discarding the nine of hearts. So you lead a heart to his ace, he returns a diamond for you to ruff, and the king of hearts is the setting trick.

#17
                                           North
                                           ♠ A 9 6 4
                                           ♡ Q 10 3 2
                                           ◇ 7 2
                                           ♣ 8 5 4

          West
          ♠ J 10 8 2
          ♡ 9 7 5
          ◇ Q J 4
          ♣ A 6 3

West	North	East	South
			1 ◇
Pass	1 ♡	Pass	3 ♣
Pass	3NT	Pass	4 ♣
Pass	5 ♣	All Pass	

You lead the jack of spades and declarer wins the first trick with the ace in dummy. Then he leads a club and plays the king from his hand. Declarer's bidding showed at least five cards in each minor suit. Since you have a potential diamond trick, why is he playing trumps before trying to ruff diamonds in dummy? Answer: He would like to play exactly two rounds of clubs before ruffing a diamond; thus cutting down on the chances of being overruffed. To prevent this, *let declarer win this trick with the king of clubs; hold up your ace.* When you think about it, you cannot benefit from winning the first club trick. Before explaining further, here are the four hands:

                                ♠ A 9 6 4
                                ♡ Q 10 3 2
                                ◇ 7 2
                                ♣ 8 5 4

          ♠ J 10 8 2   ♠ K Q 5 3
          ♡ 9 7 5   ♡ A J 8 6 4
          ◇ Q J 4   ◇ 9 3
          ♣ A 6 3   ♣ 10 7

                                ♠ 7
                                ♡ K
                                ◇ A K 10 8 6 5
                                ♣ K Q J 9 2

Declarer must lose one heart and one club, so the fate of the contract depends on whether or not he loses a diamond trick. If you win the first club trick, declarer can make his contract. When he regains the lead, he will cash a second high club, ruff the third round of diamonds in dummy with the eight of clubs, return to hand with a spade ruff and draw your last trump.

If you duck the first club lead, he must go down: If he leads a second club, you will win it and lead a third club; you then have a natural diamond trick with your ◇ Q J 4. If declarer tries to ruff the third round of diamonds in dummy before leading a second trump, your partner can overruff with the ten of clubs.

The next illustration of a hold-up play shows how it can prevent a squeeze:

#18

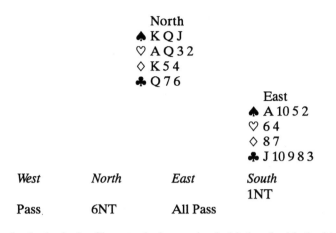

North
- ♠ K Q J
- ♡ A Q 3 2
- ◇ K 5 4
- ♣ Q 7 6

East
- ♠ A 10 5 2
- ♡ 6 4
- ◇ 8 7
- ♣ J 10 9 8 3

West	North	East	South
			1NT
Pass	6NT	All Pass	

Your partner leads the jack of hearts, declarer wins in his hand with the king and leads a spade. You should *duck*. He leads another spade. You should *duck again*. Squeeze plays rarely work unless declarer "rectifies the count" (reaches a position in which he can win all but one of the remaining tricks). Declarer is going to win two spade tricks no matter when you take your ace, so the purpose of ducking twice is to prevent declarer from rectifying the count. Now to see how these clever hold-up plays pay off:

♠ K Q J
♡ A Q 3 2
◇ K 5 4
♣ Q 7 6

♠ 6 4 3	♠ A 10 5 2
♡ J 10 9 8	♡ 6 4
◇ J 10 9 6	◇ 8 7
♣ 4 2	♣ J 10 9 8 3

♠ 9 8 7
♡ K 7 5
◇ A Q 3 2
♣ A K 5

Declarer has eleven tricks (two spades, three hearts, three diamonds and three clubs). He could win a twelfth if hearts or diamonds divided three-three, but you see they don't. So, his only chance is to lead six black cards and force West to part with a heart or a diamond. If you win the first or second spade trick, he will succeed. But if you hold up on the first two spade leads, he cannot lead a third spade without giving you two spade tricks. Since he can lead only two spades and three clubs, your partner cannot be squeezed and the contract will be set.

Reading the Location of High Cards and the Distribution

Here we are concerned with reading the clues from partner's opening lead, from partner's third-hand play and from the bidding, to discover declarer's high-card holding and/or distribution. In the next three deals it is partner's opening lead that is revealing.

#19

	North
	♠ 5 3 2
	♡ A Q
	◊ 9 7
	♣ A J 10 8 6 2

East
♠ A 9 8 4
♡ J 7 2
◊ Q 10 8 6
♣ K 5

West	North	East	South
			1♣
Pass	3♣	Pass	3NT
Pass	Pass	Pass	

Partner leads the queen of spades, you play the ace and the declarer follows suit with the six. Declarer is marked with the king of spades, so partner has at most a four-card suit. If you return a spade at trick two, you will be able to win at most two more spade tricks when you regain the lead with the king of clubs; not enough tricks to beat the contract. A better play is to try to develop three diamond tricks by leading the *ten of diamonds*. The four hands:

	♠ 5 3 2	
	♡ A Q	
	◊ 9 7	
	♣ A J 10 8 6 2	
♠ Q J 10 7		♠ A 9 8 4
♡ 9 6 5 3		♡ J 7 2
◊ K 5 4 3		◊ Q 10 8 6
♣ 4		♣ K 5
	♠ K 6	
	♡ K 10 8 4	
	◊ A J 2	
	♣ Q 9 7 3	

Although this contract can be set with any diamond lead (if you lead a low diamond and declarer plays low from his hand, partner must win with the king and switch back to spades), the ten is the proper card to lead because it leaves dummy's nine surrounded. Declarer cannot stop you from establishing three diamond tricks, which together with the ace of spades and the king of clubs will beat the contract. If declarer has the ace and king of diamonds, the contract is unbeatable.

#20

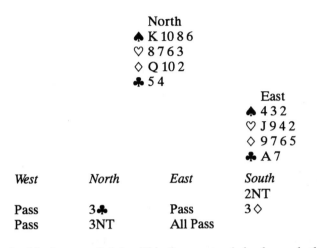

West	North	East	South
			2NT
Pass	3♣	Pass	3◇
Pass	3NT	All Pass	

The opening lead is the two of clubs. This time partner's lead reveals that declarer has a five-card club suit, so returning a club would help declarer establish his long cards in clubs. The weak heart holding in dummy suggests that the best chance to develop tricks for your side is to switch to a heart. So *lead the two of hearts*. The four hands:

```
                    ♠ K 10 8 6
                    ♡ 8 7 6 3
                    ◇ Q 10 2
                    ♣ 5 4
    ♠ J 9 7                          ♠ 4 3 2
    ♡ K 10 5                         ♡ J 9 4 2
    ◇ J 4 3                          ◇ 9 7 6 5
    ♣ K J 6 2                        ♣ A 7
                    ♠ A Q 5
                    ♡ A Q
                    ◇ A K 8
                    ♣ Q 10 9 8 3
```

With spades breaking, declarer has eight tricks (four spades, one heart and three diamonds), and he will have to drive out the king and jack of clubs before he can win a ninth. If you lead a heart at trick two, declarer will finesse the queen and partner will win with the king. Then partner will return the ten of hearts to drive out the ace. The best declarer can do is to cash his eight winners and concede down one. Note that if you do not lead a heart at trick two, there is no way to stop declarer from developing two club tricks; he will make his contract with an overtrick.

#21

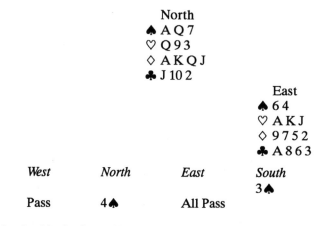

North
♠ A Q 7
♡ Q 9 3
◇ A K Q J
♣ J 10 2

East
♠ 6 4
♡ A K J
◇ 9 7 5 2
♣ A 8 6 3

West	North	East	South
			3♠
Pass	4♠	All Pass	

The opening lead is the four of hearts. Presumably partner is leading fourth-highest and can have four or five hearts. Suppose declarer plays low from dummy and you win the first two tricks with the jack and king of hearts. Partner plays the two on the second heart lead to show a five-card suit. So declarer has no more hearts and will ruff if you try to cash your ace. The only other possible tricks for the defense are in clubs. You must win two club tricks now or declarer will discard his losing clubs on the diamond suit. *Lead the three of clubs.* The four hands:

♠ A Q 7
♡ Q 9 3
◇ A K Q J
♣ J 10 2

♠ 3
♡ 10 7 5 4 2
◇ 10 8 6 3
♣ Q 9 5

♠ 6 4
♡ A K J
◇ 9 7 5 2
♣ A 8 6 3

♠ K J 10 9 8 5 2
♡ 8 6
◇ 4
♣ K 7 4

Declarer must guess whether you are underleading the ace or queen of clubs; if he puts up his king, he will make his bid with an overtrick; if he plays a low club, the defense can win the two needed club tricks. This is a good example of how leading fourth-highest from four-card or longer suits can help third hand. You learned that partner had a five-card heart suit when he played the two of hearts on the second trick. If he had only four hearts, his second play would have been some heart higher than the four; then the winning defense would be to cash a third heart trick and the ace of clubs.

You have just seen how third hand can benefit from the opening lead. Now let's see how the opening leader can benefit from partner's third-hand play.

#22

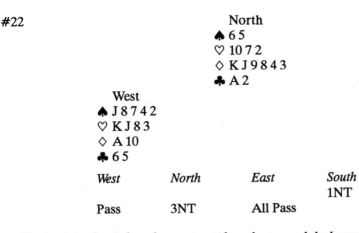

North
- ♠ 6 5
- ♡ 10 7 2
- ◇ K J 9 8 4 3
- ♣ A 2

West
- ♠ J 8 7 4 2
- ♡ K J 8 3
- ◇ A 10
- ♣ 6 5

West	North	East	South
			1NT
Pass	3NT	All Pass	

You lead the four of spades, partner plays the ten and declarer wins with the ace. What is declarer's spade holding? Since partner would not play the ten if he held the king, queen or nine, declarer must have ♠ A K Q 9. At trick two, declarer leads the queen of diamonds and you win with your ace. You can see that declarer has nine tricks (three spades, five diamonds and one club), so the only chance to beat the contract is to win the next four tricks. For this to happen partner must have ♡ A x x or better. *Lead the three of hearts.* The four hands:

```
                  ♠ 6 5
                  ♡ 10 7 2
                  ◇ K J 9 8 4 3
                  ♣ A 2
   ♠ J 8 7 4 2                    ♠ 10 3
   ♡ K J 8 3                      ♡ A 6 4
   ◇ A 10                         ◇ 5 2
   ♣ 6 5                          ♣ Q 9 8 7 4 3
                  ♠ A K Q 9
                  ♡ Q 9 5
                  ◇ Q 7 6
                  ♣ K J 10
```

When your partner wins your heart lead with the ace, he should return a heart; not a spade. He knows that the three is your lowest heart, and you would have led some higher heart if you wanted a spade led back. (See deal #13, page 88, for a more detailed explanation.)

#23   North
                                                 ♠ 9 7 3
                                                 ♡ 6 4
                                                 ◇ Q J 10 8 5 2
                                                 ♣ A Q

                West
                ♠ A Q 2
                ♡ J 8 7 5 2
                ◇ A 3
                ♣ 9 6 4

West	North	East	South
			1NT
Pass	3NT	All Pass	

You lead the five of hearts, partner plays the nine and declarer the ace. The king of diamonds is led and you take the ace. Once again your partner's third-hand play is revealing: He would not play the nine if he had the king or queen; so declarer has ♡ A K Q. You can see five diamond tricks and the ace of clubs in dummy, so you know declarer can win at least nine tricks when he regains the lead. There are 20 high-card points held between partner and declarer. Declarer's bid showed 16-18, so partner has two, three or four. What is the only holding partner can have that will set the contract? If your answer is four (or five) spades to the king, you are right. So lead the *ace of spades*. The four hands:

                                        ♠ 9 7 3
                                        ♡ 6 4
                                        ◇ Q J 10 8 5 2
                                        ♣ A Q
            ♠ A Q 2   ♠ K 10 8 4
            ♡ J 8 7 5 2   ♡ 10 9 3
            ◇ A 3   ◇ 9 6
            ♣ 9 6 4   ♣ 8 7 5 3
                                        ♠ J 6 5
                                        ♡ A K Q
                                        ◇ K 7 4
                                        ♣ K J 10 2

Partner has just what you hoped for, so leading the ace, queen and another spade beats the contract one trick. Note that if you lead anything but a spade honor, declarer has the rest of the tricks.

In the following six deals, the bidding is the main source of information to help you defeat the contracts.

#24

                        North
                        ♠ J 10 9 7
                        ♡ Q 4 2
                        ◇ A K 8
                        ♣ Q J 10

West
♠ K 8 2
♡ J 10 9 6
◇ 7 6 5 3
♣ K 4

West	North	East	South
			1♠
Pass	3♠	Pass	4♠
Pass	Pass	Pass	

You lead the jack of hearts, which is covered by dummy's queen as partner plays the three and declarer the five. The jack of spades is led, partner and declarer play low cards while you win with the king. The play to the first two tricks reveals that the declarer has the ace-king of hearts and the ace-queen of spades. If he had the ace of clubs as well, he would have tried for a slam. So your partner has the ace of clubs and you can beat the contract if declarer has as many as three clubs in his hand by leading the *king of clubs*. The four hands:

                        ♠ J 10 9 7
                        ♡ Q 4 2
                        ◇ A K 8
                        ♣ Q J 10

♠ K 8 2   ♠ 5
♡ J 10 9 6   ♡ 8 7 3
◇ 7 6 5 3   ◇ Q J 9 4
♣ K 4   ♣ A 6 5 3 2

                        ♠ A Q 6 4 3
                        ♡ A K 5
                        ◇ 10 2
                        ♣ 9 8 7

The king of clubs, ace of clubs and a club ruff will give you the three tricks you need to set the contract. Granted, it is obvious that leading the king of clubs offers the only chance to beat the contract, but it is nice to know your partner has the ace when you do it.

Declarer could have played more deceptively by winning the first heart trick in his hand with the king and leading a diamond to dummy's king before finessing in spades. This way you could not be sure whether partner has the ace of hearts or ace of clubs; but you should get it right because of partner's discouraging heart signal.

In the next deal, leading a club from K x would be a tragedy.

#25   **North**
                                                   ♠ Q J 10 7
                                                   ♡ Q 3 2
                                                   ◇ A K 5
                                                   ♣ Q J 10

                West
                ♠ K 5 2
                ♡ 10 9 8 6
                ◇ Q 8 4 3
                ♣ K 3

West	*North*	*East*	*South*
			1♠
Pass	3♠	Pass	4♠
Pass	Pass	Pass	

You lead the ten of hearts, the queen is played from dummy, partner covers with the king and declarer wins with the ace. Then he plays a diamond to dummy's ace and leads the queen of spades; partner and declarer follow with low cards while you win with the king. Before you lead to the next trick, count the points. Dummy has fifteen and you have eight, so partner and declarer have seventeen between them. Partner already played the king of hearts. If he has the ace of clubs, declarer has only ten points—not enough to open the bidding. Declarer must have the ace of clubs; so *do not lead a club*. The four hands:

                                                   ♠ Q J 10 7
                                                   ♡ Q 3 2
                                                   ◇ A K 5
                                                   ♣ Q J 10
                ♠ K 5 2   ♠ 4
                ♡ 10 9 8 6   ♡ K J 7 4
                ◇ Q 8 4 3   ◇ J 9 6
                ♣ K 3   ♣ 9 8 6 5 2
                                                   ♠ A 9 8 6 3
                                                   ♡ A 5
                                                   ◇ 10 7 2
                                                   ♣ A 7 4

Declarer has one loser in each suit. He will be set if you lead any card in your hand except a club, although a heart is the obvious choice. This deal and the previous one are not overly difficult, but they are an exercise in the thought process (counting the points) that can lead to good defensive plays.

#26

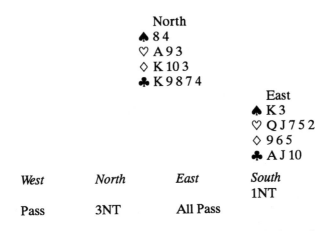

North
♠ 8 4
♡ A 9 3
◊ K 10 3
♣ K 9 8 7 4

East
♠ K 3
♡ Q J 7 5 2
◊ 9 6 5
♣ A J 10

West	North	East	South
			1NT
Pass	3NT	All Pass	

Partner leads the queen of spades, you play the king and declarer the six. You see 21 high-card points and declarer should have at least sixteen for his opening one-notrump bid. If so, partner has at most three and his spade lead was obviously from queen-jack; therefore, he has no more high cards—not even a jack. Returning a spade at trick two is futile because partner has no entry cards. Consider that declarer will most likely have to establish the club suit to make his contract, but you will win two club tricks before he can do it. Since you have the entry cards, you should try to establish your long suit. Lead the *five of hearts*.

```
                    ♠ 8 4
                    ♡ A 9 3
                    ◊ K 10 3
                    ♣ K 9 8 7 4
 ♠ Q J 10 9 5                        ♠ K 3
 ♡ 10 4                              ♡ Q J 7 5 2
 ◊ 8 7 4 2                           ◊ 9 6 5
 ♣ 6 3                               ♣ A J 10
                    ♠ A 7 6 2
                    ♡ K 8 6
                    ◊ A Q J
                    ♣ Q 5 2
```

Luckily, partner has the ten of hearts and that card will drive out the ace or king. Declarer has six winners (one spade, two hearts and three diamonds), so he needs three club tricks to fulfill his contract. Suppose declarer wins the second trick with the ace of hearts and leads a low club, which you allow him to win with the queen. He leads a club back and ducks in dummy, so you win with the jack and lead the queen of hearts to drive out the king. Since your hearts are now good and you still have the ace of clubs, declarer can win only seven tricks: down two. If partner did not have the ten of hearts, you could not beat the contract no matter what you led at trick two.

#27

North
♠ A Q J
♡ J 9 8 6 4
◇ 8 5 3
♣ Q 4

West
♠ 10 5 2
♡ K 3
◇ K J 9 7 6
♣ K 9 2

West	North	East	South
			1 ♣
1 ◇	1 ♡	Pass	2 ♣
Pass	3 ♣	Pass	3NT
Pass	Pass	Pass	

You lead the seven of diamonds, partner plays the ten and declarer wins with the queen. A spade is played and won in dummy with the jack. Next comes the queen of clubs, which you are allowed to win with the king. What do you know about declarer's points? If partner had the ace of diamonds, king of spades or ace of clubs, he surely would have won one of the first three tricks. So, declarer has those three cards, and almost surely the jack of clubs. Together with the queen of diamonds he played on the first trick, that gives him fourteen high-card points. The two-club rebid showed a six-card suit (with only five clubs, a better rebid would have been one notrump) and a minimum opening—if he had any more high cards, his hand would have been too strong to rebid just two clubs.

If you are still with me, you should realize that declarer can win a total of ten tricks when he regains the lead (three spades, two diamonds and five clubs). So the only chance to beat the contract is to win the next four tricks. The right lead, which cannot lose and may beat the contract, is the *king of hearts*. The four hands:

♠ A Q J
♡ J 9 8 6 4
◇ 8 5 3
♣ Q 4

♠ 10 5 2
♡ K 3
◇ K J 9 7 6
♣ K 9 2

♠ 8 7 6 4 3
♡ A Q 10 5
◇ 10 2
♣ 7 5

♠ K 9
♡ 7 2
◇ A Q 4
♣ A J 10 8 6 3

Partner has the magic heart holding, so you can run four heart tricks by leading the king and another heart. It was predictable that partner had the ace and queen of hearts; the ten was the key card.

#28

```
                         North
                         ♠ K 7 5 4 2
                         ♡ A 4 3
                         ◇ J 10 8
                         ♣ J 3
        West
        ♠ Q 10 3
        ♡ J 8 7 6 5
        ◇ A 6
        ♣ 10 9 4
```

West	North	East	South
			1 ◇
Pass	1 ♠	Pass	2 ♣
Pass	2 ◇	Pass	2NT
Pass	3NT	All Pass	

You lead the six of hearts, partner plays the ten and declarer wins with the king. What did you learn about declarer's heart holding from partner's third-hand play? He has the queen and nine—partner would not play the ten if he had either of those cards. At trick two, declarer leads a low diamond to dummy's jack; then he calls for the ten of diamonds, which you win with the ace. By continuing with two notrump after his partner's weak bidding, declarer should have about 16-18 high-card points. Most likely he has five diamonds and four clubs, and the diamond length is confirmed when partner plays low-high to show an odd number of diamonds; which in this case must be three (see Chapter 7 for more detailed information about Count Signals). You are at the crossroads; what do you lead at trick four?

You learned from partner's plays and the bidding that the declarer has three hearts, five diamonds and four clubs. So he has exactly one spade. If it is the ace he has at least nine tricks (two spades, three hearts and four diamonds); the contract cannot be set. But if his singleton spade is anything but the ace, you can beat the contract by *leading the queen of spades*. The four hands:

```
                         ♠ K 7 5 4 2
                         ♡ A 4 3
                         ◇ J 10 8
                         ♣ J 3
        ♠ Q 10 3                         ♠ A 9 8 6
        ♡ J 8 7 6 5                      ♡ 10 2
        ◇ A 6                            ◇ 5 3 2
        ♣ 10 9 4                         ♣ Q 8 7 6
                         ♠ J
                         ♡ K Q 9
                         ◇ K Q 9 7 4
                         ♣ A K 5 2
```

If declarer does not cover your queen-of-spades lead, you will continue with the ten and win four spade tricks. But if declarer ducks the first spade lead, partner must play the *six*—if he signals with the eight or nine, declarer can limit the defense to three spade tricks by covering the ten with the king.

Yes, declarer would have been more deceptive if he had won the first heart trick with dummy's ace.

#29
North
♠ 8
♡ A 7 6 4 3
◊ A J 3 2
♣ K 6 4

East
♠ A 6 5 4
♡ K 10 8 2
◊ 10 8 7
♣ A 5

West	North	East	South
			1 ◊
Pass	1 ♡	Pass	1 ♠
Pass	3 ◊	Pass	3NT
Pass	Pass	Pass	

Partner leads the two of clubs, the four is played from dummy and you win with your ace. Your partner has four clubs and so does the declarer. Since declarer bid one diamond instead of one club, he should have four diamonds; and he showed four spades by bidding the suit. So it is reasonably certain that his distribution is 4-1-4-4; he has a singleton heart. I have spelled it out for you, so what do you lead at trick two?

The *king of hearts* is right; the only card in your hand that will beat the contract. The four hands:

                    ♠ 8
                    ♡ A 7 6 4 3
                    ◊ A J 3 2
                    ♣ K 6 4
♠ 9 7 3 2   ♠ A 6 5 4
♡ J 9 5   ♡ K 10 8 2
◊ 5 4   ◊ 10 8 7
♣ J 9 8 2   ♣ A 5
                    ♠ K Q J 10
                    ♡ Q
                    ◊ K Q 9 6
                    ♣ Q 10 7 3

If you lead the king of hearts, declarer cannot prevent you from establishing three heart tricks, which together with the two black aces set the contract. Without the king-of-hearts lead at trick two, declarer can establish three spade tricks and make his bid with an overtrick; two overtricks if you lead a low heart.

Unusual Plays to Put Partner on Lead

The times when you would like your partner to have the lead are: when he can lead a suit to trap an enemy honor card; when he can give you a ruff; or when he can cash one or more winning tricks. Here is an example of each, showing what you must do to put your partner on lead.

#30

```
                          North
                          ♠ J 8 3
                          ♡ 7 5
                          ◇ K Q J 4
                          ♣ K J 9 2
         West
         ♠ A K Q 9 7
         ♡ A Q 4
         ◇ 5 2
         ♣ 8 6 3
```

West	North	East	South
			1 ◇
1 ♠	2 ◇	Pass	Pass
Double	3 ◇	All Pass	

You cash the king and ace of spades, your partner signaling high-low with the ten and two. As partner has a doubleton spade, you can win the first five tricks to defeat the contract if he ruffs the third spade trick and leads a heart. Since your partner may not ruff if you lead the queen of spades, *lead the nine of spades*.

```
                     ♠ J 8 3
                     ♡ 7 5
                     ◇ K Q J 4
                     ♣ K J 9 2
    ♠ A K Q 9 7                    ♠ 10 2
    ♡ A Q 4                        ♡ 10 9 8 6 2
    ◇ 5 2                          ◇ 6 3
    ♣ 8 6 3                        ♣ 10 7 5 4
                     ♠ 6 5 4
                     ♡ K J 3
                     ◇ A 10 9 8 7
                     ♣ A Q
```

The nine of spades (as opposed to the seven) is a suit-preference signal requesting a heart return (see Chapter 7), though it is hard to imagine any reason for a club return. Partner should ruff and return a heart.[1] Notice that if you do not take the first five tricks, declarer can make his bid by discarding two hearts on dummy's clubs.

---

1. In view of the East hand and dummy, a good player sitting East would ruff the third trick even if you did lead the queen. But the point here is not to give partner a problem. You know what you want done, so make it easy.

#31   North
                                       ♠ 8 4
                                       ♡ A Q 7 3
                                       ◇ K Q 10
                                       ♣ A K Q 9

            West
            ♠ A K Q J 9 3
            ♡ K 10 6 5
            ◇ 8 3 2
            ♣ —

West	North	East	South
	1♣	Pass	1◇
1♠	2♡	Pass	3◇
3♠	5◇	All Pass	

You lead the king of spades, partner plays the two and declarer the five. This strong dummy makes it obvious that the only way to beat this contract is to win two spade tricks and get a club ruff. You must get partner on lead if you are going to get a club ruff, and the only chance is to find partner with the ten of spades. So *lead the three of spades* at trick two. The four hands:

                                  ♠ 8 4
                                  ♡ A Q 7 3
                                  ◇ K Q 10
                                  ♣ A K Q 9
        ♠ A K Q J 9 3   ♠ 10 7 2
        ♡ K 10 6 5   ♡ J 9 4
        ◇ 8 3 2   ◇ 5
        ♣ —   ♣ J 8 7 6 5 2
                                  ♠ 6 5
                                  ♡ 8 2
                                  ◇ A J 9 7 6 4
                                  ♣ 10 4 3

When partner wins the second trick with the ten of spades, he should realize that the only logical reason for your desperate lead is that you have a void suit; and with ten clubs in sight, he will lead a club. If declarer has the ten of spades, he makes his contract with an overtrick. If your partner has the ten, you will beat the game. You must admit that underleading your top spades is an excellent gamble.

#32

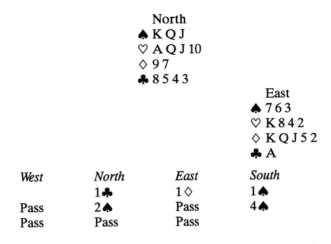

North
♠ K Q J
♡ A Q J 10
◇ 9 7
♣ 8 5 4 3

East
♠ 7 6 3
♡ K 8 4 2
◇ K Q J 5 2
♣ A

West	North	East	South
	1♣	1◇	1♠
Pass	2♠	Pass	4♠
Pass	Pass	Pass	

The opening lead is the king of clubs. Declarer must have the ace of spades and ace of diamonds for his bidding, which means you can win at most one heart and one diamond. So the best chance to beat the contract is to put partner on lead to cash a second club trick before declarer can establish the heart suit and discard one or more clubs. What card must partner have in his hand? Answer: the *ten of diamonds*. What should you lead at trick two? Answer: *a low diamond*. The four hands:

                    ♠ K Q J
                    ♡ A Q J 10
                    ◇ 9 7
                    ♣ 8 5 4 3
    ♠ 4   ♠ 7 6 3
    ♡ 7 5 3   ♡ K 8 4 2
    ◇ 10 8 4   ◇ K Q J 5 2
    ♣ K Q 10 9 6 2   ♣ A
                    ♠ A 10 9 8 5 2
                    ♡ 9 6
                    ◇ A 6 3
                    ♣ J 7

Suppose declarer wins your two-of-diamonds lead with the ace—if he ducks, partner will win with the ten and cash his club trick—and then takes a heart finesse. When you win with the king of hearts, you must *lead your other low diamond*; you will have underled the king-queen-jack twice, but it is the only way to set the contract. Note that if your first diamond lead were the king, declarer would hold up his ace; West would never get the lead and declarer would discard his losing club on the heart suit.

Helping Your Partner

Your partner may do the wrong thing if you give him the chance. If possible, do not give him the chance.

#33

                              North
                              ♠ K 4 3
                              ♡ 4 2
                              ◇ K J 10
                              ♣ Q 9 8 5 3

                                              East
                                              ♠ 7 6 5
                                              ♡ J 10 7
                                              ◇ Q 8 4 3 2
                                              ♣ 10 2

West	North	East	South
			1♠
2♡	2♠	Pass	3♠
Pass	4♠	All Pass	

Partner leads the king of clubs and you play the ten. He continues with the ace and another club; you trump the third round as declarer follows suit. What do you lead at trick four? The four hands:

                              ♠ K 4 3
                              ♡ 4 2
                              ◇ K J 10
                              ♣ Q 9 8 5 3
    ♠ 9   ♠ 7 6 5
    ♡ Q 9 8 6 5 3   ♡ J 10 7
    ◇ A 6 5   ◇ Q 8 4 3 2
    ♣ A K 7   ♣ 10 2
                              ♠ A Q J 10 8 2
                              ♡ A K
                              ◇ 9 7
                              ♣ J 6 4

Since partner bid hearts, and the dummy has weak hearts and strong diamonds, it seems that you should lead a heart. But declarer then makes his contract by drawing trumps and discarding his losing diamonds on dummy's good clubs. Should you have led a diamond? No, you are the victim, not the culprit! *Your partner should have cashed the ace of diamonds before he led the third round of clubs.*

#34

North
♠ J 10 9
♡ 2
◇ A J 7 6
♣ A K 8 5 4

West
♠ K Q 7
♡ Q 9 8 4 3
◇ 8 5
♣ Q 10 3

West	North	East	South
			1 ◇
Pass	2 ♣	Pass	2 ◇
Pass	4 ◇	Pass	5 ◇
Pass	Pass	Pass	

You lead the king of spades, partner plays the eight and declarer the three. Partner must have the ace of spades, so leading another spade is automatic, but which one? You read earlier in this book to lead the king from K Q x, and follow with the queen if you decide to lead the suit again; but not this time. The correct lead is the *seven of spades,* to eliminate a problem for your partner. The four hands:

```
              ♠ J 10 9
              ♡ 2
              ◇ A J 7 6
              ♣ A K 8 5 4
♠ K Q 7                      ♠ A 8 5 4 2
♡ Q 9 8 4 3                  ♡ J 10 7 6
◇ 8 5                        ◇ 4 2
♣ Q 10 3                     ♣ J 9
              ♠ 6 3
              ♡ A K 5
              ◇ K Q 10 9 3
              ♣ 7 6 2
```

If you lead the queen of spades at trick two, partner may decide that you have a doubleton; in which case he will overtake your queen with the ace and return a spade, hoping you can ruff. As you can see this would be fatal—declarer would discard his losing club on the third spade lead and make his contract. Note that overtaking with the ace would be the winning defense if declarer had one more spade and one fewer club. If you lead the seven of spades, partner will win with the ace and return a spade, hoping you led from ♠ K 7 and can ruff. With this defense, declarer must lose a third trick.

#35

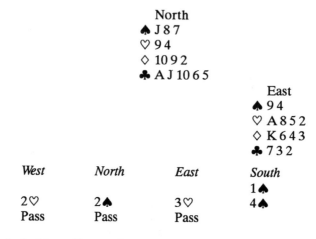

West	North	East	South
			1♠
2♡	2♠	3♡	4♠
Pass	Pass	Pass	

Partner leads the king of hearts. Partner is likely to have a six-card suit for his overcall, so declarer probably has a singleton heart. The best defense appears to be to collect any available diamond tricks before declarer is able to discard on dummy's club suit. Since partner will probably continue hearts (he doesn't know that you have four), *overtake the king-of-hearts lead with your ace and return the three of diamonds*. The four hands:

```
                        ♠ J 8 7
                        ♡ 9 4
                        ◇ 10 9 2
                        ♣ A J 10 6 5
        ♠ 5 2                            ♠ 9 4
        ♡ K Q J 10 6 3                   ♡ A 8 5 2
        ◇ A Q J                          ◇ K 6 4 3
        ♣ 8 4                            ♣ 7 3 2
                        ♠ A K Q 10 6 3
                        ♡ 7
                        ◇ 8 7 5
                        ♣ K Q 9
```

Your three-of-diamonds lead is informative. It tells your partner that you have an honor in the suit and you do not have more than four diamonds. Therefore, partner's next three plays should be the jack, ace and queen of diamonds. The only way to beat the contract is to win the first four tricks.

If you do not overtake the king of hearts at trick one, partner is unlikely to switch to a diamond from ◇ A Q J. It would be the wrong lead if you held the king of clubs instead of the king of diamonds, or other holdings.

Your play in the next deal does not prevent your partner from doing the wrong thing; it is simply a case where only you can make the play that has any chance to beat the contract.

#36

	North		
	♠ Q 2		
	♡ K Q J		
	◊ 10 5		
	♣ A Q 10 5 4 2		

West
♠ 9 7 6 4
♡ 8 5 3
◊ K 8 7 3 2
♣ 7

West	North	East	South
	1♣	Pass	2NT
Pass	3NT	All Pass	

You lead the three of diamonds, partner plays the jack and declarer the seven. Partner returns the queen of diamonds and declarer plays the nine. If a third round of diamonds is led to drive out declarer's ace, you have two good diamonds left. But you have no entry card, so leading a third round of diamonds is futile. The best chance to beat this contract is if partner has very good spades and an entry card. So a spade must be led at trick three and, with the queen in dummy, the first spade lead must come from you. Getting back to trick two, *overtake your partner's queen-of-diamonds lead with your king and switch to the seven of spades (or any spade)*. The four hands:

```
                    ♠ Q 2
                    ♡ K Q J
                    ◊ 10 5
                    ♣ A Q 10 5 4 2
    ♠ 9 7 6 4                        ♠ K J 10 3
    ♡ 8 5 3                          ♡ 10 6 4 2
    ◊ K 8 7 3 2                      ◊ Q J 4
    ♣ 7                              ♣ K 8
                    ♠ A 8 5
                    ♡ A 9 7
                    ◊ A 9 6
                    ♣ J 9 6 3
```

As you can see, declarer has only one spade stopper *if you lead the suit*. Whenever he decides to take his ace of spades, he will try the losing club finesse and wind up down two. Yes, it was lucky to find partner with such good spades. But did you ever notice that good defenders are lucky more often than poor defenders!

Killing Declarer's Discards

When you can see that declarer has, or will have, a high card which may allow him to discard a loser, you can sometimes "kill the discard" by leading the suit so your partner can ruff it. For example:

#37

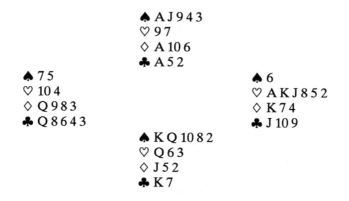

North
♠ A J 9 4 3
♡ 9 7
◇ A 10 6
♣ A 5 2

East
♠ 6
♡ A K J 8 5 2
◇ K 7 4
♣ J 10 9

West	North	East	South
		1♡	1♠
Pass	4♠	All Pass	

The opening lead is the ten of hearts. You win the first two tricks with the king and ace of hearts as declarer and partner follow suit. The only heart still missing is the queen, and declarer has it; partner would not lead the ten from Q 10 x. *Lead another heart* so partner can ruff the queen. The four hands:

              ♠ A J 9 4 3
              ♡ 9 7
              ◇ A 10 6
              ♣ A 5 2
♠ 7 5   ♠ 6
♡ 10 4   ♡ A K J 8 5 2
◇ Q 9 8 3   ◇ K 7 4
♣ Q 8 6 4 3   ♣ J 10 9
              ♠ K Q 10 8 2
              ♡ Q 6 3
              ◇ J 5 2
              ♣ K 7

When you lead the third round of hearts and partner ruffs, dummy will overruff. But declarer is left with two losing diamonds and will be set one trick. It is tempting to lead the jack of clubs at trick three, but declarer can then hold his diamond losers to one by drawing trumps and discarding one of dummy's diamonds on the queen of hearts.

#38

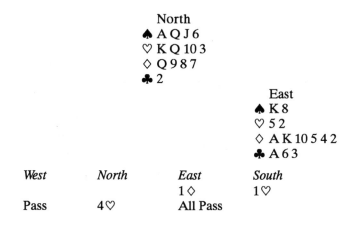

North
♠ A Q J 6
♡ K Q 10 3
◇ Q 9 8 7
♣ 2

East
♠ K 8
♡ 5 2
◇ A K 10 5 4 2
♣ A 6 3

West	North	East	South
		1◇	1♡
Pass	4♡	All Pass	

Partner leads the three of diamonds, the seven is played from dummy, you win with the king and declarer drops the six. Declarer is known to have the missing jack of diamonds, so you can win two diamond tricks. But if you cash your ace, the queen will provide declarer with a discard. So *underlead your ace-ten of diamonds at trick two and let your partner ruff.*[2] You will be left with the ace-ten over dummy's queen-nine—no discard is possible. The four hands:

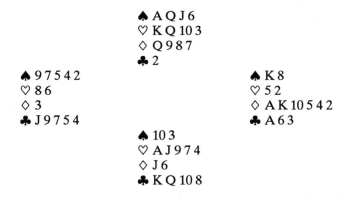

♠ A Q J 6
♡ K Q 10 3
◇ Q 9 8 7
♣ 2

♠ 9 7 5 4 2
♡ 8 6
◇ 3
♣ J 9 7 5 4

♠ K 8
♡ 5 2
◇ A K 10 5 4 2
♣ A 6 3

♠ 10 3
♡ A J 9 7 4
◇ J 6
♣ K Q 10 8

After partner ruffs your diamond lead, he should return a spade and declarer must lose a spade and a club for down one. If your second diamond play is the ace, there is no way to prevent declarer from making his contract; if you lead a third diamond, he will ruff high, draw trumps and discard his losing spade on the queen of diamonds.

---

2. Actually you should lead specifically the *five of diamonds* as a suit-preference signal requesting a spade return—see Chapter 7—which would be critical if declarer happened to have ♣ K Q J x.

#39

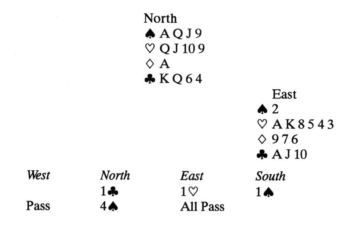

North
♠ A Q J 9
♡ Q J 10 9
◇ A
♣ K Q 6 4

East
♠ 2
♡ A K 8 5 4 3
◇ 9 7 6
♣ A J 10

West	North	East	South
	1♣	1♡	1♠
Pass	4♠	All Pass	

Partner leads the two of hearts and you win the first trick with the king. Once again, you know that partner has led a singleton and declarer has the one missing heart—partner would not lead the two if he had a doubleton. You can win two hearts and one club but, unless partner can win a trump trick (unlikely), the only chance to beat the contract is if declarer has as many as three clubs and you can win a second club trick. Even if declarer does have three clubs, you will not succeed if he can discard a club on dummy's hearts. To prevent this, you should *lead the three of hearts* at trick two. Your partner will ruff and switch to a club. When a club honor is played from dummy, win with your ace and *lead another low heart*. Declarer must ruff this with a high trump to prevent your partner from overruffing (else he is set). There is only one heart left in dummy and you still have the ace; so no discard on the heart suit is possible. The four hands:

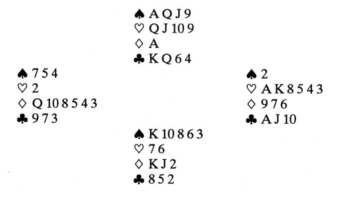

♠ A Q J 9
♡ Q J 10 9
◇ A
♣ K Q 6 4

♠ 7 5 4
♡ 2
◇ Q 10 8 5 4 3
♣ 9 7 3

♠ 2
♡ A K 8 5 4 3
◇ 9 7 6
♣ A J 10

♠ K 10 8 6 3
♡ 7 6
◇ K J 2
♣ 8 5 2

With the recommended defense, declarer must lose a second club and will be set one trick. But if you do not underlead the ace of hearts twice, declarer will have a high heart in dummy on which to discard a club.

Quiz for Chapter Four

1.

	North
	♠ A Q
	♡ 6 5 3
	◇ 8 4 2
	♣ K 10 9 7 4

	East
	♠ 8 6 5 4
	♡ A 2
	◇ J 10 9 3
	♣ A Q 3

West	North	East	South
			1NT
Pass	3NT	All Pass	

The opening one-notrump bid shows 16-18 high-card points.

Your partner leads the queen of hearts and you win with your ace. What do you lead at trick two?

2.

	North
	♠ 10 7 4
	♡ Q 10 9 7 5
	◇ 6 4 2
	♣ A 4

West	
♠ Q 8 6	
♡ A K 6	
◇ Q J 10 9	
♣ 7 5 3	

West	North	East	South
			1◇
Pass	1♡	Pass	2NT
Pass	3NT	All Pass	

You lead the queen of diamonds, partner plays the three and declarer wins with the ace. He then leads the jack of hearts. Plan your defense.

3.

	North
	♠ Q 10 7
	♡ J 3
	◇ A 10 8 5
	♣ 7 5 4 2

	East
	♠ A 2
	♡ K Q 5
	◇ J 9 7 6
	♣ 10 9 8 3

West	North	East	South
			1♠
Pass	2♠	Pass	4♠
Pass	Pass	Pass	

Your partner leads the ten of hearts, dummy plays the jack, you the queen and declarer the two. What do you lead at trick two?

4.

	North
	♠ A Q 10
	♡ 4 2
	◇ A J
	♣ K Q J 10 7 3

	East
	♠ 9 3
	♡ A K 8 6 5
	◇ K 7 2
	♣ A 8 4

West	North	East	South
	1♣	1♡	1♠
Pass	3♣	Pass	3♠
Pass	4♠	All Pass	

Your partner leads the jack of hearts and you win with the king. What do you lead at trick two?

5.   **North**
♠ Q 8 6 5 2
♥ K J 4 3
♦ 9 6
♣ 7 4

West
♠ A K J 7 3
♥ 9 6
♦ Q 10 4
♣ K 8 5

West	North	East	South
			1♥
1♠	2♥	Pass	4♥
Pass	Pass	Pass	

You lead the king of spades, partner plays the four and declarer drops the nine. What do you lead now?

6.   **North**
♠ A 9 6 4
♥ 5
♦ Q J 10 9 2
♣ K Q 9

                        East
                        ♠ 5 3 2
                        ♥ A K 7 6 2
                        ♦ 8 4
                        ♣ A J 10

West	North	East	South
	1♦	1♥	1♠
2♥	2♠	3♥	4♠
Pass	Pass	Pass	

Your partner leads the ten of hearts and you win the first trick with the king. What do you lead at trick two?

7.   **North**
♠ A K 2
♥ 10 9
♦ A K J 10 9 3
♣ 7 2

                        East
                        ♠ J 10 5
                        ♥ Q 6 4 3
                        ♦ 8 7 4 2
                        ♣ A 5

West	North	East	South
	1♦	Pass	1♠
Pass	3♦	Pass	3NT
Pass	Pass	Pass	

Your partner leads the queen of clubs, you win with your ace and declarer plays the four. What do you lead at trick two?

8.   **North**
♠ K J 9 8 5
♥ 9 6 4
♦ Q 10 2
♣ A K

West
♠ A 10 2
♥ Q J 10 8 3
♦ K 4
♣ J 9 5

West	North	East	South
	1♠	Pass	1NT
Pass	Pass	Pass	

You lead the queen of hearts, partner plays the two and declarer wins with the ace. Then declarer leads the queen of spades. Plan your defense. (If you duck, he leads another spade.)

Quiz Answers for Chapter Four

1.

	North	
	♠ A Q	
	♡ 6 5 3	
	◇ 8 4 2	
	♣ K 10 9 7 4	
West		East
♠ 10 9 3 2		♠ 8 6 5 4
♡ Q J 9 7 4		♡ A 2
◇ 7 6		◇ J 10 9 3
♣ 8 5		♣ A Q 3
	South	
	♠ K J 7	
	♡ K 10 8	
	◇ A K Q 5	
	♣ J 6 2	

West	North	East	South
			1NT
Pass	3NT	All Pass	

Your partner leads the queen of hearts and you win with your ace. What do you lead at trick two?

Lead any spade. Besides the ♡ Q J partner can have at most another jack—you can see 20 high-card points and declarer should have at least sixteen for his bid. So establishing the heart suit will do no good because partner has no entry card.

The best plan is to knock out dummy's entries and hold declarer to as few club tricks as possible. Assuming you lead a spade at trick two, declarer's predictable line of play is to win in the dummy, lead a diamond to his hand, and then finesse the jack of clubs. Partner plays the eight, so you hold up. You win the second club lead (though here it works out equally well if you win the first club and duck the second). Now lead another spade to remove dummy's last entry card. This defense limits declarer to one club trick. Altogether he can win only eight tricks: three spades, one heart, three diamonds and one club.

2.

	North	
	♠ 10 7 4	
	♡ Q 10 9 7 5	
	◇ 6 4 2	
	♣ A 4	
West		East
♠ Q 8 6		♠ 9 5 3 2
♡ A K 6		♡ 8 4 2
◇ Q J 10 9		◇ 8 3
♣ 7 5 3		♣ Q J 10 9
	South	
	♠ A K J	
	♡ J 3	
	◇ A K 7 5	
	♣ K 8 6 2	

West	North	East	South
			1◇
Pass	1♡	Pass	2NT
Pass	3NT	All Pass	

You lead the queen of diamonds, partner plays the three and declarer wins with the ace. He then leads the jack of hearts. Plan your defense.

Duck the jack-of-hearts lead to break declarer's communication with dummy's heart suit. Since he has only two hearts, this limits him to one heart trick. He has seven tricks in all (two spades, one heart, two diamonds and two clubs) and he may find a way to finagle an eighth trick, but he cannot make his contract.

If you mistakenly win the first heart trick, when declarer regains the lead he will play his second heart to drive out your remaining honor. With the ace of clubs still in dummy, he can win three heart tricks; just enough to make his contract.

3. | | North | |
    |---|---|---|
    | | ♠ Q 10 7 | |
    | | ♡ J 3 | |
    | | ◇ A 10 8 5 | |
    | | ♣ 7 5 4 2 | |

West		East
♠ 6 4 3		♠ A 2
♡ 10 9 8 7		♡ K Q 5
◇ Q 4 2		◇ J 9 7 6
♣ K Q 6		♣ 10 9 8 3

	South	
	♠ K J 9 8 5	
	♡ A 6 4 2	
	◇ K 3	
	♣ A J	

West	North	East	South
			1♠
Pass	2♠	Pass	4♠
Pass	Pass	Pass	

Your partner leads the ten of hearts, dummy plays the jack, you the queen and declarer the two. What do you lead at trick two?

Lead the ace and another spade. It should be obvious that declarer is holding up with his ace of hearts (partner would not underlead the ace) and is planning to ruff hearts in the dummy. With the cards as shown, declarer will lose four tricks (two hearts, one spade and one club) if you lead the ace and another spade. If you do not, he can ruff two hearts in dummy and make his contract.

4. | | North | |
    |---|---|---|
    | | ♠ A Q 10 | |
    | | ♡ 4 2 | |
    | | ◇ A J | |
    | | ♣ K Q J 10 7 3 | |

West		East
♠ 6 4		♠ 9 3
♡ J 10 9		♡ A K 8 6 5
◇ Q 10 8 5 3		◇ K 7 2
♣ 9 6 5		♣ A 8 4

	South	
	♠ K J 8 7 5 2	
	♡ Q 7 3	
	◇ 9 6 4	
	♣ 2	

West	North	East	South
	1♣	1♡	1♠
Pass	3♣	Pass	3♠
Pass	4♠	All Pass	

Your partner leads the jack of hearts and you win with the king. What do you lead at trick two?

Lead the two of diamonds (the king or seven would also get the job done, but the two is normal). You have three tricks and the only other reasonable hope for a trick is in diamonds. Declarer will be able to discard any losing diamonds on dummy's clubs if you give him the time. Also note that you must lead a diamond before cashing your second heart—otherwise he will discard a diamond from the dummy on his queen of hearts. If partner does not have the queen of diamonds, the contract cannot be set whether or not you lead a diamond. Since he does, your partner's queen will drive out the ace and you will be able to cash a diamond trick when you regain the lead.

5.

	North	
	♠ Q 8 6 5 2	
	♡ K J 4 3	
	◊ 9 6	
	♣ 7 4	

West	East
♠ A K J 7 3	♠ 4
♡ 9 6	♡ 5 2
◊ Q 10 4	◊ K 8 7 3
♣ K 8 5	♣ J 10 9 6 3 2

	South
	♠ 10 9
	♡ A Q 10 8 7
	◊ A J 5 2
	♣ A Q

West	North	East	South
			1♡
1♠	2♡	Pass	4♡
Pass	Pass	Pass	

You lead the king of spades, partner plays the four and declarer drops the nine. What do you lead now?

Lead the three of spades for partner to ruff. (If partner held ♠ 10 4, he would have played the ten; so he should have a single-ton.) This kills the discard—dummy's queen of spades becomes useless—and declarer must lose four tricks: two spades, one dia-mond and one club.

If you play the ace of spades at trick two, or if you lead another suit, declarer will be able to discard his club loser on the queen of spades after drawing trumps.

If partner's first spade play were the ten, you would not know who had the singleton. Only when the missing card is higher than the one your partner played can you be sure.

6.

	North	
	♠ A 9 6 4	
	♡ 5	
	◊ Q J 10 9 2	
	♣ K Q 9	

West	East
♠ 7	♠ 5 3 2
♡ 10 9 8 4	♡ A K 7 6 2
◊ A 6 5 3	◊ 8 4
♣ 8 6 4 3	♣ A J 10

	South
	♠ K Q J 10 8
	♡ Q J 3
	◊ K 7
	♣ 7 5 2

West	North	East	South
	1◊	1♡	1♠
2♡	2♠	3♡	4♠
Pass	Pass	Pass	

Your partner leads the ten of hearts and you win with the king. What do you lead at trick two?

Lead the jack of clubs to drive out the king (or queen) from dummy. This leaves you with the ace-ten of clubs behind the queen-nine. The stage is set for you to win two club tricks if partner has the ace or king of diamonds and declarer has at least three clubs. Note that if you do not underlead your ace of clubs at trick two, it is impossible to win two club tricks; declarer will be able to discard his second club loser on the diamond suit.

7.

```
              North
              ♠ A K 2
              ♡ 10 9
              ◇ A K J 10 9 3
              ♣ 7 2
West                          East
♠ 7 6 4                       ♠ J 10 5
♡ A J 8 5                     ♡ Q 6 4 3
◇ 6                           ◇ 8 7 4 2
♣ Q J 10 9 3                  ♣ A 5
              South
              ♠ Q 9 8 3
              ♡ K 7 2
              ◇ Q 5
              ♣ K 8 6 4
```

West	North	East	South
	1 ◇	Pass	1 ♠
Pass	3 ◇	Pass	3NT
Pass	Pass	Pass	

Your partner leads the queen of clubs, you win with your ace and declarer plays the four. What do you lead at trick two?

Lead the queen of hearts. Declarer is marked with the king of clubs, so you know he can win at least nine tricks if he gains the lead. If declarer has ♡ K 8 x or better, the contract cannot be set no matter what you lead. It is a long shot, but if he has ♡ K x x (no eight-spot), four heart tricks can be won *provided you lead the queen.*

8.

```
              North
              ♠ K J 9 8 5
              ♡ 9 6 4
              ◇ Q 10 2
              ♣ A K
West                          East
♠ A 10 2                      ♠ 7 4 3
♡ Q J 10 8 3                  ♡ 2
◇ K 4                         ◇ A J 8 7 6 3
♣ J 9 5                       ♣ Q 8 2
              South
              ♠ Q 6
              ♡ A K 7 5
              ◇ 9 5
              ♣ 10 7 6 4 3
```

West	North	East	South
	1 ♠	Pass	1NT
Pass	Pass	Pass	

You lead the queen of hearts, partner plays the two and declarer wins with the ace. Then declarer leads the queen of spades. Plan your defense. (If you duck, he leads another spade.)

It makes no difference whether you win the first, second or third spade lead, but you must follow by *leading the king of diamonds.* Declarer has already shown up with the ace of hearts and the queen of spades, and he must have the king of hearts; partner would not play the two of hearts on the first trick if had the king. In view of his weak one-notrump response, he can hardly have any more high cards. So, playing partner for the ace-jack of diamonds, you lead the king and another diamond. Fortunately partner has a six-card suit and the contract is set one trick. Note that if you lead another heart when you take your ace of spades, declarer will win eight tricks: four spades, two hearts and two clubs.

5

Second-Hand Play

This is one of the most difficult area of defense for the average player. He learns the rules "cover an honor with an honor" and "second hand low," but soon finds out that there are many exceptions; he is baffled when to do which. To add to this, second hand must play "in tempo" when he decides not to cover an honor with an honor, or to play second hand low; hesitating and then making the right play may be no better than making the wrong play.

To get started, here is a suit combination showing the merits of covering an honor with an honor and second hand low.

```
                    Dummy
                    J 7 6
                                  You
                                  A 9 2
```

If declarer leads the jack from dummy, cover with the ace; if he leads a low card, play the two. Now let's move to the other side of the table.

```
                    Dummy
                    J 7 6
       You
       K 10 4
```

If declarer leads the queen from his hand (an unlikely play), cover with the king; if he leads a low card, play the four. Here are the four hands to show how these rules work together.

```
                    North
                    J 7 6
       West                        East
       K 10 4                      A 9 2
                    South
                    Q 8 5 3
```

If East and West play as described above, declarer must lose three tricks.

Before getting into full deals, here are several suit combinations showing the normal play for second hand. The recommended plays are not 100 percent correct all of the time, but the exceptions are rare and some of them are noted later in this chapter.

Table of Fundamentals

Numbers 1 through 17 are about whether or not to cover honor cards, and numbers 18 through 30 are about whether or not to play second hand low. The underlined card is led, and you are second hand. Your objective is to hold the declarer to as few tricks as possible in the suit being led. There are no clues from the bidding to suggest that declarer has extreme length or shortness (with the exception of #16 and #17), so assume he has two, three or four cards in the suit.

1.	Dummy Q 3 2 You K 7 6	*Cover with the king.* The purpose of covering an honor with an honor is to promote lower cards into tricks. For example, if declarer has A J 9 and partner has 10 x x x, the ten is promoted if you cover with the queen; declarer can win only two tricks. If declarer has A J 10, he can win three tricks whether or not you cover.
2.	Dummy Q J 9 You K 6 2	*Play the two.* If you cover and declarer has the ace but not the ten, he will be able to win an extra trick by taking his ace and then finessing dummy's nine. So you should not cover the queen, but you should cover on the second round if the jack is led.
3.	Dummy 10 9 7 You Q 3 2	*Play the two.* If you cover and declarer has K x x, he can eventually score a trick with the nine. When dummy has a two-card sequence—Q J x, J 10 x or 10 9 x— do not cover the first honor (unless you have two higher honors), wait for the second to be led and then cover.
4.	Dummy Q J 3 You K 2	*Cover with the king.* With a doubleton it is right to cover, because if you don't, declarer may next lead the three. Then you must play the king on the three and there is no chance to promote a trick for partner.
5.	Dummy 10 5 4 You Q 7 2	*Cover with the queen.* If declarer has A J 8 or K J 8, he can win only one trick if you cover, but two if you don't.
6.	Dummy A J 3 You Q 7 4	*Play the four.* Leading the jack is an illogical play unless declarer has K 10 9; if you cover with the queen, he wins three tricks in the suit without guessing. If you play a low card without hestitating, he may go up with his king and finesse your partner for the queen.
7.	Dummy K 10 7 You J 6 5	*Play the five.* Again, it seems declarer is hoping you fall into his trap and cover the honor. He might have something like A 9 8; if you cover with the jack, he will win with the ace and finesse your partner out of his queen.
8.	You K 8 3	Dummy A 8 3 Declarer Q	*Play the three.* Declarer is unlikely to lead the queen without the jack. So do not cover the queen, but cover on the second round if the jack is led. If you hold K 9 x or K 10 x, you can safely cover on the first round.
9.	You K 6 2	Dummy A J 4 Declarer Q	*Cover with the king.* If partner has the ten, you gain a trick. If declarer has the ten, it does not make any difference whether or not you cover.

10.	Dummy	*Cover with the king*. You gain a trick if partner holds
	A J 4	Q 9 x. If declarer has the nine or queen, it makes no
You		difference whether or not you cover.
K 6 2		
	Declarer	
	<u>10</u>	

11.	Dummy	*Cover with the king*. You will promote a trick if partner
	A J 10 8	has 9 x x x. If you hold K x x x (or longer), you should
You		not cover; you cannot promote a trick for partner, and if
K 7 5		declarer has a doubleton, he can win only three tricks.
	Declarer	
	<u>Q</u>	

12.	Dummy	*Cover with the queen*. You save a trick if partner has the
	A K 9 7	ten. If dummy holds A K 10 8, you should also cover
You		(partner might have 9 x x x); but if dummy holds
Q 4 2		A K 10 9, you should play low.
	Declarer	
	<u>J</u>	

13.	Dummy	*Play the five*. You cannot gain by covering unless de-
	A 4 3	clarer has made a ridiculous lead of the jack from K J x.
You		He may have K J 10, and if you play the five in tempo,
Q 8 5		he may go up with the ace and finesse your partner for
	Declarer	the queen. It would also cost a trick to cover if declarer
	<u>J</u>	has J 10 x.

14.	Dummy	This is a tough decision. If declarer is leading from J x,
	A 10 2	J x x or J x x x, you gain a trick by covering with the
You		queen; but leading the jack from these holdings is a
Q 5 4		doubtful play (an honor lead is usually backed up by an
	Declarer	adjacent card). If declarer has K J 9 and you play low
	<u>J</u>	without hesitating, he may go up with dummy's ace and
		finesse your partner for the queen. What should you do?
		In most cases, I would play low *promptly*, but nobody
		knows. Help!

15.	Dummy	*Play the two*. If declarer has 10 9 x, he cannot win a
	K 7 4	trick if you play low; but if you cover, later he can win a
You		trick with his nine. If he has A 10 9, you lose a trick if
Q 8 2		you cover; and if he has A J 10, you remove the guess if
	Declarer	you cover. In all cases, it is right to play low.
	<u>10</u>	

In #16, the declarer has opened the bidding with one spade, so assume he has five or six spades. In #17, declarer has opened the bidding with three spades, so assume he has seven spades. The rest of the illustrations, from #18 on, deal with whether to play second hand low or second hand high; assume declarer does not have extreme length or shortness in the suit.

16. Dummy
    ♠ Q 8 6 5 3

    You
    ♠ K 7

Play the seven promptly. The purpose of covering an honor is to promote lower cards into tricks. In this case, you know your partner has at most one spade, so there is nothing to promote. On the other side, you will lose a trick if you cover and partner has the singleton ace. If partner is void, declarer has eleven trumps and the odds favor his playing the ace—hoping for a one-one split. His reason for leading the queen is to tempt you to make a mistake and cover.

17. Dummy
    ♠ J 7

    You
    ♠ Q 5 4

Play the four promptly. Again, partner probably has a singleton spade; if so, you cannot gain by covering with your queen. If you play low and declarer has seven spades headed by the A K 10, he will probably put up the ace and cash the king, hoping the queen will drop. Another nightmarish thought: Partner might have the singleton king!

18. Dummy
    8 4 2

    You
    A 7 3

Play the three in most cases. Exceptional circumstances, where going up with the ace is right, will be shown later in this chapter.

19. Dummy
    K Q 7 5

    You
    A 10 8 2

Play the two. If you play the ace and declarer has the jack, he will win three tricks. If you play low and let him win the first trick with the jack, he can win only two tricks.

20. Dummy
    A Q 8 4

    You
    K 10 6 3

Play the three. If declarer has J x, playing the king will give him a third trick in the suit, while playing low will limit him to two. Another possibility is declarer having x x x and partner J x. Since he must always lose at least one trick in the suit, and can take a finesse on the second round, leading low from the dummy is a good deceptive play. Your hand might go up with the king—especially when it is a doubleton.

21. Dummy
    Q 8 6

    You
    K J 2

Play the two. If declarer has A 9 x, he can win only one trick if you play low; if you waste your jack, he can win two tricks.

22. Dummy
    7 5 2

    You
    Q J 3

Play the three. Whatever honors declarer has lie behind you, so he can win the same number of tricks in the suit whether or not you split your honors (unless he has K 10 doubleton, when he will go up with the king, not take the terrible percentage play of finessing the ten). The advantage of playing low is that declarer doesn't know you have both of those cards, and he may choose the wrong line of play. For example, if you play low and he has K 10 8 x, he may finesse the eight. Or with A K 10,

			he may shun the finesse. If you split your honors, he is more likely to read the situation and gain a trick.
23.	Dummy A 4 2 You Q J 3		*Play the queen (or the jack).*[1] If you play low and declarer has the K 10, he can win a third trick by finessing the ten. With the ace (or king) in the dummy, you should split your honors.
24.	Dummy A 7 5 You K 8 3		*Play the three promptly* (unless one trick is enough to beat the contract). If declarer has the queen, he can win a trick with it whether or not you play your king. But he may have Q 10 x and guess to play the ten; or he may not even have the queen.
25.	You A J 9 4 3	Dummy K Q 7 2 Declarer 6	*Play the three.* Many players would rush in with the ace for fear declarer has a singleton. That would be the right play if you see that it will beat the contract, but your goal is to limit declarer to as few tricks as possible. If he has a singleton, he can win two tricks if you play the ace, but only one trick if you play low. If he has two or more cards in the suit, he can win two tricks whether or not you go up with your ace.
26.	You K 4 3	Dummy Q 10 7 Declarer 5	*Play the three.* If declarer has A x x and you play low without hesitating, he will have to guess whether to play the ten or queen. If you are thinking he may have A x and you will lose your king, you have forgotten the goal is to limit declarer to as few tricks as possible. If you play the king, he has two tricks; if you play low, he may misguess and play the ten.
27.	You Q J 8	Dummy A K 10 Declarer 4	*Play the eight.* Declarer can win a trick with the ten whether you play low or split your honors. But there is a fair chance he will not finesse the ten if you play low the first time. Note, though, that if the dummy has A 10 x, you should play the queen (or jack).[1]
28.	You K J 4	Dummy A 10 7 Declarer 2	*Play the four.* If declarer has the queen, he can win a trick with the ten by finessing; and he might do that! But then there is nothing you can do to win more than one trick. However, declarer may decide to play the ace and lead toward his queen, hoping your partner has the king. If you play the jack, you solve his problem. Note that if declarer has Q x x, he is misplaying the suit; the correct first play is low from the dummy.

---

1. When second hand decides to split his honors, it is debatable whether he should play the high card or the low card from a sequence headed by the king, queen, jack or ten. My recommendation is that you play the top card of a sequence (as if leading the suit); however, there is no universal agreement. Some authorities recommend the low card of the sequence, and others recommend the high card. This is a good point to discuss with your regular partners.

29.		Dummy	*Play the three.* If declarer does not have the ten, his best
		A J 9	chance to win a second trick is to finesse the nine. This
	You		will succeed if you have Q 10 or K 10, while finessing
	K Q 3		the jack will succeed only if you have the K Q. Playing
		Declarer	the queen or king might be right from Q 10 x or K 10 x
		2	to try to mislead declarer, but from K Q x, play low.

30.		Dummy	*Play the four.* Suppose declarer wins the first trick with
		K Q 10	the king, returns to his hand in another suit and leads
	You		a second low card in this suit. *Play the seven* without
	A 7 4		huddling and make him guess whether to play you for
		Declarer	the jack or ace.
		2	

Second Hand High

The following eight deals show a variety of reasons for second hand to play high.

#1

                              North
                              ♠ A K Q
                              ♡ 10 5
                              ◇ A K Q J 3
                              ♣ Q 9 8
                                                    East
                                                    ♠ J 6 2
                                                    ♡ Q J 9 3
                                                    ◇ 8 7
                                                    ♣ A J 10 7

West	North	East	South
	1 ◇	Pass	1NT
Pass	3NT	All Pass	

West leads the ten of spades, declarer wins with the queen in the dummy and calls for the eight of clubs. Before you decide whether or not to play your ace, consider that you can see eight tricks in dummy. If declarer has the ace of hearts, you cannot beat the hand. Also, declarer's one-notrump response implied that he does not have a four-card major suit. So you should assume that your partner has ♡ A x x x. *Go up with your ace of clubs and lead the queen of hearts.* The four hands:

                              ♠ A K Q
                              ♡ 10 5
                              ◇ A K Q J 3
                              ♣ Q 9 8
        ♠ 10 9 8 5   ♠ J 6 2
        ♡ A 8 7 4   ♡ Q J 9 3
        ◇ 6 4 2   ◇ 8 7
        ♣ 6 3   ♣ A J 10 7
                              ♠ 7 4 3
                              ♡ K 6 2
                              ◇ 10 9 5
                              ♣ K 5 4 2

As you can see, this defense beats the contract. But if you don't take your ace of clubs at trick two, declarer will win with the king and run his nine tricks.

#2

North
♠ J 9 8
♡ Q J 8 3
◇ A 10
♣ 10 7 5 2

East
♠ 6 5
♡ 10 7 2
◇ J 9 6 3 2
♣ A 9 6

West	North	East	South
			2NT
Pass	3♣	Pass	3◇
Pass	3NT	All Pass	

Partner leads the three of spades and the first trick is won in dummy with the eight. The two of clubs is led and you should *grab your ace and return a spade*. If your goal is to help your partner establish his long suit, make every effort to get the lead as soon as possible and return his suit. The four hands:

♠ J 9 8
♡ Q J 8 3
◇ A 10
♣ 10 7 5 2

♠ A Q 4 3 2
♡ 9 6 5
◇ 8 7 5
♣ 4 3

♠ 6 5
♡ 10 7 2
◇ J 9 6 3 2
♣ A 9 6

♠ K 10 7
♡ A K 4
◇ K Q 4
♣ K Q J 8

Declarer has eight winners (one spade, four hearts and three diamonds) and is trying to "steal" a club trick. If you duck, he will take his nine tricks. If you go up with your ace and lead a spade, partner will set the contract by running four spade tricks.

It was lucky that declarer had no more spade stoppers and partner could run four spade tricks. In the next deal, the declarer has a second stopper in partner's suit, but the same strategy will beat the contract.

#3

North
♠ J 10 4
♡ K Q 10 3
◇ 8 7 5
♣ A 8 3

                                        East
                                        ♠ 9 5
                                        ♡ 8 6 4
                                        ◇ A 6 2
                                        ♣ Q 7 5 4 2

West	*North*	*East*	*South*
			1NT
Pass	2♣	Pass	2◇
Pass	3NT	All Pass	

Partner leads the six of spades and the first trick is won in dummy with the ten. Then the five of diamonds is led. Consistent with the advice given in #2, *go up with your ace of diamonds and return a spade*. This is the winning defense, but before showing you the four hands, suppose the bidding goes the same way and you have the king of diamonds, instead of the ace.

#4

North
♠ J 10 4
♡ K Q 10 3
◇ 8 7 5
♣ A 8 3

                                        East
                                        ♠ 9 5
                                        ♡ 8 6 4
                                        ◇ K 6 2
                                        ♣ Q 7 5 4 2

Again partner leads a spade which is won with dummy's ten, and the five of diamonds is led. *Go up with your king of diamonds and, if it wins the trick, lead a spade.* Now let's look at the four hands:

♠ J 10 4
♡ K Q 10 3
◇ 8 7 5
♣ A 8 3

♠ K 8 7 6 3   ♠ 9 5
♡ 9 7 2   ♡ 8 6 4
◇ A 10 4   ◇ K 6 2
♣ J 9   ♣ Q 7 5 4 2

♠ A Q 2
♡ A J 5
◇ Q J 9 3
♣ K 10 6

Declarer has eight tricks (two spades, four hearts and two clubs). If you play a low diamond at trick two, there is no way to set the contract. But if you play your high diamond (be it the ace or king) and return a spade, it will establish three spade winners for partner and he will always get them because he has a diamond entry. Note that going up with the king is unlikely to help declarer: If he has strong diamonds (such as A Q, A Q J or A J 10), he can always finesse.

#5

North
♠ A K Q J 8
♡ 7 6 3
◇ Q 10 9
♣ 8 3

West
♠ 10 4
♡ K Q 4
◇ A J 3
♣ J 9 7 5 2

West	*North*	*East*	*South*
			1 ◇
Pass	1 ♠	Pass	1NT
Pass	3NT	All Pass	

You lead the five of clubs, partner plays the ten and declarer wins with the king. The two of diamonds is led and it is your play. Consider that declarer has the ace and queen of clubs (partner would not have played the ten with either of those cards) and five spade tricks. If you duck this trick and partner does not have the king, declarer will win with the queen and have nine tricks. The best chance to beat the contract is to find partner with four or five hearts headed by the ace. So, *win with the ace of diamonds at trick two and lead the king of hearts.* The four hands:

```
                ♠ A K Q J 8
                ♡ 7 6 3
                ◇ Q 10 9
                ♣ 8 3
  ♠ 10 4                          ♠ 9 5 3 2
  ♡ K Q 4                         ♡ A 10 8 2
  ◇ A J 3                         ◇ 7 5
  ♣ J 9 7 5 2                     ♣ 10 6 4
                ♠ 7 6
                ♡ J 9 5
                ◇ K 8 6 4 2
                ♣ A K Q
```

Partner does have four hearts to the ace, so the defense can run five tricks. Declarer's low diamond lead at trick two was an attempt to catch your napping. If you just count the tricks, you should know that this is a time to play *second hand high*.

#6   North
                                                                ♠ A K 10 9 2
                                                                ♡ 6 4
                                                                ◇ J 5 3
                                                                ♣ 10 6 2

                              West
                              ♠ Q 6
                              ♡ Q J 10 2
                              ◇ Q 9 4
                              ♣ K Q J 9

West	North	East	South
			1♡
Pass	1♠	Pass	1NT
Pass	Pass	Pass	

You start with, in order, the king, jack and queen of clubs. Partner follows suit throughout and declarer wins the third trick with the ace. At trick four, he leads the five of spades and you must *play the queen* in an effort to block his communication with the dummy. If partner has ♠ J x x x, you limit declarer to two spade tricks. The four hands:

                                          ♠ A K 10 9 2
                                          ♡ 6 4
                                          ◇ J 5 3
                                          ♣ 10 6 2
          ♠ Q 6   ♠ J 8 4 3
          ♡ Q J 10 2   ♡ 9 7
          ◇ Q 9 4   ◇ A 10 7 2
          ♣ K Q J 9   ♣ 7 4 3
                                          ♠ 7 5
                                          ♡ A K 8 5 3
                                          ◇ K 8 6
                                          ♣ A 8 5

Declarer has five winners (two spades, two hearts and one club) and cannot be prevented from scoring a trick with the king of diamonds. If you fail to play the queen of spades when he leads the suit, he will play the ten and can win a third and maybe a fourth spade trick—depending on whether or not your partner takes his jack. Note that playing the queen of spades cannot cost you a trick, no matter how the suit divides.

In the next hand there is a similar problem, but the winning play is less obvious.

#7

                                    North
                                    ♠ J 7
                                    ♡ A Q 10 9 6
                                    ◊ 6 3 2
                                    ♣ 8 7 4

        West
        ♠ K 9 6 5 2
        ♡ K 7 5
        ◊ 8 5 4
        ♣ K 10

West	North	East	South
			1♣
Pass	1♡	Pass	2NT
Pass	3NT	All Pass	

You lead the five of spades, dummy plays the jack and partner's queen wins the first trick. Partner wins the second trick with the ten of spades, and leads a third spade to declarer's ace; a diamond is discarded from dummy. Now declarer leads the two of hearts and you must *play second hand high (the king)* to beat the contract. The four hands:

                                    ♠ J 7
                                    ♡ A Q 10 9 6
                                    ◊ 6 3 2
                                    ♣ 8 7 4

        ♠ K 9 6 5 2   ♠ Q 10 8
        ♡ K 7 5   ♡ J 8 3
        ◊ 8 5 4   ◊ J 10 9 7
        ♣ K 10   ♣ Q 9 2

                                    ♠ A 4 3
                                    ♡ 4 2
                                    ◊ A K Q
                                    ♣ A J 6 5 3

Declarer has five winners outside the heart suit (one spade, three diamonds and one club), so he needs four heart tricks to make his contract. Playing the king of hearts at trick four foils his plan. If he ducks your king, you can set him by cashing two more spade tricks. If he plays the ace, he cannot win more than two heart tricks.

If you play a low heart at trick two, he will finesse the ten and it's all over. Partner will win with the jack, but declarer can take four heart tricks by finessing again on the next round.

Going up with the king may seem like a risky play, but it will not make any difference if declarer has the jack. And if the declarer has three low cards, his normal play would be to win with the ace and finesse on the second round—partner will score a trick with his doubleton jack and you will break even.

#8   North
                                                  ♠ 7 5
                                                  ♡ Q 10 6 4 2
                                                  ◇ A 9 8
                                                  ♣ 5 3 2
                                                                        East
                                                                        ♠ 10 6 4
                                                                        ♡ 7 3
                                                                        ◇ Q 10 5 3 2
                                                                        ♣ Q 8 7

West	North	East	South
			1♡
1♠	2♡	Pass	4♡
Pass	Pass	Pass	

Partner leads the king of spades, which wins the first trick, and follows with the jack of spades, which is won by declarer with the ace. Two high trumps are cashed, partner discards a spade on the second heart, and then declarer cashes the king of diamonds, the ace of diamonds, and ruffs the third round of diamonds in his hand. At trick eight, he leads a spade and ruffs in dummy; and at trick nine, he leads the two of clubs. You should be aware that declarer has "stripped the hand" (he has no more spades or diamonds in either hand). He is planning to endplay your partner. To prevent this, you must *play your queen of clubs (second hand high)* when the low club is led from dummy. The four hands:

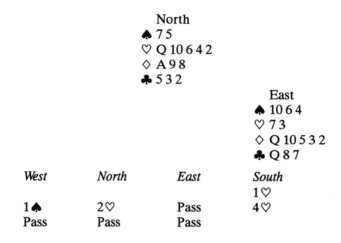

                                    ♠ 7 5
                                    ♡ Q 10 6 4 2
                                    ◇ A 9 8
                                    ♣ 5 3 2
        ♠ K Q J 9 3   ♠ 10 6 4
        ♡ 8   ♡ 7 3
        ◇ J 7 6   ◇ Q 10 5 3 2
        ♣ A J 10 4   ♣ Q 8 7
                                    ♠ A 8 2
                                    ♡ A K J 9 5
                                    ◇ K 4
                                    ♣ K 9 6

Whether declarer ducks your queen of clubs or covers with the king, the defense can win three club tricks and beat the contract. If you do not play your queen of clubs, declarer will insert the nine. Partner can win with the ten, but you collect only one more trick whether partner leads a club or a spade.

Second Hand Low

The next thirteen deals show cases where it is tempting, but wrong, to play second hand high.

#9

North
♠ A Q 7
♡ A K Q 2
◇ 10 8 5
♣ A Q 3

East
♠ 8 2
♡ 10 5 3
◇ A 9 6 4
♣ K 7 6 4

West	North	East	South
	2NT	Pass	3♠
Pass	4♠	Pass	6♠
Pass	Pass	Pass	

Your partner leads the jack of clubs, the queen is played from dummy, you cover with the king and declarer ruffs. Declarer cashes the ace and queen of spades as partner follows to the first and discards a club on the second. Then he leads the five of diamonds from dummy. You must *play a low diamond promptly*. If you have been counting the tricks, declarer has eleven (seven spades, three hearts and one club). If he has the king of diamonds, you cannot beat him if you play your ace, but may if you play low and he has the king and jack. The four hands:

♠ A Q 7
♡ A K Q 2
◇ 10 8 5
♣ A Q 3

♠ 4
♡ J 9 8 6
◇ Q 3
♣ J 10 9 8 5 2

♠ 8 2
♡ 10 5 3
◇ A 9 6 4
♣ K 7 6 4

♠ K J 10 9 6 5 3
♡ 7 4
◇ K J 7 2
♣ —

As you can see, declarer can discard two diamonds on the third high heart and the ace of clubs, but must *guess* whether to play the king or jack of diamonds to make his contract. If you go up with the ace, or huddle before playing low, you solve his problem.

#10   North
                                         ♠ 2
                                         ♡ J 10 5 4
                                         ◇ Q 8 4 2
                                         ♣ A 6 5 4

                                                             East
                                                             ♠ A J 8 5 3
                                                             ♡ A 2
                                                             ◇ 10 7 6 3
                                                             ♣ Q 10

West	North	East	South
			1♠
Pass	1NT	Pass	2♡
Pass	3♡	Pass	4♡
Pass	Pass	Pass	

Your partner makes the good lead of the seven of hearts. You win with the ace and return the two of hearts; partner plays the eight and declarer wins in dummy with the jack. At trick three, he leads the two of spades and you must *play a low spade*. With a singleton in dummy, it is tempting to go up with the ace of spades. But declarer bid the suit and he cannot ruff all of his spades in dummy; you will win a trick with your ace eventually. The four hands:

                              ♠ 2
                              ♡ J 10 5 4
                              ◇ Q 8 4 2
                              ♣ A 6 5 4

        ♠ 10 4   ♠ A J 8 5 3
        ♡ 8 7   ♡ A 2
        ◇ K J 9 5   ◇ 10 7 6 3
        ♣ K J 9 8 3   ♣ Q 10

                              ♠ K Q 9 7 6
                              ♡ K Q 9 6 3
                              ◇ A
                              ♣ 7 2

Declarer has one club loser and has already lost to the ace of hearts, so he must hold his spade losers to one if he is going to make his contract. Assuming you played low and let him win the third trick with the king of spades, he is left with ♠ Q 9 7 6. He can ruff only two in dummy, so you will eventually win two spade tricks with your ace and jack. If you rose with your ace of spades at trick three, declarer plays low and keeps ♠ K Q 9 7; he can ruff the two low spades in dummy and therefore lose only one spade trick.

#11

	North		
	♠ K Q 4 2		
	♡ 8 6 5		
	◇ K Q 10		
	♣ K 6 3		

West
♠ 7 5
♡ J 3 2
◇ A 9 5 2
♣ Q J 10 4

West	*North*	*East*	*South*
			1♠
Pass	3♠	Pass	4NT
Pass	5♣	Pass	6♠
Pass	Pass	Pass	

You lead the queen of clubs. Declarer wins in his hand with the ace, plays a spade to dummy's king and a spade to his ace, partner discarding the three of diamonds on the second spade. Now declarer leads the seven of diamonds. Using Blackwood and then jumping to a slam with two quick losers in an unbid suit when an ace is missing is bad bidding. So declarer predictably has a singleton diamond. If you duck his diamond lead you will lose your ace, but declarer can win only one diamond trick. If you play your ace and he has two losers in the side suits, he can discard them on the king and queen. Since you know declarer has three aces (he would not bid six off two aces), no second trick is cashable if you play your ace; so the right play is *a low diamond*. The four hands:

	♠ K Q 4 2	
	♡ 8 6 5	
	◇ K Q 10	
	♣ K 6 3	

♠ 7 5		♠ 6
♡ J 3 2		♡ Q 10 9 7
◇ A 9 5 2		◇ J 8 6 4 3
♣ Q J 10 4		♣ 9 8 2

	♠ A J 10 9 8 3	
	♡ A K 4	
	◇ 7	
	♣ A 7 5	

If you play a low diamond when declarer leads the seven, he will be set. If he goes up with the king or queen, he avoids a diamond loser but must lose a heart and a club for down one. However, he needs two discards to make his contract, so his right play is to finesse the ten; that way he succeeds if you have the jack.

If you rise with the ace of diamonds, it is the only trick you will get; declarer will discard his two losers on the king and queen of diamonds and make his slam.

#12   **North**
                                                        ♠ K J 4 2
                                                        ♡ 8 6 5
                                                        ◇ K J 10
                                                        ♣ K Q 7

            West
            ♠ 7 5
            ♡ J 10 3
            ◇ A 9 5 2
            ♣ J 10 9 2

West	*North*	*East*	*South*
			1♠
Pass	3♠	Pass	4NT
Pass	5♣	Pass	6♠
Pass	Pass	Pass	

You lead the jack of clubs. Declarer wins in his hand with the ace, plays a spade to dummy's king and a spade to his ace; partner discards a club on the second spade. Now declarer leads the seven of diamonds and again the question is whether or not to go up with your ace. If you think declarer has more than one diamond, it would be routine to play low; but for the same reasons given in the last hand, you should assume that he has a singleton. If you have a second trick, you should go up with your ace. Since you do not, you should *play a low diamond without hesitating*. If declarer has a singleton diamond and ♡ A x x, you will beat the contract one trick whether you go up with the ace or not. But if you go up with your ace and he has only one heart loser (♡ A K x, ♡ A Q x or ♡ A x), he will discard his loser on the king of diamonds; the only chance to beat him is to play a low diamond and hope he makes the wrong guess. The four hands:

                                ♠ K J 4 2
                                ♡ 8 6 5
                                ◇ K J 10
                                ♣ K Q 7
          ♠ 7 5   ♠ 6
          ♡ J 10 3   ♡ Q 9 7 2
          ◇ A 9 5 2   ◇ Q 8 6 4 3
          ♣ J 10 9 2   ♣ 8 6 4
                                ♠ A Q 10 9 8 3
                                ♡ A K 4
                                ◇ 7
                                ♣ A 5 3

Declarer has only one heart loser and, as stated, if you play a low diamond when the suit is led, the fate of the contract depends on whether declarer goes up with the king or finesses.

#13

North
♠ A Q
♡ 9 6 2
◇ Q 10 9 5 4 3
♣ A 5

West
♠ J 9 6 2
♡ K 10 8 7 3
◇ K J
♣ 7 4

West	North	East	South
	1◇	Pass	1♠
Pass	2◇	Pass	3NT
Pass	Pass	Pass	

You lead the seven of hearts, partner plays the four and declarer wins with the queen. (Partner would have played the ace or jack of hearts if he had either of those cards, so declarer has them.) At trick two, declarer leads the two of diamonds. You must *play the jack of diamonds—second hand low.* If declarer had the ace of diamonds, he would almost surely lead the ace; he would not lead a low diamond. Furthermore, there is no way to beat the contract if he has the ace of diamonds. So you must play the jack and save your king for an entry card; let partner win the first diamond trick so that he can lead a heart through declarer's ace-jack. The four hands:

♠ A Q
♡ 9 6 2
◇ Q 10 9 5 4 3
♣ A 5

♠ J 9 6 2   ♠ 10 7 3
♡ K 10 8 7 3   ♡ 5 4
◇ K J   ◇ A 8 6
♣ 7 4   ♣ Q J 9 8 3

♠ K 8 5 4
♡ A Q J
◇ 7 2
♣ K 10 6 2

Declarer has only seven winners (three spades, two hearts and two clubs); he must establish diamond tricks to make his contract. If you play the king of diamonds at trick two, declarer can establish diamonds easily and make his contract with at least one overtrick. If you play the jack of diamonds and let partner win with his ace, a heart lead through declarer will establish three heart tricks for you while you still have the king of diamonds as an entry.

#14   North
                                             ♠ 9 8 7
                                             ♡ A 9 4
                                             ◇ A 9 5
                                             ♣ Q 10 7 3

                West
                ♠ Q J 10 6
                ♡ 10 7 5
                ◇ 8 6 4
                ♣ K 8 4

West	North	East	South
			1NT
Pass	3NT	All Pass	

You lead the queen of spades and win the first trick. Then you lead the ten of spades, which partner wins with the king. A third spade is played and won by declarer with the ace. At trick four, he cashes the ace of clubs, then he leads the two of clubs. You must *play low smoothly*. Declarer would not play the club suit this way if he held the jack, so partner has that card. Here are the four hands to show you that declarer must guess the club situation to make his bid.

                                 ♠ 9 8 7
                                 ♡ A 9 4
                                 ◇ A 9 5
                                 ♣ Q 10 7 3
        ♠ Q J 10 6   ♠ K 4 3
        ♡ 10 7 5   ♡ J 8 3 2
        ◇ 8 6 4   ◇ Q J 10 2
        ♣ K 8 4   ♣ J 9
                                 ♠ A 5 2
                                 ♡ K Q 6
                                 ◇ K 7 3
                                 ♣ A 6 5 2

Declarer has seven winners (one spade, three hearts, two diamonds and one club), and the only chance to make his bid is to develop two more club tricks. If you mistakenly play the king when he leads the two of clubs toward dummy, his task is easy. But if you duck without hesitating, he is likely to play the ten; your partner will win with the jack and the contract can no longer be made.

#15

North
♠ Q 10 6 3
♡ K 8 7 2
♢ 9 5
♣ 10 6 3

West
♠ K 7
♡ Q J 10 9
♢ A 4 3
♣ 9 8 5 2

West	North	East	South
			2NT
Pass	3♣	Pass	3♠
Pass	4♠	All Pass	

You lead the queen of hearts. Declarer wins in his hand with the ace and leads the two of spades. Declarer would not play the suit this way if he held the ace and jack, so partner must have one or both of those cards. You should *play the seven of spades*. The four hands:

```
                    ♠ Q 10 6 3
                    ♡ K 8 7 2
                    ♢ 9 5
                    ♣ 10 6 3
    ♠ K 7                        ♠ J 8 4
    ♡ Q J 10 9                   ♡ 6 5 3
    ♢ A 4 3                      ♢ K 8 7 6 2
    ♣ 9 8 5 2                    ♣ 7 4
                    ♠ A 9 5 2
                    ♡ A 4
                    ♢ Q J 10
                    ♣ A K Q J
```

Note that declarer can make his contract unless he loses two spade tricks, and he will lose only one if you go up with your king. If you play low and he goes up with the queen, he will make his contract—but you will still get the one spade trick you are entitled to.

Now suppose you play the seven of spades, declarer finesses the ten from dummy and partner wins with the jack. Declarer can still succeed by cashing the ace and dropping your king, but he is unlikely to give you credit for ducking with a doubleton king and will probably take the percentage play: go to dummy with the king of hearts and finesse your partner for the king of spades.

Incidentally, the best way to play the spade suit is a close decision. Unless declarer can count on West playing the king from K x, cashing the ace and then leading the two is at least as good; with the spades divided as shown, this line of play would succeed with no guesswork.

#16   North
                                       ♠ 7 6 4
                                       ♡ A K J
                                       ◊ K J 2
                                       ♣ K Q 4 3

        West
        ♠ J 9 2
        ♡ 8 6 5 4
        ◊ 9 4
        ♣ A 10 8 2

West	*North*	*East*	*South*
			1NT
Pass	6NT	All Pass	

You lead the four of hearts. Declarer wins the first trick in his hand with the queen and leads the five of clubs. You must *play a low club*. Declarer wins in dummy with the king, plays a spade to the ace in his hand and leads the seven of clubs. You must *play a second low club*. You cannot prevent declarer from winning two club tricks with the king and queen, but if he has ♣ J x x or ♣ J 9 x x, he will win a third trick with the jack unless you play second hand low twice. The four hands:

                                       ♠ 7 6 4
                                       ♡ A K J
                                       ◊ K J 2
                                       ♣ K Q 4 3
        ♠ J 9 2   ♠ Q 10 8 5
        ♡ 8 6 5 4   ♡ 7 3 2
        ◊ 9 4   ◊ 7 6 5 3
        ♣ A 10 8 2   ♣ 9 6
                                       ♠ A K 3
                                       ♡ Q 10 9
                                       ◊ A Q 10 8
                                       ♣ J 7 5

Declarer needs three club tricks to make his contract. He will succeed if the suit divides three-three, or if he can drive out the ace without wasting one of his club honors. Leading a low club from his hand twice offers the best chance—you might have a singleton or doubleton ace, or make a mistake by going up with your ace with four clubs. If you duck your ace twice, declarer will lead a third round of clubs—hoping for a three-three split—and you will take two club tricks to set him.

#17

		North ♠ K 7 2 ♡ A K 7 ◇ A K 6 4 ♣ A J 9	

West
♠ Q J 10 9
♡ 9 4 2
◇ Q 9 7
♣ K Q 4

West	*North*	*East*	*South*
	2NT	Pass	3♡
Pass	4♡	Pass	4♠
Pass	6♡	All Pass	

You lead the queen of spades and declarer wins the first trick in his hand with the ace. He then cashes three rounds of hearts; partner follows suit once, then discards a low spade and a low diamond. At trick five declarer leads the two of clubs, and you should *play the four*. Declarer has eleven tricks (two spades, six hearts, two diamonds and one club); if he scores a second club trick he will make his contract. If he has the ten, all is lost. But if partner has the ten and you play low, declarer will play the nine; hoping that you have K 10 or Q 10. This is a better play than the jack, which succeeds only if you have K Q. The four hands:

	♠ K 7 2 ♡ A K 7 ◇ A K 6 4 ♣ A J 9	
♠ Q J 10 9 ♡ 9 4 2 ◇ Q 9 7 ♣ K Q 4		♠ 8 6 5 4 ♡ 5 ◇ J 10 8 3 2 ♣ 10 8 5
	♠ A 3 ♡ Q J 10 8 6 3 ◇ 5 ♣ 7 6 3 2	

Now you can see that declarer cannot make his contract unless he wins a trick with the jack of clubs. If you play a low club and he puts in the nine, he will be set. If you split your honors, there is a better chance he will play you for the king-queen.

#18   North
                                                 ♠ K J 10 2
                                                 ♡ K Q J
                                                 ◇ A J
                                                 ♣ K 5 4 3

                                                              East
                                                              ♠ 5 3
                                                              ♡ 10 8
                                                              ◇ K 9 8 4 2
                                                              ♣ A 7 6 2

West	*North*	*East*	*South*
			1♠
Pass	4NT	Pass	5♡
Pass	6♠	All Pass	

Partner leads the four of hearts and the trick is won with dummy's jack. Declarer plays a spade to his ace and a spade to dummy's king, partner following to the first and discarding the two of hearts on the second. At trick four, the three of clubs is led from dummy and it is decision time—whether to go up with your ace or play second hand low? If declarer has a singleton queen and three diamonds, the winning play would be to play the ace. But you should *play a low club* because there are more combinations where it will gain, and there is a subtle reason why you should assume declarer does not have the singleton queen; if he did, partner would have ♣ J 10 9 8 and would have found the jack of clubs a more attractive opening lead than a heart. The four hands:

                                                 ♠ K J 10 2
                                                 ♡ K Q J
                                                 ◇ A J
                                                 ♣ K 5 4 3
          ♠ 6   ♠ 5 3
          ♡ 9 7 5 4 2   ♡ 10 8
          ◇ Q 7 6 3   ◇ K 9 8 4 2
          ♣ J 9 8   ♣ A 7 6 2
                                                 ♠ A Q 9 8 7 4
                                                 ♡ A 6 3
                                                 ◇ 10 5
                                                 ♣ Q 10

If you play a low club, declarer will probably finesse the ten. This is his best play; if you have the jack of clubs, he will lose only one club trick and can discard his losing diamond on the king of clubs. As the cards lie partner will win with the jack of clubs, and the declarer will be set (down two if partner returns a diamond).

Note that declarer cannot make his contract even if he plays the queen of clubs; he can never establish a second club trick. The only way he can succeed is if you mistakenly go up with your ace of clubs.

#19
                                North
                                  ♠ A
                                  ♡ 9 8 4
                                  ◇ A 10 7 6 5 3
                                  ♣ J 5 2

West
♠ Q J 10 7
♡ J 6 3
◇ Q J 9 8
♣ 9 4

West	North	East	South
			1NT
Pass	3NT	All Pass	

Your queen-of-spades lead is won with the ace. A low diamond is led from dummy, declarer winning with the king after your partner discards the eight of clubs. Now comes the two of diamonds. *Do not split your honors—play the nine of diamonds and let him win this trick with the ten.* Since there are no side entries to dummy, this limits declarer to three diamond tricks—the king, ten and ace. If you play the queen or jack, he will let you win that trick. When he regains the lead he can win four more diamond tricks by leading his third diamond and finessing dummy's ten. The four hands:

                        ♠ A
                        ♡ 9 8 4
                        ◇ A 10 7 6 5 3
                        ♣ J 5 2

♠ Q J 10 7   ♠ 9 8 6 2
♡ J 6 3   ♡ K 10 7 5
◇ Q J 9 8   ◇ —
♣ 9 4   ♣ K Q 10 8 3
                        ♠ K 5 4 3
                        ♡ A Q 2
                        ◇ K 4 2
                        ♣ A 7 6

Since the king of hearts is onside, declarer can win five tricks outside the diamond suit and therefore needs four diamond tricks to make his contract. As long as you play second hand low to the second diamond lead, declarer will be set.

#20   North
                                          ♠ K 6 2
                                          ♡ 7 5
                                          ◇ 9 6 4
                                          ♣ A K 8 7 3

           West
           ♠ 8 7
           ♡ Q J 10 9 3
           ◇ K 3
           ♣ Q J 10 6

West	North	East	South
			1NT
Pass	3NT	All Pass	

You lead the queen of hearts, partner plays the four and declarer wins with the ace. At trick two, he leads the two of clubs. *Do not split your honors—play the six of clubs.*

If you play the six and declarer has ♣ 9 x x, he can limit you to one club trick by finessing the eight, but that is not his best play: He should play the ace or king because your partner's singleton is more apt to be the queen, jack or ten rather than the one missing spot card.

To better understand this, assume for the moment that you hold ♣ Q J x x and partner the singleton ten. If declarer finesses the eight, he will lose to the ten. His next play will be the ace or king, hoping for a three-two split; he will lose two club tricks. If he makes the right play on the first club trick, going up with the ace or king and dropping the ten, his next play will be low from dummy to his nine—a safety play so he will not lose more than one club trick if you still have ♣ Q J x.

Now back to the actual layout: If you play a club honor on the first club lead from your ♣ Q J 10 6, declarer can make the same safety play and lose only one club trick. Furthermore, your partner may have the nine of clubs. The four hands:

                                          ♠ K 6 2
                                          ♡ 7 5
                                          ◇ 9 6 4
                                          ♣ A K 8 7 3

           ♠ 8 7   ♠ 10 9 5 4 3
           ♡ Q J 10 9 3   ♡ 8 6 4
           ◇ K 3   ◇ A J 10 5
           ♣ Q J 10 6   ♣ 9

                                          ♠ A Q J
                                          ♡ A K 2
                                          ◇ Q 8 7 2
                                          ♣ 5 4 2

As you can now see, declarer needs four club tricks to make his contract. Since your partner has the nine, it is impossible for declarer to win four club tricks if you play the six at trick two. If you play a club honor, declarer can make his contract by winning with the king and leading the seven of clubs. After you win this trick, dummy retains the ♣ A 8 3 and you have ♣ Q 6; declarer can finesse the eight and win the needed four club tricks.

A similar play to second hand low is to refuse to ruff one of declarer's losing tricks. For example:

#21

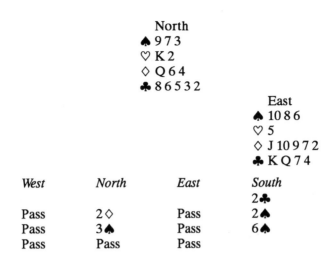

North
♠ 9 7 3
♡ K 2
◇ Q 6 4
♣ 8 6 5 3 2

East
♠ 10 8 6
♡ 5
◇ J 10 9 7 2
♣ K Q 7 4

West	North	East	South
			2♣
Pass	2◇	Pass	2♠
Pass	3♠	Pass	6♠
Pass	Pass	Pass	

Partner leads the jack of clubs and declarer wins the first trick with the ace. He then plays a low heart to dummy's king and leads the two of hearts. *Do not ruff.* Declarer obviously has one or more losing hearts in his hand that he hopes to ruff in dummy—otherwise, why did he lead hearts before drawing trumps? Since your spade spots are better than dummy's, you will be able to overruff if he tries to ruff any hearts. Here are the four hands to show you that ruffing the two of hearts is a disaster:

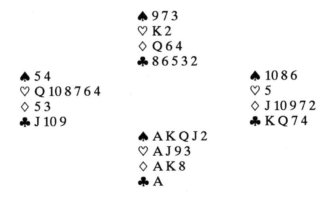

♠ 9 7 3
♡ K 2
◇ Q 6 4
♣ 8 6 5 3 2

♠ 5 4
♡ Q 10 8 7 6 4
◇ 5 3
♣ J 10 9

♠ 10 8 6
♡ 5
◇ J 10 9 7 2
♣ K Q 7 4

♠ A K Q J 2
♡ A J 9 3
◇ A K 8
♣ A

The only losers in declarer's hand are two hearts, and he can make his contract if he can ruff one of them in dummy. If you ruff the two of hearts when it is led, declarer will play a low heart from his hand and be left with ♡ A J. When he regains the lead, he will draw two rounds of trumps (exhausting your hand of spades) and ruff his losing heart in dummy.

If you do not ruff the two of hearts, declarer will win with his ace but is left with ♡ J 9; he cannot avoid losing two heart tricks. If he tries to ruff, you will overruff. If he draws trumps, your partner will win two heart tricks with the Q 10.

About Covering Honors

#22   **North**
♠ J 7 6 2
♡ Q 10 3
◇ A Q 4
♣ 10 9 8

East
♠ Q 5
♡ 9 7 5 4
◇ K 6 5 2
♣ K 7 3

West	North	East	South
			1♠
Pass	2♠	Pass	3♠
Pass	4♠	All Pass	

Partner leads the jack of diamonds, declarer wins the trick in dummy with the ace and leads the jack of spades. *Do not cover, play the five*. The only holdings that the declarer could have where leading the jack is a good play are five or six spades headed by A K 10, A 10 9 or K 10 9 (or 10 9 8 x x); in none of these cases can you gain by covering with the queen. But if you play low, you save a trick if partner has a singleton king, and put declarer to a guess if partner has a singleton or doubleton ace. The four hands:

                                        ♠ J 7 6 2
                                        ♡ Q 10 3
                                        ◇ A Q 4
                                        ♣ 10 9 8
♠ K   ♠ Q 5
♡ 8 6 2   ♡ 9 7 5 4
◇ J 10 9 7 3   ◇ K 6 5 2
♣ A J 5 4   ♣ K 7 3
                                        ♠ A 10 9 8 4 3
                                        ♡ A K J
                                        ◇ 8
                                        ♣ Q 6 2

Declarer has three losing club tricks, so the fate of the contract depends on whether you cover the jack-of-spades lead with the queen.

#23

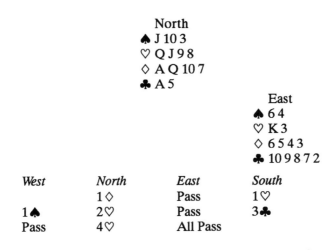

North
♠ J 10 3
♡ Q J 9 8
◇ A Q 10 7
♣ A 5

East
♠ 6 4
♡ K 3
◇ 6 5 4 3
♣ 10 9 8 7 2

West	North	East	South
	1◇	Pass	1♡
1♠	2♡	Pass	3♣
Pass	4♡	All Pass	

Your partner wins the first three tricks with the king, ace and queen of spades; you discard a low diamond on the third spade. Partner then leads a club, declarer wins with the ace in dummy and calls for the queen of hearts. *Do not cover; play the three.* If declarer has the ace and ten, your play doesn't matter. But he may have ♡ A x x x and partner ♡ 10 x x. The four hands:

♠ J 10 3
♡ Q J 9 8
◇ A Q 10 7
♣ A 5

♠ A K Q 9 5
♡ 10 7 4
◇ J 8 2
♣ 6 3

♠ 6 4
♡ K 3
◇ 6 5 4 3
♣ 10 9 8 7 2

♠ 8 7 2
♡ A 6 5 2
◇ K 9
♣ K Q J 4

If you cover the queen of hearts with the king, declarer will most likely win with the ace and finesse your partner for the ten (although he may reason that you covered with ♡ K 10 and therefore call for the jack). If you play low, he must guess whether you have ♡ K x or ♡ K x x; his next play from dummy must be a low heart to make his contract; if he leads the jack—hoping your partner began with ♡ 10 x—he will lose a heart trick. With the known spade distribution, a good declarer would more than likely play you for the heart length and go down.

#24   North
                                       ♠ A K 8
                                       ♡ J 10 4
                                       ◇ A K J 10
                                       ♣ Q J 2
                                                                East
                                                                ♠ Q J 10 4
                                                                ♡ 9 7
                                                                ◇ 9 6 5 2
                                                                ♣ K 6 3

West	North	East	South
	1◇	Pass	1NT
Pass	3NT	All Pass	

Partner leads the three of hearts, the jack is played from dummy and declarer drops the six. At trick two, the queen of clubs is led and you should *rise with the king*. When an honor card is led from two touching honors, it is normal to play low; do not cover the first honor, wait for the second. But in this case it is apparent that declarer can win nine tricks if he has the ace of clubs (two spades, one heart, four diamonds and two clubs). So you should assume that your partner has the ace. If partner also has a five- card heart suit headed by the ace or king, you will beat the contract by taking your king and leading a heart. The four hands:

```
                        ♠ A K 8
                        ♡ J 10 4
                        ◇ A K J 10
                        ♣ Q J 2
    ♠ 9 6 3                                ♠ Q J 10 4
    ♡ A 8 5 3 2                            ♡ 9 7
    ◇ 7 4                                  ◇ 9 6 5 2
    ♣ A 5 4                                ♣ K 6 3
                        ♠ 7 5 2
                        ♡ K Q 6
                        ◇ Q 8 3
                        ♣ 10 9 8 7
```

As you can see, the only defense to beat the contract is to cover the queen of clubs with your king and lead a heart. When partner gets the lead with the ace of clubs, he has enough heart tricks to set the contract.

You may think that declarer would have been more deceptive if he had led the two of clubs from dummy—instead of the queen. But you should rise with the king for the same reasons.

#25

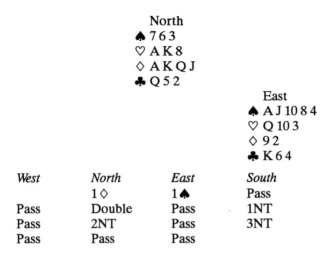

North
♠ 7 6 3
♡ A K 8
◇ A K Q J
♣ Q 5 2

East
♠ A J 10 8 4
♡ Q 10 3
◇ 9 2
♣ K 6 4

West	North	East	South
	1◇	1♠	Pass
Pass	Double	Pass	1NT
Pass	2NT	Pass	3NT
Pass	Pass	Pass	

Your partner leads the nine of spades, you play the ten and declarer wins with the king. A diamond is played over to the dummy and the queen of clubs is led. *Play a low club, do not cover the queen.* The normal play is to cover the queen with the king, but not this time. Declarer obviously has the king and queen of spades (your partner led the nine), so he cannot have the ace of clubs or he would not have passed over your one-spade bid. The reason you must not play your king of clubs is you will need it for an entry card after your spade suit is established. The four hands:

```
                    ♠ 7 6 3
                    ♡ A K 8
                    ◇ A K Q J
                    ♣ Q 5 2
♠ 9 2                                    ♠ A J 10 8 4
♡ J 9 7 5                                ♡ Q 10 3
◇ 10 7 6 4                               ◇ 9 2
♣ A 8 3                                  ♣ K 6 4
                    ♠ K Q 5
                    ♡ 6 4 2
                    ◇ 8 5 3
                    ♣ J 10 9 7
```

Your partner will capture the queen of clubs with his ace and lead another spade to drive out declarer's second stopper. Declarer can run only eight tricks, and if you do not discard any spades when he cashes his diamonds, you will beat the contract; it will be necessary to discard a heart.

It is interesting to note that if declarer led a club from his hand at trick two, your partner would have to go up with his ace and lead a spade to beat the contract.

#26   North
                                                       ♠ A 8
                                                       ♡ A 6
                                                       ◇ A K Q 10 7 3
                                                       ♣ Q 9 2
                                                                                    East
                                                                                    ♠ 7 5 4 3 2
                                                                                    ♡ Q 10
                                                                                    ◇ 9 8 6
                                                                                    ♣ K 7 4

West	North	East	South
	1◇	Pass	1NT
2♡	3NT	All Pass	

Your partner leads the eight of hearts and the trick is won with dummy's ace. You know by using the Rule of Eleven that declarer has no heart higher than the eight; if partner gets the lead, he can run the suit. At trick two declarer leads the queen of clubs. *Play a low club, do not cover the queen.* You can see eight tricks in dummy and the ace of clubs makes nine. Declarer knows your partner has all those good hearts and that he will be set in a cold contract if he takes the club finesse and your partner has the king. He has no intention of finessing. The four hands:

                                   ♠ A 8
                                   ♡ A 6
                                   ◇ A K Q 10 7 3
                                   ♣ Q 9 2
        ♠ K Q 6   ♠ 7 5 4 3 2
        ♡ K J 9 8 5 2   ♡ Q 10
        ◇ 5 4   ◇ 9 8 6
        ♣ 6 3   ♣ K 7 4
                                   ♠ J 10 9
                                   ♡ 7 4 3
                                   ◇ J 2
                                   ♣ A J 10 8 5

If declarer takes the club finesse and your partner has the king, the contract will be set two tricks. Declarer led the queen of clubs hoping you would cover if you had the king, so that he could win four overtricks. Granted declarer will make his contract even if you do not cover and he goes up with his ace, but you save all those overtricks.

Unblocking

It is sometimes necessary to get rid of a high card in your hand—play second hand high—so your partner can get the lead, or to avoid being endplayed. Here are four examples:

#27

	North
	♠ A Q 7 4
	♡ A 10 2
	◇ A Q 8 3
	♣ K 8

East
♠ J 9 6 2
♡ Q J 4
◇ K J 9 7
♣ Q 3

West	North	East	South
	1◇	Pass	1NT
Pass	3NT	All Pass	

Partner leads the seven of hearts and the first trick is won with your jack. You win the second trick with the queen of hearts, and lead the four of hearts; declarer discards a diamond and dummy wins with the ace. Partner is sitting with two good heart tricks, so you must do what you can to help him get the lead. At trick four, the king of clubs is led and you must unblock—*play your queen of clubs under the king*. The four hands:

	♠ A Q 7 4	
	♡ A 10 2	
	◇ A Q 8 3	
	♣ K 8	
♠ 10 5 3		♠ J 9 6 2
♡ K 9 8 7 5		♡ Q J 4
◇ 10 4		◇ K J 9 7
♣ J 10 2		♣ Q 3
	♠ K 8	
	♡ 6 3	
	◇ 6 5 2	
	♣ A 9 7 6 5 4	

Declarer has seven winners (three spades, one heart, one diamond and two clubs). He is hoping for a three-two club break so he can establish his long clubs, but he must give up a club trick along the way and will be set if your partner gets the lead. After cashing the king of clubs, he will lead a low club. If you do not play the queen under the king, he will duck the second trick and let you win with the queen. Since you have no more hearts, declarer will regain the lead and make his contract with an overtrick. If you do unblock the queen, his best play is the ace and another club, hoping you have the third club instead of your partner. Since partner has the third club, the contract will fail.

#28
                              North
                              ♠ A K Q J
                              ♡ 6 5
                              ◇ Q 10 7 6 2
                              ♣ A J

           West
           ♠ 10 6 5 3
           ♡ A Q 8 4 2
           ◇ K 3
           ♣ 8 7

West	North	East	South
	1 ◇	Pass	1NT
Pass	2NT	Pass	3NT
Pass	Pass	Pass	

You lead the four of hearts, partner plays the ten and declarer wins with the jack. At trick two, declarer cashes the ace of diamonds. You must unblock: *play the king of diamonds under the ace*. If declarer can establish the diamond suit, he will have more than enough tricks to make his contract. The only chance to beat the contract is for partner to get in with the jack of diamonds and play a heart through declarer's king.

Note what you have learned about declarer's hand: His remaining hearts are specifically the king and nine because partner would not have played the ten with either of those cards; and declarer would have bid one heart over one diamond with a four-card heart suit. He does not have the jack of diamonds because he would have taken a diamond finesse if he had that card. He does not have the king of clubs—in which case he can win nine tricks no matter what you do—because with it his hand would be too strong to respond one notrump. The four hands:

                              ♠ A K Q J
                              ♡ 6 5
                              ◇ Q 10 7 6 2
                              ♣ A J

           ♠ 10 6 5 3   ♠ 9 2
           ♡ A Q 8 4 2   ♡ 10 7 3
           ◇ K 3   ◇ J 9 8
           ♣ 8 7   ♣ K Q 10 6 4

                              ♠ 8 7 4
                              ♡ K J 9
                              ◇ A 5 4
                              ♣ 9 5 3 2

If you do not unblock by playing your king of diamonds under the ace, you will win the second diamond trick with your king. Since you cannot run the heart suit, declarer will make an overtrick. If you do play the king of diamonds under the ace, the declarer must give your partner the lead with the jack of diamonds before he can establish the suit. Partner will return a heart, allowing you to run four heart tricks and beat the contract.

True, declarer can make his contract if his first diamond play is a low one from his hand. *C'est la vie*.

#29

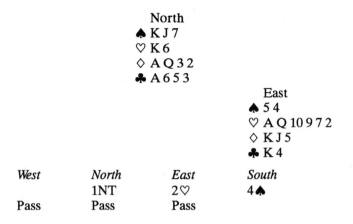

North
♠ K J 7
♡ K 6
◇ A Q 3 2
♣ A 6 5 3

East
♠ 5 4
♡ A Q 10 9 7 2
◇ K J 5
♣ K 4

West	North	East	South
	1NT	2♡	4♠
Pass	Pass	Pass	

Your partner leads the three of hearts. After the king is played from dummy, you win with the ace and lead the queen of hearts, which declarer ruffs. Declarer cashes the ace of spades and plays a spade to dummy's king; partner follows to the ace, then discards a heart. At trick five, declarer plays dummy's ace of clubs; you must unblock—*play the king*—to avoid an endplay. If you save the king, declarer will put you on lead with a club. The four hands:

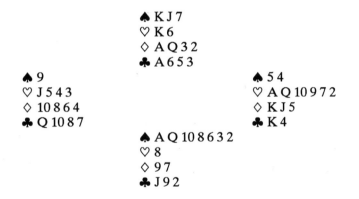

♠ K J 7
♡ K 6
◇ A Q 3 2
♣ A 6 5 3

♠ 9
♡ J 5 4 3
◇ 10 8 6 4
♣ Q 10 8 7

♠ 5 4
♡ A Q 10 9 7 2
◇ K J 5
♣ K 4

♠ A Q 10 8 6 3 2
♡ 8
◇ 9 7
♣ J 9 2

If you play the king of clubs under the ace, your partner can win two club tricks whenever that suit is led again, and you will eventually get a diamond trick to set the hand. But if you do not unblock, you will be thrown in the lead with the king of clubs and will have either to give declarer a ruff-and-discard or to lead a diamond into the ace-queen; either way, declarer makes his contract.

#30

North
♠ 7 5 3
♡ Q 9 4 3
◇ K 8 2
♣ A 6 2

West
♠ A Q 10 8 2
♡ 6 5
◇ Q 10 7
♣ J 10 9

West	North	East	South
			1♡
1♠	2♡	Pass	4♡
Pass	Pass	Pass	

You lead the jack of clubs and declarer wins in his hand with the king. At trick two, he cashes the ace of diamonds, then leads the six of diamonds. You must play *the queen of diamonds*; again, there is a danger of being endplayed. Your partner figures to have the jack of diamonds because declarer is unlikely to play the suit this way if he had it. The four hands:

```
                    ♠ 7 5 3
                    ♡ Q 9 4 3
                    ◇ K 8 2
                    ♣ A 6 2
♠ A Q 10 8 2                          ♠ J 6
♡ 6 5                                 ♡ 10 7
◇ Q 10 7                              ◇ J 5 4 3
♣ J 10 9                             ♣ Q 8 5 4 3
                    ♠ K 9 4
                    ♡ A K J 8 2
                    ◇ A 9 6
                    ♣ K 7
```

Declarer's plan is to win the third trick with the king of diamonds, draw trumps, cash the ace of clubs, ruff a club in his hand and lead his losing diamond. It is his hope that you will have to win the trick and lead a spade up to his king. This would happen if you still had the queen of diamonds in your hand. But if you unblock, partner will win the third diamond trick with the jack and lead the jack of spades; this sets the contract as declarer must lose three spade tricks.

Quiz for Chapter Five

What is your second-hand play on each of the following hands?

1.
	North		
	♠ 10 9 8 7		
	♡ 9 7		
	◊ A Q J 10		
	♣ K 6 4		

		East	
		♠ A 6 4	
		♡ J 10 2	
		◊ 8 5 3	
		♣ J 8 5 2	

West	North	East	South
			1NT
Pass	2♣	Pass	2◊
Pass	3NT	All Pass	

Your partner leads the six of hearts and declarer captures your ten with the king. He plays a diamond over to dummy's ten, and leads the ten of spades.

2.
	North		
	♠ 8 7 4		
	♡ Q 7 6		
	◊ 7 3		
	♣ K 10 9 7 2		

West			
♠ 10 6 5 3			
♡ 9 8			
◊ A Q 9 4 2			
♣ Q 3			

West	North	East	South
			2NT
Pass	3NT	All Pass	

You lead the four of diamonds, partner plays the five and declarer wins with the jack. Now he leads the ace of clubs.

3.
	North		
	♠ J 8 6 5 4		
	♡ A 7		
	◊ 2		
	♣ Q 8 6 5 2		

		East	
		♠ Q 10 9 2	
		♡ 10 3	
		◊ A 8 6 4 3	
		♣ K 10	

West	North	East	South
			1♡
Pass	1♠	Pass	2◊
Pass	2♡	All Pass	

Your partner leads the two of hearts. Declarer wins in dummy with the ace and calls for the two of diamonds.

4.
	North		
	♠ J 9 7 6		
	♡ A 2		
	◊ A 7 6		
	♣ A 8 6 5		

		East	
		♠ Q 10 5	
		♡ J 4	
		◊ Q 10 9 4 2	
		♣ 10 9 7	

West	North	East	South
			1♠
Pass	3♠	Pass	4NT
Pass	5♠	Pass	7♠
Pass	Pass	Pass	

Your partner leads the king of clubs. Declarer wins in dummy with the ace and calls for the jack of spades.

5.   North
            ♠ 8 5 2
            ♡ Q 9
            ◊ A Q 10 9 6 2
            ♣ 4 3
West
♠ 6 4 3
♡ 10 8 7 6 2
◊ K 5
♣ K J 7

West	North	East	South
			1♣
Pass	1◊	Pass	2NT
Pass	3NT	All Pass	

You lead the six of hearts: queen, king, three. Partner wins the second trick with the jack of hearts. Declarer wins the third trick with the ace of hearts; dummy discards a spade. Now declarer leads the four of diamonds.

6.   North
            ♠ 8 5 2
            ♡ J 9 3
            ◊ A K
            ♣ A K Q J 5
West
♠ 7 4
♡ A 10 6 2
◊ 5 4 3 2
♣ 10 9 8

West	North	East	South
	1♣	1♠	1NT
Pass	3NT	All Pass	

You lead the seven of spades, partner plays the nine and declarer wins with the queen. At trick two, he leads the five of hearts.

7.   North
            ♠ A 5
            ♡ 10 8 7
            ◊ A 9 6 3 2
            ♣ 7 5 4
                         East
                         ♠ 3
                         ♡ J 9 6
                         ◊ K Q J 10 4
                         ♣ A K J 8

West	North	East	South
			1◊
Pass	1NT	2♣	4♡
5♣	Double	Pass	5♡
Pass	Pass	Pass	

Your partner leads the three of clubs. You win with the king and play the ace of clubs, but declarer ruffs. He leads a spade to the ace, and calls for the five of spades.

8.   North
            ♠ 9 6 5 2
            ♡ A K
            ◊ K Q 8 4 3
            ♣ J 5
                         East
                         ♠ Q J 10 3
                         ♡ J 4 3 2
                         ◊ 10 7 6
                         ♣ 9 8

West	North	East	South
			1♣
Pass	1◊	Pass	1♠
Pass	3♠	Pass	4♠
Pass	Pass	Pass	

Your partner leads the ten of hearts. At trick two, declarer plays the nine of spades from dummy.

Quiz Answers for Chapter Five

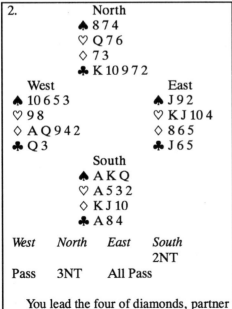

1.

	North		
	♠ 10 9 8 7		
	♡ 9 7		
	◇ A Q J 10		
	♣ K 6 4		

West		East
♠ 5 3 2		♠ A 6 4
♡ A Q 8 6 4		♡ J 10 2
◇ 6 4		◇ 8 5 3
♣ 9 7 3		♣ J 8 5 2

	South		
	♠ K Q J		
	♡ K 5 3		
	◇ K 9 7 2		
	♣ A Q 10		

West	North	East	South
			1NT
Pass	2♣	Pass	2◇
Pass	3NT	All Pass	

Your partner leads the six of hearts and declarer captures your ten with the king. He plays a diamond over to dummy's ten, and leads the ten of spades.

Go up with the ace of spades and lead the jack of hearts. If you did your detective work, you should have figured out that partner has ♡ A Q 8 x left: Partner led his fourth-highest heart, so by using the Rule of Eleven you know that declarer's king was the only heart he had higher than the six; and declarer denied a four-card major in the bidding, so partner must have at least a five-card heart suit.

Declarer's play was deceptive and probably the best chance to make his contract. He was hoping you had the ace of spades and did not play it, in which case he would run nine tricks.

2.

	North		
	♠ 8 7 4		
	♡ Q 7 6		
	◇ 7 3		
	♣ K 10 9 7 2		

West		East
♠ 10 6 5 3		♠ J 9 2
♡ 9 8		♡ K J 10 4
◇ A Q 9 4 2		◇ 8 6 5
♣ Q 3		♣ J 6 5

	South		
	♠ A K Q		
	♡ A 5 3 2		
	◇ K J 10		
	♣ A 8 4		

West	North	East	South
			2NT
Pass	3NT	All Pass	

You lead the four of diamonds, partner plays the five and declarer wins with the jack. Now he leads the ace of clubs.

Play the queen of clubs. The play to the first trick marks declarer with the king and ten of diamonds, so the next diamond lead must come from your partner. Your queen of clubs is a useless card whether declarer has the jack or not, but if you play the queen under the ace and partner has ♣ J x x, he will get the lead to play a diamond through declarer. With the cards as shown, this beats the contract.

If you do not unblock, declarer will lead a second round of clubs and duck—allowing you to win the trick with your queen. Since your partner cannot get the lead to play a diamond through declarer's king, you can no longer defeat the contract.

```
3.                    North
                      ♠ J 8 6 5 4
                      ♡ A 7
                      ◇ 2
                      ♣ Q 8 6 5 2
      West                              East
      ♠ K 7                            ♠ Q 10 9 2
      ♡ 8 6 5 2                        ♡ 10 3
      ◇ K 9 7                          ◇ A 8 6 4 3
      ♣ A J 9 4                        ♣ K 10
                      South
                      ♠ A 3
                      ♡ K Q J 9 4
                      ◇ Q J 10 5
                      ♣ 7 3

     West     North     East     South
                                  1♡
     Pass     1♠        Pass     2◇
     Pass     2♡        All Pass
```

Your partner leads the two of hearts. Declarer wins in dummy with the ace and calls for the two of diamonds.

Play a low diamond; declarer bid the suit, so you will not lose your ace. Note that if you go up with the ace of diamonds, declarer can win eight tricks no matter how you defend; he has five hearts, one spade and can develop two diamond tricks with his ◇ Q J 10.

If you correctly play a low diamond at trick two, partner will capture declarer's queen with the king and lead a second heart. Since declarer is left with ◇ J 10 5, he must now lose two more diamond tricks and will be set.

```
4.                    North
                      ♠ J 9 7 6
                      ♡ A 2
                      ◇ A 7 6
                      ♣ A 8 6 5
      West                              East
      ♠ —                              ♠ Q 10 5
      ♡ 10 9 8 7 5                     ♡ J 4
      ◇ J 5 3                          ◇ Q 10 9 4 2
      ♣ K Q J 4 3                      ♣ 10 9 7
                      South
                      ♠ A K 8 4 3 2
                      ♡ K Q 6 3
                      ◇ K 8
                      ♣ 2

     West     North     East     South
                                  1♠
     Pass     3♠        Pass     4NT
     Pass     5♠        Pass     7♠
     All Pass
```

Your partner leads the king of clubs. Declarer wins in dummy with the ace and calls for the jack of spades.

Play the five of spades. Partner is known to have a maximum of one spade, so there is no holding he can have where you would gain by covering the jack with the queen. But declarer has six spades and the odds are overwhelmingly in favor of three missing cards dividing two-one; he has no intention of finessing if you do not cover the jack with the queen. He is just giving himself an extra chance that you may have ♠ Q 10 x and cover, which would be quite a costly mistake; when partner shows out he would have a marked finesse against your ten and make his grand slam.

```
5.                North
              ♠ 8 5 2
              ♡ Q 9
              ◇ A Q 10 9 6 2
              ♣ 4 3
    West                      East
  ♠ 6 4 3                   ♠ J 10 9 7
  ♡ 10 8 7 6 2              ♡ K J 5
  ◇ K 5                     ◇ J 8 3
  ♣ K J 7                   ♣ 10 9 6
                  South
              ♠ A K Q
              ♡ A 4 3
              ◇ 7 4
              ♣ A Q 8 5 2
```

West	North	East	South
			1♣
Pass	1◇	Pass	2NT
Pass	3NT	All Pass	

You lead the six of hearts: queen, king, three. Partner wins the second trick with the jace of hearts. Declarer wins the third trick with the ace of hearts; dummy discards a spade. At trick four, declarer leads the four of diamonds.

Play the king of diamonds; second hand high to prevent declarer from conceding this trick to your partner. The only realistic chance to beat the contract is if partner has ◇ J x x. If you play the king and declarer ducks, you can cash two more heart tricks; if he covers the king with the ace, he cannot win more than two diamond tricks. In either case he is set.

If you play the five of diamonds when declarer leads the suit, he will finesse the ten. Partner can take the jack, but there is no longer a way to prevent declarer from winning five diamond tricks.

```
6.                North
              ♠ 8 5 2
              ♡ J 9 3
              ◇ A K
              ♣ A K Q J 5
    West                      East
  ♠ 7 4                     ♠ A K J 10 9
  ♡ A 10 6 2                ♡ 8 7 4
  ◇ 5 4 3 2                 ◇ Q 10 6
  ♣ 10 9 8                  ♣ 7 3
                  South
              ♠ Q 6 3
              ♡ K Q 5
              ◇ J 9 8 7
              ♣ 6 4 2
```

West	North	East	South
	1♣	1♠	1NT
Pass	3NT	All Pass	

You lead the seven of spades, partner plays the nine and declarer wins with the queen. At trick two, he leads the five of hearts.

Go up with the ace of hearts and lead a spade. You can see seven tricks in dummy and declarer won the first spade trick. If he has a second spade stopper, you cannot beat him. So the only hope is that partner can run four spade tricks. Declarer is making a sneaky play to steal a heart trick; if you do not take the ace, he will win with dummy's jack of hearts and grab his nine tricks.

Note that your partner made a good play in allowing declarer to win the first spade trick. He could see that the only chance to beat the contract was for you to have the ace of hearts and a doubleton spade.

7.   North
           ♠ A 5
           ♡ 10 8 7
           ◇ A 9 6 3 2
           ♣ 7 5 4

West   East
♠ Q 10 9 2   ♠ 3
♡ 4   ♡ J 9 6
◇ 8 7 5   ◇ K Q J 10 4
♣ Q 10 6 3 2   ♣ A K J 8

            South
           ♠ K J 8 7 6 4
           ♡ A K Q 5 3 2
           ◇ —
           ♣ 9

West	North	East	South
		1◇	1♠
Pass	1NT	2♣	4♡
5♣	Double	Pass	5♡
Pass	Pass	Pass	

Your partner leads the three of clubs. You win with the king and play the ace of clubs, but declarer ruffs. He leads a spade to the ace, and calls for the five of spades.

Do not ruff the five of spades. Declarer obviously has losing spades in his hand, or he would have drawn trumps before leading the suit. Since your hearts are higher than dummy's, he will never be able to ruff his spade losers. If you do not ruff, he will win the second spade trick with his king, but must lose two spade tricks either by your overruffing dummy, or by drawing trumps and giving your partner two natural trick with his queen-ten.

Note that if you ruff the five of spades, declarer will play a low spade from his hand—you will have ruffed a loser. The dummy now has one more trump than you, so declarer can establish his spade suit by drawing two rounds of trumps and ruffing one spade in dummy.

It was clever of partner to lead a club, instead of a diamond.

8.   North
           ♠ 9 6 5 2
           ♡ A K
           ◇ K Q 8 4 3
           ♣ J 5

West   East
♠ K   ♠ Q J 10 3
♡ 10 9 8 6   ♡ J 4 3 2
◇ A J 5 2   ◇ 10 7 6
♣ 7 6 4 2   ♣ 9 8

            South
           ♠ A 8 7 4
           ♡ Q 7 5
           ◇ 9
           ♣ A K Q 10 3

West	North	East	South
			1♣
Pass	1◇	Pass	1♠
Pass	3♠	Pass	4♠
All Pass			

Your partner leads the ten of hearts. At trick two, declarer plays the nine of spades from dummy.

Play the three of spades. If declarer has the ace and king of spades, he can finesse and win a trick with the nine. But that is not his best line of play: Your partner is more apt to have a singleton queen, jack or ten than the one missing spot card. Therefore, with ♠ A K x x, declarer should go up with his ace and, if your partner has the singleton queen, jack or ten, he can limit you to one spade trick.

It turns out that partner's singleton is the king, so splitting your honors is a disaster; declarer can maneuver to lose only two spade tricks and make his contract.

Note that if declarer leads the nine of diamonds, your partner should rise with the ace because it is apparent that declarer will not benefit from discards on the diamond suit.

6
Attitude Signals

The only signal that is used by almost all bridge players is the "attitude signal," commonly called the "come-on signal." Attitude signals apply when following to a suit led by your partner (you are third hand), and when discarding no matter who leads. They do not apply when following to a suit led by the declarer.

The attitude signal works like this: You play high-low to encourage your partner to lead a suit, and a low-high to express no interest in having the suit led. But as a rule your partner will have to make a decision whether your signal is encouraging or discouraging after seeing you play only *one card*: If the card you play is surely your lowest, it is definitely not encouraging the continuation of the suit. If there is one lower card missing, it may be encouraging; your partner must judge whether you or declarer has the lower card. If two lower cards are missing, it is highly probable that you have at least one of the lower cards and are encouraging the continuation of the suit.

Also note that there is no arbitrary rank that determines whether a card is high or low. An eight-spot is a discouraging signal if you can see all of the lower cards, and a three-spot can be an encouraging signal if the two-spot is missing; *you must study the lower cards around the table to decide*.

The requirements for signals at notrump contracts are somewhat different from the requirements at trump contracts, so they will be treated separately.

Attitude Signals at Notrump Contracts

#1

North
♠ A Q J
♡ 3 2
◇ K Q J 8 4
♣ 6 3 2

East
♠ 10 7 6 4 2
♡ 9 8 7
◇ 5
♣ A 10 9 5

West	North	East	South
			1 ◇
1 ♡	3 ◇	Pass	3NT
Pass	Pass	Pass	

Your partner leads the king of hearts. You should give him an encouraging signal if you have three or more cards headed by the ace, queen or jack. Since you do not in this deal, you should play your lowest card—*the seven of hearts*—to indicate that you have no help for him in the suit. Suppose declarer plays the four of hearts on the first trick and these are the four hands:

```
                        ♠ A Q J
                        ♡ 3 2
                        ◇ K Q J 8 4
                        ♣ 6 3 2
        ♠ 9 5 3                           ♠ 10 7 6 4 2
        ♡ K Q 10 6 5                      ♡ 9 8 7
        ◇ A 6                             ◇ 5
        ♣ 8 7 4                           ♣ A 10 9 5
                        ♠ K 8
                        ♡ A J 4
                        ◇ 10 9 7 3 2
                        ♣ K Q J
```

Your partner can see the two, three, four, five and six of hearts, so he knows the seven is your lowest heart and therefore declarer has the ace and jack. Since leading another heart into the ace-jack would be fatal, he switches to the eight of clubs. Luckily you have the ace of clubs and can return a heart through declarer's ace-jack. The heart suit is now established and your partner can beat the contract by running the rest of his hearts when he regains the lead with the ace of diamonds.

If you had ♡ J 9 7, your first play should be the nine to encourage partner to continue leading the suit; with the ♡ 9 8, you should play the eight to discourage him; with ♡ J x you should play the jack (see deal #15 on page 56).

#2   North
                                        ♠ K 8 4 3
                                        ♡ A 7 2
                                        ◇ J 10 6 3
                                        ♣ A J
                                                    East
                                                    ♠ Q J 10 9
                                                    ♡ 5 4
                                                    ◇ 8 5 2
                                                    ♣ Q 10 6 4

West	North	East	South
	1◇	Pass	2NT
Pass	3NT	All Pass	

Your partner leads the queen of hearts and the ace is played from dummy. You should *play the four* (your lowest card) on the first trick to warn partner not to lead the suit again unless he has Q J 10. The four hands:

```
                        ♠ K 8 4 3
                        ♡ A 7 2
                        ◇ J 10 6 3
                        ♣ A J
     ♠ 7 6                              ♠ Q J 10 9
     ♡ Q J 9 8 3                        ♡ 5 4
     ◇ A Q                              ◇ 8 5 2
     ♣ 9 8 5 2                          ♣ Q 10 6 4
                        ♠ A 5 2
                        ♡ K 10 6
                        ◇ K 9 7 4
                        ♣ K 7 3
```

Declarer can establish two diamond tricks to add to his six winners in the other suits, but he cannot get a ninth trick unless the defense slips. Suppose declarer takes a diamond finesse at trick two. When partner wins with his queen of diamonds he should be aware that the four was your lowest heart and shift to a club (best); he should *not lead another heart*.

Note that if you had ♡ 10 x, you should play the ten on the first trick (see deal #16 on page 57).

#3

```
                               North
                               ♠ J 5 4 2
                               ♡ K 10 6
                               ◇ J 8 7 3
                               ♣ Q 8
                                            East
                                            ♠ Q 10 8 7
                                            ♡ Q 9 8 3
                                            ◇ 6 4
                                            ♣ J 10 2
```

West	North	East	South
			1◇
Pass	1♠	Pass	2NT
Pass	3NT	All Pass	

Partner leads the four of clubs (apparently his fourth-highest) and the queen is played from dummy. You should signal by *playing the jack*. Partner knows you would play the ace or king if you had either card, so the jack shows that you have the ten. Here are the four hands so you can see how this signal helps your partner:

```
                          ♠ J 5 4 2
                          ♡ K 10 6
                          ◇ J 8 7 3
                          ♣ Q 8
        ♠ 9 6 3                              ♠ Q 10 8 7
        ♡ 7 5 2                              ♡ Q 9 8 3
        ◇ A Q                                ◇ 6 4
        ♣ K 9 6 4 3                          ♣ J 10 2
                          ♠ A K
                          ♡ A J 4
                          ◇ K 10 9 5 2
                          ♣ A 7 5
```

Declarer needs to establish diamonds to make his bid, so he will finesse for the queen of diamonds at trick two. Your partner will win with the queen and lead a low club to your ten; if declarer ducks, you will lead another club to drive out the ace. When partner regains the lead with the ace of diamonds, he has enough club tricks to set the contract.

If you held J 7 2, you could show the jack by signaling with the seven. Without the jack—from holdings such as 10 5 2, 7 5 2 or 7 2—you would of course play the two and warn partner not to lead another club from an unsafe holding.

#4   North
                                          ♠ J 5 4 2
                                          ♡ K Q 10
                                          ◇ J 8 7 3
                                          ♣ Q 7
                                                            East
                                                            ♠ Q 10 8 7
                                                            ♡ 9 8 6 3
                                                            ◇ 6 4 2
                                                            ♣ J 2

West	North	East	South
			1◇
Pass	1♠	Pass	2NT
Pass	3NT	All Pass	

This time, your partner leads the ten of clubs and the queen is played from dummy. You should *play the jack*. If partner is leading from a holding headed by the 10 9 8, it will not cost a trick to play the jack; and it will be very helpful if he is leading from K 10 9 8. Suppose these are the four hands:

```
                        ♠ J 5 4 2
                        ♡ K Q 10
                        ◇ J 8 7 3
                        ♣ Q 7
        ♠ 9 6 3                           ♠ Q 10 8 7
        ♡ 7 5 2                           ♡ 9 8 6 3
        ◇ A Q                             ◇ 6 4 2
        ♣ K 10 9 8 4                      ♣ J 2
                        ♠ A K
                        ♡ A J 4
                        ◇ K 10 9 5
                        ♣ A 6 5 3
```

If you played the jack of clubs on the first trick, partner can see that his ♣ K 9 8 are now equal cards. When he wins his first diamond trick, he will lead clubs until the ace is driven out. Once again, he will have enough club tricks to beat the contract when he regains the lead with his second high diamond. If you played the two of clubs on the first trick, he should assume that declarer has ♣ A J and not lead another club; in which case declarer would make his contract.

The play of the jack of clubs is not absolutely safe. If partner has ♣ K 10 9 5 4 and declarer ♣ A 8 6 3, partner could not continue clubs without losing a trick; but in that event you could not beat the contract if you played the two of clubs. The only successful defense is for partner to lead fourth-highest originally; this is not considered standard, but it is something good players sometimes do when lacking solidity in the suit.

#5
```
                              North
                              ♠ J 5 4 2
                              ♡ K 10 6
                              ◇ J 8 7 3
                              ♣ Q J
                                           East
                                           ♠ Q 10 8 7
                                           ♡ Q 9 8 3
                                           ◇ 6 4
                                           ♣ 10 9 2
```

West	North	East	South
			1◇
Pass	1♠	Pass	2NT
Pass	3NT	All Pass	

Partner leads the six of clubs. You should *play the ten* under dummy's jack to show that you have the nine. Using the Rule of Eleven, there are five cards higher than the six held between you, dummy and declarer. Since you can see four of the five higher cards, declarer has one; probably the ace or king. Once again, declarer takes a diamond finesse, your partner wins with the queen and leads the king of clubs. It is now reasonably clear that partner's club holding is K 8 7 6, or K 8 7 6 x, so you should *unblock by playing the nine*. The four hands:

```
                              ♠ J 5 4 2
                              ♡ K 10 6
                              ◇ J 8 7 3
                              ♣ Q J
        ♠ 9 6 3                                      ♠ Q 10 8 7
        ♡ 7 5 2                                      ♡ Q 9 8 3
        ◇ A Q                                        ◇ 6 4
        ♣ K 8 7 6 4                                  ♣ 10 9 2
                              ♠ A K
                              ♡ A J 4
                              ◇ K 10 9 5 2
                              ♣ A 5 3
```

If you do not play the ten of clubs on the first trick, partner may reason that declarer has ♣ A 10 x and not lead a second club; then the contract can no longer be set.

Also note that if you do not unblock when partner leads the king of clubs, partner will have ♣ 8 7 4 left and you will have the ♣ 9. If declarer takes his ace immediately and leads a diamond, the club suit will be blocked.

#6   North
                                      ♠ Q 5 4
                                      ♡ K 7 5
                                      ◇ Q 8 3 2
                                      ♣ K 6 4
                                                     East
                                                     ♠ A K J 10
                                                     ♡ 10 6 4 2
                                                     ◇ —
                                                     ♣ 9 7 5 3 2

West	North	East	South
			1NT
Pass	3NT	All Pass	

In this deal, you will signal to your partner when discarding. Not unexpectedly, partner leads the six of diamonds. You are aching for a spade lead, but cannot afford to waste one of your high spades; if partner gets the lead and plays a spade, you will need four spade tricks to set the contract. But there is another way to indicate that you want a spade led (besides talking about shoveling in the garden): *Instead of playing a high card in the suit you want led, play low cards in the two suits you do not want led.* Suppose you discard the two of clubs and these are the four hands:

<pre>
                      ♠ Q 5 4
                      ♡ K 7 5
                      ◊ Q 8 3 2
                      ♣ K 6 4
      ♠ 8 3 2   ♠ A K J 10
      ♡ 9 3   ♡ 10 6 4 2
      ◊ A 10 7 6 4   ◊ —
      ♣ J 10 8   ♣ 9 7 5 3 2
                      ♠ 9 7 6
                      ♡ A Q J 8
                      ◊ K J 9 5
                      ♣ A Q
</pre>

Declarer has eight tricks (four hearts, three clubs and one diamond). Seeking a second diamond trick to make his contract, he leads the suit at trick two, your partner wins with the ace, and you *discard the two of hearts.* You have told your partner you are not interested in clubs or hearts, so it should be automatic for him to lead a spade. You take your four spade tricks and beat the contract one trick. Be sure to see that you could not set the contract if you discarded a spade at either opportunity.

#7

<pre>
                              North
                              ♠ Q J 10 6 5
                              ♡ Q 10 7
                              ◊ A K Q
                              ♣ A 8
                                        East
                                        ♠ 8 4 3
                                        ♡ A J 9 2
                                        ◊ J 8 6 5
                                        ♣ 7 2
</pre>

West	North	East	South
	1♠	Pass	1NT
Pass	3NT	All Pass	

Partner leads the queen of clubs, the ace is played from dummy and you drop the two. The five of spades is led to declarer's king and partner's ace. Partner now leads the king of hearts and you must *play the two*; if you signal with the nine and partner has a doubleton heart, you can win only three heart tricks. Once again, do not signal with a card that may be the setting trick. The four hands:

♠ Q J 10 6 5
♡ Q 10 7
◇ A K Q
♣ A 8

♠ A 9 2   ♠ 8 4 3
♡ K 5   ♡ A J 9 2
◇ 7 4 3   ◇ J 8 6 5
♣ Q J 10 9 3   ♣ 7 2

♠ K 7
♡ 8 6 4 3
◇ 10 9 2
♣ K 6 5 4

Your partner knows declarer has the king of clubs (you played the two) and can see that nine tricks are available if declarer regains the lead. Since the only chance to beat the contract is to win four heart tricks, he makes a good play by leading the king of hearts. When your partner wins the trick with the king of hearts, he will realize that you have the ace and probably played the two because you could not spare a higher card to signal; he will continue the suit to the dismay of the declarer.

#8   North
                                          ♠ A 2
                                          ♡ A Q
                                          ◇ K Q J 10 8 5
                                          ♣ 9 6 3

                  West
                  ♠ J 9 7 6 3
                  ♡ 4 2
                  ◇ 7 4
                  ♣ A Q 10 5

West	North	East	South
	1 ◇	Pass	1NT
Pass	3 ◇	Pass	3NT
Pass	Pass	Pass	

You lead the six of spades. Partner wins the first trick with the king and returns the ten of spades, declarer following suit with the five and eight. It is obvious that declarer has the queen of spades. To have any chance to beat this contract, partner must have the ace of diamonds and he must switch to a club when he gets the lead. Now let's get back to trick two where partner led the ten of spades: You should *play the jack of spades*, which informs your partner that you do not have the queen. The four hands:

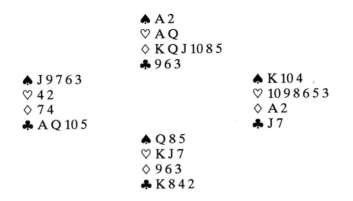

                    ♠ A 2
                    ♡ A Q
                    ◇ K Q J 10 8 5
                    ♣ 9 6 3
    ♠ J 9 7 6 3   ♠ K 10 4
    ♡ 4 2   ♡ 10 9 8 6 5 3
    ◇ 7 4   ◇ A 2
    ♣ A Q 10 5   ♣ J 7
                    ♠ Q 8 5
                    ♡ K J 7
                    ◇ 9 6 3
                    ♣ K 8 4 2

Suppose declarer leads the king of diamonds at trick three, which wins the trick, and your partner wins the next diamond with the ace. It is obvious to partner that the only chance to beat the contract is to win the next three tricks. Since your play of the jack of spades told him you do not have the queen, he should shift to the jack of clubs as the only hope. You cannot be prevented from winning three club tricks and the contract is set. The next deal is similar to the last, but the discouraging signal is given by a discard.

#9   North
                                    ♠ 7 2
                                    ♡ 8 7 5
                                    ◇ A K J 10 4 3
                                    ♣ A K
        West
        ♠ J 10 6 5 4
        ♡ A Q J 2
        ◇ 7
        ♣ 8 5 3

West	*North*	*East*	*South*
	1 ◇	Pass	1NT
Pass	3 ◇	Pass	3NT
Pass	Pass	Pass	

You lead the five of spades, partner plays the king and declarer wins with the ace. Your partner would not play the king of spades if he had the queen, so declarer has her majesty. The only chance to beat the contract is if partner has a diamond stopper and he can be persuaded to switch to a heart when he gets the lead. But your partner does not know that declarer has the queen of spades, so he will return a spade when he gets the lead with the queen of diamonds unless you tell him not to. At tricks two and three, declarer cashes the ace and king of diamonds—partner and declarer both follow suit—and you have a chance to give your partner a signal: *Discard the jack of spades; although any spade discard should discourage partner from leading the suit.* If you had four good spade tricks, you certainly would not throw one of them away. When the third round of diamonds is led and partner wins with the queen, you can throw another spade to make sure partner gets the message that you do not want him to lead a spade. The four hands:

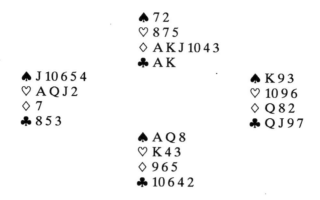

After your spade discards, partner knows as well as you that declarer has the queen of spades and that nine tricks are available once he regains the lead. The only hope to beat the contract is to win the next four heart tricks, so he should lead the ten of hearts.

Attitude Signals at Trump Contracts

At notrump contracts, signals to encourage your partner to lead a suit—come-on signals—are given when you have high-card strength. At trump contracts, you often do the same, but it is sometimes right to give an encouraging signal with a doubleton or with a worthless three-card or longer suit; and it is sometimes right to give a discouraging signal with strength. In other words: *An attitude signal is meant to inform your partner whether or not you think he should lead the suit; it does not necessarily describe your strength in the suit.*

The first deal shows two come-on signals: The first when following suit and the second by a discard.

#10
```
                          North
                          ♠ J 9 2
                          ♡ J 10 6
                          ◇ Q J 10 3
                          ♣ K 7 4
                                              East
                                              ♠ 7 4 3
                                              ♡ 7 2
                                              ◇ A 9 6
                                              ♣ 10 9 8 5 2
```

West	North	East	South
			1♠
2♡	2♠	All Pass	

Your partner leads the king of hearts and you *play the seven* to encourage him to continue leading the suit because you hope to ruff the third round. But partner wins the next two tricks with the ace and queen of hearts. Since there is no need to ruff the third heart lead, you should *discard the nine of diamonds* to encourage partner to lead that suit. The four hands:

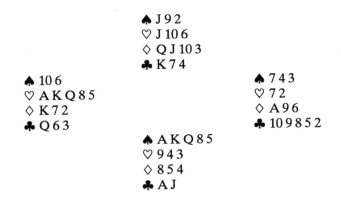

♠ J 9 2
♥ J 10 6
♦ Q J 10 3
♣ K 7 4

♠ 10 6
♥ A K Q 8 5
♦ K 7 2
♣ Q 6 3

♠ 7 4 3
♥ 7 2
♦ A 9 6
♣ 10 9 8 5 2

♠ A K Q 8 5
♥ 9 4 3
♦ 8 5 4
♣ A J

At trick four, partner leads a diamond—something he would be unlikely to do without your signal—and he chooses the *two of diamonds* to indicate that he has the king (low from strength). The rest is easy. You win with the ace of diamonds and return a diamond. Partner wins with the king and leads a third diamond to give you a ruff.

#11

North
♠ J 10 7 3
♥ 6 2
♦ A Q J 10
♣ K J 4

East
♠ Q 5
♥ 9 8
♦ K 7 4
♣ Q 10 8 6 3 2

West	North	East	South
			1♠
2♥	3♠	Pass	4♠
Pass	Pass	Pass	

Partner leads the king of hearts and then the ace of hearts. You should *play high-low—first the nine, then the eight*—because you want him to continue leading the suit so you can score a trick by overruffing dummy with the queen of spades. The four hands:

♠ J 10 7 3
♥ 6 2
♦ A Q J 10
♣ K J 4

♠ 8 2
♥ A K J 10 7 4
♦ 9 6 5 3
♣ 5

♠ Q 5
♥ 9 8
♦ K 7 4
♣ Q 10 8 6 3 2

♠ A K 9 6 4
♥ Q 5 3
♦ 8 2
♣ A 9 7

Declarer ruffs your partner's third heart lead in dummy with the jack and you overruff with the queen. Declarer must still lose a diamond trick, so the contract is set one trick.

#12   North
                                             ♠ 10 9 6 3
                                             ♡ 5 4
                                             ◇ A J
                                             ♣ 9 8 5 3 2
                                                                    East
                                                                    ♠ 7 4
                                                                    ♡ Q 9 2
                                                                    ◇ Q 10 8 7 3 2
                                                                    ♣ 7 6

West	North	East	South
			1♠
2♡	2♠	Pass	4♠
Pass	Pass	Pass	

Your partner leads the king of hearts, but this time you *should not play high-low*. If you play the nine followed by the two, he may lead a third heart, expecting you to have a doubleton and the ability to overruff the dummy, as you did in the last deal. With the cards as follows, leading a third round of hearts is a disaster.

                                             ♠ 10 9 6 3
                                             ♡ 5 4
                                             ◇ A J
                                             ♣ 9 8 5 3 2
      ♠ 8 5   ♠ 7 4
      ♡ A K 10 8 7 6   ♡ Q 9 2
      ◇ 9 4   ◇ Q 10 8 7 3 2
      ♣ K Q 10   ♣ 7 6
                                             ♠ A K Q J 2
                                             ♡ J 3
                                             ◇ K 6 5
                                             ♣ A J 4

If partner plays king, ace and another heart, he gives the declarer a ruff-and-discard; he will ruff the third heart in dummy and discard a club loser from his hand. If your partner does not lead a third heart, declarer will lose four tricks (two hearts and two clubs) and the contract will be set. If dummy had three hearts, it would be right to play the nine followed by the two to encourage partner to lead a third heart, but not when partner has bid the suit and the dummy has a doubleton.

If your first heart play is the two, you might be thinking: Isn't it possible that partner will not cash his ace of hearts and then lose it? With the cards as shown you can see that he will not lose his ace, and with a six-card suit he should cash it anyway as it cannot establish a trick for declarer if you have three cards in the suit.

Another possibility you might have considered is to play the nine followed by the *queen*. But this is wrong because that is the way you should play with a doubleton; remember, you should not play high-low with Q x because playing the queen promises the jack (or a singleton queen).

In the next deal, you have four hearts and there is a simple solution:

#13

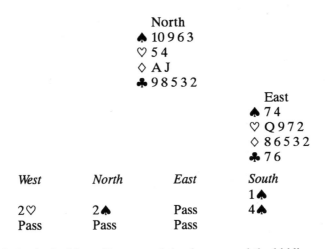

North
♠ 10 9 6 3
♡ 5 4
◇ A J
♣ 9 8 5 3 2

East
♠ 7 4
♡ Q 9 7 2
◇ 8 6 5 3 2
♣ 7 6

West	North	East	South
			1♠
2♡	2♠	Pass	4♠
Pass	Pass	Pass	

Partner again leads the king of hearts and the dummy and the bidding are the same. But your hand is different and partner might lose his second heart trick if he does not cash his ace at trick two. So to encourage partner to lead a second round of hearts, *play the seven of hearts*; then when partner leads the ace, *play the nine* to discourage him from leading a third round. The four hands:

```
                    ♠ 10 9 6 3
                    ♡ 5 4
                    ◇ A J
                    ♣ 9 8 5 3 2
        ♠ 8 5                        ♠ 7 4
        ♡ A K 10 8 6                 ♡ Q 9 7 2
        ◇ 9 7 4                      ◇ 8 6 5 3 2
        ♣ K Q 10                     ♣ 7 6
                    ♠ A K Q J 2
                    ♡ J 3
                    ◇ K Q 10
                    ♣ A J 4
```

Declarer has the same four losers as in the preceding hand, but note that he can make his contract if your partner does not cash his second heart. Declarer will draw two rounds of trumps, then discard a heart from dummy on his third high diamond. Your partner must lead exactly two rounds of hearts to beat the contract. If you signal as recommended above, your partner will cash his ace of hearts and then switch suits.

#14

North
♠ K J 9 3
♡ J 8 5 2
◇ 8 7
♣ 10 6 2

East
♠ 5
♡ Q 9 3
◇ J 10 6 4 2
♣ Q J 9 8

West	North	East	South
			1♠
Pass	2♠	Pass	4♠
Pass	Pass	Pass	

Your partner leads the king of hearts and you should *play the three*. It is wrong to give a come-on signal with Q x x when an honor in dummy will be established if partner leads the ace next. For example:

♠ K J 9 3
♡ J 8 5 2
◇ 8 7
♣ 10 6 2

♠ 8 7 2
♡ A K 6 4
◇ 9 5
♣ A 7 5 3

♠ 5
♡ Q 9 3
◇ J 10 6 4 2
♣ Q J 9 8

♠ A Q 10 6 4
♡ 10 7
◇ A K Q 3
♣ K 4

Declarer has four losers (two hearts and two clubs). Suppose you play the nine of hearts and partner continues with the ace. It does not matter whether or not he leads a third heart; the declarer can lead a third round of hearts himself and ruff in his hand. This establishes the jack of hearts as a parking place for one of his losing clubs. If partner leads a spade or a diamond at trick two, you can set the contract if you win with your queen of hearts the second time the suit is led; a shift to the queen of clubs then ends declarer's hopes.

#15

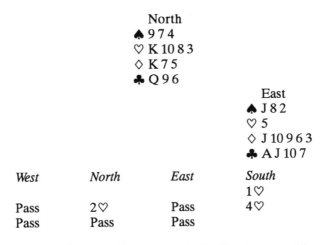

North
♠ 9 7 4
♡ K 10 8 3
◇ K 7 5
♣ Q 9 6

East
♠ J 8 2
♡ 5
◇ J 10 9 6 3
♣ A J 10 7

West	North	East	South
			1♡
Pass	2♡	Pass	4♡
Pass	Pass	Pass	

Partner leads the king of spades. Partner may be leading from ace-king or king-queen.[1] The question is how do you signal when you have the jack? If you play the eight and partner has ♠ A K 10 x, you will regret it; but if partner has ♠ K Q x x, a spade continuation would be good! Since the dummy does not appear as though it will provide any discard, it is unlikely that declarer will be able to get rid of any spade loser even if partner does not lead another spade (although it is possible—if declarer has ◇ A or ◇ A Q). There is no way to know for sure whether a spade continuation is right or wrong, but it is more likely to cost a trick than gain a trick, so *play the two of spades*. The four hands:

♠ 9 7 4
♡ K 10 8 3
◇ K 7 5
♣ Q 9 6

♠ A K 10 3
♡ 7 2
◇ Q 8 4
♣ 8 5 4 2

♠ J 8 2
♡ 5
◇ J 10 9 6 3
♣ A J 10 7

♠ Q 6 5
♡ A Q J 9 6 4
◇ A 2
♣ K 3

Declarer must lose three spade tricks and the ace of clubs unless your partner leads a spade at trick two, so playing the two of spades to discourage another spade lead is right this time.

If you held a doubleton ♠ 8 2, you should usually play the eight, hoping to ruff the third round; although you will regret it if declarer ducks with A J x and partner continues the suit.

With a doubleton ♠ J 2 it is an even more doubtful decision. Signaling with the jack should work out better most of the time, although it may cost a trick if declarer has A 10 x.

---

1. If your partnership agreement is to lead the ace from ace-king on opening lead versus suit contracts and your partner leads the king, you know he has king-queen and should give an encouraging signal; play the eight from J 8 2. This convention is covered in *Conventional Leads and Signals* on page 382.

#16   **North**
                                           ♠ A 5 4
                                           ♡ K J 10 2
                                           ◇ 6 3
                                           ♣ K Q J 7

                                                            East
                                                            ♠ J 9 2
                                                            ♡ 7 3
                                                            ◇ A 8 5 4
                                                            ♣ A 10 9 6

West	North	East	South
	1♣	Pass	1♡
Pass	2♡	Pass	4♡
Pass	Pass	Pass	

The opening lead is the king of spades. This time, with the ace of spades in the dummy, partner is marked with the queen and you definitely want him to continue leading the suit. Whether declarer plays the ace from dummy or ducks, you should *play the nine*. The four hands:

                          ♠ A 5 4
                          ♡ K J 10 2
                          ◇ 6 3
                          ♣ K Q J 7
     ♠ K Q 10 8   ♠ J 9 2
     ♡ 9 6   ♡ 7 3
     ◇ J 10 7 2   ◇ A 8 5 4
     ♣ 8 4 3   ♣ A 10 9 6
                          ♠ 7 6 3
                          ♡ A Q 8 5 4
                          ◇ K Q 9
                          ♣ 5 2

Suppose declarer lets your partner win the first spade trick with the king—this is his best play. If a spade is not led at trick two, declarer can make his contract by discarding a spade on the third round of clubs or diamonds. But with your encouraging signal, partner will lead another spade and you will be able cash a second spade trick as soon as you get the lead with one of your aces.

#17

North
♠ A 5 4
♡ K J 10 2
◇ 6 3
♣ K Q J 7

East
♠ 9 2
♡ 7 3
◇ A 9 8 5 4
♣ A 10 9 6

West	North	East	South
	1♣	Pass	1♡
Pass	2♡	Pass	4♡
Pass	Pass	Pass	

The opening lead is the king of spades. The bidding, dummy's cards and the opening lead are the same as last hand, but this time you do not have the jack of spades. If declarer plays low from dummy, you should *play the two*. If partner has the king-queen-jack of spades, he will almost surely lead the suit again anyway; but if he does not have the jack, you certainly do not want him to lead another spade. The four hands:

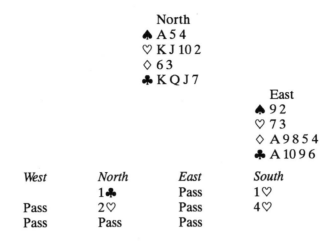

♠ A 5 4
♡ K J 10 2
◇ 6 3
♣ K Q J 7

♠ K Q 10 8
♡ 9 6
◇ J 10 7 2
♣ 8 4 3

♠ 9 2
♡ 7 3
◇ A 9 8 5 4
♣ A 10 9 6

♠ J 7 6 3
♡ A Q 8 5 4
◇ K Q
♣ 5 2

Note that if you play the nine of spades, partner will continue the suit and declarer will get an unearned trick with the jack and make his contract. So it is not always right to play high-low with a doubleton. If you play the two of spades, partner will lead another suit—it does not matter which one, although a diamond is correct in view of dummy. Declarer then cannot avoid four losers (two spades, one diamond and one club).

Another interesting point is, what should you do if declarer wins the first trick with the ace of spades? Since you have two aces and are a big favorite to get the lead before partner, and declarer would probably duck if he had ♠ J x x, it is right to *signal with the nine*. If you have no entry cards, or maybe just one ace, there is a danger that your partner may get the lead before you and lead another spade thinking that you have the jack. So, without the two aces, it is a problem; it is probably better to play safe and *signal with the two*.

#18

North
♠ A K 8 7
♡ 6
◇ Q J 10 3
♣ A 9 8 2

East
♠ J 6 5 2
♡ J 10 9 8
◇ 8 2
♣ K 7 6

West	North	East	South
	1♣	Pass	1♡
Pass	1♠	Pass	3♡
Pass	3NT	Pass	4♡
Pass	Pass	Pass	

Your partner leads the king of diamonds and you should *play the two*. You have a natural heart trick and cannot gain by ruffing the third round of diamonds. It is important to recognize that declarer may be able to discard one or more club losers on dummy's diamonds if he is given time. You want a club lead at trick two and will probably get it if you do not encourage a diamond lead. The four hands:

```
                    ♠ A K 8 7
                    ♡ 6
                    ◇ Q J 10 3
                    ♣ A 9 8 2
   ♠ Q 10 9 3                        ♠ J 6 5 2
   ♡ 5 4                             ♡ J 10 9 8
   ◇ A K 9 4                         ◇ 8 2
   ♣ J 4 3                           ♣ K 7 6
                    ♠ 4
                    ♡ A K Q 7 3 2
                    ◇ 7 6 5
                    ♣ Q 10 5
```

Your two-of-diamonds play tells your partner not to lead another diamond, but it does not tell him which suit to lead. However, since dummy has stronger spades than clubs, he should lead a club. Declarer's best play is to duck the club lead and let you win with the king. Then you will beat the contract if you return a diamond so partner can win a trick with the ace; if you do not lead a diamond, declarer can make his contract by discarding one diamond on dummy's king of spades and the other on the fourth club.

If you play the eight of diamonds at trick one, partner will continue the suit and declarer will succeed by drawing trumps and discarding one club on the second high spade and another on the fourth diamond. So this is another case where it is wrong to play high-low with a doubleton.

#19

North
♠ K 4 2
♡ A K Q 5
◇ Q J 3
♣ A Q 8

East
♠ A J 10
♡ 10 8 3
◇ 10 4 2
♣ 7 6 5 3

West	North	East	South
	2NT	Pass	4♠
Pass	Pass	Pass	

Your partner leads the king of diamonds, and the question is: What do you want him to lead at trick two? The correct answer is most emphatically the ace of diamonds, so you should signal with the *ten of diamonds*. You have two natural trump tricks and it should be apparent that you cannot win any tricks in hearts or clubs, so the only good chance to beat the contract is to win two diamond tricks. If declarer gets the lead before you get your two diamond tricks, he may be able to get rid of a losing diamond by discarding on hearts or clubs. The four hands:

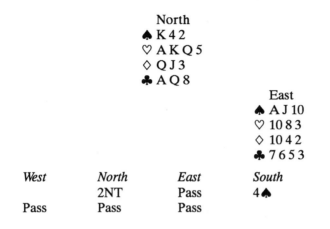

```
              ♠ K 4 2
              ♡ A K Q 5
              ◇ Q J 3
              ♣ A Q 8
♠ 7                        ♠ A J 10
♡ 9 6 4                    ♡ 10 8 3
◇ A K 8 7 5                ◇ 10 4 2
♣ J 10 9 2                 ♣ 7 6 5 3
              ♠ Q 9 8 6 5 3
              ♡ J 7 2
              ◇ 9 6
              ♣ K 4
```

If you play the two of diamonds on the first trick, your partner would probably switch to the jack of clubs. Declarer will cash three rounds of clubs and discard his losing diamond; the contract can no longer be set. If you are thinking your partner should have cashed his ace of diamonds even if you gave him a discouraging signal, let me show you a different layout in which a club switch is the winning defense:

                              ♠ K 4 2
                              ♡ A K Q 5
                              ◇ Q J 3
                              ♣ A Q 8
        ♠ 7   ♠ A 6 3
        ♡ 9 6 4   ♡ 10 8 3
        ◇ A K 8 7 5   ◇ 10 4 2
        ♣ J 10 9 2   ♣ K 6 5 3
                              ♠ Q J 10 9 8 5
                              ♡ J 7 2
                              ◇ 9 6
                              ♣ 7 4

Again partner leads the king of diamonds, but with the king of clubs instead of the jack-ten of spades, you should *play the two of diamonds*. If partner switches to the jack of clubs, the defense can win four tricks. But if West cashes the ace of diamonds at trick two, declarer can make his contract by discarding a losing club on the queen of diamonds.

#20   North
                                             ♠ J 10 8 3
                                             ♡ K Q 10 9
                                             ◇ 7 6 2
                                             ♣ A 4
                                                              East
                                                              ♠ 7 5 4
                                                              ♡ A J 3
                                                              ◇ 10 9 4
                                                              ♣ 9 7 5 2

        West   North   East   South
                                                        1NT
        Pass   2♣   Pass   2♠
        Pass   4♠   All Pass

Your partner leads the jack of clubs and the ace is played from dummy. You should *play the seven of clubs*; the purpose of encouraging the club lead is to discourage your partner from shifting to a diamond, the obvious weak suit in the dummy. If you play a low club and partner gets the lead with a high spade, he may lead a diamond, fearing declarer will discard losing diamonds on dummy's hearts. The four hands:

                              ♠ J 10 8 3
                              ♡ K Q 10 9
                              ◇ 7 6 2
                              ♣ A 4
        ♠ K 2   ♠ 7 5 4
        ♡ 6 5 4   ♡ A J 3
        ◇ K J 8 3   ◇ 10 9 4
        ♣ J 10 8 6   ♣ 9 7 5 2
                              ♠ A Q 9 6
                              ♡ 8 7 2
                              ◇ A Q 5
                              ♣ K Q 3

Suppose declarer takes a spade finesse at trick two and your partner gets the lead with the king. He sees strong hearts in dummy and is unaware that you have the ace and jack, so it is logical for him to lead the three of diamonds if you gave him a discouraging signal in clubs. But with the encouraging signal, he will lead another club and the contract will be set.

In the next deal, the dummy and partner's hands are the same, but the diamond switch is needed to beat the contract.

#21

                                North
                                ♠ J 10 8 3
                                ♡ K Q 10 9
                                ◇ 7 6 2
                                ♣ A 4
                                                        East
                                                        ♠ 7 5 4
                                                        ♡ 7 3 2
                                                        ◇ A 10 9
                                                        ♣ Q 9 7 2

West	North	East	South
			1NT
Pass	2♣	Pass	2♠
Pass	4♠	All Pass	

Again partner leads the jack of clubs and the ace is played from dummy, but this time you have three low hearts and the ace of diamonds. Seeing the danger that declarer will be able to discard one or more losing diamonds on dummy's hearts, you should *play the two of clubs*, which will discourage partner from leading a club and, consequently, encourage him to lead a diamond. The four hands:

                                ♠ J 10 8 3
                                ♡ K Q 10 9
                                ◇ 7 6 2
                                ♣ A 4
        ♠ K 2   ♠ 7 5 4
        ♡ 6 5 4   ♡ 7 3 2
        ◇ K J 8 3   ◇ A 10 9
        ♣ J 10 8 5   ♣ Q 9 7 2
                                ♠ A Q 9 6
                                ♡ A J 8
                                ◇ Q 5 4
                                ♣ K 6 3

As in the last deal, partner will get the lead with the king of spades. But now he must shift to a diamond to set the contract. If he does not, declarer will discard one of his three losing diamonds on dummy's fourth heart.

#22   North
                                             ♠ Q 10 9
                                             ♡ J 9 3 2
                                             ◇ A Q 7 4
                                             ♣ K Q
                                                                        East
                                                                        ♠ 8 7 6 5 2
                                                                        ♡ A 5
                                                                        ◇ K 9 3
                                                                        ♣ J 6 4

West	North	East	South
	1◇	Pass	1♡
Pass	2♡	Pass	4♡
Pass	Pass	Pass	

Partner leads the ace of spades, which is more than likely from a short suit—doubleton or singleton. If it is a doubleton, you want partner to continue the suit so you can give him a ruff when you get the lead with the ace of hearts. So, *play the eight of spades*. The four hands:

                                             ♠ Q 10 9
                                             ♡ J 9 3 2
                                             ◇ A Q 7 4
                                             ♣ K Q
            ♠ A 4   ♠ 8 7 6 5 2
            ♡ 10 4   ♡ A 5
            ◇ 8 6 2   ◇ K 9 3
            ♣ 10 9 8 7 5 2   ♣ J 6 4
                                             ♠ K J 3
                                             ♡ K Q 8 7 6
                                             ◇ J 10 5
                                             ♣ A 3

The ace of spades turns out to be the winning lead. With your encouragement, partner continues the suit at trick two. When trumps are led, you rush in with your ace of hearts and give him the ruff. Declarer must still lose a diamond trick and go down one.

#23   North
                                             ♠ K 9 5
                                             ♡ A K Q J 10
                                             ◇ J 3
                                             ♣ Q 6 4
                                                                        East
                                                                        ♠ 6 3
                                                                        ♡ 9 8 5 2
                                                                        ◇ A 8 7 2
                                                                        ♣ A K J

West	North	East	South
			3♠
Pass	4♠	All Pass	

The opening lead is the king of diamonds, and it appears that the only chance to beat this contract is to win the first four tricks. Since you want your partner to lead a club at trick two, not a diamond, you should *play the two of diamonds*; even though you have the ace. Before showing the four hands, here is a little test for you: Partner leads the two of clubs at trick two, you win with the jack and cash the king of clubs. Which ace do you play at trick four? Why?

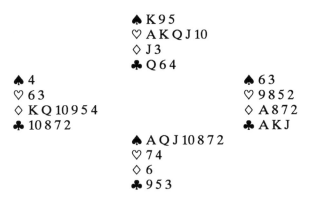

♠ K 9 5
♡ A K Q J 10
◇ J 3
♣ Q 6 4

♠ 4
♡ 6 3
◇ K Q 10 9 5 4
♣ 10 8 7 2

♠ 6 3
♡ 9 8 5 2
◇ A 8 7 2
♣ A K J

♠ A Q J 10 8 7 2
♡ 7 4
◇ 6
♣ 9 5 3

You should know to lead the ace of clubs at trick four because partner led the two of clubs at trick two; he would not lead the two if he had a five-card suit, so declarer must have another club.

#24

North
♠ 10 9 8
♡ K J 7
◇ J 5 2
♣ K Q 10 5

East
♠ 5 2
♡ A Q 10
◇ A 7 6 3
♣ 9 8 7 4

West	North	East	South
			1♠
Pass	2♠	All Pass	

Your partner leads the king of diamonds and you want him to lead a heart at trick two, so *play the three*. Another test is coming up, so read carefully. Partner switches to the four of hearts, the jack is played from dummy and you win with the queen. Presumably partner has the queen of diamonds, so underlead your ace of diamonds to put him on lead. Partner wins with the queen of diamonds and leads the three of hearts to dummy's king and your ace. What do you lead now? If the card you lead wins the trick, what do you lead next? The four hands:

```
                              ♠ 10 9 8
                              ♡ K J 7
                              ◊ J 5 2
                              ♣ K Q 10 5
        ♠ J 4 3                                    ♠ 5 2
        ♡ 9 8 6 4 3                                ♡ A Q 10
        ◊ K Q 10                                   ◊ A 7 6 3
        ♣ J 2                                      ♣ 9 8 7 4
                              ♠ A K Q 7 6
                              ♡ 5 2
                              ◊ 9 8 4
                              ♣ A 6 3
```

The only way to beat the contract is to cash the ace of diamonds at trick five and to lead your fourth diamond at trick six. You should know that declarer has a doubleton heart because partner showed five when he led the four and then the three. After winning the fifth trick with the ace of diamonds, the only source of tricks left is the trump suit (declarer must have the ace of clubs for his bid). So you should *lead the thirteenth diamond* and hope you can promote a trump trick for your partner. If you defend this way, partner will win the setting trick with the jack of spades. (For more about trump-promotion plays, see Chapter 8.)

#25   North
                                       ♠ K 9 4 3
                                       ♡ A K
                                       ◊ A Q J 8 6
                                       ♣ 7 5

            West
            ♠ 5
            ♡ Q 10 8
            ◊ K 9 7 4 3 2
            ♣ K Q J

West	North	East	South
	1◊	Pass	1♠
Pass	4♠	All Pass	

This time you are on the other side of the table. It is your partner who will be doing the signaling. You lead the king of clubs, partner plays the two and declarer the three. Either the declarer has the ace and is holding up, or partner has it and wants you to shift to another suit. In neither case can another club lead be right. The best chance to beat the contract is if partner is void in diamonds. So *lead the two of diamonds.*[2] The four hands:

---

2. The two of diamonds is a suit-preference signal (see next chapter). If partner ruffs as you hope, you are requesting him to return a club. You may think this is obvious, but it is possible that you led from K x of clubs; in which case you would lead a high diamond to warn partner not to underlead his ace of clubs.

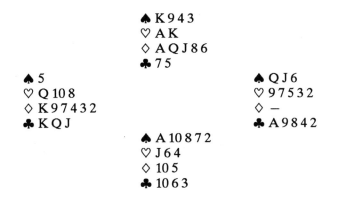

A low diamond is played from the dummy and your partner ruffs. Since you are marked with the queen of clubs, he underleads his ace of clubs to put you back on lead to give him another ruff—the only defense to beat the contract.

#26

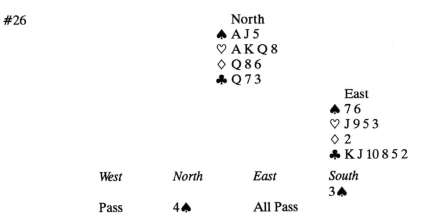

West	North	East	South
			3♠
Pass	4♠	All Pass	

Your partner wins the first trick with the king of diamonds and, seeing your two-spot, switches to the ace of clubs. Since you want him to lead a diamond at trick three, not a club, you must *play the two of clubs*. The four hands:

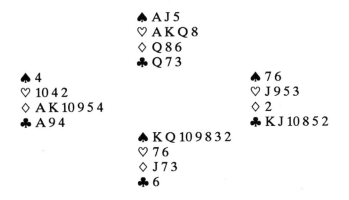

Your partner knew either you or declarer had a singleton diamond, and he defended well by cashing the ace of clubs to find out who. When you play the two of clubs, he will next cash the ace of diamonds and then give you a ruff to set the hand.

You might have held ◇ x x x ♣ K J 10 x and declarer ◇ x ♣ x x x, in which case you would give partner an encouraging signal—*the jack*—when he leads the ace of clubs. Partner would then lead the nine of clubs (an indication that he has no more than three clubs; he would lead his lowest if he had four) and, with the knowledge that declarer began with three clubs, you will win two more club tricks.

Signaling with Honor Cards

The next five deals are all trump contracts, but the technique for signaling with honor cards is much the same as at notrump contracts.

#27

	North
	♠ Q J 10
	♡ 9 4
	◇ 10 8 7
	♣ K J 6 4 3

	East
	♠ 9 8
	♡ 8 6 5 3 2
	◇ Q J 2
	♣ 8 7 5

West	North	East	South
			1♠
Double	2♠	Pass	4♠
Pass	Pass	Pass	

Your partner leads the king of diamonds and you should *signal with the queen. Playing the queen guarantees the jack* (unless you have a singleton queen), and your partner may underlead his ace if he wishes to put you on lead. The four hands:

	♠ Q J 10	
	♡ 9 4	
	◇ 10 8 7	
	♣ K J 6 4 3	
♠ 6 5		♠ 9 8
♡ A Q 7		♡ 8 6 5 3 2
◇ A K 5 4 3		◇ Q J 2
♣ 10 9 2		♣ 8 7 5
	♠ A K 7 4 3 2	
	♡ K J 10	
	◇ 9 6	
	♣ A Q	

At trick two, your partner should lead the four of diamonds so you can get the lead and play a heart through declarer's king. As you can see, the only way to beat the contract is to win the first four tricks; otherwise declarer will discard his losers on the club suit.

#28

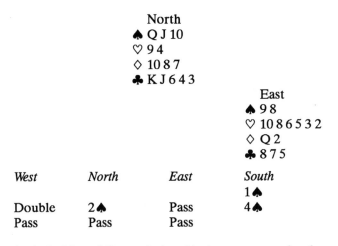

North
♠ Q J 10
♡ 9 4
◊ 10 8 7
♣ K J 6 4 3

East
♠ 9 8
♡ 10 8 6 5 3 2
◊ Q 2
♣ 8 7 5

West	North	East	South
			1♠
Double	2♠	Pass	4♠
Pass	Pass	Pass	

Again partner leads the king of diamonds, but this time you must *play the two*. If you play the queen, partner will think you have the jack and probably underlead his ace. Note that partner may continue with the ace of diamonds even if you play the two, and in the following layout he should. The four hands:

♠ Q J 10
♡ 9 4
◊ 10 8 7
♣ K J 6 4 3

♠ 6 5
♡ A Q 7
◊ A K 5 4 3
♣ 10 9 2

♠ 9 8
♡ 10 8 6 5 3 2
◊ Q 2
♣ 8 7 5

♠ A K 7 4 3 2
♡ K J
◊ J 9 6
♣ A Q

Your partner probably will read your two-of-diamonds play to be from ◊ J x x, but it could be from Q x or a singleton. In none of these cases will he lose by cashing the ace of diamonds at trick two. When he plays the ace and your queen drops, he will lead a third diamond to give you a ruff. Then you will return a heart and set the contract two tricks.

On another day your partner may lead the king and you will get a bad result by playing the low card from Q x; he may decide against playing his ace and declarer may make an unmakable contract. But this is accepted as the best way to play: There is only one situation in which you may signal with the queen from Q x: *if the jack is in the dummy*. For example: If partner leads the king and the dummy has J x x, play the queen from Q x if you want partner to continue with the ace and then give you a ruff.

#29

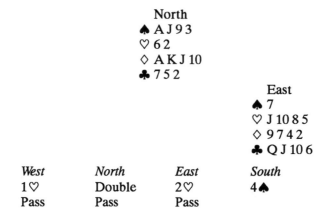

North
♠ A J 9 3
♡ 6 2
◇ A K J 10
♣ 7 5 2

East
♠ 7
♡ J 10 8 5
◇ 9 7 4 2
♣ Q J 10 6

West	*North*	*East*	*South*
1♡	Double	2♡	4♠
Pass	Pass	Pass	

Your partner leads the king of hearts and you should *play the jack*. Since you have raised hearts, your partner will not read you for a doubleton. Playing the jack denies the queen, but promises the ten. This information can be important. The four hands:

```
              ♠ A J 9 3
              ♡ 6 2
              ◇ A K J 10
              ♣ 7 5 2
♠ 6 2                        ♠ 7
♡ A K Q 7 3                  ♡ J 10 8 5
◇ 5 3                        ◇ 9 7 4 2
♣ A 9 8 4                    ♣ Q J 10 6
              ♠ K Q 10 8 5 4
              ♡ 9 4
              ◇ Q 8 6
              ♣ K 3
```

Your partner should underlead the ace-queen of hearts at trick two so you can win with the ten and lead a club. If declarer gets the lead before you take four tricks, he will make his contract by drawing trumps and discarding one of his losers on dummy's fourth diamond.

Note that if your partner had ♡ A K x x x and you signaled with the jack of hearts, he would know declarer had the queen and would not underlead his ace.

#30

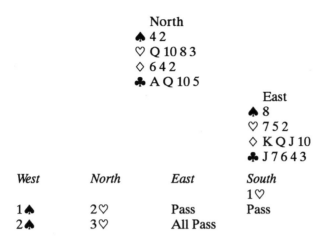

West	North	East	South
			1♡
1♠	2♡	Pass	Pass
2♠	3♡	All Pass	

Your partner leads the king of spades and then the ace of spades. You should *discard the king of diamonds* to show that you control the suit from the king on down, and to encourage him to lead a diamond. The four hands:

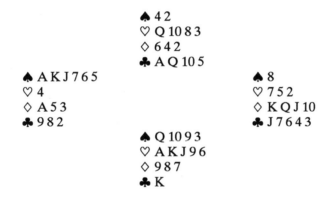

The only way to beat this contract is to win the first five tricks (two spades and three diamonds), so it is imperative that your partner leads a diamond at trick three. Without your signal, probably partner would lead a third spade hoping for a trump trick.

#31

North
♠ K 9 4 3
♡ 7 5 2
◇ A 8 4
♣ A K Q

East
♠ 10 5
♡ Q J 4 3
◇ Q J 10 9 7
♣ 7 6

West	North	East	South
	1NT	Pass	3♠
Pass	4♠	All Pass	

The opening lead is the ten of clubs. At trick two, declarer leads the ace of diamonds. You should *play the queen of diamonds*, under the ace, to tell your partner that you have the jack and ten. This turns out to be very important as it enables your partner to avoid being endplayed. The four hands:

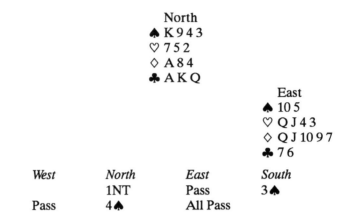

♠ K 9 4 3
♡ 7 5 2
◇ A 8 4
♣ A K Q

♠ J 7
♡ A 9 8 6
◇ K 3
♣ 10 9 8 5 2

♠ 10 5
♡ Q J 4 3
◇ Q J 10 9 7
♣ 7 6

♠ A Q 8 6 2
♡ K 10
◇ 6 5 2
♣ J 4 3

Declarer has four losers (two hearts and two diamonds) and will be set with the ace of hearts offside unless he can force your partner to lead a heart or give a ruff-and-discard. When declarer cashes the ace of diamonds and you signal with the queen, partner should know that it is safe to play the king of diamonds. If he does not unblock, declarer will succeed by drawing trumps, cashing two more rounds of clubs and then leading a diamond. If partner still has the lone king, he must win the trick and lead a heart or a club; in either case declarer will make his contract. But if partner unblocked, you will win two diamond tricks and lead a heart through declarer's king.

True, declarer probably would have done better by playing the first diamond *from his hand*. Then West would have to play before seeing his partner's signal. The key point, though, is that against both notrump and trump contracts, the way to describe your holding when you have a sequence of honor cards is to play the highest card of the sequence—from K Q J 10, play king; from Q J 10 9, play the queen; from K J 10 9, play the jack; and from A 10 9 8, play the ten. *An honor signal always denies possession of the card above the one you play.*

Provided you are giving a come-on signal, the rule about playing the high card of a sequence also applies to sequences headed by spot cards. For example: If you hold K 8 7 6, *play the eight* if you want to encourage partner to lead the suit, or *play the six* to discourage him. Playing the seven might be considered sadistic—making it harder for partner to recognize whether or not you want him to lead the suit.

When not to Signal

Knowing when *not* to signal is just as important as knowing when to signal. Average players tend to be wasteful in signaling—they often lose a trick or pinpoint the winning line of play to declarer. *Never signal at the expense of a trick.* The final three deals illustrate situations in which a signal is tempting but wrong.

#32

```
                        North
                        ♠ A J 3
                        ♡ K 8 6 5
                        ♢ Q 7 4 2
                        ♣ K 4
                                        East
                                        ♠ 10 8 7 5
                                        ♡ A Q 10 9 3
                                        ♢ 6
                                        ♣ 7 6 2
```

West	North	East	South
			1 ◊
Pass	1 ♡	Pass	3 ◊
Pass	4NT	Pass	5 ♡
Pass	6 ◊	All Pass	

Partner leads the queen of clubs. Declarer wins the first trick in dummy with the king, leads a diamond to the ace and cashes the king of diamonds. You must discard and it is tempting to play the ten of hearts to encourage your partner to lead the suit. But this is a slam contract and your partner is unlikely to get the lead. The trouble with playing a high heart is you are telling the declarer that you have the ace and that could help him to make his contract. So on the second diamond lead you should *discard a club (or a low heart)*. The four hands:

```
                        ♠ A J 3
                        ♡ K 8 6 5
                        ♢ Q 7 4 2
                        ♣ K 4
        ♠ Q 9 4 2                       ♠ 10 8 7 5
        ♡ 7 2                           ♡ A Q 10 9 3
        ♢ 9 3                           ♢ 6
        ♣ Q J 10 9 5                    ♣ 7 6 2
                        ♠ K 6
                        ♡ J 4
                        ♢ A K J 10 8 5
                        ♣ A 8 3
```

Declarer's only losers are the two hearts and he has a choice of plays: He can lead a heart and hope your partner has the ace, or he can cash the king of spades and then finesse the jack; if the spade finesse works, he can discard one of his losing hearts. If you signaled with the ten of hearts and he trusts you, he will make his contract by taking the spade finesse. If you don't signal, he may do the right thing anyway; but at least you will not have helped him. *Do not give an honest signal when the only player you can help is the declarer.*

You may be thinking you would have doubled six diamonds to request a heart opening lead! It could be the winning decision, but it is dangerous. Declarer may have the king of hearts, a singleton heart, or even a void suit; if you double six diamonds and he redoubles and makes his contract, the double would be costly. Another thought: The opponents may run to six notrump (which would be played by North) and make it—although they cannot win more than eleven tricks in this layout.

If the opponents reached six notrump played by South, then you should double for a heart lead.

#33

```
                                North
                              ♠ A 6 3
                              ♡ K 10 7
                              ◇ J 8 2
                              ♣ 9 6 5 3
                                                    East
                                                  ♠ 5
                                                  ♡ A Q 8 3
                                                  ◇ 9 7 6 4
                                                  ♣ Q 8 7 4
```

West	North	East	South
			1♠
Pass	2♠	Pass	4♠
Pass	Pass	Pass	

Your partner wins the first trick with the king of clubs. He continues with the ace of clubs, which is ruffed by declarer. Declarer cashes the king of spades and leads another spade to the ace. *Do not discard the eight of hearts* as it may be a trick. You should *discard a low diamond*. The four hands:

```
                              ♠ A 6 3
                              ♡ K 10 7
                              ◇ J 8 2
                              ♣ 9 6 5 3
        ♠ 10 8 7                              ♠ 5
        ♡ J 5 4                               ♡ A Q 8 3
        ◇ 10 5 3                              ◇ 9 7 6 4
        ♣ A K J 2                             ♣ Q 8 7 4
                              ♠ K Q J 9 4 2
                              ♡ 9 6 2
                              ◇ A K Q
                              ♣ 10
```

Declarer will lose three heart tricks if he is forced to lead the suit himself and you do not signal with the eight of hearts. It makes no difference how he plays the suit, but suppose after drawing trumps he leads the two of hearts, partner plays the four, dummy the ten and you the queen. Now you exit with a diamond or a club. The remaining hearts are:

```
                                North
                              ♡ K 7
        West                                    East
        ♡ J 5                                  ♡ A 8 3
                                South
                              ♡ 9 6
```

You will eventually get two more heart tricks and set the contract, provided you still have that precious eight-spot.

#34

```
                          North
                          ♠ 10 7 6 3
                          ♡ Q 8 5
                          ◇ A 10 9
                          ♣ 5 4 2
                                          East
                                          ♠ Q 8 4 2
                                          ♡ 7 2
                                          ◇ J 6 5 3
                                          ♣ A 10 9
```

West	North	East	South
			1♡
Pass	2♡	Pass	4♡
Pass	Pass	Pass	

Your partner leads the king of spades and it is tempting to give an encouraging signal with the eight. But the eight might be an important card, so *the four will have to do*. When you wish to encourage your partner to continue leading a suit, you should always signal with the highest card you can spare (for example, from Q 8 7 2 you should play the eight, not the seven); but this time you cannot spare the eight-spot. The four hands:

```
                     ♠ 10 7 6 3
                     ♡ Q 8 5
                     ◇ A 10 9
                     ♣ 5 4 2
    ♠ A K 5                              ♠ Q 8 4 2
    ♡ 9 6 4                              ♡ 7 2
    ◇ Q 7 2                              ◇ J 6 5 3
    ♣ 8 7 6 3                            ♣ A 10 9
                     ♠ J 9
                     ♡ A K J 10 3
                     ◇ K 8 4
                     ♣ K Q J
```

If you signal with the eight and partner continues with the ace, the remaining spades are the 10 7 in the dummy and the Q 4 in your hand. Declarer will be able to establish the dummy's fourth spade to discard a diamond and make his contract. If you do not waste the eight, declarer will have to lose a diamond trick eventually and be set.

Quiz for Chapter Six

1.
$$\text{North}$$
♠ Q 10 5
♡ J 10 3
◇ A K Q J
♣ A Q 2

$$\text{East}$$
♠ J 3 2
♡ K 8
◇ 9 6 4 2
♣ 8 6 5 4

West	North	East	South
	1◇	Pass	1♡
1♠	2NT	Pass	3♡
Pass	4♡	All Pass	

Your partner leads the king of spades. Which spade do you play?

2.
$$\text{North}$$
♠ K 4 2
♡ J 8 5
◇ K Q J 10
♣ A Q 9

$$\text{East}$$
♠ 7 6
♡ Q 10 9 2
◇ A 8 5
♣ K J 7 3

West	North	East	South
	1NT	Pass	4♠
Pass	Pass	Pass	

Your partner leads the king of hearts. Which heart do you play?

3.
$$\text{North}$$
♠ 9 8 5 2
♡ K J 7
◇ K 4 3
♣ 7 4 3

$$\text{East}$$
♠ 3
♡ Q 2
◇ A 7 6 5 2
♣ Q J 10 9 8

West	North	East	South
1♠	Pass	1NT	2♡
2♠	3♡	All Pass	

Your partner wins the first trick with the king of spades and then leads the ace of spades. What do you discard?

4.
$$\text{North}$$
♠ Q 10
♡ K 6 4
◇ K J 9 8 3
♣ A 5 4

$$\text{West}$$
♠ K 6
♡ 10 5 3 2
◇ 7 4 2
♣ Q 9 8 2

West	North	East	South
			1♠
Pass	2◇	Pass	2♠
Pass	4♠	All Pass	

You lead the two of clubs, the ace is put up from dummy, partner plays the six and declarer the three. The queen of spades is led and you win with the king. What do you lead now?

5.

```
              North
              ♠ 7 6 5 3
              ♡ A
              ◇ A Q 8 2
              ♣ Q 10 7 3
                          East
                          ♠ Q J 10
                          ♡ Q 10 9 7
                          ◇ K 10 9 5
                          ♣ 8 2
```

West	North	East	South
	1◇	Pass	1♠
Pass	2♠	Pass	4♠
Pass	Pass	Pass	

Your partner leads the king of clubs. Which club do you play?

6.

```
              North
              ♠ 7 2
              ♡ 9 4
              ◇ A 10 5
              ♣ K J 10 8 6 3
      West
      ♠ 10 8 6 5 3
      ♡ A Q 7
      ◇ 8 7 6
      ♣ 7 4
```

West	North	East	South
			1NT
Pass	3NT	All Pass	

You lead the five of spades, partner plays the queen and declarer wins with the ace. The queen of clubs is led. Partner wins with the ace of clubs and leads the king of spades. Which spade do you play?

7.

```
              North
              ♠ K 9 8 4
              ♡ A 7 2
              ◇ K Q 10 6
              ♣ 10 5
      West
      ♠ 7 6
      ♡ K 8 4 3
      ◇ 9 5 4 2
      ♣ A K 3
```

West	North	East	South
	1◇	Pass	1♠
Pass	2♠	Pass	4♠
Pass	Pass	Pass	

You lead the king of clubs and your partner plays the queen. What do you lead now?

8.

```
              North
              ♠ K Q J
              ♡ 10 9 8 7
              ◇ A J 9 6
              ♣ Q 3
      West
      ♠ 10 8 7 6 5
      ♡ A 4 2
      ◇ 3
      ♣ 10 7 5 2
```

West	North	East	South
			1♡
Pass	3♡	Pass	4NT
Pass	5◇	Pass	5♡
Pass	Pass	Pass	

You lead the three of diamonds, the six is played from dummy, partner puts in the ten and declarer wins with the king. The king of hearts is led. Plan your defense.

Quiz Answers for Chapter Six

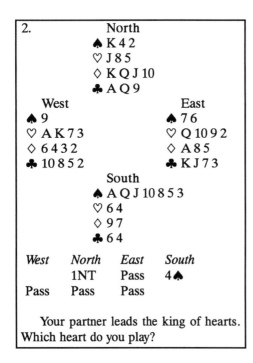

1.   North
                     ♠ Q 10 5
                     ♡ J 10 3
                     ◇ A K Q J
                     ♣ A Q 2
     West   East
     ♠ A K 9 7 6   ♠ J 3 2
     ♡ A 4   ♡ K 8
     ◇ 10 8 5   ◇ 9 6 4 2
     ♣ 10 9 3   ♣ 8 6 5 4
                     South
                     ♠ 8 4
                     ♡ Q 9 7 6 5 2
                     ◇ 7 3
                     ♣ K J 7

West	North	East	South
	1◇	Pass	1♡
1♠	2NT	Pass	3♡
Pass	4♡	All Pass	

Your partner leads the king of spades.
Which spade do you play?

Play the jack of spades. It is clear that you are not going to win any tricks in clubs or diamonds and may not get a second spade trick unless your partner takes it right away. If you signal with the three of spades, your partner may read it as a come-on signal and cash the ace, but why be ambiguous when you can be emphatic—the jack of spades is of no value.

Note that if you play a low spade and partner leads a club at trick two, declarer can discard his losing spade on the diamond suit and make his contract.

There is an amusing story about this hand involving a husband and wife in one of my classes. The husband led the king of spades and his wife properly signaled with the jack. But when he continued with the ace and another spade and his wife did not ruff, he yelled so the whole class could hear: "What the hell are you doing?" Since his wife played high-low, he expected her to have a doubleton and to ruff the third spade. Was his face red when he learned the result!

2.   North
                     ♠ K 4 2
                     ♡ J 8 5
                     ◇ K Q J 10
                     ♣ A Q 9
     West   East
     ♠ 9   ♠ 7 6
     ♡ A K 7 3   ♡ Q 10 9 2
     ◇ 6 4 3 2   ◇ A 8 5
     ♣ 10 8 5 2   ♣ K J 7 3
                     South
                     ♠ A Q J 10 8 5 3
                     ♡ 6 4
                     ◇ 9 7
                     ♣ 6 4

West	North	East	South
	1NT	Pass	4♠
Pass	Pass	Pass	

Your partner leads the king of hearts.
Which heart do you play?

Play the two of hearts, to discourage your partner from leading another heart. If a club trick is needed to beat this contract, you won't get it unless your partner leads a club before he relinquishes the lead. The strong diamonds in the dummy make a club switch obvious, and partner should lead the two of clubs (something he would not do if he had more than four clubs, so you know declarer cannot have a singleton club). Declarer will probably finesse the queen of clubs—it would not help him to do otherwise—and the defense can win four tricks (two hearts, one diamond and one club) before he can discard any of his losers on the diamond suit.

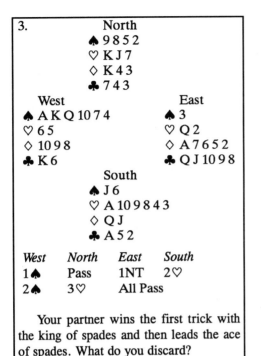

3.

	North	
	♠ 9 8 5 2	
	♡ K J 7	
	◇ K 4 3	
	♣ 7 4 3	
West		East
♠ A K Q 10 7 4		♠ 3
♡ 6 5		♡ Q 2
◇ 10 9 8		◇ A 7 6 5 2
♣ K 6		♣ Q J 10 9 8
	South	
	♠ J 6	
	♡ A 10 9 8 4 3	
	◇ Q J	
	♣ A 5 2	

West	North	East	South
1♠	Pass	1NT	2♡
2♠	3♡	All Pass	

Your partner wins the first trick with the king of spades and then leads the ace of spades. What do you discard?

Discard the queen of clubs. Your honor signal says that you control the suit from the queen on down. This makes it easy for your partner to switch to the king of clubs, and to lead another club if declarer ducks. The club lead is needed to win two club tricks, which together with two spades and one diamond set the contract by one trick. Without a club lead at trick three, declarer can maneuver to discard a losing club on dummy's king of diamonds.

4.

	North	
	♠ Q 10	
	♡ K 6 4	
	◇ K J 9 8 3	
	♣ A 5 4	
West		East
♠ K 6		♠ 8 5 3
♡ 10 5 3 2		♡ A Q 9 7
◇ 7 4 2		◇ 6 5
♣ Q 9 8 2		♣ K 10 7 6
	South	
	♠ A J 9 7 4 2	
	♡ J 8	
	◇ A Q 10	
	♣ J 3	

West	North	East	South
			1♠
Pass	2◇	Pass	2♠
Pass	4♠	All Pass	

You lead the two of clubs, the ace is put up from dummy, partner plays the six and declarer the three. The queen of spades is led and you win with the king. What do you lead now?

Lead the two of hearts. The six was your partner's lowest club—he did not encourage you to lead another club—so switching suits is in order. You should reason that if declarer has any diamond losers, there is no hurry to get them. But he may be able to discard heart losers on dummy's good diamond suit. Hence the decision to lead a heart instead of a diamond. Your partner cannot win the two heart tricks you need to beat the contract unless you lead a heart.

5.   North
                          ♠ 7 6 5 3
                          ♡ A
                          ◇ A Q 8 2
                          ♣ Q 10 7 3
       West   East
       ♠ 4   ♠ Q J 10
       ♡ J 8 5 4 2   ♡ Q 10 9 7
       ◇ 7 6 3   ◇ K 10 9 5
       ♣ A K 9 4   ♣ 8 2
                          South
                          ♠ A K 9 8 2
                          ♡ K 6 3
                          ◇ J 4
                          ♣ J 6 5

West	North	East	South
	1◇	Pass	1♠
Pass	2♠	Pass	4♠
Pass	Pass	Pass	

       Your partner leads the king of clubs.
       Which club do you play?

Play the two of clubs. You have a natural spade trick and will not gain by ruffing the third round of clubs. However, you could lose if partner continues clubs, because the fourth club in dummy sets up for a discard; with the cards as shown declarer would be able to discard his losing diamond on the queen of clubs.

But if you play the two of clubs, partner should switch to a diamond because there is no logical reason to lead hearts. Declarer will probably play a low diamond from the dummy (no other play is better), and you will win with the king. Now lead a club. You will eventually get a spade trick to set the contract one trick.

6.   North
                          ♠ 7 2
                          ♡ 9 4
                          ◇ A 10 5
                          ♣ K J 10 8 6 3
       West   East
       ♠ 10 8 6 5 3   ♠ K Q 9
       ♡ A Q 7   ♡ J 10 6 2
       ◇ 8 7 6   ◇ 9 4 3 2
       ♣ 7 4   ♣ A 5
                          South
                          ♠ A J 4
                          ♡ K 8 5 3
                          ◇ K Q J
                          ♣ Q 9 2

West	North	East	South
			1NT
Pass	3NT	All Pass	

       You lead the five of spades, partner plays the queen and declarer wins with the ace. The queen of clubs is led. Partner wins with the ace of clubs and leads the king of spades. Which spade do you play?

Play the ten of spades. You know the declarer has the jack of spades because your partner played the queen on the first trick. With all those club tricks staring you in the face, it should be clear that declarer will be able to win at least nine tricks when he regains the lead. But your partner does not know that declarer has the jack of spades, so he will lead another spade unless you tell him not to. Your strange play of the ten could hardly mean anything except it is your highest spade; you do not have the jack. Your partner can see as well as you that declarer will make his contract if he regains the lead. If he gets your message, he will switch to the jack of hearts; and this will beat the contract.

```
7.              North
              ♠ K 9 8 4
              ♡ A 7 2
              ◇ K Q 10 6
              ♣ 10 5
   West                      East
   ♠ 7 6                     ♠ 3
   ♡ K 8 4 3                 ♡ J 10 9 5
   ◇ 9 5 4 2                 ◇ A 8 3
   ♣ A K 3                   ♣ Q J 8 7 2
              South
              ♠ A Q J 10 5 2
              ♡ Q 6
              ◇ J 7
              ♣ 9 6 4

   West    North    East    South
           1◇       Pass    1♠
   Pass    2♠       Pass    4♠
   Pass    Pass     Pass
```

You lead the king of clubs and your partner plays the queen. What do you lead now?

Play the three of clubs to put your partner on lead so he can switch to a heart—your partner must have the jack of clubs to play the queen. It is clear that a heart should be led at trick three because it looks as though declarer will be able to discard at least one heart on dummy's diamonds if you give him time. If declarer has the queen of hearts, the first heart lead must come from your partner. With the cards as shown, partner will win the second trick with the jack of clubs and lead the jack of hearts. This defense is necessary to beat the contract.

```
8.              North
              ♠ K Q J
              ♡ 10 9 8 7
              ◇ A J 9 6
              ♣ Q 3
   West                      East
   ♠ 10 8 7 6 5              ♠ A 9 3 2
   ♡ A 4 2                   ♡ 5
   ◇ 3                       ◇ Q 10 7 5 4
   ♣ 10 7 5 2               ♣ 8 6 4
              South
              ♠ 4
              ♡ K Q J 6 3
              ◇ K 8 2
              ♣ A K J 9

   West    North    East    South
                            1♡
   Pass    3♡       Pass    4NT
   Pass    5◇       Pass    5♡
   Pass    Pass     Pass
```

You lead the three of diamonds, the six is played from dummy, partner puts in the ten and declarer wins with the king. The king of hearts is led. Plan your defense.

Duck the king-of-hearts lead. The declarer would have bid a slam unless two aces were missing, so partner predictably has an ace. In any case, it is unlikely that you can beat this contract unless your partner has the ace of spades or the ace of clubs; so you can put him in the lead to give you a diamond ruff. The trouble with winning the first trick with the ace of hearts is you do not know which ace your partner has. But the bidding indicates that partner probably has a singleton heart. By ducking the first heart lead and winning the second, you give your partner a chance to give you a signal. With the actual distribution, he will play the nine of spades on the second heart trick. Then you will lead a spade to partner's ace, and he will give you your diamond ruff.

7

Count Signals and Suit-Preference Signals

The **Count Signal** tells partner whether you have an even number or an odd number of cards in a suit. To give *a Count Signal in a non-trump suit*:

(1) With an odd number of cards in the suit, play low-high, starting with your lowest card.

(2) With an even number of cards in the suit, play high-low, but *do not signal with a high card that may waste a trick*. Generally you should start your high-low signal with the highest card you can spare. For example, play the six from 6 3, the eight (or seven[1]) from 8 7 5 3, or the four from 10 4 3 2 or Q 10 4 2.

A Count Signal *in the trump suit* (sometimes called a "Trump Echo") is just the opposite. You play high-low with an odd number of cards, and low-high with an even number. The reason for this is the higher card of a doubleton may be of value (even a spot card may produce a trick by an overruff or a trump-promotion play), while you can usually spare the middle card from three.

The **Suit-Preference Signal** is a way to indicate, by the rank of the card you play, which of the other suits you want your partner to lead.

How can you tell when a signal is for attitude, count or suit preference? This is something you and your partner must know if you are going to use these signals effectively. The primary signal is for attitude; if an attitude signal can apply, it does apply. Attitude signals are used when partner leads a suit—you are third hand—or when you are discarding (regardless of who led to the trick).

Count signals are normally used only when you are following to a suit led by declarer (you are second or fourth hand). Exceptionally count signals may be used in attitude-signal situations provided your attitude about the suit is apparent or already known.

Count signals in a trump suit may be used any time trumps are played, whether you are following suit, leading trumps or ruffing.

Suit-preference signals are used when leading a suit, following suit or discarding, but only when both partners know that the attitude signal and the count signal are useless information.

Count signals and suit-preference signals are vitally important to good defense. Some of the following illustrations show how to give the signals, while others show how to read them when your partner gives the signals. It is surprising to me that many competent bridge players ignore these signals. I hope you and your regular partners will study this chapter and use them.

---

1. Many players, especially experts, prefer to play their *second-highest* from four cards, provided partner will have no problem reading it. This sometimes helps when it is necessary to distinguish between two and four cards.

Count Signals by Second- and Fourth-Hand

#1

                                North
                                ♠ 7 3 2
                                ♡ A 4
                                ◇ Q J 10 8 5
                                ♣ 6 5 3

                                                    East
                                                    ♠ J 6
                                                    ♡ K 7 5 2
                                                    ◇ A 7 6
                                                    ♣ J 10 9 8

West	North	East	South
			2NT
Pass	3NT	All Pass	

Your partner leads the jack of hearts. You win the first trick with the king and return a heart to drive out dummy's ace; declarer follows suit with low hearts. Your goal now should be to limit declarer to as few diamond tricks as possible: If he has ◇ K x x x, you cannot stop him from winning four diamond tricks; if he has ◇ K x x, you can limit him to two diamond tricks by holding up your ace twice; and if he has ◇ K x, you can limit him to one diamond trick by winning the second diamond trick. So what you need to know is how many diamonds the declarer has! He won't tell you, but your partner will by playing high-low with an even number and low-high with an odd number.

At trick three, declarer leads a low diamond from dummy to his king and your partner plays the three. Then declarer leads the two of diamonds and partner plays the four. There is one diamond missing and you know your partner has it because he played low-high to show an odd number. So you should *win the second diamond trick*. The four hands:

                                ♠ 7 3 2
                                ♡ A 4
                                ◇ Q J 10 8 5
                                ♣ 6 5 3

        ♠ Q 10 8 5   ♠ J 6
        ♡ J 10 9 6   ♡ K 7 5 2
        ◇ 9 4 3   ◇ A 7 6
        ♣ 7 4   ♣ J 10 9 8

                                ♠ A K 9 4
                                ♡ Q 8 3
                                ◇ K 2
                                ♣ A K Q 2

Since neither clubs nor spades divide three-three, declarer can win only eight tricks (two spades, two hearts, one diamond and three clubs). If you did not play count signals and ducked the second diamond lead to guard against declarer's having three diamonds, he would make his contract.

Often you must decide whether partner has an odd or even number of cards in a suit before he has a chance to play a second card. For example:

#2

```
                        North
                        ♠ 8 7 3
                        ♡ K Q 10 2
                        ◇ 9 6 5 4
                        ♣ Q 2
        West
        ♠ Q 10 6 5
        ♡ A 9 4
        ◇ 8 3 2
        ♣ K 7 3
```

West	North	East	South
			1◇
Pass	1♡	Pass	2NT
Pass	3NT	All Pass	

You lead the five of spades, partner plays the jack and declarer wins with the ace. The jack of hearts is led and the proper time to take your ace is when declarer plays his last card in the suit, so you follow suit with the four and observe that partner plays the five. Now declarer leads the six of hearts. How many hearts do you think your partner has? The 8, 7 and 3 are still missing. If partner held 8 7 5 3, he would have played the eight the first time, so he must have 8 7 5. This tells you declarer began with three, so *you should duck the second heart lead*. The four hands:

```
                        ♠ 8 7 3
                        ♡ K Q 10 2
                        ◇ 9 6 5 4
                        ♣ Q 2
    ♠ Q 10 6 5                          ♠ J 9 4 2
    ♡ A 9 4                             ♡ 8 7 5
    ◇ 8 3 2                             ◇ 10 7
    ♣ K 7 3                             ♣ A 6 5 4
                        ♠ A K
                        ♡ J 6 3
                        ◇ A K Q J
                        ♣ J 10 9 8
```

After you duck the second heart lead, declarer can win only eight tricks (two spades, two hearts and four diamonds). If you win the second heart lead, he can win three heart tricks and make his contract.

Note that the declarer deliberately concealed the three of hearts in an effort to make you think your partner was starting a high-low signal. This shows the importance of giving a clear signal. If partner foolishly played the five from 8 7 5 3, you would be unable to read it.

#3

North
♠ K Q 10 9
♡ J 10 2
◇ 8 5 2
♣ J 4 3

East
♠ A 7 3
♡ Q 8 6
◇ 9 6 4 3
♣ Q 9 5

West	North	East	South
			1◇
Pass	1♠	Pass	2NT
Pass	3NT	All Pass	

Partner leads the three of hearts, the jack is put up from the dummy and you must *play a low heart*. The declarer is marked with the ace or king of hearts (or both), so you will not lose a trick by ducking, but you will deprive declarer of an entry to dummy. Now you must decide when to take your ace of spades. Suppose the king of spades is led from dummy. You play low, declarer plays the five and partner the eight. Partner's eight of spades must be the start of a high-low to show an even number of spades—probably four based on the bidding. Declarer next leads the nine of spades and you should *take your ace*. Declarer must have the jack of spades to be playing this way, and if you duck again, he will win two spade tricks when he is entitled to just one. The four hands:

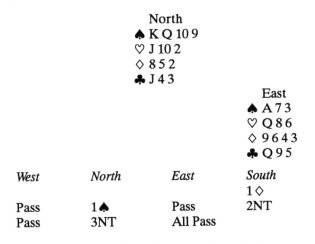

♠ K Q 10 9
♡ J 10 2
◇ 8 5 2
♣ J 4 3

♠ 8 6 4 2
♡ K 9 5 3
◇ 10 7
♣ K 10 8

♠ A 7 3
♡ Q 8 6
◇ 9 6 4 3
♣ Q 9 5

♠ J 5
♡ A 7 4
◇ A K Q J
♣ A 7 6 2

This good defense limits declarer to just one spade trick (plus two hearts, four diamonds and one club), so the contract cannot be made.

There are times when it is impossible to tell whether partner has an odd or even number of cards when you have seen only one card. For example, suppose the spade holding in this hand were:

North
♠ K Q J 10

East
♠ A 9 7 6

Dummy leads the king of spades, you play the nine, declarer the two and partner the four. Then the queen of spades is led. Partner would play the four from 4 3 or 8 5 4. There is no way to tell. Fortunately, such cases are rare.

The count signal is equally important when defending trump contracts.

#4
                           North
                           ♠ 5 3 2
                           ♡ 8 6 4
                           ◊ K 10 9 5
                           ♣ K Q J

                                            East
                                        ♠ 9 7 4
                                      ♡ 7 3
                                      ◊ A 8 7 2
                                      ♣ A 10 8 5

West	North	East	South
			1♡
Pass	2♡	Pass	4♡
Pass	Pass	Pass	

Partner leads the queen of spades, you play the four and declarer wins with the ace. He leads the three of clubs and partner *plays the two* to show an odd number. Here again you must figure out how many cards partner has in the suit when he has played only one card. You can rule out a singleton in partner's hand (he would have led it if he wanted a ruff), so partner has either three or five clubs. If partner has three clubs, your play will not matter—declarer would also have three clubs. The critical situation is when partner has five clubs, in which case declarer has only one and you must *win the first club trick with your ace*. The four hands:

                          ♠ 5 3 2
                          ♡ 8 6 4
                          ◊ K 10 9 5
                          ♣ K Q J

♠ Q J 10 8   ♠ 9 7 4
♡ A 5   ♡ 7 3
◊ 6 3   ◊ A 8 7 2
♣ 9 7 6 4 2   ♣ A 10 8 5

                          ♠ A K 6
                          ♡ K Q J 10 9 2
                          ◊ Q J 4
                          ♣ 3

After winning with the ace of clubs, you should lead the nine of spades to drive out the king and inform partner that declarer has a third spade in his hand (if you began with four, you would lead back your lowest spade). Now the contract can be set because declarer cannot get to dummy in time to discard his spade loser. However, if he is tricky and leads the two of hearts towards dummy's eight, your partner must go up with the ace of hearts and cash his spade trick.

#5

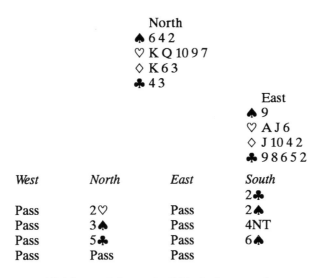

North
♠ 6 4 2
♡ K Q 10 9 7
◇ K 6 3
♣ 4 3

East
♠ 9
♡ A J 6
◇ J 10 4 2
♣ 9 8 6 5 2

West	North	East	South
			2♣
Pass	2♡	Pass	2♠
Pass	3♠	Pass	4NT
Pass	5♣	Pass	6♠
Pass	Pass	Pass	

After the strong, artificial two-club opening bid, declarer reaches a contract of six spades and your partner leads the queen of clubs. Declarer wins the first trick with the ace and draws three rounds of trumps; partner follows suit throughout and you discard two clubs. At trick five, declarer leads a low heart, partner *plays the two* to show an odd number, the king is played from dummy and you must decide whether to win with the ace or hold up. If partner has a singleton, declarer has four and you will win two heart tricks whether you hold up or not (also, partner would have led a heart if he had a singleton). Therefore, it is apparent that partner has three hearts and declarer two. You must *hold up your ace—play the six—*to deprive declarer of an entry. The four hands:

```
                    ♠ 6 4 2
                    ♡ K Q 10 9 7
                    ◇ K 6 3
                    ♣ 4 3
  ♠ 7 5 3                           ♠ 9
  ♡ 8 3 2                           ♡ A J 6
  ◇ Q 8 5                           ◇ J 10 4 2
  ♣ Q J 10 7                        ♣ 9 8 6 5 2
                    ♠ A K Q J 10 8
                    ♡ 5 4
                    ◇ A 9 7
                    ♣ A K
```

If you win the first heart trick with the ace, declarer will win whatever you lead back in his hand, play his second heart to dummy's queen, and ruff the third round. The remaining hearts in dummy will now be good, so he can lead a diamond to dummy's king and discard his diamond loser. But if you duck the first round of hearts, you eliminate a crucial entry to dummy; he must lose a heart and a diamond.

In the next deal, the count signal is needed in two suits.

#6   North
                                ♠ 7 3 2
                                ♡ Q 8 4
                                ◇ Q J 10 5
                                ♣ Q J 4

                                                East
                                                ♠ Q J 9 8 6
                                                ♡ A
                                                ◇ A 8 6
                                                ♣ A 10 5 2

West	North	East	South
		1♠	Double
Pass	2◇	Pass	2♡
Pass	3♡	Pass	4♡
Pass	Pass	Pass	

Your partner leads the ten of spades, you play the jack and declarer wins with the ace. Partner would have led a low spade from ♠ 10 x x, so he should have a doubleton and declarer ♠ A K x. If declarer loses a spade trick (in addition to your three aces), he will be set. To make his contract, declarer must discard a spade on one of dummy's high clubs or diamonds.

At trick two, declarer leads the king of diamonds and partner *plays the nine* to show an even number. Partner should have four diamonds and the declarer two (declarer would not lead diamonds before drawing trumps if he had four); so you should *duck the first diamond trick*. Now declarer leads the king of clubs and partner *plays the three* to show an odd number, which is predictably five (if partner has three clubs, so does declarer and it doesn't matter whether you take your ace or duck). So, assuming declarer has a singleton club, you should *win the first club trick* and lead a spade to drive out the king. Whatever declarer leads next, you will regain the lead and set the hand by winning three more tricks with your two red aces and the high spade. Here are the four hands:

```
                      ♠ 7 3 2
                      ♡ Q 8 4
                      ◇ Q J 10 5
                      ♣ Q J 4
    ♠ 10 4                              ♠ Q J 9 8 6
    ♡ 6 5                               ♡ A
    ◇ 9 7 3 2                           ◇ A 8 6
    ♣ 9 8 7 6 3                         ♣ A 10 5 2
                      ♠ A K 5
                      ♡ K J 10 9 7 3 2
                      ◇ K 4
                      ♣ K
```

If either you do not duck the first diamond lead or you do duck the first club lead, declarer will make his contract. How in the world would anybody (even an expert) know to make these plays if it were not for the count signal?

#7   North
                                         ♠ 8 5 3
                                         ♡ J 6 4
                                         ◊ A Q 10 9 5
                                         ♣ 6 2
                                                              East
                                                              ♠ 9 6 2
                                                              ♡ Q 9 8
                                                              ◊ K 4
                                                              ♣ K J 9 7 5

West	North	East	South
			1♣
Pass	1◊	Pass	2NT
Pass	3NT	All Pass	

Partner leads the four of spades, you play the nine and declarer wins with the queen. At trick two, he leads the jack of diamonds, partner *plays the eight* and dummy the five. You should play the *four of diamonds*. Partner has clearly shown an even number of diamonds. Whether partner has two or four diamonds, declarer's next play will probably be to finesse again (assuming you did not hesitate). In the likely event that partner has four diamonds, your ducking play will limit declarer to one diamond trick if he finesses again. The four hands:

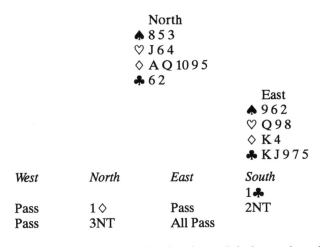

                          ♠ 8 5 3
                          ♡ J 6 4
                          ◊ A Q 10 9 5
                          ♣ 6 2
        ♠ K 10 7 4   ♠ 9 6 2
        ♡ 10 3 2   ♡ Q 9 8
        ◊ 8 7 6 2   ◊ K 4
        ♣ Q 3   ♣ K J 9 7 5
                          ♠ A Q J
                          ♡ A K 7 5
                          ◊ J 3
                          ♣ A 10 8 4

Note that if you win the first diamond trick, declarer has an easy road to nine tricks (two spades, two hearts, four diamonds and one club). Holding up the king of diamonds is a gamble, but a good one. If declarer next plays the ace, he will win five diamond tricks (the fifth diamond is merely an overtrick), but if he repeats the finesse, he will win only one diamond and be set; probably down two.

As you may have observed from these first seven hands, the time when count signals are most useful is when the declarer has led a suit in which your partner has (or may have) a high card; your play helps him decide when to play his high card and limit declarer to as few tricks as possible. But there are times when the information given by a count signal will be useful to declarer but not to your partner. In such cases you should vary your strategy to mislead the declarer as to whether you have an odd or even number of cards. For example:

#8   North
                                            ♠ J 3
                                            ♡ K 10 7 5
                                            ◇ 8 7 4
                                            ♣ A 9 6 3
                                                              East
                                                              ♠ A 9 7 6
                                                              ♡ 8 3
                                                              ◇ Q J 9 2
                                                              ♣ Q J 10

West	*North*	*East*	*South*
			1 ◇
Pass	1 ♡	Pass	2NT
Pass	3NT	All Pass	

Partner leads the five of spades and you win the first trick with the ace. You return the six of spades, declarer wins with the king and partner plays the two. At trick three, declarer plays the queen of hearts. An accurate count signal will not help your partner but may help declarer, so the better strategy is usually to *play the three*. Look at the four hands to see why:

                                            ♠ J 3
                                            ♡ K 10 7 5
                                            ◇ 8 7 4
                                            ♣ A 9 6 3
          ♠ Q 10 8 5 2   ♠ A 9 7 6
          ♡ J 9 6 4   ♡ 8 3
          ◇ 10 5   ◇ Q J 9 2
          ♣ 4 2   ♣ Q J 10
                                            ♠ K 4
                                            ♡ A Q 2
                                            ◇ A K 6 3
                                            ♣ K 8 7 5

Declarer needs four heart tricks to make his contract. After the queen of hearts, assume declarer continues with the ace of hearts and a third heart toward dummy. If you have played high-low to show an even number *and he believes you*, he will finesse the ten and make his contract. Declarer's normal percentage play is to go up with the king, something he probably would do if you misguided him by playing low-high.

Another strategy here—which might be called reverse psychology—is to give an honest count signal (play the eight of hearts and then the three of hearts) in the expectation that declarer will not believe you. Which would you do?

Here is another example in which you should not make a normal count signal, but the reason is to preserve important spot cards, rather than psychological.

#9

North
- ♠ A 7 5
- ♡ 10 8 4
- ◇ A K 7 4 3
- ♣ K 3

West
- ♠ 4 3 2
- ♡ K Q J 9
- ◇ Q 9 8 5
- ♣ 6 2

West	North	East	South
	1◇	Pass	2NT
Pass	3NT	All Pass	

You win the first two tricks with the king and jack of hearts, then lead the queen of hearts; partner follows suit throughout and declarer wins with the ace. At trick four, he leads the two of diamonds. You should *play the five; do not give a count signal if the card you play may cost a trick*. The four hands:

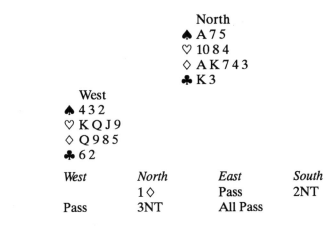

                  ♠ A 7 5
                  ♡ 10 8 4
                  ◇ A K 7 4 3
                  ♣ K 3
♠ 4 3 2   ♠ J 9 8 6
♡ K Q J 9   ♡ 6 5 2
◇ Q 9 8 5   ◇ 10
♣ 6 2   ♣ Q J 10 9 7
                  ♠ K Q 10
                  ♡ A 7 3
                  ◇ J 6 2
                  ♣ A 8 5 4

Declarer has eight tricks (three spades, one heart, two diamonds and two clubs) and his only chance for a ninth is a third diamond trick. Suppose you mistakenly play the nine (or eight) of diamonds at trick four. Declarer will win with the king and, seeing the ten drop, lead a low diamond to his jack. You can win with the queen, but now you are left with the ◇ 8 5 in front of dummy's ◇ A 7 4. After you cash your fourth heart, declarer will regain the lead and win the rest of the diamond tricks by finessing the seven. If you play the five on the first diamond lead, the contract is hopeless.

Count Signals by Third Hand

In a vast majority of cases a signal by third-hand is for attitude. But there are times when an attitude signal is not needed (your partner already knows, or will know no matter which card you play, that you have no high cards in the suit), so you can employ the count signal.[2] For example:

#10
                                    North
                                    ♠ Q 9 4 2
                                    ♡ Q J 4
                                    ◇ J 5
                                    ♣ K J 9 3
                                                            East
                                                            ♠ 10 7 6
                                                            ♡ 9 5 2
                                                            ◇ Q 10 9 8
                                                            ♣ 8 7 2

West	North	East	South
			1NT
Pass	2♣	Pass	2◇
Pass	3NT	All Pass	

Partner leads the seven of hearts and the queen is played from dummy. If you had the ace or king of hearts, you would play it. No matter which spot card you decide to play, your partner will assume that you don't have the ace or king. So an attitude signal is meaningless and you can use the count signal. Play the *two of hearts* on the first trick to show an odd number. Here are the four hands so you can see how this helps your partner.

                                    ♠ Q 9 4 2
                                    ♡ Q J 4
                                    ◇ J 5
                                    ♣ K J 9 3
        ♠ A 8 5   ♠ 10 7 6
        ♡ K 10 8 7 3   ♡ 9 5 2
        ◇ 7 4 3   ◇ Q 10 9 8
        ♣ A 6   ♣ 8 7 2
                                    ♠ K J 3
                                    ♡ A 6
                                    ◇ A K 6 2
                                    ♣ Q 10 5 4

Suppose declarer leads a low club from dummy at trick two and your partner captures the queen with his ace. Your two-of-hearts signal showed an odd number of hearts, which must be three (declarer denied four hearts in the bidding), so your partner should know that declarer now has the lone ace. He should lead a heart at trick three to establish the suit. When

---

2. Some players have problems recognizing when a third-hand signal is for count. If you are in this category, you might do better to play count signals only when declarer has led the suit—second or fourth hand—until you get more experience.

he regains the lead with the ace of spades, he can run three heart tricks and beat the contract.
In the next deal you have a doubleton heart.

#11

North
♠ Q 9 4 2
♡ Q J 4
◇ J 5
♣ K J 9 3

East
♠ J 10 7 6
♡ 9 2
◇ Q 10 9 8
♣ 8 7 2

West	North	East	South
			1NT
Pass	2♣	Pass	2◇
Pass	3NT	All Pass	

Again your partner leads the seven of hearts and the queen is played from dummy, but this time you must *play the nine* to show an even number of hearts. The four hands:

♠ Q 9 4 2
♡ Q J 4
◇ J 5
♣ K J 9 3

♠ A 8 5
♡ K 10 8 7 3
◇ 7 4 3
♣ A 6

♠ J 10 7 6
♡ 9 2
◇ Q 10 9 8
♣ 8 7 2

♠ K 3
♡ A 6 5
◇ A K 6 2
♣ Q 10 5 4

At trick two, declarer leads a club from dummy to his queen and your partner's ace. Your nine-of- hearts signal showed an even number of hearts (which must be two), so your partner knows that the declarer began with three and he therefore should not lead another heart. Note that if partner leads a diamond, declarer can be held to eight tricks (one spade, two hearts, two diamonds and three clubs). But if partner leads another heart, declarer can win a ninth trick with dummy's jack of hearts.

#12

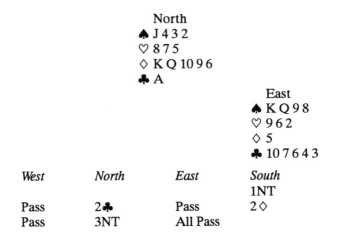

	West	North	East	South
				1NT
	Pass	2♣	Pass	2◇
	Pass	3NT	All Pass	

As you were informed in Chapter 1, page 3, the opening lead of an ace against a notrump contract indicates a very strong suit (usually with four honor cards) and asks partner to play the missing honor if he has it, *or else give count*. So, if your partner leads the ace of hearts, you should *play the two* to show an odd number of hearts. The four hands:

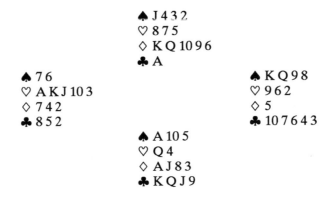

Your partner knows the missing five hearts are divided three-two—declarer denied a four-card major in the bidding—and your play of the two shows an odd number, which must be three (without the queen). Therefore your partner knows that declarer began with ♡ Q x and he will set the contract by winning the first five heart tricks.

Now let's change the hand so the declarer has three hearts:

♠ J 4 3 2
♡ 8 7 5
◇ K Q 10 9 6
♣ A

♠ 7 6   ♠ Q 9 8 5
♡ A K J 10 3   ♡ 9 2
◇ 7 4 2   ◇ A 5
♣ 8 5 2   ♣ 10 7 6 4 3

♠ A K 10
♡ Q 6 4
◇ J 8 3
♣ K Q J 9

Again your partner leads the ace of hearts, but this time you should *play the nine* to show an even number of hearts. Now your partner knows you have a doubleton and the declarer has ♡ Q x x. The only way to win more than two heart tricks is for you to get the lead and play a heart through declarer. Since you have the ace of diamonds, the contract can be set two tricks if partner leads anything but a heart at trick two.

The next deal shows an unusual use of the count signal to convey the winning defense to partner.

#13

North
♠ A Q 6 3
♡ A K J 10 9
♢ 10 7 4
♣ 8

West
♠ 8 7 2
♡ 5 4 3
♢ K J
♣ Q J 10 9 6

West	North	East	South
	1♡	Pass	1♠
Pass	3♠	Pass	4♠
Pass	Pass	Pass	

You lead the queen of clubs to partner's ace. He returns the two of diamonds (low from strength, so he must have the ace or queen) and declarer plays the three. You should *win with the king and return the jack*, to tell your partner that you have a doubleton. The four hands:

```
                 ♠ A Q 6 3
                 ♡ A K J 10 9
                 ♢ 10 7 4
                 ♣ 8
 ♠ 8 7 2                        ♠ 4
 ♡ 5 4 3                        ♡ 8 7 6 2
 ♢ K J                          ♢ A 6 5 2
 ♣ Q J 10 9 6                   ♣ A 5 4 3
                 ♠ K J 10 9 5
                 ♡ Q
                 ♢ Q 9 8 3
                 ♣ K 7 2
```

If you play high-low (first the king and then the jack), partner will win the second diamond trick with the ace and return a diamond for you to ruff. Note that if your partner does not win the second diamond trick and lead a third diamond for you to ruff, declarer can get rid of his losing diamonds by discarding on the heart suit. It is true that if you play the jack first and then the king, partner could overtake your king with the ace, but this would be a disaster if you began with ♢ K J x (although you might return the spot card from ♢ K J x to eliminate an unnecessary problem for your partner).

If you think that declarer could make life more difficult for the defenders by playing the queen of diamonds at trick two (sort of anti-count warfare), you are right; but it is clearly not the percentage play.

#14   North
                                       ♠ K Q 9 2
                                       ♡ 4
                                       ◇ Q J 10
                                       ♣ A 10 8 5 3
                                                           East
                                                           ♠ 6
                                                           ♡ A Q J 9 7 2
                                                           ◇ A K 6 2
                                                           ♣ K 4

West	North	East	South
		1♡	3♠
4♡	4♠	5♡	5♠
Pass	Pass	Double	All Pass

After winning your partner's queen-of-clubs opening lead with dummy's ace, declarer cashes the king of spades and partner follows suit. Now declarer leads a club, you win with the king and partner follows with the jack. At trick four, you cash the king of diamonds and partner *plays the nine* to show an even number, which must be four. You already know partner began with one spade and two clubs, so his ten red cards must be six hearts and four diamonds. Therefore, declarer is void in hearts and has one more diamond. To beat the contract, your next play must be the ace of diamonds. The four hands:

                                       ♠ K Q 9 2
                                       ♡ 4
                                       ◇ Q J 10
                                       ♣ A 10 8 5 3
        ♠ 3   ♠ 6
        ♡ K 10 8 6 5 3   ♡ A Q J 9 7 2
        ◇ 9 8 7 4   ◇ A K 6 2
        ♣ Q J   ♣ K 4
                                       ♠ A J 10 8 7 5 4
                                       ♡ —
                                       ◇ 5 3
                                       ♣ 9 7 6 2

Note that if you try to cash the ace of hearts before winning the second diamond trick, declarer will ruff and discard his losing diamond on dummy's fifth club. You must admit that it would be tempting to play the ace of hearts before the ace of diamonds if it were not for the count signal.

Count Signals in the Trump Suit

As you read earlier, the way to give a count signal in the trump suit is the opposite from non-trump suits: *You play high-low with an odd number, and low-high with an even number.*

This signal may be used when making an opening lead to help your partner to count the distribution of the other suits (i.e., lead the nine from 9 8 4, but lead the two from 9 8 4 2 or 6 2). However, count signals in the trump suit also help the declarer to count the distribution, so some expert partnerships prefer not to have any agreement on which trump card to lead.

Almost all good players agree that count signals in the trump suit are very good *when following suit, or when ruffing a trick.* Sometimes this information helps your partner to count the distribution, but its most important usage is to let your partner know how many trumps you have when he is deciding whether or not to give you a ruff. For example:

#15
```
                              North
                              ♠ J 8 4
                              ♡ 7 6 4 2
                              ◇ Q 9 8 7 5
                              ♣ A
                                               East
                                               ♠ A 5
                                               ♡ K 9 8
                                               ◇ A 6 4 2
                                               ♣ 7 5 3 2
```

West	North	East	South
			1♠
Pass	2♠	Pass	4♠
Pass	Pass	Pass	

Your partner leads the three of diamonds, you win with the ace and declarer plays the jack. Partner would not lead the three from either K 3 or 10 3, and is unlikely to lead it from K 10 3, so declarer most likely has K J 10 and your partner a singleton. You lead the six of diamonds and partner ruffs with the *seven of spades*. He returns the queen of hearts. Declarer wins with the ace and leads the king of spades. Partner follows with the *two of spades* to show an odd number and you win the trick with your ace. Knowing that partner has a third trump, you should *lead another diamond*. The four hands:

```
                              ♠ J 8 4
                              ♡ 7 6 4 2
                              ◇ Q 9 8 7 5
                              ♣ A
        ♠ 7 6 2                                ♠ A 5
        ♡ Q J 10 5 3                           ♡ K 9 8
        ◇ 3                                     ◇ A 6 4 2
        ♣ J 9 8 4                               ♣ 7 5 3 2
                              ♠ K Q 10 9 3
                              ♡ A
                              ◇ K J 10
                              ♣ K Q 10 6
```

The second diamond ruff sets the contract. This may seem to be an easy defense, but it would not be without the count signal. Suppose partner has only two trumps:

                                ♠ J 8 4
                                ♡ 7 6 4 2
                                ◇ Q 9 8 7 5
                                ♣ A
        ♠ 6 2   ♠ A 5
        ♡ Q J 10 5   ♡ K 9 8
        ◇ 3   ◇ A 6 4 2
        ♣ Q J 9 8 6 4   ♣ 7 5 3 2
                                ♠ K Q 10 9 7 3
                                ♡ A 3
                                ◇ K J 10
                                ♣ K 10

With only two trumps, your partner will *ruff your diamond return with the two of spades.*
When declarer gets the lead with the ace of hearts and leads the king of spades, partner will
play the six (playing low-high shows an even number, obviously two). Since you know partner
does not have another trump, you beat the contract by *cashing the king of hearts.* If you
mistakenly lead another diamond, declarer will make his contract by discarding his losing
heart on dummy's long diamonds.

#16   North
                                        ♠ A 9 8 3
                                        ♡ K Q 5
                                        ◇ A Q J 10
                                        ♣ K 6
                West
                ♠ K J
                ♡ 10 9 8 7 6
                ◇ 5 2
                ♣ 10 7 4 3

West	North	East	South
	1 ◇	Pass	1 ♠
Pass	4 ♠	All Pass	

You lead the ten of hearts, the king is played from dummy and partner wins the trick with
the ace. Back comes the two of hearts, which is won by declarer with the jack. The fact that
partner returned the two makes it clear that he has no more hearts. Declarer leads a low spade
to dummy's ace and partner *plays the four.* The three of spades is led from dummy, partner
plays the two and you capture declarer's queen with the king. Partner's high-low signal shows
that he has a third trump, so *lead a heart* and he will ruff it. The four hands:

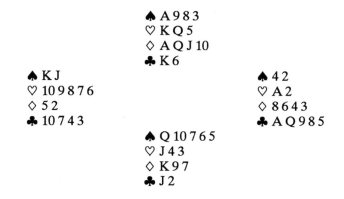

After the heart ruff, declarer must lose another trick to the ace of clubs and go down one. Once again, suppose partner had only two trumps.

The first four tricks are played the same as before, but this time partner *plays the two of spades and then the four*. This shows a doubleton trump, so you know he cannot ruff the third round of hearts. Therefore, you *lead a club at trick five*, and this turns out to be the winning defense—partner will cash two club tricks. Note that if you do not lead a club, declarer can discard one of his club losers on the fourth round of diamonds and make his contract.

Suit-Preference Signals by a Player on Lead

When leading a suit that you expect your partner to ruff, the size of the card you lead is an indication of which suit you want him to lead back. For example:

#17

```
                              North
                              ♠ Q 7 2
                              ♡ K J 9 5
                              ◇ K 6 3
                              ♣ K Q 7
                                                      East
                                                      ♠ A J 9 6 4 3
                                                      ♡ —
                                                      ◇ Q 8 4 2
                                                      ♣ A 10 3
```

West	*North*	*East*	*South*
	1♣	1♠	2♡
Pass	3♡	Pass	4♡
Pass	Pass	Pass	

Partner leads the eight of spades, you play the ace and declarer the ten. Although partner may be leading from ♠ 8 5, you should return a spade in the hope that he has led a singleton and can ruff. If he does have a singleton, you can give him a second ruff if he returns a club. So this is an ideal situation for the suit-preference signal, and here is how it works.

There are always two suits besides the one you lead and the trump suit. In this case they are diamonds and clubs, but in another deal they might be any two suits. These two suits are called the "higher-ranking suit" and the "lower-ranking suit." If you want your partner to return the higher-ranking suit, lead the highest card you can spare. If you want him to return the lower-ranking suit, lead the lowest card. If you have no particular desire for him to lead either suit, lead back a middle card.

In this case you want a club return—the lower-ranking suit—so *lead the three of spades.* The four hands:

```
                              ♠ Q 7 2
                              ♡ K J 9 5
                              ◇ K 6 3
                              ♣ K Q 7
        ♠ 8                                           ♠ A J 9 6 4 3
        ♡ 7 4 2                                       ♡ —
        ◇ J 10 9                                      ◇ Q 8 4 2
        ♣ 9 8 6 5 4 2                                 ♣ A 10 3
                              ♠ K 10 5
                              ♡ A Q 10 8 6 3
                              ◇ A 7 5
                              ♣ J
```

When partner ruffs the spade, he will return a club. You win with the ace and give him a second spade ruff. If you held the ace of diamonds instead of the ace of clubs, you would lead the jack of spades at trick two to ask for a diamond return. If you didn't have either minor-suit ace, you would lead the six of spades; partner should recognize the six as neither your highest nor lowest spade and his best strategy would be a trump return just in case you had the ace of hearts.

Sometimes it is necessary to underlead an ace to comply with partner's suit-preference signal. For example:

#18

North
♠ K Q 8 5
♡ K Q J 10
◇ K 9 3
♣ 7 4

West
♠ 10 6 2
♡ 9
◇ 8 7 5 4
♣ A 10 8 5 3

West	North	East	South
			1♠
Pass	3♠	Pass	4♠
Pass	Pass	Pass	

You lead the nine of hearts, partner wins with the ace and *returns the two of hearts*. This is clearly a signal for you to return the lower-ranking suit and, since you have the ace of clubs, partner predictably has the king. So ruff with the six of spades and *lead the five of clubs*. The four hands:

♠ K Q 8 5
♡ K Q J 10
◇ K 9 3
♣ 7 4

♠ 10 6 2   ♠ 7
♡ 9   ♡ A 7 5 4 2
◇ 8 7 5 4   ◇ 10 6
♣ A 10 8 5 3   ♣ K J 9 6 2

♠ A J 9 4 3
♡ 8 6 3
◇ A Q J 2
♣ Q

When partner wins the third trick with the king of clubs, he will lead another heart to give you a second ruff; the only way to beat the contract. If you did not have had the ace of clubs, partner could not get the lead with the king, but he clearly preferred a club return as opposed to a diamond.

#19   North
                                             ♠ J 9 3
                                             ♡ K 6 5 2
                                             ◇ 10 4
                                             ♣ K J 10 5
                                                            East
                                                            ♠ Q 5
                                                            ♡ 10 7 4 3
                                                            ◇ A K 7
                                                            ♣ A 9 7 2

West	North	East	South
		1♣	1♠
Pass	2♠	All Pass	

Partner leads the queen of clubs, the king is played from dummy and you win with the ace. Since you bid clubs, there is no certainty that partner has led a singleton (he may have led from ♣ Q x), but you need a lot of tricks to beat two spades and should assume he has led a singleton. You might think it a good idea to play the king of diamonds first so partner will know what to lead after he ruffs your club return. But don't do it! You can tell your partner to return a diamond by the suit-preference signal and, if he has three spades and you do not waste one of your high diamonds, you can give him *three* ruffs. So, *return the two of clubs*. The four hands:

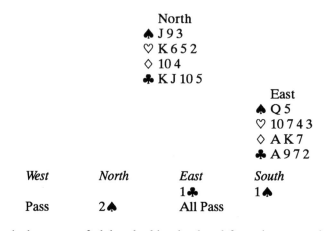

                                             ♠ J 9 3
                                             ♡ K 6 5 2
                                             ◇ 10 4
                                             ♣ K J 10 5
        ♠ 7 6 2   ♠ Q 5
        ♡ Q J 9 8   ♡ 10 7 4 3
        ◇ J 9 8 6 3   ◇ A K 7
        ♣ Q   ♣ A 9 7 2
                                             ♠ A K 10 8 4
                                             ♡ A
                                             ◇ Q 5 2
                                             ♣ 8 6 4 3

Partner should ruff the two of clubs with the seven of spades (the beginning of a trump echo to show he has three trumps) and lead a diamond. When you win the trick with your king, partner learns that you have the ace as well. So, lead another club, which partner ruffs with the two; then he leads another diamond to your ace and you give him a third ruff. You have just set the contract by winning the first six tricks.

In the next deal, a suit-preference signal is used to stop partner from leading a suit.

#20

North
♠ A Q 7
♡ A 10 9 2
◇ K J 10 8
♣ 6 3

East
♠ J 5 4
♡ K 6
◇ A 9 3 2
♣ J 9 8 2

West	North	East	South
	1◇	Pass	1♡
Pass	2♡	Pass	4♡
Pass	Pass	Pass	

Partner leads the seven of diamonds, which you should assume is a singleton; he would be unlikely to lead dummy's bid suit with a doubleton. So you win the first trick and return a diamond, but which one? Although you do not have the king of spades, you should *play the nine of diamonds*; the reason being to discourage partner from leading a club, which might jeopardize a trick, when a spade lead is safe. The four hands:

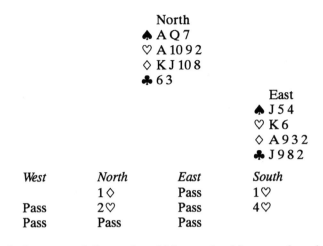

♠ A Q 7
♡ A 10 9 2
◇ K J 10 8
♣ 6 3

♠ K 9 8 6 3
♡ 5 4
◇ 7
♣ K 10 7 5 4

♠ J 5 4
♡ K 6
◇ A 9 3 2
♣ J 9 8 2

♠ 10 2
♡ Q J 8 7 3
◇ Q 6 5 4
♣ A Q

Partner should ruff your nine-of-diamonds lead and heed your signal by returning a spade, even though he has the king. Declarer can win a trick with the queen of spades, but his other two finesses will fail and the contract is defeated. Note that if you return the three of diamonds at trick two and partner reads this as a suit-preference signal asking for the lower-ranking suit, he might lead a club and give declarer the contract.

#21   North
                                 ♠ K Q 5
                                 ♡ Q J 7 6
                                 ◇ 9 8 3
                                 ♣ 7 6 2

            West
            ♠ 9 2
            ♡ A K 10 2
            ◇ A J 10
            ♣ K J 8 5

West	*North*	*East*	*South*
			1♠
Double	2♠	Pass	Pass
Double	Pass	3♣	3♠
Pass	Pass	Pass	

You lead the king of hearts and partner plays the nine as a come-on signal. Therefore, you continue with the ace of hearts and partner plays the five. Of course, you will play a third heart for partner to ruff, but which suit do you want him to lead back? The right answer is a diamond, so that you can lead a fourth round of hearts for partner to ruff. Declarer will overruff, but this prevents him from discarding a loser on dummy's fourth heart. So, *lead the ten of hearts* at trick three. The four hands:

                                 ♠ K Q 5
                                 ♡ Q J 7 6
                                 ◇ 9 8 3
                                 ♣ 7 6 2
            ♠ 9 2   ♠ J 8
            ♡ A K 10 2   ♡ 9 5
            ◇ A J 10   ◇ 7 6 5 4
            ♣ K J 8 5   ♣ Q 10 9 4 3
                                 ♠ A 10 7 6 4 3
                                 ♡ 8 4 3
                                 ◇ K Q 2
                                 ♣ A

After ruffing the third round of hearts, partner follows your signal and leads a diamond. Declarer plays the king and you win with the ace. You then lead the two of hearts, partner ruffs and declarer overruffs. Now declarer must lose another trick and go down one.

In rare cases, a suit-preference signal can be used when you lead a suit that you do not expect your partner to ruff. For example:

#22

                          North
                          ♠ A Q 5
                          ♡ 10 7
                          ◇ J 9 6 3
                          ♣ J 8 5 2

        West
        ♠ 6 3
        ♡ A K 9 4 3
        ◇ A Q 7 2
        ♣ 10 4

West	North	East	South
			1♠
2♡	2♠	Pass	4♠
Pass	Pass	Pass	

You lead the king of hearts and partner plays the queen, an honor signal to tell you he has the jack. Since a diamond lead from partner at trick three would be nice, you should underlead the ace of hearts. But lead the *nine of hearts* so partner will know to lead a diamond instead of a club. The four hands:

                          ♠ A Q 5
                          ♡ 10 7
                          ◇ J 9 6 3
                          ♣ J 8 5 2

        ♠ 6 3   ♠ 7 4
        ♡ A K 9 4 3   ♡ Q J 5 2
        ◇ A Q 7 2   ◇ 10 8 5
        ♣ 10 4   ♣ 9 7 6 3

                          ♠ K J 10 9 8 2
                          ♡ 8 6
                          ◇ K 4
                          ♣ A K Q

It takes a diamond lead from partner at trick three to beat the contract; otherwise declarer can discard one of his losing diamonds on the jack of clubs. The dummy has similar holdings in the minor suits, so partner would not know whether you wanted a diamond or a club lead if it were not for the suit-preference signal.

Suit-Preference Signals when Partner Leads

A suit-preference signal applies only when an attitude signal or a count signal would be useless. It is in third-hand situations that a partnership misunderstanding is most apt to take place. Here is an example of what happened to me in a rubber-bridge game. My partner was a reasonably good player who just recently learned how (or how *not*) to play suit-preference signals.

#23

```
                          North
                          ♠ J 8 7
                          ♡ K Q 2
                          ◇ J 6 3
                          ♣ 9 7 5 4
        West
        ♠ 10 6 3
        ♡ 10 7 5 4 3
        ◇ A K 8
        ♣ K 2
```

West	North	East	South
			1♠
Pass	2♠	Pass	4♠
Pass	Pass	Pass	

My partner led the king of diamonds and I played the two. Thinking that my two-of-diamonds play was a suit-preference signal, he switched to the king of clubs. The four hands:

```
                          ♠ J 8 7
                          ♡ K Q 2
                          ◇ J 6 3
                          ♣ 9 7 5 4
        ♠ 10 6 3                        ♠ 5 2
        ♡ 10 7 5 4 3                    ♡ A J 9
        ◇ A K 8                         ◇ 9 4 2
        ♣ K 2                           ♣ J 10 8 6 3
                          ♠ A K Q 9 4
                          ♡ 8 6
                          ◇ Q 10 7 5
                          ♣ A Q
```

As you can see, the declarer would be set if my partner led anything but a club. My play of the two of diamonds indicated that I did not think he should lead another diamond. Since this was an attitude-signal situation, there was no way I could tell him which other suit to lead.

Partner's king-of-clubs shift could have been the winning defense, but it was an inferior play and one that he would not have made if he hadn't confused the signals.

Now let's look at some third-hand situations where attitude and count signals would be illogical, and suit-preference signals do apply. The first two deals show cases where partner leads a singleton in a suit in which dummy has great strength.

#24

North
♠ K 10 9 3
♡ Q 2
◇ K 6 4
♣ K Q J 5

East
♠ 5 2
♡ A 7
◇ 8 7 5 2
♣ 10 8 6 4 3

West	*North*	*East*	*South*
	1♣	Pass	1♠
2♡	2♠	Pass	4♠
Pass	Pass	Pass	

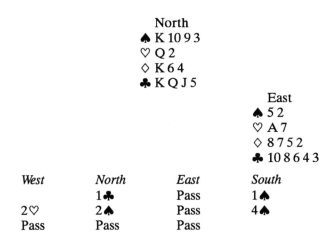

Your partner leads the ace of clubs, which is predictably a singleton because the dummy bid clubs. The dummy has all the high clubs, so an attitude signal is useless; and partner is not interested in how many clubs you have, so a count signal is equally useless. He wants to know how to put you on lead so you can give him a club ruff. This is an ideal situation for a suit-preference signal, so *play the ten of clubs* to tell your partner to lead the higher-ranking suit; in this case hearts.

♠ K 10 9 3
♡ Q 2
◇ K 6 4
♣ K Q J 5

♠ 7 6
♡ K J 10 9 8 3
◇ Q J 9 3
♣ A

♠ 5 2
♡ A 7
◇ 8 7 5 2
♣ 10 8 6 4 3

♠ A Q J 8 4
♡ 6 5 4
◇ A 10
♣ 9 7 2

Seeing your ten-of-clubs signal, partner should lead a heart to your ace. After you give him the club ruff, he will set the contract by cashing the king of hearts. Note how tempting it would be for partner to lead a diamond at trick two instead of a heart, if it were not for the suit-preference signal.

#25

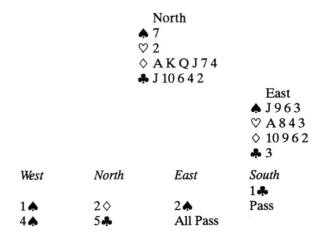

North
♠ 7
♡ 2
◇ A K Q J 7 4
♣ J 10 6 4 2

East
♠ J 9 6 3
♡ A 8 4 3
◇ 10 9 6 2
♣ 3

West	North	East	South
			1♣
1♠	2◇	2♠	Pass
4♠	5♣	All Pass	

Partner leads the five of diamonds (clearly a singleton), the ace is played from dummy and you should play *the two of diamonds* to tell your partner that you have an entry in the lower-ranking suit; which in this case is obviously the ace of hearts. The four hands:

                      ♠ 7
                      ♡ 2
                      ◇ A K Q J 7 4
                      ♣ J 10 6 4 2
♠ K Q 10 8 5 4   ♠ J 9 6 3
♡ K 10 7 6   ♡ A 8 4 3
◇ 5   ◇ 10 9 6 2
♣ A 8   ♣ 3
                      ♠ A 2
                      ♡ Q J 9 5
                      ◇ 8 3
                      ♣ K Q 9 7 5

Heeding your suit-preference signal, partner will lead a heart when he gains the lead with the ace of clubs. You win with the ace of hearts and return a diamond for partner to ruff, defeating the contract. If you had the ace of spades, instead of the ace of hearts, you would play the ten of diamonds on the first trick.

Another time the suit-preference signal can be used by third hand is when removing declarer's last stopper in a notrump contract. For example:

#26

North
♠ K 10 6
♡ 7 5 2
◇ A J 9 7 2
♣ 6 4

West
♠ A 9 2
♡ Q J 8 6 4 3
◇ 8 3
♣ 7 5

West	North	East	South
			1NT
Pass	2NT	All Pass	

You lead the six of hearts, partner plays the ace and declarer the ten. Partner returns the nine of hearts and declarer plays the king. If partner should get the lead, you surely want him to lead a spade. So play *the queen of hearts* under the king. If you held the ace of clubs instead of the ace of spades, you would play the three of hearts. The four hands:

```
                    ♠ K 10 6
                    ♡ 7 5 2
                    ◇ A J 9 7 2
                    ♣ 6 4
  ♠ A 9 2                          ♠ J 8 5
  ♡ Q J 8 6 4 3                    ♡ A 9
  ◇ 8 3                            ◇ K 6 4
  ♣ 7 5                            ♣ J 10 9 8 3
                    ♠ Q 7 4 3
                    ♡ K 10
                    ◇ Q 10 5
                    ♣ A K Q 2
```

Assume declarer takes the losing diamond finesse at trick three. Partner will win with the king and return a spade to set the contract two tricks. If partner returned a club (which would certainly be a more tempting choice if it were not for the suit-preference signal), declarer would make his contract.

In the next deal, you will give an attitude signal first, then follow up with a suit-preference signal:

#27   North
                                           ♠ K J 10 8
                                           ♡ A J 3
                                           ◇ 9 7 4
                                           ♣ K J 3
                                                                          East
                                                                          ♠ A 9 5 4
                                                                          ♡ 6
                                                                          ◇ J 8 6 5 2
                                                                          ♣ Q 10 8

West	North	East	South
			1♡
Pass	1♠	Pass	2♡
Pass	4♡	All Pass	

Partner leads the ace of diamonds and you give a discouraging signal with the two. Then partner leads the king of diamonds to show a doubleton. It is obvious that the contract can be set if partner leads a spade; you will win with the ace and give him a diamond ruff. So *play the jack of diamonds under partner's king*, a suit-preference signal asking partner to lead the higher-ranking suit. Without your signal, he would probably lead a club because of the weaker club holding in dummy. Here are the four hands to show you that this is the only defense to beat the contract.

                                           ♠ K J 10 8
                                           ♡ A J 3
                                           ◇ 9 7 4
                                           ♣ K J 3
            ♠ 6 3 2   ♠ A 9 5 4
            ♡ 10 7 4   ♡ 6
            ◇ A K   ◇ J 8 6 5 2
            ♣ 9 7 5 4 2   ♣ Q 10 8
                                           ♠ Q 7
                                           ♡ K Q 9 8 5 2
                                           ◇ Q 10 3
                                           ♣ A 6

In the next example, dummy is strong in the suit your partnership bid and raised.

#28

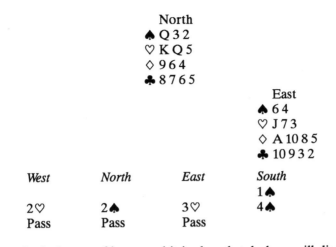

North
♠ Q 3 2
♡ K Q 5
◇ 9 6 4
♣ 8 7 6 5

East
♠ 6 4
♡ J 7 3
◇ A 10 8 5
♣ 10 9 3 2

West	North	East	South
			1♠
2♡	2♠	3♡	4♠
Pass	Pass	Pass	

Your partner leads the ace of hearts and it is clear that declarer will discard one or two losers on dummy's top hearts if he is given the chance. So you should *play the jack of hearts*, telling partner to switch to the higher-ranking suit, diamonds. The four hands:

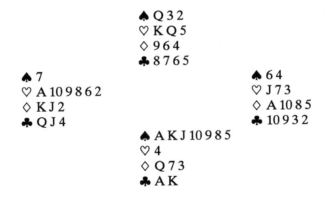

♠ Q 3 2
♡ K Q 5
◇ 9 6 4
♣ 8 7 6 5

♠ 7
♡ A 10 9 8 6 2
◇ K J 2
♣ Q J 4

♠ 6 4
♡ J 7 3
◇ A 10 8 5
♣ 10 9 3 2

♠ A K J 10 9 8 5
♡ 4
◇ Q 7 3
♣ A K

Since you raised hearts, partner knows that you have three cards in the suit and that you played the jack as a suit-preference signal. He should therefore lead the two of diamonds. Partner would not lead his lowest diamond unless he wanted you to return the suit, so you should win the second trick with the ace of diamonds and lead another diamond. With the cards as shown, partner will win two more diamond tricks and set the contract.

If you had not raised hearts, playing the jack of hearts on the first trick would be wrong (partner would probably lead another heart hoping you could ruff); you should play the three of hearts—an attitude signal—which leaves partner to guess whether to switch to a club or a diamond, or to lead another heart hoping you can ruff.

Both a suit-preference signal and an attitude signal can be used at a suit contract when the opening leader holds the lead in a suit bid by his partner: Since third hand is known to have a long suit, he plays the highest card he can spare or his lowest card as suit preference, and *plays a middle card as a come-on signal*. For example:

#29

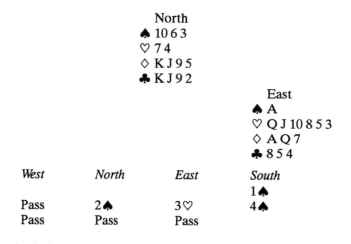

North
♠ 10 6 3
♡ 7 4
◇ K J 9 5
♣ K J 9 2

East
♠ A
♡ Q J 10 8 5 3
◇ A Q 7
♣ 8 5 4

West	North	East	South
			1♠
Pass	2♠	3♡	4♠
Pass	Pass	Pass	

Your partner leads the ace of hearts because you bid the suit, so declarer has the king and one trick may already have been wasted. But it looks like you can still beat the contract if declarer has at least two diamonds and partner leads the suit. So *play the queen of hearts* on the first trick to deny possession of the king and ask partner to switch to the higher-ranking suit. The four hands:

```
                      ♠ 10 6 3
                      ♡ 7 4
                      ◇ K J 9 5
                      ♣ K J 9 2
   ♠ 5 4                              ♠ A
   ♡ A 6 2                            ♡ Q J 10 8 5 3
   ◇ 10 8 4 2                         ◇ A Q 7
   ♣ 10 7 6 3                         ♣ 8 5 4
                      ♠ K Q J 9 8 7 2
                      ♡ K 9
                      ◇ 6 3
                      ♣ A Q
```

Partner certainly should get the message and switch to the two of diamonds so you can take your two diamond tricks before declarer has a chance to discard on the club suit. How would you signal if partner led the ace of hearts and you held the following East hand?

```
                      ♠ 10 6 3
                      ♡ 7 4
                      ◇ K J 9 5
                      ♣ K J 9 2
   ♠ 5 4                              ♠ 2
   ♡ A 6 2                            ♡ K Q J 8 5 3
   ◇ 10 8 4 2                         ◇ A Q 7
   ♣ 10 7 6 3                         ♣ 8 5 4
                      ♠ A K Q J 9 8 7
                      ♡ 10 9
                      ◇ 6 3
                      ♣ A Q
```

Again you want your partner to switch to a diamond, so play *the queen of hearts*. True, this denies the king, but sometimes it pays to lie. Only if partner leads a diamond at trick two can you win three more tricks and set the contract.

Based on what I said earlier, playing the king would also call for a diamond lead; if you wanted a heart continuation you would play a middle card—the eight. But the queen is the superior play because partner is less likely to misread the meaning of your signal.

Probably the time that a third-hand signal is most apt to be misunderstood is when the opening leader wins the first trick and the dummy has a singleton. Under these conditions suit preference *and* attitude signals are used: an unusually high card asks for the higher-ranking suit, the lowest card asks for the lower ranking suit, and a middle card is a come-on signal. In the next two deals, the challenge is to read your partner's signal.

#30

North
♠ 7
♡ Q 9 5 4
♢ A Q J 2
♣ K J 8 3

West
♠ A J 9 6
♡ 2
♢ 10 8 5 4 3
♣ 7 5 4

West	North	East	South
	1♢	1♠	2♡
2♠	4♡	4♠	5♡
Pass	Pass	Pass	

You lead the ace of spades and partner plays the king. This is obviously a suit-preference signal asking for the higher-ranking suit to be led. Partner is known to have a fist full of spades and would play a middle card if he wanted a spade continuation. The right switch is the *four of diamonds*. The four hands:

```
              ♠ 7
              ♡ Q 9 5 4
              ♢ A Q J 2
              ♣ K J 8 3
♠ A J 9 6                    ♠ K Q 10 8 5 2
♡ 2                          ♡ 6 3
♢ 10 8 5 4 3                 ♢ K 7
♣ 7 5 4                      ♣ A 9 6
              ♠ 4 3
              ♡ A K J 10 8 7
              ♢ 9 6
              ♣ Q 10 2
```

With the diamond lead at trick two, East can win two more tricks with the king of diamonds and the ace of clubs. With any other lead, declarer can succeed by drawing trumps and eventually discarding his losing diamond on the fourth round of clubs.

If third hand had this same spade holding in a different deal and wanted partner to lead another spade, he would signal with the ten, or maybe the eight. If he wanted a club lead, he would play the two.

Of course, if third hand has a short suit, or even a four- or five-card suit with a high card he cannot afford to play without jeopardizing a trick, he cannot be so emphatic with his signals. For example:

#31

                                      North
                                      ♠ A Q
                                      ♡ 7
                                      ◇ K Q J 8 3
                                      ♣ A J 10 5 4

                    West
                    ♠ 4 3
                    ♡ A K J 10 5 4
                    ◇ 7 2
                    ♣ 8 6 2

West	North	East	South
	1◇	Pass	1♠
2♡	3♣	Pass	3♠
Pass	4♠	Pass	4NT
Pass	5♡	Pass	6♠
Pass	Pass	Pass	

You lead the king of hearts, partner plays the eight and declarer the three. Partner might have played the eight from ♡ 8 6 2 or ♡ 9 8 6. His signal is ambiguous; there is no sure way to know whether he wants you to switch to the higher-ranking suit, or to lead another heart.

Fortunately you can usually figure it out based on logic. A diamond lead will be right if partner has the ace of diamonds (but declarer would not bid a slam off two aces), or if partner is void in diamonds; which is also unlikely because declarer would have supported diamonds if he had ◇ A x x x. The most common reason to continue leading a suit in which the dummy has a singleton is to promote a trump trick. In this case, leading the ace of hearts will force dummy to ruff with the ace or queen and beat the contract if partner has ♠ J x x. Since winning a trump trick offers the only good chance to get another trick, *lead the ace of hearts*. The four hands:

                                      ♠ A Q
                                      ♡ 7
                                      ◇ K Q J 8 3
                                      ♣ A J 10 5 4
        ♠ 4 3   ♠ J 10 6
        ♡ A K J 10 5 4   ♡ 8 6 2
        ◇ 7 2   ◇ 10 9 5 4
        ♣ 8 6 2   ♣ 9 7 3
                                      ♠ K 9 8 7 5 2
                                      ♡ Q 9 3
                                      ◇ A 6
                                      ♣ K Q

The ace-of-hearts lead forces declarer to ruff in dummy and promotes a trump trick for partner. With any other lead, declarer is left with three high trumps; he will make his contract by drawing your partner's trumps with the ace, queen and king, and discarding his losing hearts on dummy's winners.

Note that six clubs or six diamonds can be made, but these contracts are hard to reach.

A suit-preference signal by third hand can also apply when partner knows, or will know, your exact holding in a suit. For example:

#32

			North
			♠ J 10 9 8
			♡ J 10 8 7
			◇ K J 9
			♣ J 6

East
♠ A K Q 6 5 3
♡ 6
◇ A Q 8
♣ 5 4 2

West	North	East	South
		1♠	2♡
2♠	3♡	4♠	5♡
Double	Pass	Pass	Pass

Partner leads the seven of spades. The standard third-hand play is the queen from ace-king-queen to help your partner determine your holding in the suit. But since partner has raised spades, you know declarer is void and your partner will know your exact spade holding when declarer ruffs. *When your partner knows (or will know) your exact holding in a suit, there is no need for a standard third-hand play, an attitude signal or a count signal; but a suit-preference signal can be useful.* If partner should get the lead, you want him to lead a diamond—the higher-ranking suit—so *play the ace of spades* on the first trick. Playing the queen would ask for a club lead. Playing the king would be neutral (no preference). The four hands:

	♠ J 10 9 8	
	♡ J 10 8 7	
	◇ K J 9	
	♣ J 6	
♠ 7 4 2		♠ A K Q 6 5 3
♡ A		♡ 6
◇ 10 5 4 3 2		◇ A Q 8
♣ K 9 7 3		♣ 5 4 2
	♠ —	
	♡ K Q 9 5 4 3 2	
	◇ 7 6	
	♣ A Q 10 8	

Declarer will lead a trump to your partner's ace at trick two. If partner leads a club, declarer will avoid a club loser. Worse yet, declarer will be able to establish a spade trick by ruffing finesses to get rid of a diamond loser and make his contract.

If your partner reads your signal and leads a diamond at trick three, the contract can be set two tricks.

Suit-Preference Signals when Declarer Leads

All of the suit-preference signals so far have been when you or your partner are leading a suit. When declarer leads a suit (you are second or fourth hand), it is normal to use count signals when following suit or attitude signals when discarding. Suit-preference signals may be used only when partner already knows (or will know immediately) the information provided by the normal signal. The final four deals show situations where suit preference is appropriate.

#33

```
                        North
                        ♠ K J 6 4
                        ♡ 3
                        ◇ K J 4 2
                        ♣ K 10 4 2
                                            East
                                            ♠ A Q 2
                                            ♡ K Q J 10 8 6 2
                                            ◇ 9 8 7
                                            ♣ —
```

West	North	East	South
		1♡	2♣
Pass	2♡	3♡	4♣
4♡	5♣	All Pass	

Partner leads the four of hearts, you play the ten and declarer wins with the ace. At trick two, a club is led and partner wins with the ace. You are anxious for a spade lead and have three choices of signals: You can discard a high spade, but the only one you can spare is the two. Or a low diamond, but the lowest one you have is the seven and partner may think it is a come-on signal. So, the best choice is to give a suit-preference signal by discarding a heart. Which heart would you discard?

Right—the *king!* That play should wake up your partner. If he doesn't lead a spade, get another partner. The four hands:

```
                        ♠ K J 6 4
                        ♡ 3
                        ◇ K J 4 2
                        ♣ K 10 4 2
        ♠ 9 7 5 3                           ♠ A Q 2
        ♡ 9 7 5 4                           ♡ K Q J 10 8 6 2
        ◇ 10 5 3                            ◇ 9 8 7
        ♣ A 6                               ♣ —
                        ♠ 10 8
                        ♡ A
                        ◇ A Q 6
                        ♣ Q J 9 8 7 5 3
```

If your partner does not lead a spade at trick three, declarer will fulfill his contract by discarding one of his losing spades on dummy's fourth diamond.

#34

North
♠ 6 5 4
♡ 8
◇ A K J 10 9 8 3
♣ 7 2

West
♠ A Q 10 2
♡ J 7 6 5 2
◇ —
♣ 8 6 5 3

West	North	East	South
			1NT
Pass	3◇	Pass	3NT
Pass	Pass	Pass	

You lead the five of hearts, partner plays the nine and declarer wins with the king. The play at trick one reveals that partner has the ten of hearts, and declarer has the ace and queen. To beat the contract, partner must have the guarded queen of diamonds and switch to a spade when he gets the lead. At trick two, declarer plays the five of diamonds. To discourage your partner from returning a heart, all you have to do is discard any heart. However, the size of the heart you discard should be suit preference; you can give two signals at once. Since you want partner to lead a spade, discard the *jack of hearts*; if you wanted a club lead, you would discard the two of hearts. The four hands:

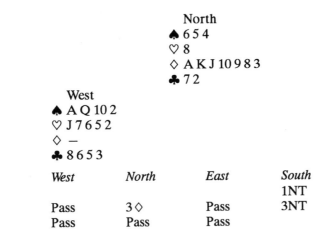

♠ 6 5 4
♡ 8
◇ A K J 10 9 8 3
♣ 7 2

♠ A Q 10 2   ♠ J 8 7
♡ J 7 6 5 2   ♡ 10 9 3
◇ —   ◇ Q 4 2
♣ 8 6 5 3   ♣ K Q J 10

♠ K 9 3
♡ A K Q 4
◇ 7 6 5
♣ A 9 4

When partner gets the lead with the queen of diamonds, he should obey orders and lead a spade. But he had better lead the *jack* as it is the only card in his hand that enables you to win four spade tricks and set the contract.

The next deal is another example where your partner knows your exact holding in a suit (see deal #32), but this time you give a suit-preference signal by discarding in a suit led by the declarer.

#35   North
                                      ♠ A 10 9 8
                                      ♡ 8 6 5
                                      ◇ 10 9 7
                                      ♣ J 10 3

              West
              ♠ J
              ♡ A K J 10 9 2
              ◇ 8 5
              ♣ A Q 4 2

West	North	East	South
			1♠
2♡	2♠	Pass	4♠
Pass	Pass	Pass	

You start with your two top hearts, declarer ruffing the second. Declarer leads a spade to dummy's ace, then plays another spade, which your partner wins with the king. Partner knows your exact heart holding—♡ J 10 9 2—so whichever heart you discard is a suit-preference signal. If you want the higher-ranking suit led, discard the jack; if you want the lower-ranking suit led, discard the two; and if you have no preference, discard the nine or ten. Since you want a club lead, *discard the two of hearts*. The four hands:

                              ♠ A 10 9 8
                              ♡ 8 6 5
                              ◇ 10 9 7
                              ♣ J 10 3
         ♠ J   ♠ K 5 3
         ♡ A K J 10 9 2   ♡ Q 7 4
         ◇ 8 5   ◇ 6 4 2
         ♣ A Q 4 2   ♣ 9 8 6 5
                              ♠ Q 7 6 4 2
                              ♡ 3
                              ◇ A K Q J 3
                              ♣ K 7

If your partner does not lead a club, declarer can make his contract by drawing the last trump and discarding two of dummy's clubs on his long diamonds. He will lose one heart, one spade and only one club.

In this last deal, a suit-preference signal is given *after* a count signal:

#36

North
♠ 7 4 2
♡ Q J 6
◇ Q J
♣ K J 10 9 5

East
♠ 10 5
♡ A 9 4 2
◇ 8 7 6 3
♣ 8 3 2

West	North	East	South
			1NT
Pass	3NT	All Pass	

Partner leads the six of spades, you play the ten and declarer wins with the king. A low club is led and this trick is won with dummy's nine; you play the two to show an odd number. Then declarer plays the five of clubs from dummy, and *the next club you play is a suit-preference signal.* So *play the eight of clubs* to ask for a heart lead. If you held the ace of diamonds, you would play the three of clubs. The four hands:

♠ 7 4 2
♡ Q J 6
◇ Q J
♣ K J 10 9 5

♠ A J 8 6 3
♡ 10 7 5
◇ 9 4 2
♣ A 4

♠ 10 5
♡ A 9 4 2
◇ 8 7 6 3
♣ 8 3 2

♠ K Q 9
♡ K 8 3
◇ A K 10 5
♣ Q 7 6

Note that your partner, West, could tell by your play of the ten of spades that declarer has the queen-nine, so he knows the only chance to beat the contract is to put you on lead to play a spade through declarer. (An expert sitting West would be watching his partner's second club play like a hawk.) Since the eight is obviously your highest club, partner should lead a heart. After you win with the ace of hearts and return a spade, the contract is set two tricks. If partner leads anything but a heart, declarer has at least nine tricks (one spade, four diamonds and four clubs).

Quiz for Chapter Seven

1.

North
♠ J 7 2
♡ 5 4 3
◇ Q J 4
♣ K Q J 2

West
♠ 10 5
♡ Q J 10 9 8
◇ A 9 8 6 2
♣ 3

West	North	East	South
			1♠
Pass	2♠	Pass	4♠
Pass	Pass	Pass	

You lead the three of clubs. Partner captures dummy's king with his ace and returns the four of clubs, which you ruff. What do you lead now?

2.

North
♠ K 10 8
♡ K 10 9 5
◇ 7 3
♣ 8 7 5 2

West
♠ A 6 4
♡ 8 2
◇ Q 5 4 2
♣ J 10 9 3

West	North	East	South
			1♡
Pass	2♡	Pass	4♡
Pass	Pass	Pass	

You lead the jack of clubs, partner wins with the ace and declarer plays the four. Partner leads the king of clubs and declarer plays the six. Which club do you play?

3.

North
♠ A K Q J
♡ J 10 8 2
◇ 9 7 6
♣ Q 8

West
♠ 3
♡ K 6 4
◇ K 10 8 4 2
♣ K 5 4 3

West	North	East	South
			1♡
Pass	3♡	Pass	4♡
Pass	Pass	Pass	

You lead the three of spades, partner plays the two and declarer the four. The jack of hearts is led, partner and declarer play low hearts and you win with the king. What do you lead now?

4.

North
♠ K Q 2
♡ A J 8
◇ 10 5
♣ Q J 9 8 3

West
♠ 6
♡ 9 5 4
◇ 9 8 4 3
♣ A K 7 6 2

West	North	East	South
	1♣	Pass	1♠
Pass	2♠	Pass	4NT
Pass	5◇	Pass	6♠
Pass	Pass	Pass	

You lead the king of clubs, partner plays the four and declarer the five. What do you lead now?

5.

                    North
                    ♠ K Q 2
                    ♡ A 10 8 5
                    ◇ Q 6 4 3
                    ♣ 7 4

                                      East
                                      ♠ J 9 7 6 3
                                      ♡ K 4 3
                                      ◇ 10 7 5
                                      ♣ 9 2

West	North	East	South
			1NT
Pass	2♣	Pass	2◇
Pass	3NT	All Pass	

Your partner leads the ace of clubs. Which club do you play, and why?

6.

                    North
                    ♠ A K Q
                    ♡ 7
                    ◇ A Q J 9 2
                    ♣ 8 6 5 4
      West
      ♠ 4
      ♡ A K J 9 5 4
      ◇ 6 5
      ♣ Q 7 3 2

West	North	East	South
			1♠
2♡	3◇	Pass	4♣
Pass	4NT	Pass	5◇
Pass	6♠	All Pass	

You lead the king of hearts, partner plays the eight and declarer the two. What do you lead now?

7.

                    North
                    ♠ Q 10 5
                    ♡ J 10 9
                    ◇ A Q 6 3
                    ♣ Q J 2
      West
      ♠ K 8 2
      ♡ A Q 7 5 4
      ◇ 5 2
      ♣ 10 7 6

West	North	East	South
			1NT
Pass	3NT	All Pass	

You lead the five of hearts, partner plays the two and declarer the three. The queen of spades is led from dummy and you win the second trick with the king. What do you lead now?

8.

                    North
                    ♠ 9 7 6
                    ♡ K 4
                    ◇ A J 9 8 7 5
                    ♣ K 4
      West
      ♠ Q 8 5 4 2
      ♡ A 10
      ◇ 3 2
      ♣ 8 5 3 2

West	North	East	South
			1♡
Pass	2◇	Pass	2NT
Pass	3NT	All Pass	

You lead the four of spades, partner plays the ace and declarer the ten. The three of spades is returned, declarer plays the jack and you win with the queen. What do you lead now?

Quiz Answers for Chapter Seven

1.   **North**
       ♠ J 7 2
       ♡ 5 4 3
       ◇ Q J 4
       ♣ K Q J 2

West   **East**
♠ 10 5   ♠ 8 3
♡ Q J 10 9 8   ♡ 7 6
◇ A 9 8 6 2   ◇ K 7 5 3
♣ 3   ♣ A 9 8 5 4

       South
       ♠ A K Q 9 6 4
       ♡ A K 2
       ◇ 10
       ♣ 10 7 6

West	North	East	South
			1♠
Pass	2♠	Pass	4♠
Pass	Pass	Pass	

You lead the three of clubs: king, ace, six. Partner returns the four of clubs, which you ruff. What do you lead now?

Lead the six of diamonds. The four is partner's lowest club, so he wants you to lead back the lower-ranking suit. Since you have the ace of diamonds, he must have the king. *Without the ace or king of diamonds, he should not lead back his lowest club.* Partner will win the third trick with the king of diamonds and give you another club ruff; the only defense to beat the contract.

2.   **North**
       ♠ K 10 8
       ♡ K 10 9 5
       ◇ 7 3
       ♣ 8 7 5 2

West   **East**
♠ A 6 4   ♠ J 9 7 5 2
♡ 8 2   ♡ 6 4
◇ Q 5 4 2   ◇ 10 9 8 6
♣ J 10 9 3   ♣ A K

       South
       ♠ Q 3
       ♡ A Q J 7 3
       ◇ A K J
       ♣ Q 6 4

West	North	East	South
			1♡
Pass	2♡	Pass	4♡
Pass	Pass	Pass	

You lead the jack of clubs: two, ace, four. Partner leads the king of clubs and declarer plays the six. Which club do you play?

Play the ten of clubs, a suit-preference signal asking partner to lead the higher-ranking suit. Partner has shown a doubleton club by playing high-low. If he leads a spade at trick three, you can win with the ace and give him a club ruff.

If you held the ace of diamonds instead of the ace of spades, you would play your lowest club under partner's king. Note that if you were not playing suit-preference signals, partner would probably lead the ten of diamonds and declarer would make his contract.

3.

	North
	♠ A K Q J
	♡ J 10 8 2
	◇ 9 7 6
	♣ Q 8

West		East
♠ 3		♠ 10 9 7 6 2
♡ K 6 4		♡ 3
◇ K 10 8 4 2		◇ Q J 5 3
♣ K 5 4 3		♣ A 7 2

	South
	♠ 8 5 4
	♡ A Q 9 7 5
	◇ A
	♣ J 10 9 6

West	North	East	South
			1♡
Pass	3♡	Pass	4♡
Pass	Pass	Pass	

You lead the three of spades, partner plays the two and declarer the four. The jack of hearts is led, partner and declarer play low hearts and you win with the king. What do you lead now?

Lead the three of clubs. Partner's two-of-spades was a suit-preference signal asking you to switch to the lower-ranking suit when you get the lead. When you lead the club and he wins with the ace, he will return a spade for you to ruff. You will cash the king of clubs to set the contract.

If partner held the ace of diamonds instead of the ace of clubs, he would play the ten of spades on the first trick. If he did not have either ace, he would play his middle spade—the seven.

4.

	North
	♠ K Q 2
	♡ A J 8
	◇ 10 5
	♣ Q J 9 8 3

West		East
♠ 6		♠ 8 5 3
♡ 9 5 4		♡ 10 7 6 3 2
◇ 9 8 4 3		◇ Q J 7 6
♣ A K 7 6 2		♣ 4

	South
	♠ A J 10 9 7 4
	♡ K Q
	◇ A K 2
	♣ 10 5

West	North	East	South
	1♣	Pass	1♠
Pass	2♠	Pass	4NT
Pass	5◇	Pass	6♠
Pass	Pass	Pass	

You lead the king of clubs, partner plays the four and declarer the five. What do you lead now?

Lead the ace of clubs (or any club). As recommended earlier, your partner should always play the higher card from a doubleton (except from Q x) when you lead the king and dummy has length in the suit. If he held ♣ 10 4, he would play the ten on the first trick. So declarer has another club in his hand. With the cards as shown, declarer can discard his losing club on the third round of hearts if you don't lead a club at trick two.

If partner's first club play were the ten, you could not be sure who had the singleton. In that case, you would have to guess what to do next.

5.   North
                    ♠ K Q 2
                    ♡ A 10 8 5
                    ◇ Q 6 4 3
                    ♣ 7 4
     West   East
     ♠ 8 5 4   ♠ J 9 7 6 3
     ♡ 9 7 6   ♡ K 4 3
     ◇ 8 2   ◇ 10 7 5
     ♣ A K Q 10 3   ♣ 9 2
                    South
                    ♠ A 10
                    ♡ Q J 2
                    ◇ A K J 9
                    ♣ J 8 6 5

West	North	East	South
			1NT
Pass	2♣	Pass	2◇
Pass	3NT	All Pass	

Your partner leads the ace of clubs. Which club do you play? Why?

Play the nine of clubs. The opening lead of an ace against a notrump contract asks you to play the king, queen, or jack if you have one, or else *give count*. (Giving count if you have no honor card is not 100 percent standard; the old-fashioned way is always to play your highest card. This is a good point to discuss with your regular partners. See #12 on page 246.) Therefore, your nine-of-clubs play is a count signal to show an even number. From this, your partner can deduce that you have a doubleton and declarer has ♣ J x x x. He knows he cannot run five club tricks, so he should not lead a club at trick two. Although any lead but a club will beat the contract, suppose he leads a spade. Declarer has eight tricks if he takes them, but he may try the losing heart finesse. You will win with the king of hearts and lead the two of clubs to beat the contract two tricks.

6.   North
                    ♠ A K Q
                    ♡ 7
                    ◇ A Q J 9 2
                    ♣ 8 6 5 4
     West   East
     ♠ 4   ♠ 10 9 5 2
     ♡ A K J 9 5 4   ♡ 10 8 6 3
     ◇ 6 5   ◇ 8 7 4 3
     ♣ Q 7 3 2   ♣ 10
                    South
                    ♠ J 8 7 6 3
                    ♡ Q 2
                    ◇ K 10
                    ♣ A K J 9

West	North	East	South
			1♠
2♡	3◇	Pass	4♣
Pass	4NT	Pass	5◇
Pass	6♠	All Pass	

You lead the king of hearts, partner plays the eight and declarer the two. What do you lead now?

Lead the ace of hearts. As you were informed earlier: When you lead a high card and dummy has a singleton, partner plays the highest card he can spare or his lowest card as suit preference, and plays a middle card as a come-on signal. The eight of hearts appears to be a middle card. It could also be partner's highest (he might have ♡ 8 6 3), but if he has a diamond trick, he will win it whether you lead the suit or not. It is more likely that he has a trump holding that can be promoted into a trick if you lead the ace of hearts to force declarer to ruff with one of dummy's high trumps. As you can see in this layout, the ace-of-hearts lead is needed to beat the contract.

7.

	North	
	♠ Q 10 5	
	♡ J 10 9	
	◇ A Q 6 3	
	♣ Q J 2	
West		East
♠ K 8 2		♠ 7 4 3
♡ A Q 7 5 4		♡ 8 6 2
◇ 5 2		◇ K 8 7 4
♣ 10 7 6		♣ 9 5 3
	South	
	♠ A J 9 6	
	♡ K 3	
	◇ J 10 9	
	♣ A K 8 4	

West	North	East	South
			1NT
Pass	3NT	All Pass	

You lead the five of hearts, partner plays the two and declarer the three. The queen of spades is led from dummy and you win the second trick with the king. What do you lead now?

Lead the ace of hearts. It is obvious that partner cannot have a high heart (he would have played the king on the first trick if he had it), so an attitude signal would have been useless; his play of the two of hearts was a count signal showing an odd number of hearts. He might have a singleton, but then declarer would have four and there is virtually no hope of beating the contract no matter what you lead. However, your partner probably has three hearts, in which case declarer is sitting with the lone king and you can win the next four heart tricks. Note that declarer can run nine tricks (three spades, one heart, one diamond and four clubs) if you lead anything but the ace of hearts at trick three.

8.

	North	
	♠ 9 7 6	
	♡ K 4	
	◇ A J 9 8 7 5	
	♣ K 4	
West		East
♠ Q 8 5 4 2		♠ A 3
♡ A 10		♡ J 9 7 6
◇ 3 2		◇ K 6 4
♣ 8 5 3 2		♣ J 9 7 6
	South	
	♠ K J 10	
	♡ Q 8 5 3 2	
	◇ Q 10	
	♣ A Q 10	

West	North	East	South
			1♡
Pass	2◇	Pass	2NT
Pass	3NT	All Pass	

You lead the four of spades, partner plays the ace and declarer the ten. The three of spades is returned, declarer plays the jack and you win with the queen. What do you lead now?

Lead the eight of spades, a suit-preference signal asking partner to play the higher-ranking suit if he gets the lead. Declarer has no choice but to try the diamond finesse. Partner will win with his king and follow your instructions by leading a heart. Note that if partner does not lead a heart, declarer can run nine tricks (one spade, five diamonds and three clubs).

If you held a club entry instead, you would signal by leading the two of spades at trick three.

8

Defensive Trump Tricks

This chapter deals exclusively with various ways to win tricks in the enemy trump suit, and there are many, as you shall see. To get started:

Giving Partner a Ruff

#1

North
♠ 4 2
♡ 9 7 3
◊ Q J 7 6 5
♣ K J 10

West
♠ A 10 8 7 5
♡ A Q J 2
◊ 3
♣ 6 4 3

West	North	East	South
			1♠
Pass	1NT	Pass	3◊
Pass	4◊	Pass	5◊
Pass	Pass	Pass	

You lead the ace of hearts and partner gives you a come-on signal by playing the eight. Should you lead another heart? No! You can see seven spades between your hand and dummy, and declarer should have five spades for his opening bid; so partner is marked with a singleton. *Lead the ace and another spade* to give him a ruff. The four hands:

♠ 4 2
♡ 9 7 3
◊ Q J 7 6 5
♣ K J 10

♠ A 10 8 7 5
♡ A Q J 2
◊ 3
♣ 6 4 3

♠ 3
♡ K 10 8 6 5
◊ 9 4
♣ 9 8 7 5 2

♠ K Q J 9 6
♡ 4
◊ A K 10 8 2
♣ A Q

The contract cannot be set without the spade ruff. In case you are wondering why partner encouraged you to lead another heart when he had a singleton spade, it is because he did not know that you had the ace of spades.

#2

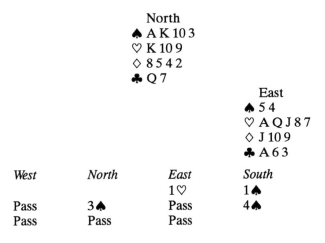

North
♠ A K 10 3
♡ K 10 9
♦ 8 5 4 2
♣ Q 7

East
♠ 5 4
♡ A Q J 8 7
♦ J 10 9
♣ A 6 3

West	North	East	South
		1♡	1♠
Pass	3♠	Pass	4♠
Pass	Pass	Pass	

Partner leads the five of hearts, the nine is played from dummy, you win with the jack and declarer drops the two. Should you play the ace and another heart so partner can ruff, or sit back and wait with ♡ A Q behind ♡ K 10?

Three hearts are still missing: the six, four and three. If you play as recommended in Chapter 1—lead the lowest card from three low versus a trump contract—you know your partner cannot have more than two hearts; he would not lead the five from any combination including the six, or from ♡ 5 4 3. So, *cash the ace of hearts and lead a third heart to give him a ruff*. The four hands:

♠ A K 10 3
♡ K 10 9
♦ 8 5 4 2
♣ Q 7

♠ 8 2
♡ 5 4
♦ Q 7 6 3
♣ 10 9 8 5 2

♠ 5 4
♡ A Q J 8 7
♦ J 10 9
♣ A 6 3

♠ Q J 9 7 6
♡ 6 3 2
♦ A K
♣ K J 4

With this layout, you must give your partner a heart ruff to beat the contract; otherwise declarer will be able to make his contract by drawing trumps and eventually discarding a heart in dummy on the third round of clubs.

If you change the cards so declarer has ♡ x x and ♦ A K x, he will make his contract if you cash the ace of hearts, but will be set if you lead any other suit. This shows an advantage of leading low from three spot cards—if your agreement were to lead high or middle, the winning defense would be guesswork.

#3

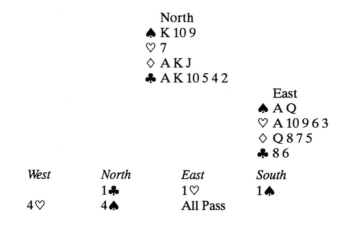

North
♠ K 10 9
♡ 7
◇ A K J
♣ A K 10 5 4 2

East
♠ A Q
♡ A 10 9 6 3
◇ Q 8 7 5
♣ 8 6

West	North	East	South
	1♣	1♡	1♠
4♡	4♠	All Pass	

Partner leads the queen of hearts, you win with the ace and declarer plays the king. You can forget about winning a trick with your queen of diamonds (dummy's long club suit will provide ample discards), so the only good chance to beat the contract is to give your partner a ruff. If partner had a singleton, he would have led it. But he may have a doubleton diamond and three trumps—that is, his distribution may be 3-6-2-2—in which case you can beat the contract if you *lead a diamond at trick two, and then continue to lead diamonds each time you gain the lead with your high trumps.* The four hands:

♠ K 10 9
♡ 7
◇ A K J
♣ A K 10 5 4 2

♠ 6 5 2
♡ Q J 8 5 4 2
◇ 9 3
♣ 9 7

♠ A Q
♡ A 10 9 6 3
◇ Q 8 7 5
♣ 8 6

♠ J 8 7 4 3
♡ K
◇ 10 6 4 2
♣ Q J 3

Partner will ruff the third round of diamonds to beat the contract by one trick. Note that if partner has only two trumps, the contract cannot be set no matter what you lead.

Getting a Ruff

The next five deals show how and when to put partner on lead so you can get the ruff.

#4

North
♠ J 10 9 5
♡ 6 2
♢ A K
♣ A K Q 10 3

East
♠ A 6
♡ A 10 9 5
♢ Q 10 8 7 4 3
♣ 2

West	North	East	South
	1♣	1♢	1♠
2♢	4♠	All Pass	

Partner leads the king of hearts. To get a ruff, you must first get rid of all the cards you have in a suit and then put your partner in the lead. In this case, *overtake partner's king of hearts with your ace and lead your singleton club*. Then, when you regain the lead with the ace of spades, play a heart. Partner will win the trick and give you a club ruff. The four hands:

♠ J 10 9 5
♡ 6 2
♢ A K
♣ A K Q 10 3

♠ 4 3
♡ K Q J 8
♢ J 9 2
♣ 9 6 5 4

♠ A 6
♡ A 10 9 5
♢ Q 10 8 7 4 3
♣ 2

♠ K Q 8 7 2
♡ 7 4 3
♢ 6 5
♣ J 8 7

Sometimes giving partner a ruff isn't the right defense, until later.

#5   **North**
                                      ♠ Q 6 3
                                      ♡ J 7 6
                                      ◇ A Q 9
                                      ♣ K Q 9 6

                                                          East
                                                          ♠ A 9 7
                                                          ♡ A Q 5 2
                                                          ◇ 10
                                                          ♣ 10 8 7 4 3

West	North	East	South
	1♣	Pass	1♠
Pass	1NT	Pass	3♣
Pass	3♠	Pass	4♠
Pass	Pass	Pass	

Partner leads the ten of hearts, you win with the ace and declarer plays the king. The bidding suggests that declarer has five spades and four clubs, in which case partner has two spades and is void in clubs. This means you will be able to give your partner only one club ruff, which together with the ace of hearts and ace of spades gives you three tricks. The best chance to win a fourth trick is to *lead your singleton diamond at trick two*. When you regain the lead with the ace of spades, *lead a club for partner to ruff*. He will return a diamond for you to ruff, the fourth defensive trick. The four hands:

                                      ♠ Q 6 3
                                      ♡ J 7 6
                                      ◇ A Q 9
                                      ♣ K Q 9 6
       ♠ 4 2   ♠ A 9 7
       ♡ 10 9 8 4 3   ♡ A Q 5 2
       ◇ K 8 6 5 3 2   ◇ 10
       ♣ —   ♣ 10 8 7 4 3
                                      ♠ K J 10 8 5
                                      ♡ K
                                      ◇ J 7 4
                                      ♣ A J 5 2

Without your diamond lead at trick two, declarer has an easy road to ten tricks.
In the next deal, you must create an entry to your partner's hand to get a ruff.

#6

North
♠ 9 8 5 4
♡ 8 5
♢ A K
♣ K Q 10 9 8

West
♠ A Q 7
♡ A Q 2
♢ Q 10 9 8 6 4
♣ 6

West	North	East	South
			1♠
2♢	3♠	Pass	4♠
Pass	Pass	Pass	

You lead the six of clubs and the first trick is won in dummy with the eight. A spade is led to declarer's jack and your queen. It is apparent that declarer is planning to draw trumps and then discard losing hearts on dummy's club suit. Since declarer must have the king of hearts for his opening bid, you cannot win more than one heart trick; the only chance to beat the contract is to put partner in the lead to give you a club ruff. Which is the only card partner might have to get the lead? Answer: *the jack of hearts*. What should you lead at trick three? Answer: *the queen of hearts*. The four hands:

```
                     ♠ 9 8 5 4
                     ♡ 8 5
                     ♢ A K
                     ♣ K Q 10 9 8
   ♠ A Q 7                              ♠ 2
   ♡ A Q 2                              ♡ J 9 7 4 3
   ♢ Q 10 9 8 6 4                       ♢ J 7 5
   ♣ 6                                  ♣ 7 5 4 3
                     ♠ K J 10 6 3
                     ♡ K 10 6
                     ♢ 3 2
                     ♣ A J 2
```

On your queen-of-hearts lead partner should signal with the nine—an attitude signal which must show the jack (without the jack partner would play his lowest, or play the ten if he held ♡ 10 9).

Declarer must play the king of hearts on your queen (else you have four tricks). Then, when you regain the lead with the ace of spades, you can play the two of hearts. Partner wins with the jack and gives you a club ruff.

Sometimes the chance of getting a ruff is remote (partner must have some precise holding that may not materialize), but you should try if it is the only chance to set the contract. For example:

#7   North
                                            ♠ K 7 6
                                            ♡ K Q
                                            ◇ K Q J 3
                                            ♣ A K J 7
                                                                        East
                                                                        ♠ 8 4 2
                                                                        ♡ A 8 3 2
                                                                        ◇ 10 5
                                                                        ♣ 9 6 5 4

West	North	East	South
	2NT	Pass	3♠
Pass	4♠	All Pass	

Partner leads the jack of hearts and you win with your ace. Can you dream up a holding for partner that offers a chance to beat the contract?

Answer: Three or four diamonds to the ace and the ace of spades. So go for it! *Lead the ten of diamonds* and hope you can win a trump trick by ruffing the third round. The four hands:

                                            ♠ K 7 6
                                            ♡ K Q
                                            ◇ K Q J 3
                                            ♣ A K J 7
        ♠ A 5   ♠ 8 4 2
        ♡ J 10 9 7 4   ♡ A 8 3 2
        ◇ A 9 2   ◇ 10 5
        ♣ Q 8 3   ♣ 9 6 5 4
                                            ♠ Q J 10 9 3
                                            ♡ 6 5
                                            ◇ 8 7 6 4
                                            ♣ 10 2

Partner should win your ten-of-diamonds lead with the ace and return a diamond. Then, when he regains the lead with the ace of spades, he will play a third diamond, which you will ruff. Lucky, yes, but the diamond ruff offers the only good chance to beat the contract.

#8   North
                                            ♠ A J 9 6 4
                                            ♡ K 3
                                            ◇ A K Q
                                            ♣ 7 5 2
        West
        ♠ K Q
        ♡ 8 6 2
        ◇ J 10 7 6 5 4 3
        ♣ 9

West	North	East	South
			3♡
Pass	4♡	All Pass	

You lead your singleton club. Partner wins the first trick with the queen, then leads the ace of clubs; declarer follows suit with the three and four. What do you discard on the second club lead?

Declarer is known to have the jack of clubs (partner would not have won the first trick with the queen if he had the jack), so partner will win the first three club tricks and you can get a spade ruff if you *discard first the king and then the queen of spades on the second and third rounds of clubs*. The four hands:

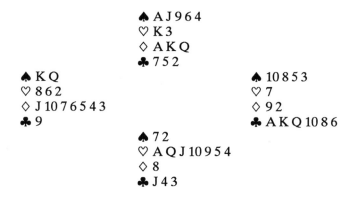

On the bidding you should know that you can never win a spade trick with the king or queen: Declarer has three clubs and probably seven hearts, so, if he has any losing spades, he will discard them on dummy's diamonds. The king and queen of spades are useless cards, so throw them away and get a ruff.

Trump-Promotion Plays

#9

North
♠ A K
♡ Q 10 7 2
◇ Q 9 6
♣ A K J 2

East
♠ 7 4
♡ A K J 3
◇ J 10 8 4
♣ 9 6 5

West	North	East	South
	1♣	Pass	1♠
Pass	2NT	Pass	4♠
Pass	Pass	Pass	

Partner leads the nine of hearts, the ten is put in from the dummy, you win with the jack and declarer plays the four. You win the next two tricks with the king and ace of hearts; partner discards the two of diamonds on the third round. Partner implied he has nothing in diamonds, so the only chance for another trick is in the trump suit. *Lead your fourth heart* in the hope of creating a trump trick for partner. The four hands:

```
                              ♠ A K
                              ♡ Q 10 7 2
                              ◇ Q 9 6
                              ♣ A K J 2
        ♠ J 3 2                                           ♠ 7 4
        ♡ 9 6                                             ♡ A K J 3
        ◇ K 5 2                                           ◇ J 10 8 4
        ♣ 10 8 7 4 3                                      ♣ 9 6 5
                              ♠ Q 10 9 8 6 5
                              ♡ 8 5 4
                              ◇ A 7 3
                              ♣ Q
```

If declarer ruffs the fourth round of hearts with any spade except the queen, partner will overruff with the jack. If declarer ruffs with the queen, partner will discard and eventually win a trick with the jack—this is a trump-promotion play. Note that partner made a good signal when he discarded the two of diamonds on the third round of hearts; he knew that a diamond lead *might* beat the contract, but he also knew that a fourth heart lead would *positively* beat the contract.

#10   North
                                                     ♠ A K Q 3
                                                     ♡ 7
                                                     ◇ K 6 5 4
                                                     ♣ K J 10 2
                                                                        East
                                                                        ♠ J 9 6
                                                                        ♡ 8 4
                                                                        ◇ A Q J 8 2
                                                                        ♣ A 7 5

West	North	East	South
		1◇	4♡
Pass	Pass	Pass	

Partner leads the nine of diamonds, the four is played from dummy and you win with the jack. Assuming that partner would not lead the nine if he had more than two diamonds, you cash the ace of diamonds and everyone follows suit. If partner has ♡ K, ♡ Q x, ♡ J x x or ♡ 10 x x x, you can promote his honor into a trick by leading another diamond; but don't do it yet! *First cash the ace of clubs and then lead the third round of diamonds*. The four hands:

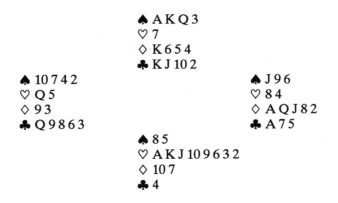

♠ A K Q 3
♡ 7
◇ K 6 5 4
♣ K J 10 2

♠ 10 7 4 2
♡ Q 5
◇ 9 3
♣ Q 9 8 6 3

♠ J 9 6
♡ 8 4
◇ A Q J 8 2
♣ A 7 5

♠ 8 5
♡ A K J 10 9 6 3 2
◇ 10 7
♣ 4

If you lead the third diamond before cashing the ace of clubs, declarer will make his contract by discarding his lone club and letting your partner ruff.

So remember: When you try for a trump-promotion play and the hand on your right has a higher card in the suit than the one you lead, the declarer may be able to discard a loser instead of ruffing. In such cases it may be important to cash any side winners before trying for the trump-promotion play.

There are times when you should not try a trump-promotion play. For example:

#11

North
♠ A J 10 2
♡ K 7 6
◇ K J 10
♣ A 4 2

East
♠ K
♡ A Q 10 9 3 2
◇ A 6 4
♣ 10 9 8

West	North	East	South
	1NT	2♡	3♠
Pass	4♠	All Pass	

Partner leads the jack of hearts, the king is played from dummy and you win with the ace. You cash the queen of hearts as everyone follows suit. If you lead a third round of hearts and partner has the queen of spades, he will be able to overruff declarer; but that doesn't help the defense. If partner has two or more spades including the queen, declarer will be set even if you do not lead a heart. In view of the bidding, though, it is hard to imagine that declarer does not have the queen of spades, and consider what will happen if you lead a heart at trick three and declarer does have it. He will ruff high and when your partner does not overruff, he will reason that you have the king; he will play a spade to the ace instead of taking the normal finesse. So, *lead the ten of clubs* at trick three and hope that declarer doesn't figure out why you didn't lead the third heart. The four hands:

```
                              ♠ A J 10 2
                              ♡ K 7 6
                              ◇ K J 10
                              ♣ A 4 2
        ♠ 8 5 3                                    ♠ K
        ♡ J 4                                      ♡ A Q 10 9 3 2
        ◇ 9 8 5 3                                  ◇ A 6 4
        ♣ 7 6 5 3                                  ♣ 10 9 8
                              ♠ Q 9 7 6 4
                              ♡ 8 5
                              ◇ Q 7 2
                              ♣ K Q J
```

As you can see, the fate of the contract hinges on declarer's dropping the king of spades. A good player might reason that you have the blank king because you did not lead a third heart. But if you do lead a third heart and your partner does not overruff, even a not-so-good player will drop your king.

#12   North
                                       ♠ 8 7 2
                                       ♡ K 6
                                       ◇ A K Q 3
                                       ♣ 8 6 5 4
                                                          East
                                                          ♠ Q 3
                                                          ♡ Q 10 9 8 5 4
                                                          ◇ 9 7 6
                                                          ♣ 10 2

West	North	East	South
			1♠
Pass	2◇	Pass	2♠
Pass	4♠	All Pass	

Partner leads, in order, the king of clubs, the ace of clubs and the queen of clubs. You discard the four of hearts on the third lead, and declarer follows suit throughout. Then partner leads the jack of clubs. The only chance to beat the contract is to win a trump trick, so you should *ruff the jack of clubs with the queen of spades* and hope it promotes a spade trick for partner. The four hands:

```
                              ♠ 8 7 2
                              ♡ K 6
                              ◇ A K Q 3
                              ♣ 8 6 5 4
        ♠ J 6                                      ♠ Q 3
        ♡ 7 3 2                                    ♡ Q 10 9 8 5 4
        ◇ 10 8 5 4                                 ◇ 9 7 6
        ♣ A K Q J                                  ♣ 10 2
                              ♠ A K 10 9 5 4
                              ♡ A J
                              ◇ J 2
                              ♣ 9 7 3
```

When declarer overruffs your queen of spades with the ace or king, your partner's jack becomes the setting trick. This is the first example of a trump-promotion play called the "uppercut."

#13

North
♠ 10 9
♡ 10 6 4
◇ A K Q J 5
♣ K J 2

West
♠ J 8 3
♡ A K Q 9 8 7
◇ 6 3 2
♣ A

West	North	East	South
	1◇	Pass	1♠
2♡	Pass	Pass	4♠
Pass	Pass	Pass	

Your first two leads are the king and ace of hearts, partner playing high-low and declarer following suit. It appears the only chance to beat the contract is to win a trump trick. Which insignificant card in your partner's hand will beat the contract? Answer: the *seven of spades*, so he can ruff your next heart lead and promote your jack of spades into a trick. What do you lead at trick three? Answer: the *ace of clubs*. At trick four, you should *lead a low heart*. The four hands:

```
                    ♠ 10 9
                    ♡ 10 6 4
                    ◇ A K Q J 5
                    ♣ K J 2
   ♠ J 8 3                          ♠ 7
   ♡ A K Q 9 8 7                    ♡ 5 2
   ◇ 6 3 2                          ◇ 10 9 7 4
   ♣ A                              ♣ 8 7 6 5 4 3
                    ♠ A K Q 6 5 4 2
                    ♡ J 3
                    ◇ 8
                    ♣ Q 10 9
```

If you lead the third round of hearts before cashing the ace of clubs, declarer can make his contract by overruffing the seven of spades, cashing his two other high spades, and discarding his three clubs on dummy's diamond suit before you can ruff with the jack of spades. Also, it is important to lead a low heart at trick four; if you lead the queen, partner may get careless and not ruff.

#14   **North**
                                       ♠ 9 7
                                       ♡ K Q 2
                                       ◇ K Q J 4
                                       ♣ Q J 9 8
                                                        East
                                                        ♠ A K 10 6 5
                                                        ♡ J 10 4
                                                        ◇ 8 2
                                                        ♣ A 7 3

West	North	East	South
	1◇	1♠	2♡
Pass	3♡	Pass	4♡
Pass	Pass	Pass	

Partner leads the jack of spades. You win the first trick with the king as declarer follows with the two. When you cash the ace of spades at trick two, declarer follows with the three and partner with the eight. Partner has shown a doubleton spade (he would lead his lowest card from J x x), so you can promote a trump trick for yourself if partner has any heart—even the three-spot—by leading a third spade for him to ruff. So how do you defend? *First cash the ace of clubs, then lead a low spade.* The four hands:

                                       ♠ 9 7
                                       ♡ K Q 2
                                       ◇ K Q J 4
                                       ♣ Q J 9 8
        ♠ J 8   ♠ A K 10 6 5
        ♡ 3   ♡ J 10 4
        ◇ 9 7 6 5 3   ◇ 8 2
        ♣ K 10 6 4 2   ♣ A 7 3
                                       ♠ Q 4 3 2
                                       ♡ A 9 8 7 6 5
                                       ◇ A 10
                                       ♣ 5

When partner ruffs your third spade lead with the three of hearts and dummy overruffs with the queen, your ♡ J 10 4 is promoted into a trick. But if you lead the third spade before cashing the ace of clubs, declarer will make his contract by overruffing with the queen of hearts, cashing two high trumps (immaterial, but good technique), and discarding his losing club on the third round of diamonds.

Another interesting point: Partner does not know that you have a potential trump trick, so when you play the ace of clubs he should give a come-on signal. Of course, you ignore his signal and lead a spade at trick four.

#15   **North**
                                       ♠ 10 6 4 2
                                       ♡ 7 6 5 3
                                       ◇ A Q J
                                       ♣ A Q

                                                          East
                                                          ♠ A 5
                                                          ♡ A 4
                                                          ◇ 10 9 7 3
                                                          ♣ 10 8 6 4 2

West	North	East	South
	1◇	Pass	1♠
Pass	2♠	All Pass	

Partner leads the king of hearts, you overtake with the ace and return the four of hearts. Partner wins the second heart trick with the nine and cashes the queen of hearts. You discard the discouraging two of clubs and declarer follows with the jack. At trick four, partner leads the ten of hearts. Dummy's strong holdings in the minor suits indicate that no more tricks are available except in the trump suit. Should you ruff partner's high heart with the ace or the five, or just discard?

Answer: *Ruff with the ace*, so that if partner has any trump honors, they can be won separately. The four hands:

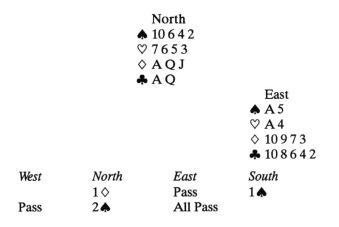

                          ♠ 10 6 4 2
                          ♡ 7 6 5 3
                          ◇ A Q J
                          ♣ A Q
        ♠ Q J 3   ♠ A 5
        ♡ K Q 10 9   ♡ A 4
        ◇ K 8 4   ◇ 10 9 7 3
        ♣ 9 7 5   ♣ 10 8 6 4 2
                          ♠ K 9 8 7
                          ♡ J 8 2
                          ◇ 6 5 2
                          ♣ K J 3

After ruffing with the ace of spades, you should return a spade and partner will get two more trump tricks. Note that if you do not ruff with the ace, declarer will lose only two trump tricks and make his contract.

#16

                                        North
                                        ♠ 7 3 2
                                        ♡ K 8 5 2
                                        ◇ A K J
                                        ♣ A Q 4

                                                              East
                                                              ♠ Q 6
                                                              ♡ A Q 9
                                                              ◇ 7 5
                                                              ♣ J 10 9 7 6 3

West	North	East	South
	1NT	Pass	3♠
Pass	3NT	Pass	4◇
Pass	4♠	All Pass	

Partner leads the three of hearts and you win the first trick with the queen. You can win one more heart trick—partner would not lead his lowest if he held more than four—and since no tricks are available in the minor suits, you must win two trump tricks to beat the contract. Here is a tough question: Can you figure out a trump holding partner can have that needs a trump-promotion play to win two tricks?

The answer is ♠ A 9 x or ♠ K 9 x. To set the stage for the trump promotion, you must do your part. *Cash the ace of hearts at trick two and then lead the nine of hearts.* The four hands:

                                        ♠ 7 3 2
                                        ♡ K 8 5 2
                                        ◇ A K J
                                        ♣ A Q 4
        ♠ K 9 4   ♠ Q 6
        ♡ J 6 4 3   ♡ A Q 9
        ◇ 8 4   ◇ 7 5
        ♣ K 8 5 2   ♣ J 10 9 7 6 3
                                        ♠ A J 10 8 5
                                        ♡ 10 7
                                        ◇ Q 10 9 6 3 2
                                        ♣ —

When declarer wins the third trick in dummy with the king of hearts, he can do not better than lead a spade and finesse the ten. Partner wins with the king, leads his fourth heart and you execute an uppercut by ruffing with the queen of spades. If declarer overruffs with the ace, he is left with ♠ J 8 5; so partner's ♠ 9 4 is now a trick.

Good defenders have learned to *beware the ruff-and-discard*. It is usually wrong to lead a suit in which the dummy and declarer are both void if there are still trumps in both of their hands, because declarer may gain a trick by ruffing in one hand and discarding a loser in the other. But if declarer has no losers in the side suits, giving him a ruff-and-discard cannot cost a trick and may promote a trump trick for your side; it is often a good play. Here are several examples:

#17

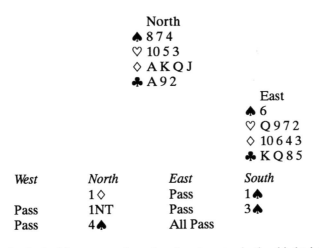

North
♠ 8 7 4
♡ 10 5 3
◇ A K Q J
♣ A 9 2

East
♠ 6
♡ Q 9 7 2
◇ 10 6 4 3
♣ K Q 8 5

West	North	East	South
	1◇	Pass	1♠
Pass	1NT	Pass	3♠
Pass	4♠	All Pass	

Your partner leads the king, ace and another heart; you win the third trick with the queen as declarer follows suit throughout. It is apparent that declarer has no losers in the side suits (he will discard any club losers on dummy's diamonds), and therefore he cannot gain if you give him a ruff-and-discard. *Lead your thirteenth heart* and hope it will promote a trump trick for partner. The four hands:

♠ 8 7 4
♡ 10 5 3
◇ A K Q J
♣ A 9 2

♠ J 5 2
♡ A K 6
◇ 9 8 5
♣ 10 7 4 3

♠ 6
♡ Q 9 7 2
◇ 10 6 4 3
♣ K Q 8 5

♠ A K Q 10 9 3
♡ J 8 4
◇ 7 2
♣ J 6

When you lead a heart at trick four, partner's jack of spades is promoted into the setting trick. Granted, partner might not have had a possible trump trick, but there was nothing to lose by trying.

#18   North
                                       ♠ 6 5 3
                                       ♡ A K
                                       ◇ A K J 9 4 2
                                       ♣ Q 5

             West
             ♠ A J
             ♡ 9 8 7 4
             ◇ Q
             ♣ A K 10 7 3 2

             West   North   East   South
                           1 ◇   Pass   1 ♠
             2 ♣   3 ◇   Pass   3 ♠
             Pass   4 ♠   All Pass

You win the first two tricks with the king and ace of clubs, partner playing the four and six, declarer the eight and jack. Partner did not high-low and therefore has the one missing club. Since you have the ace of spades, it is still possible to promote a trump trick if partner has ♠ 10 x—provided you *lead a club at trick three* to get the missing club out of partner's hand. Suppose declarer ruffs your third club lead in dummy and plays a spade to his king and your ace. Now *lead another club*. Partner will ruff with the ten (if he has it) and promote your jack of spades into the setting trick. The four hands:

                                       ♠ 6 5 3
                                       ♡ A K
                                       ◇ A K J 9 4 2
                                       ♣ Q 5
             ♠ A J   ♠ 10 4
             ♡ 9 8 7 4   ♡ Q J 3 2
             ◇ Q   ◇ 8 7 6 5
             ♣ A K 10 7 3 2   ♣ 9 6 4
                                       ♠ K Q 9 8 7 2
                                       ♡ 10 6 5
                                       ◇ 10 3
                                       ♣ J 8

It was fortunate that partner had the ten of spades, but without your continuous club leads declarer would make a contract that should be set.

#19

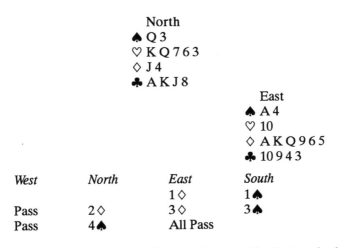

North
♠ Q 3
♡ K Q 7 6 3
◇ J 4
♣ A K J 8

East
♠ A 4
♡ 10
◇ A K Q 9 6 5
♣ 10 9 4 3

West	North	East	South
		1 ◇	1 ♠
Pass	2 ◇	3 ◇	3 ♠
Pass	4 ♠	All Pass	

This deal is similar to the last one, with an added wrinkle. Partner leads the two of diamonds to your queen. You win the next trick with the ace of diamonds and partner follows with the seven; so one diamond is missing and partner has it. The only source of tricks left is the trump suit—the bidding marks declarer with the ace of hearts—so you should *lead a third diamond*. Suppose declarer ruffs in his hand, plays a club to dummy's king, and leads the three of spades. *Play the four of spades* (you must save the ace to capture the queen). Let's assume declarer wins this trick with the jack. When the declarer plays another spade to dummy's queen and your ace, *lead another round of diamonds* in the hope that it will promote a trump trick for partner. The four hands:

                     ♠ Q 3
                     ♡ K Q 7 6 3
                     ◇ J 4
                     ♣ A K J 8
    ♠ 10 8 2   ♠ A 4
    ♡ J 9 5 4 2   ♡ 10
    ◇ 10 7 2   ◇ A K Q 9 6 5
    ♣ 6 5   ♣ 10 9 4 3
                     ♠ K J 9 7 6 5
                     ♡ A 8
                     ◇ 8 3
                     ♣ Q 7 2

At the point that you lead the fourth round of diamonds, declarer has ♠ K 9 7 and partner has ♠ 10; so the ten is promoted into the setting trick. Note that if you played the ace of spades when declarer led the three from dummy, he would play a low spade from his hand; since he retains his three high spades, there is no way to promote a trump trick.

#20   **North**
                                             ♠ J 6 2
                                             ♡ J 8 6 2
                                             ◇ J 5 3
                                             ♣ A Q 10

                West
                ♠ 9 7
                ♡ Q 4
                ◇ K 9 8 6 2
                ♣ J 6 5 3

West	*North*	*East*	*South*
			1 ♡
Pass	2 ♡	2 ♠	4 ♡
Pass	Pass	Pass	

You lead the nine of spades and partner wins the first trick with the queen. He cashes the ace and king of spades, declarer following suit. Which card would you play on the third spade lead?

You know that your queen of hearts can be promoted into a trick if partner leads a fourth round of spades, but your partner does not know that. So, discard the *two of diamonds* on the third trick. Once you tell him not to switch to a diamond, he should infer that you want another spade lead. The four hands:

                                    ♠ J 6 2
                                    ♡ J 8 6 2
                                    ◇ J 5 3
                                    ♣ A Q 10
        ♠ 9 7   ♠ A K Q 8 3
        ♡ Q 4   ♡ 5
        ◇ K 9 8 6 2   ◇ 10 7 4
        ♣ J 6 5 3   ♣ 9 8 4 2
                                    ♠ 10 5 4
                                    ♡ A K 10 9 7 3
                                    ◇ A Q
                                    ♣ K 7

When partner leads the fourth round of spades, declarer cannot avoid a trump loser and the contract is set. If partner leads any other suit, declarer has the rest of the tricks.

The next deal is a true story about the late Harry Fishbein, one of the all-time great bridge players and a very humorous fellow. This happened many years ago in a high-stake rubber-bridge game. Harry was sitting West and his partner was one of the worst players in the club.

#21

<table>
<tr><td></td><td colspan="4">North</td></tr>
<tr><td></td><td colspan="4">♠ K 10 6 3</td></tr>
<tr><td></td><td colspan="4">♡ 8 5</td></tr>
<tr><td></td><td colspan="4">◇ Q 7 4</td></tr>
<tr><td></td><td colspan="4">♣ A K Q 2</td></tr>
</table>

West
♠ A Q J 9 8 7
♡ J 6 3
◇ 9 5
♣ 8 7

West	North	East	South
	1♣	1◇	1♡
1♠	1NT	2♠	4♡
Pass	Pass	Pass	

Harry led the nine of diamonds. His partner captured dummy's queen with his king and won the next two tricks with the ace and jack of diamonds. Harry had to make a discard on the third diamond. He knew declarer was void in spades (his partner would not have raised him with fewer than three) and that a fourth diamond lead was needed to promote his jack of hearts into a trick. He thought about discarding his lowest spade, but it was the seven. His partner was notorious for not paying any attention to the spot cards and might assume his seven to be a come-on signal and lead a spade. So he thought up a signal that would wake the devil: *He discarded the ace of spades.* The four hands:

```
                        ♠ K 10 6 3
                        ♡ 8 5
                        ◇ Q 7 4
                        ♣ A K Q 2
     ♠ A Q J 9 8 7                      ♠ 5 4 2
     ♡ J 6 3                            ♡ 4
     ◇ 9 5                              ◇ A K J 10 2
     ♣ 8 7                              ♣ J 10 9 6
                        ♠ —
                        ♡ A K Q 10 9 7 2
                        ◇ 8 6 3
                        ♣ 5 4 3
```

Now that the king of spades in dummy is high, his partner should realize that it is impossible to win any tricks in the side suits. So it is obvious that he should lead another diamond and hope to promote a trump trick for Harry. Alas, the story would not be humorous if Harry's partner led another diamond. He led a *spade* and declarer made his contract!

When not to Ruff, and When not to Overruff

It is not always right to ruff with what appears to be a worthless trump. For example:

#22

```
                              North
                              ♠ 9 8 7
                              ♡ K 10 9
                              ◇ A 7 4
                              ♣ A Q 5 3
                                              East
                                              ♠ 4 3 2
                                              ♡ 8 6 5 3 2
                                              ◇ —
                                              ♣ K 10 7 6 2
```

West	North	East	South
			1♠
Pass	2NT	Pass	3◇
Pass	3♠	Pass	4NT
Pass	5♡	Pass	6♠
Pass	Pass	Pass	

Partner leads the queen of diamonds and the four is played from dummy. *Do not ruff.* Since declarer bid the suit, partner will not lead it unless he has ◇ Q J 10 9 or ◇ Q J 10 8. If you ruff, you will be ruffing one of declarer's losing tricks. Before explaining further, here are the four hands:

```
                              ♠ 9 8 7
                              ♡ K 10 9
                              ◇ A 7 4
                              ♣ A Q 5 3
        ♠ 6 5                                    ♠ 4 3 2
        ♡ 7 4                                    ♡ 8 6 5 3 2
        ◇ Q J 10 9 6 3                           ◇ —
        ♣ J 9 8                                  ♣ K 10 7 6 2
                              ♠ A K Q J 10
                              ♡ A Q J
                              ◇ K 8 5 2
                              ♣ 4
```

Suppose you discard a heart or club on the first trick and let declarer win it with his king of diamonds. If declarer leads diamonds again before drawing trumps, you will ruff dummy's ace. If he draws trumps, he will be left with two unavoidable diamond losers. Either way, the contract will be set.

If you mistakenly ruff the first trick, declarer can make his contract. He will play a low diamond from his hand and be left with ◇ K x x opposite ◇ A x. The dummy now has one more trump than you, so declarer will draw two rounds of trumps and eventually ruff the fourth round of diamonds in the dummy.

When you have a natural trump trick and an opportunity to overruff presents itself, a common way to promote a trump trick is to discard instead. For example:

#23

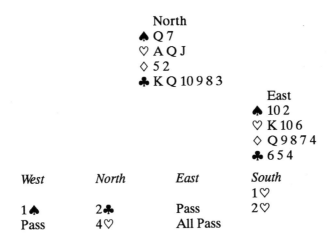

West	North	East	South
			1♡
1♠	2♣	Pass	2♡
Pass	4♡	All Pass	

Partner leads the king and ace of spades. Seeing you play high-low, he continues with the jack of spades, which is ruffed in dummy with the jack of hearts. Overruffing with the king will net you only one heart trick, while discarding a club or diamond will net you two; so *do not overruff*. The four hands:

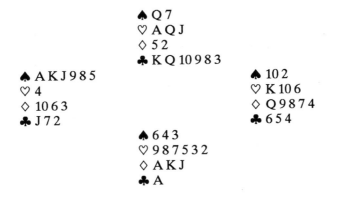

When you have a natural trump trick, such as the king of hearts in this deal, and have an opportunity to overruff, you may promote a lower trump by not overruffing. In this case, the ten of hearts is promoted. This, of course, is a fundamental illustration and I know you would pass the test if you were East. Now for some less obvious situations.

#24   North
                                       ♠ —
                                       ♡ A Q J 7 6
                                       ◇ Q 9 2
                                       ♣ A 10 8 4 3
                West
                ♠ K 8 2
                ♡ 10 9 5 4
                ◇ 8 3
                ♣ K 7 6 5

West	North	East	South
		1◇	3♠
Pass	Pass	Pass	

You lead the eight of diamonds. Partner wins the first trick with the ten, the second trick with the king of diamonds, and leads the ace of diamonds, which is ruffed by declarer with the queen. *Do not overruff.* Suppose you discard a low club on the third round of diamonds. Declarer leads the jack of spades, you play the two and partner wins with the ace. Partner leads another diamond and declarer ruffs this one with the ten. Again, *do not overruff* and your eight-spot is promoted into a winner. The four hands:

                                       ♠ —
                                       ♡ A Q J 7 6
                                       ◇ Q 9 2
                                       ♣ A 10 8 4 3
        ♠ K 8 2   ♠ A 5
        ♡ 10 9 5 4   ♡ 8 3
        ◇ 8 3   ◇ A K J 10 7 5
        ♣ K 7 6 5   ♣ Q J 2
                                       ♠ Q J 10 9 7 6 4 3
                                       ♡ K 2
                                       ◇ 6 4
                                       ♣ 9

In the early plays, declarer ruffed with the queen of spades, led the jack of spades and ruffed with the ten of spades, so he is left with ♠ 9 7 6 4 3 and you with ♠ K 8. You will win two more spade tricks and set the contract. Declarer would make his contract if you overruffed at either opportunity.

#25

North
♠ A Q 8
♡ 6 3
◇ Q 9 6 5 3
♣ K Q 2

West
♠ 7 6 4
♡ Q 7 5 2
◇ 8
♣ 10 9 8 6 3

West	North	East	South
	1◇	Pass	1♡
Pass	1NT	2◇	4♡
Pass	Pass	Pass	

You lead the eight of diamonds. Partner wins the first trick with the ten and leads the king of diamonds, which declarer ruffs with the nine of hearts. *Discard a spade; do not overruff with the queen.* Now declarer cashes the ace and king of hearts before leading the jack to your queen. Partner follows with the eight of hearts, then discards a low spade on the second heart and a low diamond on the third. Now you lead a club. Partner wins with his ace and plays another diamond. The four hands:

North
♠ A Q 8
♡ 6 3
◇ Q 9 6 5 3
♣ K Q 2

West
♠ 7 6 4
♡ Q 7 5 2
◇ 8
♣ 10 9 8 6 3

East
♠ J 10 9 3
♡ 8
◇ A K J 10 7 2
♣ A 5

South
♠ K 5 2
♡ A K J 10 9 4
◇ 4
♣ J 7 4

Declarer has lost three tricks so far (one heart, one diamond and one club) and has played the nine, ace, king and jack of hearts. He now holds the ♡ 10 4 and you have ♡ 7. Your partner's last diamond lead enables you to score the setting trick with the seven of hearts.

#26   North
                                           ♠ A 3 2
                                           ♡ Q 6 4
                                           ◇ A K
                                           ♣ A K J 10 7

                    West
                    ♠ K 9 7
                    ♡ 9 3
                    ◇ J 8 7 5
                    ♣ J 6 4 3

West	North	East	South
	2NT	Pass	3♠
Pass	4♠	All Pass	

You lead the nine of hearts. Partner wins the first three tricks with the ten, king and ace of hearts. Then he leads a fourth heart, which declarer ruffs with the queen of spades. Would you overruff with the king or discard?

If you *do not overruff*, you have a sure trump trick. The four hands:

                                    ♠ A 3 2
                                    ♡ Q 6 4
                                    ◇ A K
                                    ♣ A K J 10 7
        ♠ K 9 7   ♠ 5
        ♡ 9 3   ♡ A K J 10 2
        ◇ J 8 7 5   ◇ 10 9 6 2
        ♣ Q 6 4 3   ♣ 8 5 2
                                    ♠ Q J 10 8 6 4
                                    ♡ 8 7 5
                                    ◇ Q 4 3
                                    ♣ 9

If you overruff the queen with the king, declarer will overruff your king with dummy's ace and draw your last two trumps with his jack and ten. But if you do not overruff, declarer is left with ♠ J 10 8 6 4 and you have ♠ K 9 7; he must lose a spade trick.

The key play was partner's fourth heart lead. Without it declarer could avoid a spade loser by finessing through you for the king.

Forcing Declarer to Ruff

When you have length in the enemy trump suit, it is sometimes good strategy to lead a long side suit. The plan is to force the declarer to ruff one or more times so you can take control of the trump suit—get to the point where he must concede a trick to you with a long trump. This strategy, sometimes called "the forcing game," is illustrated in the next six deals:

#27

```
                        North
                        ♠ 10 8 5
                        ♡ K Q 4
                        ◇ K J 9
                        ♣ 10 9 3 2
        West
        ♠ 6 4 3 2
        ♡ A 8
        ◇ 7 6
        ♣ A K J 8 7
```

West	North	East	South
			1♠
2♣	2♠	Pass	4♠
Pass	Pass	Pass	

You win the first two tricks with the king and ace of clubs, partner and declarer both following suit. If declarer has only five spades, you can force him to ruff twice. Then you will have one more trump than he, and the contract will fail. Since the ten and nine of clubs are still in dummy you must *lead a low club* at trick three for partner to ruff. Declarer will overruff, but he is now down to four spades and you have the high club. When he cashes his first high spade and your partner shows out, he learns that you began with four spades and he cannot afford to draw all of your trumps, so he does the best he can and leads a heart. You take the ace of hearts and *lead the jack of clubs*. If declarer discards, it is the setting trick; if he ruffs, he will be down to two trumps and you still have three. The best declarer can do is down one.

```
                        ♠ 10 8 5
                        ♡ K Q 4
                        ◇ K J 9
                        ♣ 10 9 3 2
        ♠ 6 4 3 2                      ♠ 7
        ♡ A 8                          ♡ 10 6 5 3
        ◇ 7 6                          ◇ 10 8 5 4 3 2
        ♣ A K J 8 7                    ♣ 6 5
                        ♠ A K Q J 9
                        ♡ J 9 7 2
                        ◇ A Q
                        ♣ Q 4
```

Note that this defense will not work if declarer has six trumps. But in this case no defense will beat the contract.

#28   North
                                            ♠ 10 8 5
                                            ♡ K Q 4
                                            ◇ K J 9 2
                                            ♣ 10 7 3
                West
                ♠ A 4 3 2
                ♡ 9 8
                ◇ 7 6
                ♣ K J 9 6 5

West	North	East	South
			1♠
Pass	2♠	Pass	4♠
Pass	Pass	Pass	

Following the strategy that you should lead a long suit when you have length in the enemy trump suit, you open with the six of clubs. The lead is somewhat risky, but bridge is not a game for cowards and this time you get lucky. Partner wins the first trick with the ace and returns a club. You capture declarer's queen with your king and lead the jack of clubs to force declarer to ruff. Note that both declarer and dummy are now out of clubs. Declarer leads the king of spades at trick four and *you must duck*. He continues with the queen of spades and *you must duck again*. Before continuing the explanation, here are the four hands:

                                            ♠ 10 8 5
                                            ♡ K Q 4
                                            ◇ K J 9 2
                                            ♣ 10 7 3
        ♠ A 4 3 2   ♠ 7
        ♡ 9 8   ♡ 10 6 5 3
        ◇ 7 6   ◇ 10 8 5 4 3
        ♣ K J 9 6 5   ♣ A 8 2
                                            ♠ K Q J 9 6
                                            ♡ A J 7 2
                                            ◇ A Q
                                            ♣ Q 4

If you mistakenly win the first or second spade lead and play a club, declarer will ruff in dummy and use the long spades in his hand to draw your trumps. But if you duck the first two spade leads, you are left with ♠ A 4 and declarer with ♠ J 9. If he leads a third round of spades, you will win with the ace. Then the dummy will be out of trumps and another club lead will force declarer to ruff with his last trump; he will go down two. Declarer can do better if he does not lead a third trump and starts cashing his winners; you will eventually ruff with your low trump and set the contract one trick.

#29

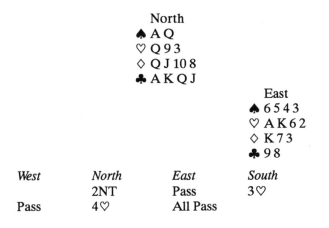

North
♠ A Q
♡ Q 9 3
◇ Q J 10 8
♣ A K Q J

East
♠ 6 5 4 3
♡ A K 6 2
◇ K 7 3
♣ 9 8

West	North	East	South
	2NT	Pass	3♡
Pass	4♡	All Pass	

Partner leads the ten of spades and the ace is played from dummy. The three of hearts is led, you play low and declarer wins with the jack as partner follows suit. Another heart is led, partner discards the nine of diamonds and you capture dummy's queen with your king. Partner signaled that he has the ace of diamonds, so declarer is down off the top if has two diamonds. But you also can set the contract if declarer has a singleton diamond and you can force him to ruff diamonds twice; in which case you can win a third trump trick. If you lead a low diamond at trick four, it won't work. After partner wins with the ace and returns a diamond, you must play your king to force declarer to ruff; since the dummy is left with the high diamond, you cannot force him to ruff again. The only way to beat the contract is to *lead the king of diamonds at trick four*. The four hands:

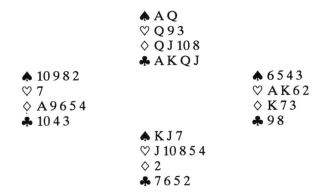

♠ A Q
♡ Q 9 3
◇ Q J 10 8
♣ A K Q J

♠ 10 9 8 2
♡ 7
◇ A 9 6 5 4
♣ 10 4 3

♠ 6 5 4 3
♡ A K 6 2
◇ K 7 3
♣ 9 8

♠ K J 7
♡ J 10 8 5 4
◇ 2
♣ 7 6 5 2

After cashing the king of diamonds, lead another diamond and declarer must ruff (else he is down). Declarer has already lost two tricks and has remaining ♡ 10 8, while you have ♡ A 6. If he abandons trumps and starts cashing his winners, you can ruff the third round of clubs with your low heart. If he leads another heart, you will take your ace and promote your low heart into a winner by leading another diamond, which forces declarer to ruff with his last trump.

Although uncommon, it is possible to force declarer to lose trump control even when he has a six-card suit. For example:

#30

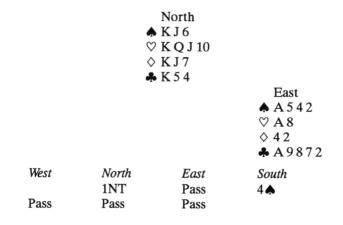

North
♠ K J 6
♡ K Q J 10
◇ K J 7
♣ K 5 4

East
♠ A 5 4 2
♡ A 8
◇ 4 2
♣ A 9 8 7 2

West	North	East	South
	1NT	Pass	4♠
Pass	Pass	Pass	

Partner leads the queen of clubs and is allowed to win the first trick. He continues with the jack of clubs; declarer plays low from dummy and ruffs in his hand. Declarer leads a low spade, partner discards a heart and *you allow dummy's king to win the trick.* Another spade is led and *again you hold up your ace.* Before explaining further, here are the four hands:

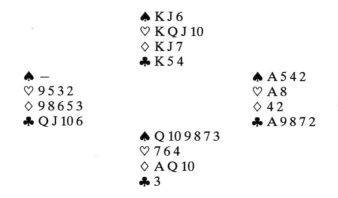

♠ K J 6
♡ K Q J 10
◇ K J 7
♣ K 5 4

♠ —
♡ 9 5 3 2
◇ 9 8 6 5 3
♣ Q J 10 6

♠ A 5 4 2
♡ A 8
◇ 4 2
♣ A 9 8 7 2

♠ Q 10 9 8 7 3
♡ 7 6 4
◇ A Q 10
♣ 3

Although declarer cannot make his contract no matter how he plays, let's say he leads a heart at trick five. You take the ace and lead another club which declarer ruffs. Declarer has ruffed two clubs and led trumps twice, so he is down to ♠ Q 10 and you still have ♠ A 5. If he plays another spade, you can set him two tricks by winning with the ace and leading a club; if he starts cashing winners in the other suits, you will eventually ruff with your low trump.

If you have four trumps and the enemy trump suit divides four-four, you must make declarer ruff in both hands to promote an extra trump trick. For example:

#31   North
                                       ♠ K Q 8 4
                                       ♡ Q 10 7 2
                                       ◇ 8 3
                                       ♣ K 9 5

          West
          ♠ 10 2
          ♡ A 6 5 3
          ◇ A K Q 10 9
          ♣ 6 4

West	North	East	South
			1NT
2◇	3◇	Pass	3♡
Pass	4♡	All Pass	

You win the first two tricks with the king and ace of diamonds as partner and declarer both follow suit. Declarer's one-notrump bid shows 16-18 points, so he should have all of the missing high cards (except maybe a jack). The only chance to beat the contract is to win two trump tricks. *Lead the queen of diamonds* at trick three to force the dummy to ruff. When declarer leads trumps, *duck the first two rounds*. The four hands:

                                   ♠ K Q 8 4
                                   ♡ Q 10 7 2
                                   ◇ 8 3
                                   ♣ K 9 5
          ♠ 10 2   ♠ J 9 5 3
          ♡ A 6 5 3   ♡ 4
          ◇ A K Q 10 9   ◇ 6 4 2
          ♣ 6 4   ♣ 10 8 7 3 2
                                   ♠ A 7 6
                                   ♡ K J 9 8
                                   ◇ J 7 5
                                   ♣ A Q J

After ruffing the third round of diamonds in dummy, declarer's best play it to try to draw the trumps. When you duck the second round of hearts and your partner shows out, he knows he cannot make his contract. If he leads a third trump, you will win with the ace and lead a diamond to force him to ruff with his last trump; then he will go down two tricks. Declarer's proper play is to cash his side winners and let you ruff to go down one.

Sometimes it is your partner who has the long trumps, and he needs your help to force declarer to ruff. For example:

#32   North
                                              ♠ 8 4
                                              ♡ Q J 9 7
                                              ◇ A Q
                                              ♣ A Q J 4 2
            West
            ♠ A K J 9 5
            ♡ 8
            ◇ 1 0 7 6 4 3
            ♣ 6 3

West	North	East	South
	1♣	Pass	1♡
1♠	3♡	3♠	4♡
Pass	Pass	Pass	

You win the first two tricks with the king and ace of spades. Partner plays the ten and three; declarer follows suit twice. Since partner raised your suit, his high-low in spades cannot be a doubleton; yet he wants you to lead another one. He would not encourage giving declarer a ruff-and-discard if he held a minor-suit king, so he probably has four hearts and wants to promote a trump trick with a long heart as was done in #31—by forcing declarer to ruff in both hands. So obey orders: *lead any spade at trick three*. The four hands:

                                              ♠ 8 4
                                              ♡ Q J 9 7
                                              ◇ A Q
                                              ♣ A Q J 4 2
            ♠ A K J 9 5   ♠ Q 10 7 3
            ♡ 8   ♡ A 6 5 2
            ◇ 1 0 7 6 4 3   ◇ 9 8 2
            ♣ 6 3   ♣ 8 5
                                              ♠ 6 2
                                              ♡ K 10 4 3
                                              ◇ K J 5
                                              ♣ K 10 9 7

As was predictable from partner's signal, he does have four hearts and neither minor-suit king. By leading a third spade to force declarer to ruff in one hand or the other, the contract can be set by the same defense as in the last hand, partner holding up his ace of trumps twice.

In the last six deals, the defense caused declarer to lose control of the trump suit by forcing him to ruff. In the next three, forcing the dummy to ruff will prevent declarer from finessing against your trump holding, or will promote an intermediate trump into a trick.

#33

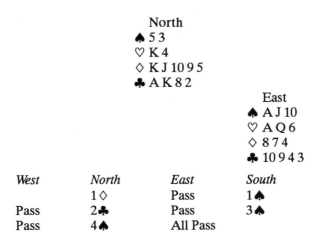

North
♠ 5 3
♡ K 4
◇ K J 10 9 5
♣ A K 8 2

East
♠ A J 10
♡ A Q 6
◇ 8 7 4
♣ 10 9 4 3

West	North	East	South
	1◇	Pass	1♠
Pass	2♣	Pass	3♠
Pass	4♠	All Pass	

Partner leads the jack of hearts, the king is played from dummy and you win with your ace. If declarer has as many as three hearts in his hand, you can force the dummy to ruff the third round; then you will win two spade tricks because declarer cannot lead spades from dummy twice. So, *lead the queen and another heart to force dummy to ruff*. The four hands:

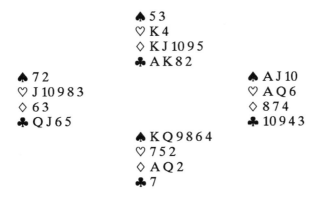

♠ 5 3
♡ K 4
◇ K J 10 9 5
♣ A K 8 2

♠ 7 2
♡ J 10 9 8 3
◇ 6 3
♣ Q J 6 5

♠ A J 10
♡ A Q 6
◇ 8 7 4
♣ 10 9 4 3

♠ K Q 9 8 6 4
♡ 7 5 2
◇ A Q 2
♣ 7

Declarer does have three hearts and ruffs the third round in dummy. Now he can lead through your ♠ A J 10 only once and you will win two spade tricks. If you do not lead the third heart, declarer will discard his losing heart on the king of clubs, and hold his spade losers to one by leading spades from dummy twice.

#34   North
                                                 ♠ A Q J
                                                 ♡ 6
                                                 ◇ K Q J 10 7
                                                 ♣ A 7 5 3

                                                                    East
                                                                    ♠ 10 9 7 4
                                                                    ♡ A 3 2
                                                                    ◇ 4 2
                                                                    ♣ J 10 8 2

West	North	East	South
			1♠
Pass	2◇	Pass	2♠
Pass	4NT	Pass	5◇
Pass	6♠	All Pass	

Partner leads the king of hearts. If you can force the declarer to ruff a heart with one of dummy's high spades, you have a natural trump trick. So, to make sure a heart is led at trick two, *overtake the king of hearts with the ace and lead another one yourself*. The four hands:

                                ♠ A Q J
                                ♡ 6
                                ◇ K Q J 10 7
                                ♣ A 7 5 3
        ♠ —   ♠ 10 9 7 4
        ♡ K Q 9 7 5 4   ♡ A 3 2
        ◇ 9 6 5 3   ◇ 4 2
        ♣ 9 6 4   ♣ J 10 8 2
                                ♠ K 8 6 5 3 2
                                ♡ J 10 8
                                ◇ A 8
                                ♣ K Q

Once the dummy is forced to ruff, declarer will be set. But if a heart is not led at trick two, declarer will have enough high spades to draw all of your trumps and discard his losing hearts on dummy's winners.

#35   North
                                                 ♠ K Q J 10
                                                 ♡ 7
                                                 ◇ A Q 9 2
                                                 ♣ J 10 8 7

        West
        ♠ A 9 7
        ♡ K Q J 10 6
        ◇ 6 4
        ♣ A 9 2

West	North	East	South
1♡	Double	3♡	3♠
Pass	4♠	All Pass	

You lead the king of hearts and it wins the first trick. If declarer has at least three hearts in his hand, you can force dummy to ruff twice and your nine of spades is promoted into a trick. So, *lead a heart at trick two.* When you regain the lead, *play a third round of hearts.* The four hands:

```
                        ♠ K Q J 10
                        ♡ 7
                        ◇ A Q 9 2
                        ♣ J 10 8 7
        ♠ A 9 7                            ♠ 3
        ♡ K Q J 10 6                       ♡ A 9 5 2
        ◇ 6 4                              ◇ 8 7 5 3
        ♣ A 9 2                            ♣ 6 5 4 3
                        ♠ 8 6 5 4 2
                        ♡ 8 4 3
                        ◇ K J 10
                        ♣ K Q
```

In the last deal of this chapter, you must make the unusual play of holding up the ace of trumps twice, even though you have only three trumps.

#36

```
                        North
                        ♠ A J 10
                        ♡ J 9 6 3
                        ◇ 9 6
                        ♣ K Q J 10
                                        East
                                        ♠ 8 6 5
                                        ♡ A 5 2
                                        ◇ A K Q J
                                        ♣ 7 5 4
```

West	North	East	South
		1◇	Double
Pass	2◇	Pass	2♡
Pass	4♡	All Pass	

Partner leads the two of diamonds and you can see three tricks (two diamonds and one heart). The bidding indicates that partner does not have any high cards, so the only reasonable chance to beat the contract is to win a second trump trick. Partner's opening lead marks declarer with at least three diamonds, so the best defense is to win the first two diamond tricks and lead a third diamond to force dummy to ruff. At trick four, the six of hearts is led from the dummy. You play low, declarer wins with the king and partner drops the *eight.* Then declarer leads the queen of hearts and partner plays the *five* (by playing high-low he has shown a third trump—see Chapter 7, Count Signals), so declarer has bid a three-card heart suit. If you win this trick with your ace of hearts, declarer can make his contract no matter what you lead because of the lucky three-three heart break. The winning defense is to *duck the second heart lead,* even though you are left with the lone ace. The four hands:

                                ♠ A J 10
                                ♡ J 9 6 3
                                ◊ 9 6
                                ♣ K Q J 10
        ♠ 7 4 3 2   ♠ 8 6 5
        ♡ 8 7 5   ♡ A 4 2
        ◊ 10 4 3 2   ◊ A K Q J
        ♣ 9 6   ♣ 7 5 4
                                ♠ K Q 9
                                ♡ K Q 10
                                ◊ 8 7 5
                                ♣ A 8 3 2

After forcing dummy to ruff once and ducking two rounds of hearts, everyone has one heart left. If declarer leads another heart, you can take your ace and win a trick with your high diamond. If instead he cashes his side winners, partner will be able to ruff the third round of clubs.

If you are thinking that South should have bid three clubs, not two hearts, you may be right. But bidding a three-card suit in this auction is a conceivable action. You must trust partner's signal rather than the opponent's bid.

Quiz for Chapter Eight

1.

North
♠ 3
♡ K Q
♢ A K Q 10 2
♣ K Q J 5 4

East
♠ A
♡ A 10 7 6 4
♢ 9 8 5
♣ A 8 7 2

West	North	East	South
	1♢	1♡	4♠
Pass	Pass	Pass	

Partner leads the two of hearts. Plan your defense.

2.

North
♠ A Q 7
♡ J 10 9 2
♢ 8 3
♣ Q J 6 4

West
♠ 4 3 2
♡ A 7 4 3
♢ A K J 10 4
♣ 5

West	North	East	South
			1NT
2♢	3♢	Pass	3♡
Pass	4♡	All Pass	

The one-notrump opening bid shows 16-18 high-card points. You win the first two tricks with the king and ace of diamonds; partner plays two-six and declarer plays five-queen. Plan your defense.

3.

North
♠ Q 9 8 4
♡ K J 10 2
♢ A Q 10 3
♣ 6

East
♠ A 3
♡ A 9 8 6 5 4
♢ 2
♣ 10 9 7 5

West	North	East	South
			1♠
Pass	3♠	Pass	4♠
Pass	Pass	Pass	

Partner leads the three of hearts, you win with the ace and declarer drops the queen. Plan your defense.

4.

North
♠ A K 4
♡ K Q 10 3
♢ Q 10 9 5
♣ K Q

East
♠ Q 8
♡ A 2
♢ 7 4
♣ A J 10 9 6 5 3

West	North	East	South
	1♢	2♣	2♠
Pass	4♠	All Pass	

Partner leads the seven of clubs, you win with the ace and declarer plays the two. Plan your defense.

5.   North
                  ♠ 8 4 3
                  ♡ A K Q 7
                  ◇ J 5
                  ♣ A K Q J
                                East
                                ♠ 9 2
                                ♡ J 6 5
                                ◇ K Q 8 7 2
                                ♣ 9 4 3

West	North	East	South
	1♣	Pass	1♡
1♠	4♡	All Pass	

Partner leads the king, ace and queen of spades. What do you play on the third spade lead?

6.   North
                  ♠ A 9 4 3
                  ♡ 5
                  ◇ A K Q 8 4 2
                  ♣ 7 4
                                East
                                ♠ J 10 8
                                ♡ A Q 10 6 4
                                ◇ J 6 5
                                ♣ A J

West	North	East	South
	1◇	1♡	1♠
2♡	3♠	Pass	4♠
Pass	Pass	Pass	

Partner leads the king of clubs. Plan your defense.

7.   North
                  ♠ J 10 6 2
                  ♡ A Q 3 2
                  ◇ J
                  ♣ K J 7 4
West
♠ A Q
♡ 10 8
◇ A K 10 4 3 2
♣ 9 6 5

West	North	East	South
			1♣
1◇	1♡	Pass	1♠
2◇	3♠	Pass	4♠
Pass	Pass	Pass	

You lead the king of diamonds, partner plays the five and declarer the seven. Plan your defense.

8.   North
                  ♠ 10 9 6 5
                  ♡ J 3
                  ◇ K Q 8 5
                  ♣ A K Q
                                East
                                ♠ A
                                ♡ A K 10 9 8 4
                                ◇ 4 3
                                ♣ J 7 6 3

West	North	East	South
	1◇	1♡	1♠
Pass	2♠	Pass	4♠
Pass	Pass	Pass	

Partner leads the two of hearts. You win with the king and cash the ace of hearts, declarer playing the seven and queen, and partner following to the second trick with the five. Plan your defense.

Quiz Answers for Chapter Eight

1.

North
- ♠ 3
- ♡ K Q
- ◇ A K Q 10 2
- ♣ K Q J 5 4

West
- ♠ J 7 5
- ♡ J 9 8 2
- ◇ J 6 4 3
- ♣ 10 3

East
- ♠ A
- ♡ A 10 7 6 4
- ◇ 9 8 5
- ♣ A 8 7 2

South
- ♠ K Q 10 9 8 6 4 2
- ♡ 5 3
- ◇ 7
- ♣ 9 6

West	North	East	South
	1◇	1♡	4♠
Pass	Pass	Pass	

Partner leads the two of hearts. Plan your defense.

The only chance to beat the contract is to win a second trump trick. If partner does not have a natural trump trick, maybe you can help him promote one. Partner probably would have led a club if he had a singleton, so the best chance is that he has a doubleton club and the perfect trump holding (such as ♠ J x x or ♠ 10 x x x). After winning the first trick with the ace of hearts, *lead the ace of clubs*. Partner will signal with the ten; then you *lead another club*. When declarer leads a spade from the dummy and you win with the ace, *lead a third round of clubs*. With the cards as shown, this defense beats the contract; partner's jack of spades is promoted into the setting trick.

2.

North
- ♠ A Q 7
- ♡ J 10 9 2
- ◇ 8 3
- ♣ Q J 6 4

West
- ♠ 4 3 2
- ♡ A 7 4 3
- ◇ A K J 10 4
- ♣ 5

East
- ♠ J 10 9 5
- ♡ 5
- ◇ 9 7 6 2
- ♣ 10 8 7 3

South
- ♠ K 8 6
- ♡ K Q 8 6
- ◇ Q 5
- ♣ A K 9 2

West	North	East	South
			1NT
2◇	3◇	Pass	3♡
Pass	4♡	All Pass	

You win the first two tricks with the king and ace of diamonds; partner plays two-six, and declarer plays five-queen. Plan your defense.

Declarer should have the ace of clubs and all of the missing kings for his opening bid, so the only chance to beat the contract is to promote a second trump trick. *Lead a third round of diamonds*; declarer has no losers in the side suits, so a ruff-and-discard cannot help him. After ruffing the third trick (it makes no difference which hand ruffs), declarer will lead trumps. You must *duck the first two trump leads*, leaving declarer with two trumps in one hand and one in the other. If he leads a third trump, you can set him two tricks by winning with the ace and leading a diamond. If declarer abandons the trump suit and starts cashing his high cards, you can set him one trick by ruffing the second club lead.

3.	North
	♠ Q 9 8 4
	♡ K J 10 2
	◇ A Q 10 3
	♣ 6

West	East
♠ 6 5	♠ A 3
♡ 3	♡ A 9 8 6 5 4
◇ K J 9 8 7	◇ 2
♣ J 8 4 3 2	♣ 10 9 7 5

South
♠ K J 10 7 2
♡ Q 7
◇ 6 5 4
♣ A K Q

West	North	East	South
			1♠
Pass	3♠	Pass	4♠
Pass	Pass	Pass	

Partner leads the three of hearts, you win with the ace and declarer drops the queen. Plan your defense.

It is clear that partner has led a singleton—if he had ♡ 7 3, he would have led the seven—so you can give him a heart ruff; but that will not beat the contract. The best chance for a fourth trick is to get a diamond ruff. So don't lead a heart at trick two, *lead your singleton diamond.* When you regain the lead with the ace of spades, give your partner the heart ruff, and he will return a diamond for you to ruff.

4.	North
	♠ A K 4
	♡ K Q 10 3
	◇ Q 10 9 5
	♣ K Q

West	East
♠ 5 2	♠ Q 8
♡ J 9 8 7 6 4	♡ A 2
◇ 8 6 3 2	◇ 7 4
♣ 7	♣ A J 10 9 6 5 3

South
♠ J 10 9 7 6 3
♡ 5
◇ A K J
♣ 8 4 2

West	North	East	South
	1◇	2♣	2♠
Pass	4♠	All Pass	

Partner leads the seven of clubs, you win with the ace and declarer plays the two. Plan your defense.

The best chance to beat the contract is for partner to have a singleton club and at least two spades; any two spades except the three and two will do. *Lead the jack of clubs at trick two.* Partner will ruff with the two of spades and, reading your jack-of-clubs lead as a suit-preference signal (asking for the higher-ranking suit), he will return a heart. When you win with the ace and *lead another club,* partner will ruff with the five to force dummy to overruff with the king. This uppercut play promotes your queen of spades into the setting trick.

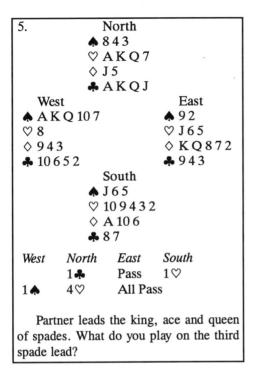

5. North
    ♠ 8 4 3
    ♡ A K Q 7
    ◇ J 5
    ♣ A K Q J

West
♠ A K Q 10 7
♡ 8
◇ 9 4 3
♣ 10 6 5 2

East
♠ 9 2
♡ J 6 5
◇ K Q 8 7 2
♣ 9 4 3

South
♠ J 6 5
♡ 10 9 4 3 2
◇ A 10 6
♣ 8 7

West	North	East	South
	1♣	Pass	1♡
1♠	4♡	All Pass	

Partner leads the king, ace and queen of spades. What do you play on the third spade lead?

Play the two of diamonds. Presumably partner will win a third spade trick with the queen and the question is: what do you want him to lead at trick four? Declarer is almost certain to have the ace of diamonds for his bid, but, even if you did not know this, the only fail-safe defense is a *fourth round of spades* to promote your jack of hearts. When partner sees your two of diamonds along with the strong clubs in dummy, he should realize that you want another spade led. With any other lead, declarer will draw trumps and discard his losing diamonds on dummy's clubs.

Note that if declarer has only four hearts, partner's fourth spade lead would cost you a diamond trick. But in that case you break even because you win a trick with the jack of hearts instead.

6. North
    ♠ A 9 4 3
    ♡ 5
    ◇ A K Q 8 4 2
    ♣ 7 4

West
♠ 2
♡ 8 7 2
◇ 10 9 7
♣ K Q 10 8 3 2

East
♠ J 10 8
♡ A Q 10 6 4
◇ J 6 5
♣ A J

South
♠ K Q 7 6 5
♡ K J 9 3
◇ 3
♣ 9 6 5

West	North	East	South
	1◇	1♡	1♠
2♡	3♠	Pass	4♠
Pass	Pass	Pass	

Partner leads the king of clubs. Plan your defense.

Overtake partner's king of clubs with your ace, cash the ace of hearts and lead the jack of clubs. Seeing that no more tricks are available outside the trump suit, partner should overtake your jack of clubs with his queen and lead a third club. If declarer ruffs low, you will overruff; if he ruffs with the ace, your ♠ J 10 8 becomes a natural trick.

Note that if you do not cash the ace of hearts before leading the jack of clubs, declarer can make his contract by discarding a heart from dummy on partner's third club lead.

7.   North
                      ♠ J 10 6 2
                      ♡ A Q 3 2
                      ◇ J
                      ♣ K J 7 4
        West   East
        ♠ A Q   ♠ 7 5 3
        ♡ 10 8   ♡ J 9 6 4
        ◇ A K 10 4 3 2   ◇ 9 8 6 5
        ♣ 9 6 5   ♣ 8 2
                      South
                      ♠ K 9 8 4
                      ♡ K 7 5
                      ◇ Q 7
                      ♣ A Q 10 3

West	North	East	South
			1♣
1◇	1♡	Pass	1♠
2◇	3♠	Pass	4♠
Pass	Pass	Pass	

You lead the king of diamonds, partner plays the five and declarer the seven. Plan your defense.

The bidding tells you that partner is unlikely to have any significant high cards, so you will need three trump tricks to beat the contract. Declarer opened the bidding with one club and is a favorite to have a four-card club suit. If so, your partner has a doubleton club and you can give him a ruff. *Lead a club at trick two.* When you regain the lead with the queen and ace of spades, *lead clubs twice more* and partner will ruff the third round.

8.   North
                      ♠ 10 9 6 5
                      ♡ J 3
                      ◇ K Q 8 5
                      ♣ A K Q
        West   East
        ♠ Q 3   ♠ A
        ♡ 6 5 2   ♡ A K 10 9 8 4
        ◇ 10 6 2   ◇ 4 3
        ♣ 10 8 5 4 2   ♣ J 7 6 3
                      South
                      ♠ K J 8 7 4 2
                      ♡ Q 7
                      ◇ A J 9 7
                      ♣ 9

West	North	East	South
	1◇	1♡	1♠
Pass	2♠	Pass	4♠
Pass	Pass	Pass	

Partner leads the two of hearts. You win with the king and cash the ace of hearts, declarer playing the seven and queen, and partner following to the second trick with the five. Plan your defense.

The bidding marks declarer with the ace of diamonds, so the only source of tricks left is the trump suit. Partner must have a natural trump trick or a holding that can be promoted into a trick to set the contract. He led the two of hearts and followed with the five to show that he has the one missing heart. So, *lead a third round of hearts* to get rid of the heart in partner's hand and set the stage for a trump-promotion play. When you get the lead with the ace of spades, *play another heart.* This promotes partner's queen of spades and is the only defense to beat the contract.

9

Discarding and Deception

Accurate Discarding

When you cannot follow suit, your play in a non-trump suit is a "discard." Choosing the right discard is not always easy, but often crucial; a careless or impetuous discard can give away the contract. Perhaps more errors are made in this area of defense than any other, so take your time and plan your discards carefully. The first seven illustrations show how to discard accurately.

#1

```
                         North
                         ♠ J 4
                         ♡ A J 10 6
                         ◇ K Q 9 2
                         ♣ 7 5 3
                                         East
                                         ♠ 8 3
                                         ♡ K Q 9 4
                                         ◇ J 10 7 6
                                         ♣ K Q J
```

West	North	East	South
			1♠
Pass	2◇	Pass	3♠
Pass	4♠	Pass	5♣
Pass	5♡	Double	6♠
Pass	Pass	Pass	

Partner leads the three of hearts, the ten is played from dummy and you win with the queen. Then you lead the king of clubs, declarer wins with the ace and partner follows with the two. Declarer proceeds to play three high trumps. Partner follows suit throughout, a club is thrown from dummy and you must discard on the third spade. A good general rule is to "keep the dummy covered" (keep equal length with dummy's long suits). So *discard a club; do not discard a heart or a diamond*. If declarer leads a fourth trump and pitches a club from dummy, *discard another club*. In the following layout, declarer can make his bid if you discard a heart or a diamond.

                                                    ♠ J 4
                                                    ♡ A J 10 6
                                                    ◇ K Q 9 2
                                                    ♣ 7 5 3

                        ♠ 9 5 2   ♠ 8 3
                        ♡ 8 7 3   ♡ K Q 9 4
                        ◇ 5 3   ◇ J 10 7 6
                        ♣ 10 8 6 4 2   ♣ K Q J

                                                    ♠ A K Q 10 7 6
                                                    ♡ 5 2
                                                    ◇ A 8 4
                                                    ♣ A 9

Fortunately partner has the ten of clubs and therefore declarer has one more inescapable loser. If you discard a diamond on the third or fourth trump lead, declarer can discard his losing club on dummy's fourth diamond. If you discard a heart, he can establish the fourth heart for a discard by cashing the ace and ruffing the third round. As long as you keep equal length with dummy's suits, the contract cannot be made.

#2   North
                                                    ♠ A Q 6 5
                                                    ♡ K 7 3
                                                    ◇ 9 3 2
                                                    ♣ A 8 4

                                                                        East
                                                                        ♠ 10 4 3 2
                                                                        ♡ J 10 9 5
                                                                        ◇ A 5
                                                                        ♣ Q J 6

West	North	East	South
	1♣	Pass	1♡
Pass	1♠	Pass	2NT
Pass	3NT	All Pass	

Partner leads the six of diamonds. You win the first trick with the ace and return the five of diamonds, on which declarer plays the jack and partner the queen. Partner then leads the four of diamonds, which reveals that he began with a five-card suit, but more importantly it is a suit-preference signal indicating strength in clubs (see topic, Chapter 7). On this trick you should *discard a club*. You should keep four spades because there are four in dummy, and keep four hearts because declarer bid the suit. The club discard is the safest; it will cost a trick only if declarer has ♣ K 10 x or ♣ K 10 x x. The four hands:

```
                         ♠ A Q 6 5
                         ♡ K 7 3
                         ◇ 9 3 2
                         ♣ A 8 4
♠ J 8                                        ♠ 10 4 3 2
♡ 4 2                                        ♡ J 10 9 5
◇ Q 10 7 6 4                                 ◇ A 5
♣ K 10 9 3                                   ♣ Q J 6
                         ♠ K 9 7
                         ♡ A Q 8 6
                         ◇ K J 8
                         ♣ 7 5 2
```

Declarer has eight winners (three spades, three hearts, one diamond and one club) and, once you discard a club at trick three, he cannot legitimately win a ninth.

#3   North
                                      ♠ Q 5 3 2
                                      ♡ 9
                                      ◇ A K Q 7
                                      ♣ A K Q 2
                                                     East
                                                     ♠ 8 7 6 4
                                                     ♡ Q
                                                     ◇ J 9 8 2
                                                     ♣ J 10 7 6

West	*North*	*East*	*South*
3♡	Double	Pass	4♠
Pass	4NT	Pass	5◇
Pass	6♠	All Pass	

Partner wins the first trick with the king of hearts and continues with the ace of hearts. Declarer ruffs in dummy with the queen of spades, so what do you discard?

"A trump," you say? *That's right!* The four hands:

```
                         ♠ Q 5 3 2
                         ♡ 9
                         ◇ A K Q 7
                         ♣ A K Q 2
♠ 9                                          ♠ 8 7 6 4
♡ A K J 10 7 5 4                             ♡ Q
◇ 6 3                                        ◇ J 9 8 2
♣ 8 5 3                                      ♣ J 10 7 6
                         ♠ A K J 10
                         ♡ 8 6 3 2
                         ◇ 10 5 4
                         ♣ 9 4
```

After ruffing the second heart lead with the queen of spades, declarer is left with two heart losers and can discard one of them on dummy's third high club. If you discard a diamond or club on the second heart lead, he can draw all of your trumps and discard his second heart loser on the fourth round of the suit in which you made the discard. By underruffing and subsequently keeping equal length with dummy's minor suits, you will set the contract.

#4   North
                                             ♠ K Q 2
                                             ♡ 7 2
                                             ◇ 9 7 6 5 3
                                             ♣ J 8 4
                    West
                    ♠ 7 4
                    ♡ Q 10 9 3
                    ◇ 10 8 2
                    ♣ A K Q 9

West	North	East	South
			1♠
Pass	2♠	Pass	4♠
Pass	Pass	Pass	

You win the first three tricks with the king, ace and queen of clubs as partner and declarer both follow suit. At trick four, you lead a trump and declarer proceeds to lead five rounds of spades, partner following three times. What three discards do you make? Why?

Before answering, here are the four hands:

                                             ♠ K Q 2
                                             ♡ 7 2
                                             ◇ 9 7 6 5 3
                                             ♣ J 8 4
          ♠ 7 4   ♠ 9 5 3
          ♡ Q 10 9 3   ♡ J 8 6 5 4
          ◇ 10 8 2   ◇ Q J
          ♣ A K Q 9   ♣ 10 6 3
                                             ♠ A J 10 8 6
                                             ♡ A K
                                             ◇ A K 4
                                             ♣ 7 5 2

You may discard two hearts and one club or three hearts, but *do not discard a diamond*. As you can see, you will win a diamond trick and beat the contract as long as you keep three diamonds. Declarer cannot have more than two hearts; if he did, he would have ruffed a heart (or two) in dummy before drawing trumps. So the only thing in your hand that might be of value is your diamond holding.

#5

```
                              North
                              ♠ Q J 10 5
                              ♡ A J 10 9
                              ◇ K 2
                              ♣ Q 6 3
            West
            ♠ 8 6
            ♡ 7 4 3 2
            ◇ Q 10 9 5
            ♣ J 10 9
```

West	North	East	South
			1♠
Pass	3♠	Pass	4♠
Pass	Pass	Pass	

You lead the jack of clubs and are allowed to win the first trick. So you continue with the ten of clubs and partner wins the next two club tricks with the king and ace before exiting with a spade. Declarer wins and leads two more rounds of spades; partner shows out on the third round. Assuming declarer will lead out all five of his trumps, which three discards should you make? The four hands:

```
                         ♠ Q J 10 5
                         ♡ A J 10 9
                         ◇ K 2
                         ♣ Q 6 3
      ♠ 8 6                              ♠ 4 3
      ♡ 7 4 3 2                          ♡ Q 5
      ◇ Q 10 9 5                         ◇ J 8 7 6 4
      ♣ J 10 9                           ♣ A K 8 2
                         ♠ A K 9 7 2
                         ♡ K 8 6
                         ◇ A 3
                         ♣ 7 5 4
```

Two things should be clear: Declarer must have a possible loser in his hand or he would have claimed; and he has no diamond losers because he would have ruffed them in dummy. Therefore he must have a possible heart loser and you should envision what you now see; declarer has three hearts to the king and must guess which way to finesse for the queen. Your best strategy is usually to *discard only diamonds*; if you don't discard any hearts, declarer is more likely to play you for the queen.[1]

---

1. There is a considerable amount of psychology in an ending such as this, and it is not clearly wrong to discard a heart. A deceptive defender might discard a heart from Q x x or Q x x x to disguise his holding; so choosing to discard a heart from x x x or x x x x could outfox a clever declarer.

#6   North
                                               ♠ 9 8 2
                                               ♡ K Q
                                               ◇ A K Q 9 8 5
                                               ♣ 10 4
                West
                ♠ K Q J 10 6 4
                ♡ A 9 3
                ◇ 2
                ♣ K 7 5

West	North	East	South
	1◇	Pass	1♡
1♠	2◇	Pass	2NT
Pass	3NT	All Pass	

You win the first trick with the king of spades and continue with the queen; partner follows suit and declarer wins with the ace. Then declarer cashes the jack of diamonds and leads another diamond. You should realize that he intends to run all six diamonds and you must make five discards. *Now is the time to organize a plan.*

You have four safe discards—two hearts, one club and one spade; if you discard two spades, declarer can lead a heart and you won't have enough spades left to set him. So you should realize that you must blank your king of clubs and hope that partner has the queen, or that declarer has the ace-queen and takes the finesse. If your first four discards are two hearts, one club and one spade and then you squirm in your chair before you discard a second club, a good psychologist may read that you blanked the king and play a club to his ace. A more deceptive procedure is to *discard the second club before the last diamond is led*: A good rotation of discards would be a low heart, a low club, a low heart, a low club and a low spade. The four hands:

                                        ♠ 9 8 2
                                        ♡ K Q
                                        ◇ A K Q 9 8 5
                                        ♣ 10 4
        ♠ K Q J 10 6 4   ♠ 5 3
        ♡ A 9 3   ♡ 10 8 4
        ◇ 2   ◇ 10 7 6
        ♣ K 7 5   ♣ J 9 6 3 2
                                        ♠ A 7
                                        ♡ J 7 6 5 2
                                        ◇ J 4 3
                                        ♣ A Q 8

It turns out that declarer does have the queen of clubs and once you discard two clubs, he can make his contract by cashing the ace of clubs and dropping your king; but he may take the finesse! Be sure to see that if you do not blank the king of clubs, declarer cannot go wrong; he will lead a heart and you will not have enough spade tricks to set the contract.

#7

North
♠ A 6 5 2
♡ J 3
◇ A K J 10 7
♣ K 10

West
♠ Q J 8
♡ 10 9 8 7 2
◇ 6
♣ 8 7 4 3

West	North	East	South
			1NT
Pass	2♣	Pass	2◇
Pass	3◇	Pass	3NT
Pass	6NT	All Pass	

To make the right discard this time, you must count the declarer's hand. You lead the ten of hearts to partner's ace and declarer's queen. Partner returns a heart, which declarer wins with the king, so you know he has no more hearts. Now declarer leads the queen of diamonds and continues to cash four of his five diamond tricks; you discard three hearts and declarer throws a club on the fourth diamond. You now hold ♠ Q J 8 and ♣ 8 7 4 3. The four low clubs may seem unimportant, but the key to beating the contract is to make the right discard on the fifth diamond. Declarer has shown up with two hearts and three diamonds. Since he told you in the bidding that he has no four-card major, his apparent distribution is three spades, two hearts, three diamonds and five clubs. Having discarded one club on the fourth round of diamonds, he now has the same distribution as you—three spades and four clubs. On the last diamond partner throws a heart, declarer discards a spade and *you must do the same*; your club holding is the only chance to provide a club stopper, so you must rely on partner to protect the spades. The four hands:

♠ A 6 5 2
♡ J 3
◇ A K J 10 7
♣ K 10

♠ Q J 8   ♠ 7 4 3
♡ 10 9 8 7 2   ♡ A 6 5 4
◇ 6   ◇ 8 5 3 2
♣ 8 7 4 3   ♣ J 9

♠ K 10 9
♡ K Q
◇ Q 9 4
♣ A Q 6 5 2

As you can see, your club holding is indeed crucial and if you discard a club declarer will win four club tricks to make his contract. Actually, your spade discard is without risk—partner is known to have three spades including at least one higher than dummy's six-spot, so declarer cannot win a third spade trick. Declarer could have played the hand better (but you will always beat the contract if you follow his discard on the fifth diamond). He should play off the king and ace of spades before cashing the fifth diamond; the queen-jack might be doubleton. Also, the fifth diamond will squeeze East if he has ♠ Q J x and four clubs, and this is easier to read after the king and ace of spades have been played.

Discarding to Help Partner

Another duty when discarding is to help your partner with his discards. Here are five examples:

#8

```
                        North
                        ♠ K J
                        ♡ 10 6
                        ◊ 7 4 3
                        ♣ A K J 10 9 8
                                        East
                                        ♠ 7 6 4 3
                                        ♡ J 8 2
                                        ◊ Q J 10 9
                                        ♣ 7 2
```

West	North	East	South
			2NT
Pass	4♣ (a)	Pass	4NT (b)
Pass	7NT	All Pass	

(a) Gerber
(b) Three aces

Partner leads the ten of spades and declarer wins in his hand with the ace. He then starts running the club suit and you have no discarding problems, but your partner may have. Your discard on the third club lead should be the *queen of diamonds*. This is a signal to tell partner that you have control of that suit from the queen down. Here are the four hands so you can see how this helps your partner.

```
                        ♠ K J
                        ♡ 10 6
                        ◊ 7 4 3
                        ♣ A K J 10 9 8
        ♠ 10 9 8 5 2                        ♠ 7 6 4 3
        ♡ 9 7 4 3                           ♡ J 8 2
        ◊ K 5                               ◊ Q J 10 9
        ♣ 6 4                               ♣ 7 2
                        ♠ A Q
                        ♡ A K Q 5
                        ◊ A 8 6 2
                        ♣ Q 5 3
```

Declarer has twelve winners (two spades, three hearts, one diamond and six clubs) and cannot get another unless West discards a heart; in which case he will win a fourth heart trick with the five. Hoping for a defensive error, declarer should cash six clubs and two spades before touching the red suits. At trick eight, West must discard from ♡ 9 7 4 3 ◊ K 5. Without the queen-of-diamonds signal it would tempting to throw a heart and save ◊ K 5, but knowing that partner controls the diamond suit it is obvious that West should discard a diamond and hold onto four hearts.

#9

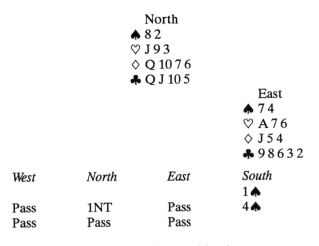

North
♠ 8 2
♡ J 9 3
◇ Q 10 7 6
♣ Q J 10 5

East
♠ 7 4
♡ A 7 6
◇ J 5 4
♣ 9 8 6 3 2

West	North	East	South
			1♠
Pass	1NT	Pass	4♠
Pass	Pass	Pass	

Partner leads the king of hearts. He continues with a heart to your ace, and you lead a third heart to his queen, declarer following suit throughout. Partner exits with the ten of spades, which declarer wins with the jack. Declarer starts running the spade suit, partner shows out on the third lead, so declarer has a seven-card suit. You have no discarding problems (you have a handful of losers), but why isn't declarer claiming the contract? Why is he leading spades after the missing trumps have been drawn?

Answer: He obviously has a loser in his hand and he intends to run all of his spades to give your partner a chance to make a faulty discard.

When you stop to think about it, you can figure out the exact problem. Declarer followed suit to three heart tricks and has a seven-card spade suit, so he has three cards in the minor suits. If your partner had the ace of diamonds or ace of clubs, he would have cashed it at trick four. So declarer has either ◇ A x and ♣ A or ◇ A and ♣ A x. When declarer cashes his last spade at trick ten, your partner must discard from ◇ K x ♣ K x; he needs your help to figure out declarer's distribution. Your first three discards should be the *four of diamonds, five of diamonds and jack of diamonds*. This reveals to partner that you began with three diamonds, and therefore declarer has two. The four hands:

♠ 8 2
♡ J 9 3
◇ Q 10 7 6
♣ Q J 10 5

♠ 10 9
♡ K Q 10 5
◇ K 9 8 3
♣ K 7 4

♠ 7 4
♡ A 7 6
◇ J 5 4
♣ 9 8 6 3 2

♠ A K Q J 6 5 3
♡ 8 4 2
◇ A 2
♣ A

In situations like this, the best way to help your partner to count the hand is to discard one suit completely, and since you have three diamonds and five clubs, you should discard diamonds—the shorter suit. Partner can see eight diamonds and knows that five are missing; when you discard three diamonds and then stop, he can deduce that declarer has the remaining two and will hold ◇ K x. If you discard haphazardly, there is an even chance he will make the wrong discard.

#10

North
♠ A J
♡ Q 9 8 7
◇ A 10 9 4
♣ 9 3 2

East
♠ Q 9 6 4 3
♡ K 10 6 2
◇ 5
♣ Q J 7

West	North	East	South
			1◇
Pass	1♡	Pass	1NT
Pass	2NT	Pass	3NT
Pass	Pass	Pass	

Partner leads the six of clubs and your jack forces out declarer's king. A diamond is led, partner plays the jack and dummy the ace. Then the declarer plays the ten of diamonds from dummy. Which card should you discard?

You should discard *the queen of clubs* to eliminate a problem for partner. Before explaining further, here are the four hands:

♠ A J
♡ Q 9 8 7
◇ A 10 9 4
♣ 9 3 2

♠ 10 7 5	♠ Q 9 6 4 3
♡ 4 3	♡ K 10 6 2
◇ Q J 2	◇ 5
♣ A 10 8 6 5	♣ Q J 7

♠ K 8 2
♡ A J 5
◇ K 8 7 6 3
♣ K 4

Declarer will make his contract unless your partner cashes his four club tricks when he gets the lead with the queen of diamonds. By using the Rule of Eleven, you know that declarer was dealt only one club higher than the six and he has already played it, so partner now has ♣ A 10 8 or ♣ A 10 8 x. If you do not discard the queen of clubs, partner may not lead the suit again for fear declarer still has ♣ Q x.

To show you that the winning defense could be for partner not to lead another club, suppose these were the four hands:

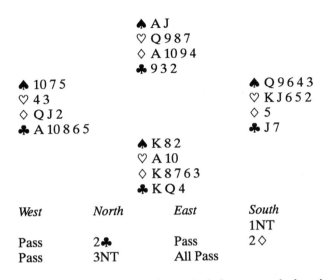

<pre>
                          ♠ A J
                          ♡ Q 9 8 7
                          ◇ A 10 9 4
                          ♣ 9 3 2
       ♠ 10 7 5   ♠ Q 9 6 4 3
       ♡ 4 3   ♡ K J 6 5 2
       ◇ Q J 2   ◇ 5
       ♣ A 10 8 6 5   ♣ J 7
                          ♠ K 8 2
                          ♡ A 10
                          ◇ K 8 7 6 3
                          ♣ K Q 4
</pre>

West	North	East	South
			1NT
Pass	2♣	Pass	2◇
Pass	3NT	All Pass	

Again partner leads the six of clubs and your jack forces out declarer's king. Now you should discard the six of hearts on the second diamond lead. When partner gets the lead with the queen of diamonds, he will probably read your six as encouraging and lead a heart; although he can beat the contract by leading anything but a club.

From partner's point of view, it is unlikely, but possible, that declarer has ♣ K Q and you ♣ J x x. In that case, you can reveal that you began with three clubs by throwing a club on the second diamond; something you most emphatically should not do if it is your last club.

#11

<pre>
                          North
                          ♠ J 9 7 2
                          ♡ K J 10 9 3
                          ◇ A J
                          ♣ K 8
                                           East
                                           ♠ 6
                                           ♡ Q 8 7 4 2
                                           ◇ 10 9 5 3
                                           ♣ A Q 2
</pre>

West	North	East	South
			2♠ (a)
Pass	4♠	All Pass	

(a) Weak Two-Bid

Partner leads the king of diamonds and the first trick is won in dummy with the ace. Declarer plays the ace and king of spades, partner following with the three and queen. You must discard on the second spade, but before you do consider: Partner is marked with the ace of hearts (the weak-two bidder should not have a side ace together with the ace and king of spades), and if he has two hearts, declarer has a singleton. It looks like the declarer will lose one diamond and two clubs, so if he leads a heart, you want partner to win with his ace. But if declarer leads a heart, partner may play low, hoping declarer will misguess and play the jack. Of course, declarer would go up with the king and make his contract. What can you do to alert partner that he should go up with his ace of hearts?

Answer: *Discard the queen of hearts* on the second spade lead. The four hands:

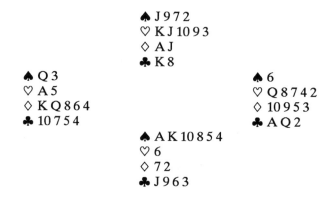

♠ J 9 7 2
♡ K J 10 9 3
◇ A J
♣ K 8

♠ Q 3
♡ A 5
◇ K Q 8 6 4
♣ 10 7 5 4

♠ 6
♡ Q 8 7 4 2
◇ 10 9 5 3
♣ A Q 2

♠ A K 10 8 5 4
♡ 6
◇ 7 2
♣ J 9 6 3

With the queen of hearts gone, partner knows that only one heart trick is available. So, when declarer leads his singleton heart, he will win with the ace, cash his high diamond and lead a club.

If you think declarer made a mistake by cashing the second spade and giving you an opportunity to signal before he led a heart, you are right.

Furthermore, partner probably should go up with the ace of hearts even if declarer plays two rounds of trumps and you do not discard the queen of hearts; he should envision that four tricks are available (one heart, one diamond and two clubs). But your partner might be sleeping and the queen-of-hearts discard should wake him up!

#12

North
♠ A J 8 3
♡ 10 5 3
◇ 6 4
♣ A K 7 2

East
♠ Q 10 9 7
♡ A 6
◇ K 2
♣ Q J 8 5 3

West	North	East	South
	1♣	Pass	1◇
Pass	1♠	Pass	2NT
Pass	3NT	All Pass	

Partner leads the four of hearts, you win with the ace and declarer plays the nine. You return the six of hearts, declarer plays the jack and partner wins with the queen. Next, partner leads the two of hearts, showing that he began with a five-card suit, and you must make a discard. Consider that in top tricks declarer can win a maximum of two spades, two clubs and one heart, so he needs four diamond tricks to make his contract. If he has ◇ A Q J 10 you cannot stop him, so partner must have a diamond honor in order to beat the contract. If partner has ◇ Q x, ◇ J x x or ◇ 10 x x x, declarer must lose a diamond trick before he can run the suit, and with careful play he can manage to lose the trick to your king unless you get rid of it. The king of diamonds is a useless card. In fact it is worse than useless—it is in an obstruction. So *discard the king of diamonds at trick three*. The four hands:

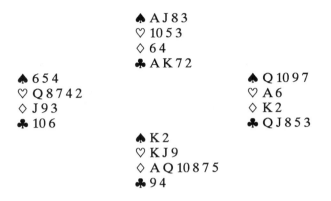

Once you discard the king of diamonds, declarer can win at most eight tricks—whether he puts partner on lead in diamonds, or endplays you in clubs to get an extra spade trick.

If you do not discard the king of diamonds, declarer can make his contract by conceding a diamond trick to you: He can play a spade to dummy's ace, lead a diamond and finesse the queen (if you play the king, he will duck), return to dummy with the ace of clubs, and lead another diamond, which he will duck when you play the king. By this clever line of play declarer keeps your partner from getting the lead and establishes five diamond tricks; he winds up making his contract with an overtrick.

Of course, declarer did not have to depend on your failure to discard the king of diamonds *if he had won the second heart trick with his king*.

Deception

Now we get into various ways to deceive the declarer. All of these contracts can be made, and more than likely would be made without a deceptive play. In other words, you are going to create an optional line of play for declarer that will fail. Here are 18 illustrations on the subject, the first nine dealing with "falsecards" as you follow suit:

#13

North
♠ A K 10 8
♡ 7
◇ A K Q 10 8
♣ 6 5 2

West
♠ J 9 5 4
♡ Q J 9 8 5
◇ 7 6
♣ 4 3

West	North	East	South
	1◇	Pass	1♠
Pass	4♠	Pass	5♣
Pass	6♠	All Pass	

You lead the queen of hearts and partner wins the first trick with the ace. He returns the queen of clubs, which declarer wins with the ace. Then declarer leads a low spade toward dummy. Declarer probably has four spades to the queen, and if both you and partner follow with low spades, his normal play to guard against a four-one split is to win the first spade trick with the ace or king, and the second with the queen. Your partner will show out on the second spade lead, so declarer has a marked finesse against your jack. If his first two plays are the ace and the king, you will win a trick with the jack; but he won't play that way if the ♠ J 9 x are missing because if your partner has those cards, there is no way to escape losing a spade trick. But if the three missing spades are J x x, he can avoid a spade loser no matter who has the long spades if he guesses which spade honor to play second. To give the declarer this option, you must *play the nine of spades on the first spade trick*. The four hands:

```
                        ♠ A K 10 8
                        ♡ 7
                        ◇ A K Q 10 8
                        ♣ 6 5 2
        ♠ J 9 5 4                              ♠ 2
        ♡ Q J 9 8 5                            ♡ A 6 4 3 2
        ◇ 7 6                                  ◇ 9 5 4
        ♣ 4 3                                  ♣ Q J 10 7
                        ♠ Q 7 6 3
                        ♡ K 10
                        ◇ J 3 2
                        ♣ A K 9 8
```

Declarer's second spade play automatically will be to the queen unless you play the nine of spades on the first spade trick. But if your first spade play is the nine, he must guess whether you have a singleton nine or partner has a singleton two. He may guess right, but chances are he will not.

#14   North
                                        ♠ A J
                                        ♡ 8 5 2
                                        ◇ Q 9 7 6 4
                                        ♣ A 9 2

        West
        ♠ Q 10 9 2
        ♡ J 10 9
        ◇ K 5 3
        ♣ 8 7 6

West	North	East	South
			1♠
Pass	2◇	Pass	2♠
Pass	3♠	Pass	4♠
Pass	Pass	Pass	

You lead the jack of hearts. Declarer wins with the ace and leads the three of spades. The best guess is that he has six spades to the king and will surely finesse the jack if you play the two. But if the declarer's goal is to limit his spade losers to one and you falsecard by *playing the ten (or the nine)*, he has a choice of plays to guard against a four-one break: If you have ♠ Q 10 9 x, he must finesse the jack; if you have a singleton ten and partner ♠ Q 9 x x, he must go up with the ace and finesse through your partner. The four hands:

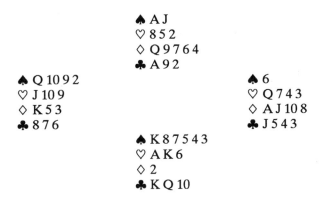

```
                        ♠ A J
                        ♡ 8 5 2
                        ◊ Q 9 7 6 4
                        ♣ A 9 2
     ♠ Q 10 9 2                        ♠ 6
     ♡ J 10 9                          ♡ Q 7 4 3
     ◊ K 5 3                           ◊ A J 10 8
     ♣ 8 7 6                           ♣ J 5 4 3
                        ♠ K 8 7 5 4 3
                        ♡ A K 6
                        ◊ 2
                        ♣ K Q 10
```

With two losers in the red suits, declarer must limit his spade losers to one. If your first spade play is the ten or nine, there is a good chance he will go wrong.

#15
```
                                North
                                ♠ J 8 6 5
                                ♡ A Q J 2
                                ◊ 7
                                ♣ K Q J 3
        West
        ♠ 10 9 4
        ♡ 8 7 3
        ◊ K Q 10 6
        ♣ 9 5 2
```

West	North	East	South
	1♣	Pass	1♠
Pass	3♠	Pass	4◊
Pass	4♡	Pass	6♠
Pass	Pass	Pass	

You lead the king of diamonds. Declarer wins with the ace and plays a heart to dummy's ace. On a low spade from dummy, partner plays the three and declarer the queen. You should falsecard by dropping *the nine or ten of spades*. If partner has ♠ K x, declarer will avoid a spade loser by playing the ace if you play the four on the first spade trick. But if you falsecard, he may decide you were dealt ♠ 10 9 and your partner ♠ K x x; in which case he can make his contract by going to dummy and leading the jack of spades. The four hands:

```
                        ♠ J 8 6 5
                        ♡ A Q J 2
                        ◊ 7
                        ♣ K Q J 3
     ♠ 10 9 4                        ♠ K 3
     ♡ 8 7 3                         ♡ 10 6 4
     ◊ K Q 10 6                      ◊ 9 8 5 4 2
     ♣ 9 5 2                         ♣ A 7 6
                        ♠ A Q 7 2
                        ♡ K 9 5
                        ◊ A J 3
                        ♣ 10 8 4
```

This is a poor slam, requiring a lucky spade break like the one shown in the diagram; declarer can make his contract by finessing the queen of spades, then cashing the ace. But if you play the nine or ten on the first spade trick, you give declarer an optional line of play that will fail.

#16

```
                          North
                          ♠ 10 8 7
                          ♡ A 3
                          ◇ Q 7 6
                          ♣ K Q 9 5 4
                                            East
                                            ♠ A J 9
                                            ♡ K 8 5 2
                                            ◇ 10 4 3
                                            ♣ 7 6 3
```

West	North	East	South
			1♠
Pass	2♣	Pas	3♣
Pass	3♠	Pass	4♠
Pass	Pass	Pass	

Partner leads the queen of hearts and the first trick is won in dummy with the ace. Then the seven of spades is led. If declarer has ♠ K Q x x x, he will lose only one spade trick by leading toward his king-queen twice. He will surely do this if your first spade play is the nine. But if you falsecard by *playing the jack of spades*, he has an optional line of play that will lose two spade tricks. After capturing your jack of spades with his king or queen, declarer may think you have a singleton spade (or maybe ace-jack doubleton) instead of your actual holding. Having been misled into thinking your partner has the nine of spades, declarer may lead a low spade and finesse dummy's eight. The four hands:

```
                          ♠ 10 8 7
                          ♡ A 3
                          ◇ Q 7 6
                          ♣ K Q 9 5 4
         ♠ 6 4                              ♠ A J 9
         ♡ Q J 10 7 6                       ♡ K 8 5 2
         ◇ A 9 5 2                          ◇ 10 4 3
         ♣ 8 2                              ♣ 7 6 3
                          ♠ K Q 5 3 2
                          ♡ 9 4
                          ◇ K J 8
                          ♣ A J 10
```

If declarer finesses the eight of spades, you will win two spade tricks, plus one heart and one diamond; he will be set one trick. Note that finessing the eight of spades would be the only way to make the contract if you actually had a singleton jack and your partner had played well by ducking with ♠ A 9 x x. Also note that the falsecard does no damage if partner happens to have a spade honor.

#17

North
♠ A J 2
♡ 10 6 5
♢ 8 6 4 3
♣ A J 7

West
♠ Q 10 4
♡ K Q J 9
♢ J 10 5
♣ 8 3 2

West	North	East	South
			1NT
Pass	3NT	All Pass	

You start with, in order, the king, jack and queen of hearts. Partner discards the four of clubs on the third heart and declarer wins with the ace. Declarer wins the next trick by leading a low spade to dummy's jack. Then he cashes dummy's ace of spades. *You should play the queen of spades under the ace*—the card declarer knows you have—*not the ten*. The four hands:

♠ A J 2
♡ 10 6 5
♢ 8 6 4 3
♣ A J 7

♠ Q 10 4
♡ K Q J 9
♢ J 10 5
♣ 8 3 2

♠ 8 7 3
♡ 7 4
♢ K Q 9 2
♣ 9 6 5 4

♠ K 9 6 5
♡ A 8 3 2
♢ A 7
♣ K Q 10

Declarer needs four spade tricks to make his contract. If you play the ten of spades under the ace, he will play a spade to the king next—he knows you have the queen. But if you play the queen under the ace, he doesn't know whether to play you for ♠ Q 4 or ♠ Q 10 4—his next play may be to finesse the nine.

The next deceptive play actually happened. The deal was reported by the late, great B. J. Becker in his King Features Bridge Column. The words are his:

#18

                            ♠ 5
                            ♡ A K Q 8 2
                            ♢ Q 9 4
                            ♣ J 9 7 5

♠ K Q J 8 7 4   ♠ 6 2
♡ J 10 5   ♡ 9 7 3
♢ 8 2   ♢ K J 10 6 3
♣ A Q   ♣ 6 4 2

                            ♠ A 10 9 3
                            ♡ 6 4
                            ♢ A 7 5
                            ♣ K 10 8 3

West	North	East	South
1♠	2♡	Pass	2NT
Pass	Pass	Pass	

"I played in a matchpoint team-of-four event recently and my partner reached two notrump and made exactly two. The king-of-spades opening lead was taken with the ace, a heart was played to the queen, and the jack of clubs was finessed.

"West won with the queen, cashed the queen and jack of spades, and led another spade. My partner couldn't afford to fool around any longer and ran eight tricks—two spades, five hearts and a diamond.

"At the other table the bidding was identical, but the play went differently. My teammate, Bill Root, sitting West, led a spade. Declarer took it, crossed to dummy with a heart, and led the jack of clubs and finessed.

"But *West won this trick with the ace*. Root had concocted a plot to sell declarer on the idea that East had the queen of clubs. He cashed the queen and jack of spades and exited with a spade.

"South took it and ran dummy's hearts. West threw both his diamonds away.

"Ten tricks had been played. Declarer was down to three cards—the ace of diamonds and the king-ten of clubs. West three cards were two good spades and the queen of clubs.

"Declarer led a club from dummy and confidently finessed the ten, naturally assuming that East had the queen. At the same time that he finessed, South claimed the last three tricks.

"But declarer was mistaken. West took the last three tricks—a club and two spades—and declarer went down one."

Bridge sometimes attracts players from the world of physical sport. Here is an actual deal where an exceptional defensive play to beat an unbeatable contract was made by Tim McCarver—the topnotch catcher for the St. Louis Cardinals and Philadelphia Phillies, and today a celebrated baseball announcer who is considered the best in the business.

#19

♠ Q 8
♡ K Q 9 4
♢ A Q J 7
♣ A 9 3

♠ J 10 9 4　　　　　　　　　　♠ K 7 6 3 2
♡ 7 5 3 2　　　　　　　　　　♡ 10 8 6
♢ K 5 4　　　　　　　　　　　♢ 10 9 8
♣ K J　　　　　　　　　　　　♣ 8 2

♠ A 5
♡ A J
♢ 6 3 2
♣ Q 10 7 6 5 4

West	North	East	South
	1♢	Pass	2♣
Pass	2♡	Pass	2NT
Pass	3NT	All Pass	

McCarver led the jack of spades, which was covered by dummy's queen, partner's king and declarer's ace. (If North had opened the bidding with one notrump, he would have been declarer and, since East has the king of spades, would have had little trouble making twelve tricks; but if West had the king of spades, the reverse would be true.)

Declarer could see seven winners (one spade, four hearts, one diamond and one club) and knew he could make his contract if the diamond finesse succeeded. But he saw an extra chance if West had the singleton king of clubs, so he led the four of clubs at trick two. Apparently McCarver realized what he was up to and played *the king of clubs!* Believing the king to be a singleton, declarer won with dummy's ace and then took a club finesse, losing to the jack. The defenders took the next four spade tricks and set the contract.

If McCarver did not play the king on the first club trick, declarer would return to his hand twice with the ace and jack of hearts to take two diamond finesses; thus making his contract with an overtrick.

#20

North
♠ A J 9 8 3
♡ A Q 7 2
♢ 6 5
♣ K 5

East
♠ K Q 10 2
♡ J 10 9
♢ K 7 4 3
♣ 10 9

West	North	East	South
	1♠	Pass	2♣
Pass	2♡	Pass	2NT
Pass	3NT	All Pass	

Partner wins the first trick with the queen of diamonds; then he leads a low diamond, which you are allowed to win with your king. You play a third diamond. Declarer wins with the ace and discards a low spade from the dummy. Now declarer leads a low spade to dummy's eight. You should *win the trick with the king or queen, not with the ten*. This cannot cost a trick and may bamboozle declarer into trying a second spade finesse. Furthermore, *do not lead your diamond and declarer may think you have no more diamonds*; exit with the ten of clubs. The four hands:

$$\spadesuit\ A\ J\ 9\ 8\ 3$$
$$\heartsuit\ A\ Q\ 7\ 2$$
$$\diamondsuit\ 6\ 5$$
$$\clubsuit\ K\ 5$$

♠ 7 5	♠ K Q 10 2
♡ K 6 4	♡ J 10 9
◊ Q J 9 8	◊ K 7 4 3
♣ 7 6 3 2	♣ 10 9

$$\spadesuit\ 6\ 4$$
$$\heartsuit\ 8\ 5\ 3$$
$$\diamondsuit\ A\ 10\ 2$$
$$\clubsuit\ A\ Q\ J\ 8\ 4$$

Declarer has eight winners (one spade, one heart, one diamond and five clubs) and can make his contract by taking the winning heart finesse. But while running his clubs he will almost surely discard three hearts from dummy and try a second spade finesse, especially since you led him to believe that you do not have another diamond. The last four cards in dummy would be ♠ A J 9 ♡ A and declarer needs three more tricks to make his contract. If you did not have another diamond, he would succeed even if the second spade finesse failed unless you still had ♠ K 10 x or ♠ Q 10 x.

#21   North
                                                          ♠ 8 3
                                                          ♡ A Q 6 4
                                                          ◊ K 10 3
                                                          ♣ K Q 9 5

                                                                      East
                                                                      ♠ A K 6 2
                                                                      ♡ 10 9 5 3
                                                                      ◊ 8 4
                                                                      ♣ 7 6 3

West	*North*	*East*	*South*
			1◊
Pass	1♡	Pass	1NT
Pass	3NT	All Pass	

Partner leads the four of spades. Since you can see the two and three, you know partner has led from a four-card suit and declarer has three spades. So *win the first trick with the ace and return a low spade*. Here are the four hands to show you this play might gain and cannot lose:

♠ 8 3
♥ A Q 6 4
♦ K 10 3
♣ K Q 9 5

♠ J 9 7 4   ♠ A K 6 2
♥ J 8 2   ♥ 10 9 5 3
♦ A 7 6 5   ♦ 8 4
♣ 8 2   ♣ 7 6 3

♠ Q 10 5
♥ K 7
♦ Q J 9 2
♣ A J 10 4

If you win the first two tricks with the king and ace of spades, declarer will win a trick with his queen and make his contract. But if you return a low spade at trick two, he will probably finesse the ten, instead of going up with his queen. With the knowledge that declarer has three spades, you cannot lose by this play; if partner has the queen, you can always get four spade tricks.

Declarer's correct percentage play is to finesse the ten regardless of which spade honor you win at trick one; but if you win with the king, a less knowledgeable declarer may decide to play you for ace-king. Hence the falsecard of winning with the ace increases your chances of success.

Another way to deceive declarer is to "duck" (to hold up a card with which you could win the trick), as you shall see in the next four illustrations.

#22   North
                                             ♠ A J 2
                                             ♥ K 10 8
                                             ♦ A Q 10
                                             ♣ K Q 10 5
                                                                 East
                                                                 ♠ 8 7
                                                                 ♥ J 9 5 3 2
                                                                 ♦ 7 6 5
                                                                 ♣ A 4 2

West	*North*	*East*	*South*
	1♣	Pass	2NT
Pass	4NT	Pass	6NT
Pass	Pass	Pass	

Partner leads the eight of diamonds and declarer wins the first trick in his hand with the king. A low club is led to dummy's king and you should *play a low club promptly*. The four hands:

$$\spadesuit \text{ A J 2}$$
$$\heartsuit \text{ K 10 8}$$
$$\diamondsuit \text{ A Q 10}$$
$$\clubsuit \text{ K Q 10 5}$$

♠ 10 6 5 4 3   ♠ 8 7
♡ 7 4   ♡ J 9 5 3 2
◇ 8 4 3   ◇ 7 6 5
♣ J 9 6   ♣ A 4 2

♠ K Q 9
♡ A Q 6
◇ K J 9 2
♣ 8 7 3

Declarer has ten winners outside the club suit, so he needs two club tricks to make his contract. If you win the first club trick with the ace, he will probably finesse your partner for the jack when he regains the lead.[2] If you let him win the first club trick, he will return to his hand and lead a second club; not knowing whether you or your partner is holding up with the ace, he must guess whether to finesse the ten or go up with the queen.

#23   North
                                             ♠ K 5 3
                                             ♡ A Q
                                             ◇ A Q J 10 9
                                             ♣ 9 7 2

            West
            ♠ 10 8 4
            ♡ K 5 4
            ◇ 8 7 6 2
            ♣ A J 3

West	*North*	*East*	*South*
			1NT
Pass	4♣ (a)	Pass	4♡ (b)
Pass	6NT	All Pass	

(a) Gerber
(b) One ace

After learning that declarer's opening one-notrump bid shows 16-18 high-card points, you lead the two of diamonds. Declarer wins in dummy with the nine and leads a club to his king. *You should duck, playing the three of clubs.* It was easy to hold up the ace of clubs in the previous hand because you could see the king and queen in dummy. When the concealed hand plays the king, holding up an ace is a doubtful play because your partner might have the queen; but not this time. You can see 24 high-card points between your hand and dummy, so

---

2. If East does win the first trick with the ace and declarer assumes that East would always hold up his ace unless he had a doubleton ace-jack or a singleton ace, the finesse would be technically wrong—a doubleton ace-jack is more likely than a singleton ace. But declarer should run all of his side winners before he leads a second club, and with the cards as shown he learns that East began with two spades, five hearts and three diamonds, and therefore exactly three clubs; he cannot have begun with the singleton ace or doubleton ace-jack. So the only chance not to lose a second club trick is to finesse dummy's ten.

declarer would not have enough points for an opening one-notrump bid if partner had the queen of clubs. The four hands:

```
                    ♠ K 5 3
                    ♡ A Q
                    ◇ A Q J 10 9
                    ♣ 9 7 2
      ♠ 10 8 4                        ♠ 7 6 2
      ♡ K 5 4                         ♡ 10 9 8 6 3
      ◇ 8 7 6 2                       ◇ 4 3
      ♣ A J 3                         ♣ 10 6 5
                    ♠ A Q J 9
                    ♡ J 7 2
                    ◇ K 5
                    ♣ K Q 8 4
```

Declarer has ten winners (four spades, one heart and five diamonds). If you win the first club trick with the ace, he knows he can win only one club trick, and will therefore take the winning heart finesse to make his slam. If you play the three of clubs *without pause*, declarer may decide your partner has the ace of clubs. Since he does not know that the heart finesse will work, he may try for his twelfth trick by leading another club from dummy and live to regret it.

#24

```
                    North
                    ♠ K J
                    ♡ A 3
                    ◇ K 10 9 8 7
                    ♣ 6 5 4 2
      West
      ♠ 10 9 8 6 3
      ♡ J 9 4
      ◇ A 5 2
      ♣ 9 3
```

West	North	East	South
			1NT
Pass	3NT	All Pass	

You lead the ten of spades, the jack is played from dummy and partner is allowed to win the trick with the queen. He returns the seven of spades to dummy's king. A low diamond is led, partner plays the three and declarer the queen. You should *play a low diamond—hold up your ace*. Declarer will lead another diamond at trick four and *you should duck again*. If declarer has the jack of diamonds, nothing matters. But if partner has the jack, declarer is likely to misguess and finesse the ten. Then partner will return a spade to establish your suit while you still have the ace of diamonds. The four hands:

                                    ♠ K J
                                    ♡ A 3
                                    ◇ K 10 9 8 7
                                    ♣ 6 5 4 2
        ♠ 10 9 8 6 3   ♠ Q 7 2
        ♡ J 9 4   ♡ Q 8 7 6
        ◇ A 5 2   ◇ J 3
        ♣ 9 3   ♣ Q J 10 7
                                    ♠ A 5 4
                                    ♡ K 10 5 2
                                    ◇ Q 6 4
                                    ♣ A K 8

Note that if you win the first diamond trick with your ace and lead a spade, your partner will probably win a trick with his jack of diamonds; but he will have no more spades, so declarer will regain the lead and win nine tricks (two spades, two hearts, two clubs and three diamonds). It's true that declarer can make his contract with an overtrick if he goes up with dummy's king on the second diamond lead, but if he does that, he would be set if you had the jack instead of the ace. Declarer is unlikely to guess the diamond situation unless you huddle before holding up your ace.

#25   North
                                            ♠ J 10 7 3
                                            ♡ A J 10 4
                                            ◇ A Q 9 6
                                            ♣ J

            West
            ♠ A Q 6 4
            ♡ K Q 9 2
            ◇ 7 5
            ♣ A 8 3

West	*North*	*East*	*South*
	1 ◇	Pass	1 ♠
Pass	2 ♠	Pass	3 ◇
Pass	4 ♠	All Pass	

You lead the king of hearts and the first trick is won with dummy's ace. The jack of spades is led, partner and declarer follow with low cards, and you should *play a low spade; do not win the trick*. You can always beat the contract if declarer has another heart, but if he has a singleton heart, your best chance is to lull him into a false sense of security; although it is the wrong play, he may decide that your partner has the queen of spades and lead another spade. If he does, you can beat the contract by cashing your two top spades and leading a fourth round to remove all of the trumps; then you will be able to win a trick with the queen of hearts when you get the lead with the ace of clubs. The four hands:

```
              ♠ J 10 7 3
              ♡ A J 10 4
              ◇ A Q 9 6
              ♣ J
♠ A Q 6 4                    ♠ 2
♡ K Q 9 2                    ♡ 8 6 5 3
◇ 7 5                        ◇ 10 8 3
♣ A 8 3                      ♣ 9 7 5 4 2
              ♠ K 9 8 5
              ♡ 7
              ◇ K J 4 2
              ♣ K Q 10 6
```

You may think that West should double four spades! In this case it would be a mistake because declarer can make his contract by knocking out the ace of clubs early. With the knowledge that trumps are dividing badly, there is less chance he will make any mistakes. Also note that if you win the first spade lead, declarer can succeed regardless of the subsequent defense.

Another type of ducking play is common when declarer is taking a "ruffing finesse." For example:

#26

```
                      North
                      ♠ K Q 7 2
                      ♡ A J 10 9
                      ◇ 5
                      ♣ K J 8 6
                                      East
                                      ♠ 4
                                      ♡ Q 8 6 2
                                      ◇ 9 7 6 3 2
                                      ♣ Q 5 4
```

West	North	East	South
	1♣	Pass	1♠
Pass	3♠	Pass	4NT
Pass	5◇	Pass	6♠
Pass	Pass	Pass	

Partner leads the king of diamonds and declarer wins with the ace. He draws two rounds of trumps and you discard a diamond. Then he plays the king of hearts and a heart to dummy's ace; partner indicates an odd number of hearts by playing low-high. Now declarer leads the jack of hearts, and you *should not play the queen*. If you cover the jack with the queen, declarer will ruff and eventually discard a loser on the ten of hearts. True, declarer can discard a loser on the jack of hearts if you don't cover, but he doesn't know that you have the queen and may not intend to do so. The four hands:

```
                              ♠ K Q 7 2
                              ♡ A J 10 9
                              ◊ 5
                              ♣ K J 8 6
        ♠ 6 5                                        ♠ 4
        ♡ 7 4 3                                      ♡ Q 8 6 2
        ◊ K Q 10 8 4                                 ◊ 9 7 6 3 2
        ♣ A 9 7 3                                    ♣ Q 5 4
                              ♠ A J 10 9 8 3
                              ♡ K 5
                              ◊ A J
                              ♣ 10 2
```

Declarer has only two club losers. By cashing the king and ace of hearts and ruffing a third heart from dummy, he can discard one of his club losers if the queen of hearts drops, or if you kindly cover the jack with the queen. If the queen does not show up, he can still make his contract if West has the ace and queen of clubs, or just one honor and he guesses which; so his correct play is to ruff the third heart. When declarer leads a club, your partner of course should play low without hesitating in the hope declarer will misguess.

Another form of deception arises when you have a chance to overruff the dummy. For example:

#27   **North**
                                             ♠ 6 3
                                             ♡ Q 10 9 8
                                             ◊ A J
                                             ♣ A Q 10 7 2
                                                             East
                                                             ♠ 9 4
                                                             ♡ K J 6
                                                             ◊ Q 10 8 7 4 3
                                                             ♣ 9 4

West	North	East	South
	1♣	Pass	1♡
1♠	2♡	Pass	2NT
Pass	4♡	All Pass	

Partner starts with the king and ace of spades. Seeing you play high-low, he continues with the two of spades, which declarer ruffs with dummy's eight. You can win this trick by overruffing with the jack, but declarer will eventually finesse through you for the king; you will get only one trump trick. The fact that declarer bid two notrump over two hearts suggests that he has a four-card heart suit. Your best chance to win two trump tricks is to *overruff the third spade trick with the king of hearts*. Here are the four hands to show you how declarer is likely to play:

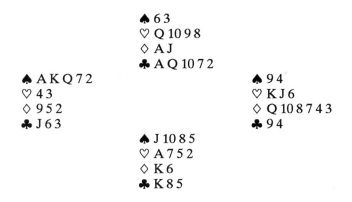

♠ 6 3
♡ Q 10 9 8
◇ A J
♣ A Q 10 7 2

♠ A K Q 7 2   ♠ 9 4
♡ 4 3   ♡ K J 6
◇ 9 5 2   ◇ Q 10 8 7 4 3
♣ J 6 3   ♣ 9 4

♠ J 10 8 5
♡ A 7 5 2
◇ K 6
♣ K 8 5

When you overruff the eight of hearts with the king, declarer is led to believe that your partner has the jack. Whether he cashes the ace of hearts first or not, he will eventually finesse dummy's ten and you will win the setting trick with the jack.

Another possibility, which would be the right play if you thought declarer had a five-card heart suit, is not to overruff the third spade trick at all. Declarer then may believe that your partner has the king and jack. Instead of taking a double finesse through you, he will probably cash the ace and lead toward the queen, and again you will win two trump tricks.

In the next deal, the way to mislead the declarer is to give a "false signal."

#28   North
                                      ♠ Q 4 2
                                      ♡ J 4
                                      ◇ A K Q J
                                      ♣ A Q J 3
                                                    East
                                                    ♠ 7 5 3
                                                    ♡ 9 6 3
                                                    ◇ 10 7 6 2
                                                    ♣ 10 8 5

West	North	East	South
	1◇	Pass	1♠
2♡	3♡	Pass	3♠
Pass	4♠	All Pass	

Bad card holders must learn to defend well, or they should give up the game. Here is an example of what can be done. Partner leads the king of hearts. Hopefully he has the ace and can win two heart tricks, but the only other defensive tricks must come from the trump suit. So you have nothing to lose by *playing high-low on the first two heart tricks* to give the impression that you have a doubleton. Partner will lead a third heart and declarer will probably ruff with the queen because he thinks you will overruff if he ruffs with a low spade. Now look at the four hands to see what might happen.

```
                        ♠ Q 4 2
                        ♡ J 4
                        ◇ A K Q J
                        ♣ A Q J 3
      ♠ A 10                            ♠ 7 5 3
      ♡ A K Q 8 7                       ♡ 9 6 3
      ◇ 8 5 4                           ◇ 10 7 6 2
      ♣ 9 6 2                           ♣ 10 8 5
                        ♠ K J 9 8 6
                        ♡ 10 5 2
                        ◇ 9 3
                        ♣ K 7 4
```

Having won the third trick with the queen of spades in dummy, declarer is now in jeopardy of losing two spade tricks. He leads a low spade to his king and your partner wins with the ace. Declarer now has ♠ J 9 8 6 and the ten, seven and five are still missing. Should he play the jack and hope to drop the ten, or should he take a finesse? The odds favor the finesse, so he is likely to go down; all because a bad card holder thought of a deceptive play.

Here is another false signal that might fool a sophisticated declarer.

```
#29                            North
                               ♠ 4 3
                               ♡ J 9 7 5
                               ◇ A K Q 8
                               ♣ J 10 6
        West
        ♠ Q 10 8 7 5 2
        ♡ 4 3
        ◇ 7 3 2
        ♣ K 8
```

West	North	East	South
			1NT
Pass	2♣	Pass	2◇
Pass	3NT	All Pass	

You lead the seven of spades to partner's ace, as declarer follows with the six. The nine of spades is returned and you capture declarer's jack with your queen. It is clear to lead another spade at trick three, and the card you lead is a suit-preference signal. But there is no advantage in asking your partner to lead a club, because if partner gains the lead in hearts, the appearance of dummy will make a club lead obvious. On the chance that declarer may have a choice of plays, you should *give a false suit-preference signal; lead the ten of spades at trick three to make declarer think your reentry is in the higher-ranking suit—hearts.* The four hands:

♠ 4 3
♡ J 9 7 5
◇ A K Q 8
♣ J 10 6

♠ Q 10 8 7 5 2   ♠ A 9
♡ 4 3   ♡ A 8 6 2
◇ 7 3 2   ◇ 10 9 6
♣ K 8   ♣ 7 5 4 3

♠ K J 6
♡ K Q 10
◇ J 5 4
♣ A Q 9 2

Declarer has six tricks (one spade, four diamonds and one club) and can win the three extra tricks he needs by taking the club finesse if it works, or by playing hearts if your partner has the ace of hearts. Your false suit-preference signal may influence him to try the club finesse.

In the last deal of this chapter, the deceptive play is a lead.

#30

North
♠ Q
♡ K 9 8 7
◇ K Q J 5 4
♣ 10 8 2

East
♠ K 7 6 3
♡ Q 4
◇ A 8 2
♣ Q 9 6 3

West	North	East	South
			1♡
Pass	2◇	Pass	2♡
Pass	4♡	All Pass	

Your partner leads the jack of spades, you play the king and declarer wins with the ace. The ace and king of hearts are cashed; partner follows to the first and then discards a spade. A low diamond is led from dummy and you win with the ace as declarer plays the ten. The only source of tricks left is clubs, and you had better get them before declarer can discard on dummy's diamonds. Since you need *three* club tricks, *lead the queen of clubs*. The four hands:

                                    ♠ Q
                                    ♡ K 9 8 7
                                    ◇ K Q J 5 4
                                    ♣ 10 8 2

    ♠ J 10 9 8 4   ♠ K 7 6 3
    ♡ 5   ♡ Q 4
    ◇ 9 7 6 3   ◇ A 8 2
    ♣ A J 5   ♣ Q 9 6 3

                                    ♠ A 5 2
                                    ♡ A J 10 6 3 2
                                    ◇ 10
                                    ♣ K 7 4

When you lead the queen of clubs at trick five, declarer may decide to duck (this would be the only way to make his contract if you had ♣ Q J 9). If he guesses correctly and plays the king, your partner should win with the ace and *lead a low club*; declarer then must guess whether to finesse the eight or go up with the ten. If declarer passes both tests, he is one hellofagood guesser.

If you lead a low club instead of the queen, declarer will play low from his hand. The defense can win only two club tricks and declarer succeeds without any guesswork.

Quiz for Chapter Nine

1.
North
♠ A K 10 5 3
♡ A Q
◇ 8 5 4
♣ 10 9 7

East
♠ Q J 9 8 7
♡ 9 7 6 4
◇ A 3
♣ A 5

West	North	East	South
	1♠	Pass	2♣
Pass	2♠	Pass	2NT
Pass	3NT	All Pass	

Partner leads the six of diamonds. You win with the ace and return the three of diamonds, declarer playing the jack and partner the queen. Partner then leads the two of diamonds. What do you discard?

2.
North
♠ A Q J
♡ A 9 8 7
◇ A K 6 5 2
♣ 7

West
♠ K 10 6
♡ 3
◇ Q J 9 8 3
♣ K Q J 2

West	North	East	South
			3♡
Pass	6♡	All Pass	

You lead the king of clubs and win the first trick. What do you lead at trick two? Why?

3.
North
♠ 7 4
♡ K Q 5 4
◇ J 8 6
♣ K 9 5 2

East
♠ Q J 10
♡ 8 6 3 2
◇ 5 3
♣ J 10 8 7

West	North	East	South
			1NT
Pass	2♣	Pass	2♠
Pass	2NT	Pass	3NT
Pass	Pass	Pass	

The opening one-notrump bid shows 16-18 high-card points. Partner wins the first four tricks with the ace, king, queen and ten of diamonds. If a spade is discarded from dummy on the fourth diamond, which two discards do you make?

4.
North
♠ 3
♡ A K 9 4
◇ J 10 5
♣ A Q J 7 2

West
♠ J 10 2
♡ Q 8 5 3
◇ A K 7 6
♣ 9 4

West	North	East	South
			3♠
Pass	4♠	All Pass	

You win the first two tricks with the king and ace of diamonds, then lead a third diamond, which declarer ruffs. He plays a heart to dummy's ace and leads the three of spades, partner plays the six and declarer the king. Which spade do you play? Why?

5.   North
                ♠ 6 5
                ♡ Q J 3
                ◊ K Q 10 7 4
                ♣ A 9 8
                                    East
                                    ♠ 8 4 2
                                    ♡ 10 9 8 2
                                    ◊ 8 6 5 3
                                    ♣ 7 6

West	North	East	South
			1♡
1♠	2◊	Pass	2NT
Pass	3♡	Pass	4♡
Pass	Pass	Pass	

Partner leads the king of spades. How do you defend with this marvelous hand?

6.   North
                ♠ A 9 5
                ♡ K J 10 7 6
                ◊ 10 3
                ♣ A 10 2
        West
        ♠ Q 7 2
        ♡ 5
        ◊ K Q J 9 4
        ♣ 8 6 4 3

West	North	East	South
			1♡
Pass	3♡	Pass	4NT
Pass	5♡	Pass	5NT
Pass	6◊	Pass	6♡
Pass	Pass	Pass	

You lead the king of diamonds. Declarer wins with the ace, cashes two high hearts and three high clubs; partner follows suit throughout. At trick seven, declarer plays a diamond to your jack. What do you lead now?

7.   North
                ♠ A 6 3
                ♡ K Q
                ◊ K J 10 8 2
                ♣ A Q 7
        West
        ♠ K Q J 10 9
        ♡ A 8 4
        ◊ 7 3
        ♣ K J 10

West	North	East	South
	1◊	Pass	1NT
2♠	3NT	All Pass	

You lead the king of spades. After holding up twice, declarer wins your third spade lead and partner discards the two of hearts. Declarer then cashes the ace and queen of diamonds, finesses the queen of clubs and proceeds to cash three more diamond winners. Which three discards do you make?

8.   North
                ♠ 10 7 2
                ♡ K 4
                ◊ J 10 5
                ♣ A K J 9 2
        West
        ♠ 8 3
        ♡ Q 10 9 2
        ◊ A K 8 4
        ♣ 7 6 5

West	North	East	South
			1♠
Pass	2♣	Pass	3♠
Pass	4♠	Pass	4NT
Pass	5◊	Pass	6♠
Pass	Pass	Pass	

You lead the king and ace of diamonds. declarer ruffing the second. He cashes the ace and king of spades, partner showing out on the second lead, so declarer has a seven-card suit. He plays out his other four spades. Regardless of what dummy and partner throw, which four discards do you make?

Quiz Answers for Chapter Nine

1.

		North	
		♠ A K 10 5 3	
		♡ A Q	
		◇ 8 5 4	
		♣ 10 9 7	

West		East
♠ 4		♠ Q J 9 8 7
♡ J 8 5 3		♡ 9 7 6 4
◇ Q 9 7 6 2		◇ A 3
♣ J 3 2		♣ A 5

		South	
		♠ 6 2	
		♡ K 10 2	
		◇ K J 10	
		♣ K Q 8 6 4	

West	North	East	South
	1♠	Pass	2♣
Pass	2♠	Pass	2NT
Pass	3NT	All Pass	

Partner leads the six of diamonds: four, ace, ten. You return the three of diamonds: jack, queen, five. Partner then leads the two of diamonds. What do you discard?

Discard the ace of clubs. Discarding the ace of clubs will waste a trick if declarer has the king, queen and jack of clubs, but it will beat the contract if partner has a club honor with which he can get the lead to cash his diamond tricks.

With the cards as shown, declarer will have eight tricks if you discard the ace of clubs (two spades, three hearts, one diamond and two clubs) and he cannot win more than two club tricks without giving your partner the lead with the jack.

If you do not discard the ace of clubs, declarer will lead clubs from dummy twice. You will win a trick with the ace of clubs, but must relinquish the lead to declarer so that he can run the rest of his clubs and make an overtrick.

Yes, declarer can make his contract if he wins the second diamond trick with the king!

2.

		North	
		♠ A Q J	
		♡ A 9 8 7	
		◇ A K 6 5 2	
		♣ 7	

West		East
♠ K 10 6		♠ 9 8 7 5 2
♡ 3		♡ 2
◇ Q J 9 8 3		◇ 10
♣ K Q J 2		♣ A 10 9 6 5 4

		South	
		♠ 4 3	
		♡ K Q J 10 6 5 4	
		◇ 7 4	
		♣ 8 3	

West	North	East	South
			3♡
Pass	6♡	All Pass	

You lead the king of clubs and win the first trick. What do you lead at trick two? Why?

Lead the ten of spades (or the six). If you don't lead a spade and declarer has more than one spade in his hand, his routine line of play will be to draw trumps and to try to establish a long card or two in diamonds; then if this fails, he will fall back on the spade finesse. An immediate spade lead will force declarer to commit himself before he discovers that diamonds are breaking badly.

Declarer's proper play is to refuse the spade finesse (only a 50-percent chance) and to try to establish the long diamond (an 84-percent chance). Of course, he will fail as the cards lie.

```
3.                 North
                   ♠ 7 4
                   ♡ K Q 5 4
                   ◇ J 8 6
                   ♣ K 9 5 2
        West                      East
        ♠ 9 8 5 2                 ♠ Q J 10
        ♡ J 10 7                  ♡ 8 6 3 2
        ◇ A K Q 10                ◇ 5 3
        ♣ 6 3                     ♣ J 10 8 7
                   South
                   ♠ A K 6 3
                   ♡ A 9
                   ◇ 9 7 4 2
                   ♣ A Q 4

   West     North     East     South
                                1NT
   Pass     2♣        Pass     2♠
   Pass     2NT       Pass     3NT
   Pass     Pass      Pass
```

Partner wins the first four tricks with the ace, king, queen and ten of diamonds. If a spade is thrown from dummy at trick four, which two discards do you make?

Discard two spades. To open the bidding with one notrump and accept partner's invitation to game, declarer should have seventeen or eighteen high-card points; since he has no diamond honors, he must have the ace-king of spades, ace of hearts and ace-queen of clubs. If his heart holding is A x, he has only eight winners (two spades, three hearts and three clubs). If you discard a heart or a club, he surely can win a ninth trick. So the only chance to beat the contract is to discard two spades and hope that partner has the nine of spades and ♡ J x x. This is another case where keeping equal length with dummy's long suits is the winning defense.

```
4.                 North
                   ♠ 3
                   ♡ A K 9 4
                   ◇ J 10 5
                   ♣ A Q J 7 2
        West                      East
        ♠ J 10 2                  ♠ A 6
        ♡ Q 8 5 3                 ♡ J 10 6 2
        ◇ A K 7 6                 ◇ Q 9 8 4
        ♣ 9 4                     ♣ 8 5 3
                   South
                   ♠ K Q 9 8 7 5 4
                   ♡ 7
                   ◇ 3 2
                   ♣ K 10 6

   West     North     East     South
                                3♠
   Pass     4♠        All Pass
```

You cash the first two diamond tricks, then lead a third diamond, which declarer ruffs. He plays a heart to dummy's ace and leads the three of spades: six, king. Which spade do you play? Why?

Play the jack or ten of spades under the king. Declarer must hold his spade losers to one if he is going to make his contract. If you play the two, his only hope is to lead a low spade next and find your partner with a doubleton ace. If you play the jack or ten under the king, he may decide that you have ♠ J 10 and partner ♠ A x x; then he will lead the queen and lose two spade tricks. By falsecarding with the jack or ten on the first spade trick, you give declarer a choice of plays, one of which will fail.

```
5.              North
              ♠ 6 5
              ♡ Q J 3
              ◇ K Q 10 7 4
              ♣ A 9 8
   West                     East
♠ A K 10 7 3              ♠ 8 4 2
♡ 6                       ♡ 10 9 8 2
◇ A 9                     ◇ 8 6 5 3
♣ Q 10 5 4 2             ♣ 7 6
              South
              ♠ Q J 9
              ♡ A K 7 5 4
              ◇ J 2
              ♣ K J 3
```

West	North	East	South
			1♡
1♠	2◇	Pass	2NT
Pass	4♡	All Pass	

Partner leads the king of spades. How do you defend with this marvelous hand?

Play the eight of spades on the first trick. The plan is to play high-low to encourage partner to lead a third spade. Declarer will think you have a doubleton spade and, more than likely, he will ruff the third round of spades with the queen or jack of hearts to prevent you from scoring a trick with a low trump. This would be the winning play if you actually did have a doubleton spade and the hearts were divided three-two. But with the cards as shown, ruffing with the queen or jack promotes your ♡ 10 9 8 2 into the setting trick.

```
6.              North
              ♠ A 9 5
              ♡ K J 10 7 6
              ◇ 10 3
              ♣ A 10 2
   West                     East
♠ Q 7 2                   ♠ J 8 6 4
♡ 5                       ♡ 8 3
◇ K Q J 9 4              ◇ 7 6 5 2
♣ 8 6 4 3               ♣ J 9 5
              South
              ♠ K 10 3
              ♡ A Q 9 4 2
              ◇ A 8
              ♣ K Q 7
```

West	North	East	South
			1♡
Pass	3♡	Pass	4NT
Pass	5♡	Pass	5NT
Pass	6◇	Pass	6♡
Pass	Pass	Pass	

You lead the king of diamonds. Declarer wins with the ace, cashes two high hearts and three high clubs; partner follows throughout. Declarer plays a diamond to your jack. What do you lead now?

Lead the queen of spades. It is apparent that declarer's line of play—stripping his hand of clubs and diamonds and throwing you on lead—is to force you to lead a spade (you must not lead a club or diamond because that would give him a ruff-and-discard). If declarer has ♠ K 10 x and you lead a low spade, he will surely avoid a spade loser by capturing your partner's jack with his king and finessing you for the queen.

If you lead the queen, he can make his contract by winning the first spade trick with dummy's ace and finessing your partner out of the jack. This is the correct percentage play—playing for split honors—but declarer may not know this; or he may deliberately go against the odds because he doesn't think you would be smart enough to lead the queen without the jack.

If declarer has any spade holding other than K 10 x, your lead of the queen will not matter.

7. **North**
    ♠ A 6 3
    ♡ K Q
    ◇ K J 10 8 2
    ♣ A Q 7

West   **East**
♠ K Q J 10 9   ♠ 8 2
♡ A 8 4   ♡ J 7 6 3 2
◇ 7 3   ◇ 9 6 4
♣ K J 10   ♣ 9 5 2

            South
            ♠ 7 5 4
            ♡ 10 9 5
            ◇ A Q 5
            ♣ 8 6 4 3

West	North	East	South
	1◇	Pass	1NT
2♠	3NT	All Pass	

You lead the king of spades. After holding up twice, declarer wins your third spade lead and partner discards the two of hearts. Declarer then cashes the ace and queen of diamonds, finesses the queen of clubs and cashes three more diamond winners. Which three discards do you make?

Discard two hearts and a club, or two clubs and a heart; do not discard a spade. Declarer has eight tricks (one spade, five diamonds and two clubs). If you discard a spade, you will have thrown away the setting trick; declarer will establish a ninth trick by leading a heart and you will not have enough spades left to set him. So you must discard one or both clubs and hope that partner has three clubs to the nine.

8. **North**
    ♠ 10 7 2
    ♡ K 4
    ◇ J 10 5
    ♣ A K J 9 2

West   **East**
♠ 8 3   ♠ 5
♡ Q 10 9 2   ♡ 8 7 6 5 3
◇ A K 8 4   ◇ Q 9 6 3 2
♣ 7 6 5   ♣ Q 4

            South
            ♠ A K Q J 9 6 4
            ♡ A J
            ◇ 7
            ♣ 10 8 3

West	North	East	South
			1♠
Pass	2♣	Pass	3♠
Pass	4♠	Pass	4NT
Pass	5◇	Pass	6♠
Pass	Pass	Pass	

You lead the king and ace of diamonds. Declarer ruffs the second and cashes his other six spades. Regardless of what dummy and partner throw, which four discards do you make?

Discard any number of hearts or diamonds; do not discard any clubs. If declarer had three hearts, he would have ruffed a heart in dummy, so he must have seven spades, two hearts, one diamond and therefore three clubs. If he had the queen of clubs, he would have claimed the contract by now; so partner has ♣ Q x and declarer can make his contract if he cashes the ace and king. But the percentage play with eight clubs is to cash one high club and then to finesse for the queen, something declarer will do unless you foolishly discard a club or two.

Random Quiz

The quizzes presented so far have dealt with the subjects of given chapters. The following 36 problems have an added challenge: *You must figure out the theme.* Your goal, as it has been throughout the book, is to beat the contract by one trick. Answers begin on page 364.

1.

```
        North
        ♠ 7 2
        ♡ K 2
        ◇ 9 8 6 3
        ♣ K Q J 10 5
                    East
                    ♠ 9 3
                    ♡ A Q 5
                    ◇ Q 10 7 4
                    ♣ A 6 4 2
```

West	North	East	South
			1♠
Pass	1NT	Double	4♠
Pass	Pass	Pass	

Your partner leads the jack of hearts and you top dummy's king with your ace. What do you lead at trick two?

3.

```
        North
        ♠ K Q 7 4
        ♡ K Q 6 4
        ◇ 8 3 2
        ♣ 9 5
                    East
                    ♠ 8 6 5 2
                    ♡ J 10 9 3
                    ◇ K Q
                    ♣ 8 7 4
```

West	North	East	South
			1NT
Pass	2♣	Pass	2◇
Pass	3NT	All Pass	

The opening one-notrump bid shows 16-18 high-card points. Your partner leads, in order, the king, ten and queen of clubs. Dummy discards a diamond and declarer wins the third trick with the ace. Declarer leads another club, which your partner wins with the jack. After dummy discards another diamond, what do you throw?

2.

```
        North
        ♠ 10 7 2
        ♡ A K
        ◇ K Q J 10 8
        ♣ K Q 3
                    East
                    ♠ Q J 9 6 5
                    ♡ Q 7 2
                    ◇ A 9 4
                    ♣ A 6
```

West	North	East	South
	1◇	1♠	1NT
Pass	3NT	All Pass	

Your partner leads the eight of spades, the two is played from dummy, you overtake with the nine and declarer wins with the ace. The three of diamonds is led, partner plays the two and dummy the king. Plan your defense.

4.

```
        North
        ♠ 10 5
        ♡ K Q 9 4
        ◇ A 7
        ♣ K Q J 10 2
                    East
                    ♠ A 9 8 4 2
                    ♡ 5
                    ◇ J 10 6 3 2
                    ♣ 6 3
```

West	North	East	South
	1♣	Pass	1♡
1♠	3♡	4♠	5♡
Pass	Pass	Pass	

Your partner leads the king of spades. Plan your defense.

How to Play a Bridge Hand

5.

	North
	♠ Q 6 2
	♡ A 10 5 4
	◇ K Q 10 9
	♣ K 3

	East
	♠ A 10 8 5
	♡ 9
	◇ 8 7 6 4 3
	♣ J 10 7

West	North	East	South
	1◇	Pass	1♡
Pass	2♡	Pass	4♡
Pass	Pass	Pass	

Your partner leads the ace of diamonds. Which diamond do you play?

6.

	North
	♠ Q 10 9
	♡ J 8 3
	◇ Q 6
	♣ A Q J 10 5

	East
	♠ A 8 7 4
	♡ A Q 9
	◇ 10 9 3
	♣ 7 6 2

West	North	East	South
			1♡
Pass	2♣	Pass	3♣
Pass	3♡	Pass	4♡
Pass	Pass	Pass	

Your partner leads the three of spades to your ace. You return the four of spades, partner wins this trick with the king and leads another spade, which is won with dummy's queen while declarer discards the three of clubs. Then the three of hearts is led from dummy. Which heart do you play?

7.

	North
	♠ K Q 9 7
	♡ 8
	◇ Q J 2
	♣ A K Q J 4

West	
♠ A	
♡ 10 3 2	
◇ A K 10 7 6 5	
♣ 9 8 2	

West	North	East	South
	1♣	Pass	1♡
2◇	2♠	Pass	4♡
Pass	Pass	Pass	

You win the first two tricks with the king and ace of diamonds; partner plays the nine and three, declarer the four and eight. Plan your defense.

8.

	North
	♠ Q 6 4
	♡ K 8 5 3
	◇ A K J 10
	♣ 7 2

West	
♠ 10 5	
♡ Q 9 4	
◇ 8 7 3 2	
♣ K 6 5 3	

West	North	East	South
	1◇	1♠	2♡
Pass	3♡	Pass	4♡
Pass	Pass	Pass	

You lead the ten of spades, dummy plays the queen and partner wins the first three tricks with the king, ace and jack as declarer follows suit. What do you discard on the third spade lead?

9.   North
♠ J 7
♥ A 9 6 4 3
♦ A Q J
♣ A K 10

East
♠ K 10 6 5
♥ K Q 8 2
♦ 6 3
♣ J 7 4

West	North	East	South
Pass	1♡	Pass	1NT
Pass	3NT	All Pass	

Your partner leads the four of spades and the seven is played from dummy. Which spade do you play?

10.   North
♠ Q 7 6 5 4
♥ A J 9 2
♦ A 8
♣ K 3

West
♠ K 10 3
♥ Q 4
♦ 10 9 7 6 2
♣ Q 8 4

West	North	East	South
	1♠	Pass	2♣
Pass	2♡	Pass	3NT
Pass	Pass	Pass	

You lead the ten of diamonds, dummy plays the eight, partner the queen and declarer the king. A club is led to dummy's king as partner follows with the ten. Another club is led, partner plays the five, declarer the jack and you win with the queen. What do you lead now?

11.   North
♠ Q 10 3
♥ Q 9
♦ A Q J 8 7
♣ K Q 5

West
♠ A 6 5
♥ K 7
♦ 6 4 3
♣ J 10 9 8 2

West	North	East	South
	1NT	2♠	4♡
4♠	Pass	Pass	5♡
Pass	Pass	Pass	

You lead the jack of clubs, dummy plays the king, partner the ace and declarer the four. Partner returns the three of clubs, declarer plays the six, you the eight and dummy the queen. The queen of hearts is led and finessed to your king. What do you lead now?

12.   North
♠ Q 6 4
♥ K J 4
♦ K Q 10 7
♣ 8 3 2

East
♠ 2
♥ A Q 10 3
♦ A 8 5
♣ Q 9 6 5 4

West	North	East	South
			4♠
Pass	Pass	Pass	

Your partner leads the three of diamonds, dummy plays the king, you the ace and declarer the two. What do you lead now?

13.   North
                    ♠ K J 7
                    ♡ K J 3
                    ◊ J 8 4
                    ♣ 10 6 5 2
                                    East
                                    ♠ 9 6
                                    ♡ 6 5 2
                                    ◊ K 10 6 5
                                    ♣ Q 7 4 3

West	North	East	South
			1♠
Pass	2♠	Pass	4♠
Pass	Pass	Pass	

Your partner leads the king of clubs. Which club do you play?

14.   North
                    ♠ K 9 6 4
                    ♡ Q 10 2
                    ◊ Q J 8
                    ♣ 8 5 3
                                    East
                                    ♠ 7 3
                                    ♡ A J 5
                                    ◊ A 10 6 4 3
                                    ♣ 10 9 7

West	North	East	South
			1♠
Pass	2♠	Pass	4♠
Pass	Pass	Pass	

Your partner leads the jack of spades and declarer wins the first two spade tricks in his hand with the ace and queen; partner follows suit. The king of diamonds is led, partner plays the two and you duck. Declarer leads another diamond, partner plays the nine and you win with the ace. What do you lead now?

15.   North
                    ♠ 8 5 4 2
                    ♡ K 6 3
                    ◊ A Q 6
                    ♣ K 4 3
                                    East
                                    ♠ J 10 9 3
                                    ♡ 9 7 5
                                    ◊ 10 4 2
                                    ♣ 10 8 6

West	North	East	South
			1NT
Pass	3NT	All Pass	

The opening one-notrump bid shows 16-18 high-card points. Your partner leads the queen of hearts, which is allowed to win the first trick. The jack of hearts is led and this trick is won with dummy's king. Then declarer leads the eight of spades from dummy. Which spade do you play?

16.   North
                    ♠ A K Q
                    ♡ 7 6 4
                    ◊ J 10 3
                    ♣ A K Q 5
            West
            ♠ 9 8 6 5
            ♡ 8 3
            ◊ A 7 6
            ♣ J 10 9 7

West	North	East	South
	1♣	1♡	1NT
Pass	3NT	All Pass	

You lead the eight of hearts, partner plays the nine and declarer the king. Declarer then leads the five of diamonds. Plan your defense.

17.
<pre>
              North
              ♠ 7 6 3
              ♡ A Q 10
              ◇ J 9 7 4
              ♣ J 8 5
West
♠ K Q 10 4 2
♡ 9 8 3
◇ 6 5 2
♣ K 7
</pre>

West	North	East	South
			1NT
Pass	2NT	Pass	3NT
Pass	Pass	Pass	

The opening one-notrump bid shows 16-18 high-card points. You lead the king of spades, partner plays the eight and declarer the five. What do you lead at trick two?

18.
<pre>
              North
              ♠ Q 3
              ♡ A 4
              ◇ A Q 10 8 2
              ♣ 9 6 5 3
                              East
                              ♠ 6 4
                              ♡ 8 7 2
                              ◇ K J 9 5
                              ♣ J 10 8 2
</pre>

West	North	East	South
			1♠
Pass	2◇	Pass	2♠
Pass	3♠	Pass	4♠
Pass	Pass	Pass	

Your partner leads the jack of hearts and dummy plays the ace. Which heart do you play?

19.
<pre>
              North
              ♠ A J
              ♡ K Q 10 8 7
              ◇ 10 8 5
              ♣ A K Q
                              East
                              ♠ K 6 2
                              ♡ A 9 5
                              ◇ Q 9 4
                              ♣ 10 7 4 3
</pre>

West	North	East	South
	1♡	Pass	1NT
Pass	3NT	All Pass	

Your partner leads the five of spades. You win the first trick with the king and return the six of spades; declarer follows with the nine and partner with the ten. A low heart is led to declarer's jack, then another heart to dummy's king and your ace. What do you lead now?

20.
<pre>
              North
              ♠ Q J 10
              ♡ A K 5
              ◇ J 10 9 8
              ♣ A K J
                              East
                              ♠ 3 2
                              ♡ Q 10 8 4
                              ◇ K 7 5
                              ♣ 9 7 6 4
</pre>

West	North	East	South
	1◇	Pass	1NT
Pass	3NT	All Pass	

Your partner leads the six of spades and the first trick is won with dummy's ten. The jack of diamonds is led. Plan your defense.

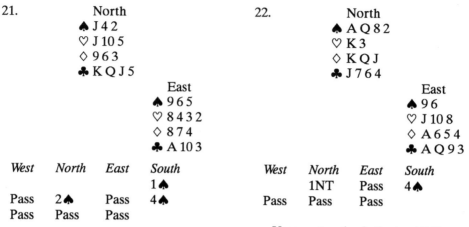

21.   North
                ♠ J 4 2
                ♡ J 10 5
                ◇ 9 6 3
                ♣ K Q J 5

                              East
                              ♠ 9 6 5
                              ♡ 8 4 3 2
                              ◇ 8 7 4
                              ♣ A 10 3

West	North	East	South
			1♠
Pass	2♠	Pass	4♠
Pass	Pass	Pass	

Your partner leads the queen of diamonds, you play the four and the first trick is won by declarer with the ace. He leads the six of clubs, partner plays the two and dummy the king. Plan your defense.

22.   North
                ♠ A Q 8 2
                ♡ K 3
                ◇ K Q J
                ♣ J 7 6 4

                              East
                              ♠ 9 6
                              ♡ J 10 8
                              ◇ A 6 5 4
                              ♣ A Q 9 3

West	North	East	South
	1NT	Pass	4♠
Pass	Pass	Pass	

Your partner leads the ten of diamonds, you play the ace and declarer the three. What do you lead now?

23.   North
                ♠ Q 9 7 6
                ♡ J 10 8
                ◇ K J 2
                ♣ J 10 5

      West
      ♠ 10 8 3
      ♡ 9
      ◇ 10 7 6 5 3
      ♣ K 8 4 2

West	North	East	South
			1♠
Pass	2♠	3♡	4♠
Pass	Pass	Pass	

You lead the nine of hearts, partner plays the ace and declarer the three. Partner returns the five of hearts, declarer plays the king and you ruff. What do you lead at trick three?

24.   North
                ♠ A 9 7
                ♡ 8 5 4
                ◇ K 2
                ♣ Q 9 6 4 3

                              East
                              ♠ J 8 5 3 2
                              ♡ 9 6 3
                              ◇ 6
                              ♣ K J 10 7

West	North	East	South
			1♡
Pass	2♡	Pass	4♡
Pass	Pass	Pass	

Your partner leads the king of spades. Declarer wins with dummy's ace, cashes the king of diamonds and leads the two of diamonds. Plan your defense.

25.
```
            North
          ♠ K 8 6 3
          ♡ 6 5 4
          ◇ A K J
          ♣ Q 10 2
                        East
                      ♠ A 10 7
                      ♡ A 8 3
                      ◇ 6 5 4 2
                      ♣ 9 8 3
```

West	North	East	South
			1♣
Pass	1♠	Pass	1NT
Pass	3NT	All Pass	

Your partner leads the king of hearts and you signal with the eight. He continues with the queen of hearts. Which heart do you play on the second trick?

26.
```
            North
          ♠ K 6
          ♡ K Q 8 3
          ◇ Q 8 7
          ♣ A 5 4 2
    West
  ♠ J 10 9 8 3
  ♡ A 10
  ◇ J 5 3
  ♣ K 7 6
```

West	North	East	South
			1♡
Pass	3♡	Pass	4♡
Pass	Pass	Pass	

You lead the jack of spades. Declarer wins the first two tricks with the queen and ace of spades; then he leads the two of hearts. Plan your defense.

27.
```
            North
          ♠ Q J 3
          ♡ 8 7 5 2
          ◇ Q 10
          ♣ K 10 9 3
    West
  ♠ K 10 7 5
  ♡ A 9 3
  ◇ 9 7 6 4 2
  ♣ 8
```

West	North	East	South
			1♡
Pass	2♡	Pass	4♡
Pass	Pass	Pass	

You lead the eight of clubs, dummy plays the nine, partner the jack and declarer wins with the ace. The king of hearts is led. Plan your defense.

28.
```
            North
          ♠ 8 2
          ♡ Q 6 4
          ◇ K Q J 9 3
          ♣ A 10 5
                        East
                      ♠ J 9 5
                      ♡ K 8 3 2
                      ◇ A 10 6 5
                      ♣ J 4
```

West	North	East	South
	1◇	Pass	1♠
Pass	1NT	Pass	4♣ (a)
Pass	4♡ (b)	Pass	6♠
Pass	Pass	Pass	

(a) Gerber
(b) One ace

Your partner leads the jack of hearts, the four is played from dummy and declarer wins with the ace. The four of diamonds is led, partner plays the eight and dummy the king. Plan your defense.

29.

North
♠ K 7
♡ Q 8 7 3
◇ A J 5
♣ K 9 6 4

West
♠ Q J 9 4
♡ 2
◇ 10 7 6 3
♣ Q 8 7 5

West	North	East	South
	1♣	Pass	1♡
Pass	2♡	Pass	4♡
Pass	Pass	Pass	

You lead the queen of spades, dummy plays the king and partner wins with the ace. Partner returns the two of spades and you win this trick with the nine. What do you lead now?

30.

North
♠ K 4
♡ 10 7 2
◇ J 9 5 2
♣ Q J 10 9

West
♠ A 3 2
♡ 9 8 6 5
◇ A K Q 10 3
♣ 7

West	North	East	South
			1♡
2◇	2♡	Pass	4♡
Pass	Pass	Pass	

You win the first two tricks with the king and ace of diamonds as partner plays high-low and declarer follows suit. What do you lead now?

31.

North
♠ A Q 7 2
♡ 9
◇ A J 3
♣ K Q J 10 5

East
♠ 8 4 3
♡ A K 10 6 5
◇ K 10 7
♣ 4 2

West	North	East	South
	1♣	1♡	1♠
2♡	4♠	All Pass	

Your partner leads the two of hearts and you win the first trick with the king. What do you lead now?

32.

North
♠ J
♡ Q J 10 9 6 3 2
◇ A J
♣ 9 5 4

West
♠ 10 7 3 2
♡ A 4
◇ 10 9 8 7 6 5
♣ 8

West	North	East	South
		1♣	4♠
Pass	Pass	Pass	

You lead the eight of clubs. Partner wins the first two tricks with the queen and ace of clubs while declarer plays the two and seven. Partner then cashes the king of clubs and declarer follows with the jack. What are your discards at tricks two and three?

33.
North
♠ Q 9 8 3
♡ 7 4
◇ A Q 2
♣ K Q 10 6

East
♠ K 5
♡ J 10 3 2
◇ J 7 6
♣ A 9 8 2

West	North	East	South
	1♣	Pass	1♠
Pass	2♠	Pass	3♣
Pass	4♠	All Pass	

Your partner leads the three of clubs and you win with the ace. What do you lead at trick two?

34.
North
♠ Q 8 4
♡ J 9 3
◇ K Q J 10 7
♣ 5 2

East
♠ A 7 5 3
♡ 8 6 4
◇ 9 3 2
♣ 10 6 4

West	North	East	South
			1NT
Pass	3NT	All Pass	

The opening one-notrump bid shows 16-18 high-card points. Your partner leads the seven of clubs and your ten is topped by declarer's jack. A diamond is led, partner plays the four and dummy the king. Which diamond do you play? The queen of diamonds is led at trick three. Which diamond do you play this time?

35.
North
♠ A K Q J 9
♡ K 7
◇ 9 6 2
♣ 8 7 2

West
♠ 10 2
♡ A J 8
◇ A Q 5
♣ Q 10 6 4 3

West	North	East	South
	1♠	Pass	2♡
Pass	2♠	Pass	2NT
Pass	3NT	All Pass	

You open with the four of clubs to partner's nine and declarer's jack. Declarer leads the three of hearts. Plan your defense.

36.
North
♠ J 6 5
♡ A K 10 3
◇ 7
♣ K Q J 9 8

East
♠ A Q 10
♡ 4 2
◇ A K J 9 6 5
♣ 10 7

West	North	East	South
	1♣	1◇	1♡
Pass	3♡	Pass	4♡
Pass	Pass	Pass	

Your partner leads the two of diamonds and you win the first trick with the king. What do you lead at trick two?

Random Quiz Answers

1.

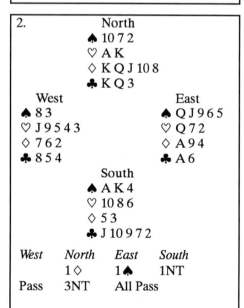

North
♠ 7 2
♡ K 2
♢ 9 8 6 3
♣ K Q J 10 5

West
♠ 8 4
♡ J 10 9 8 7
♢ K J 5 2
♣ 9 3

East
♠ 9 3
♡ A Q 5
♢ Q 10 7 4
♣ A 6 4 2

South
♠ A K Q J 10 6 5
♡ 6 4 3
♢ A
♣ 8 7

West	North	East	South
			1♠
Pass	1NT	Double	4♠
Pass	Pass	Pass	

Your partner leads the jack of hearts and you top dummy's king with your ace. What do you lead at trick two?

Lead the three of spades. Since you have the ace of clubs and partner will give you the count when the suit is led so you will know when to take your ace, declarer will be unable to discard any losers on the club suit. But if he has more than two hearts in his hand, he may be able to ruff one in dummy if you do not lead a trump.

When clubs are eventually led, partner will play the nine to show a doubleton (if he had a singleton, more than likely he would have led it). This marks declarer with a doubleton club, so you will hold up your ace until the second round. If a second round of trumps has not been led by the time you regain the lead with the ace of clubs, you should lead another trump and declarer cannot avoid losing three heart tricks.

2.

North
♠ 10 7 2
♡ A K
♢ K Q J 10 8
♣ K Q 3

West
♠ 8 3
♡ J 9 5 4 3
♢ 7 6 2
♣ 8 5 4

East
♠ Q J 9 6 5
♡ Q 7 2
♢ A 9 4
♣ A 6

South
♠ A K 4
♡ 10 8 6
♢ 5 3
♣ J 10 9 7 2

West	North	East	South
	1♢	1♠	1NT
Pass	3NT	All Pass	

Your partner leads the eight of spades: two, nine, ace. The three of diamonds is led, partner plays the two and dummy the king. Plan your defense.

Win the first diamond trick with your ace and lead the queen of spades. This assures beating the contract: Declarer can win only eight tricks (two spades, two hearts and four diamonds). When you regain the lead, your ace of clubs and three spades tricks, added to the ace of diamonds that you have already won, gives you five tricks.

Note that if you duck the first diamond trick, declarer will abandon diamonds and establish the club suit. He will make nine tricks (two spades, two hearts, one diamond and four clubs).

3.
```
                North
              ♠ K Q 7 4
              ♡ K Q 6 4
              ♢ 8 3 2
              ♣ 9 5
   West                      East
 ♠ J 9 3                   ♠ 8 6 5 2
 ♡ 7 2                     ♡ J 10 9 3
 ♢ J 9 6 5                 ♢ K Q
 ♣ K Q J 10                ♣ 8 7 4
                South
              ♠ A 10
              ♡ A 8 5
              ♢ A 10 7 4
              ♣ A 6 3 2
```

West	North	East	South
			1NT
Pass	2♣	Pass	2♢
Pass	3NT	All Pass	

Your partner leads, in order, the king, ten and queen of clubs. Dummy discards a diamond and declarer wins the third trick with the ace. Declarer leads another club, which your partner wins with the jack. After dummy discards another diamond, what do you throw?

Discard the king or queen of diamonds. Declarer must have the three missing aces for his opening notrump bid, and that gives him eight tricks (three spades, three hearts, one diamond and one club). If you discard a spade or a heart, he will surely win a fourth trick in that suit. So, the only hope is to discard a diamond and find partner with the J 9 x or better in diamonds and spades, which will stop declarer winning a second diamond trick or a fourth spade trick.

Now that you see the four hands you know that declarer will be set as long as you do not discard a spade or a heart—*keep the dummy covered.* Partner of course should lead a diamond at trick five (although a heart lead will do no damage since you have the jack-ten-nine); but a spade lead would be a disaster.

Leading the fourth round of clubs was a good play by declarer, giving his opponents a chance to make a faulty discard, or possibly to establish a squeeze.

4.
```
                North
              ♠ 10 5
              ♡ K Q 9 4
              ♢ A 7
              ♣ K Q J 10 2
   West                      East
 ♠ K Q J 7 3               ♠ A 9 8 4 2
 ♡ 7 6                     ♡ 5
 ♢ K 8                     ♢ J 10 6 3 2
 ♣ A 8 5 4                 ♣ 6 3
                South
              ♠ 6
              ♡ A J 10 8 3 2
              ♢ Q 9 5 4
              ♣ 9 7
```

West	North	East	South
	1♣	Pass	1♡
1♠	3♡	4♠	5♡
Pass	Pass	Pass	

Your partner leads the king of spades. Plan your defense.

Overtake partner's king of spades with your ace and lead the jack of diamonds. The bidding indicates that declarer has at most one spade, and he may be able to discard any diamond losers on dummy's clubs if given time. So, a diamond lead at trick two is mandatory, and you should lead the jack of diamonds in case declarer has the queen and partner the king. This turns out to be the only defense to beat the contract. After the ace of diamonds is driven out and partner eventually gets the lead with the ace of clubs, the setting trick can be won in diamonds.

```
5.                    North
                      ♠ Q 6 2
                      ♡ A 10 5 4
                      ◇ K Q 10 9
                      ♣ K 3
      West                          East
      ♠ K 9 7 3                     ♠ A 10 8 5
      ♡ J 6 2                       ♡ 9
      ◇ A                           ◇ 8 7 6 4 3
      ♣ 8 6 5 4 2                   ♣ J 10 7
                      South
                      ♠ J 4
                      ♡ K Q 8 7 3
                      ◇ J 5 2
                      ♣ A Q 9
```

West	North	East	South
	1◇	Pass	1♡
Pass	2♡	Pass	4♡
Pass	Pass	Pass	

Your partner leads the ace of diamonds. Which diamond do you play?

Play the eight of diamonds. Partner's lead of the ace of dummy's bid suit is obviously a singleton and the card you play is a suit-preference signal. Because of your eight-of-diamonds signal, partner should lead a spade at trick two (he should lead the nine of spades to make it clear that he does not want a spade returned). When you win with your ace and lead a diamond, partner will ruff and cash the king of spades to set the contract. Without a spade lead at trick two, declarer would make his contract with an overtrick.

```
6.                    North
                      ♠ Q 10 9
                      ♡ J 8 3
                      ◇ Q 6
                      ♣ A Q J 10 5
      West                          East
      ♠ K J 6 3                     ♠ A 8 7 4
      ♡ 5 2                         ♡ A Q 9
      ◇ J 7 5 4 2                   ◇ 10 9 6 3
      ♣ 8 4                         ♣ 7 6 2
                      South
                      ♠ 5 2
                      ♡ K 10 7 6 4
                      ◇ A K 8
                      ♣ K 9 3
```

West	North	East	South
			1♡
Pass	2♣	Pass	3♣
Pass	3♡	Pass	4♡
Pass	Pass	Pass	

Your partner leads the three of spades: nine, ace, two. You return the four of spades: five, king, ten. Partner leads another spade; queen, eight, three of clubs. Then the three of hearts is led from dummy. Which heart do you play?

Play the queen of hearts when the three is led from dummy. If you play the ace or a low heart and declarer has the king and ten, you will get only one heart trick. If you put up the ace, he will play low and later finesse the ten; if you play the nine, he will finesse the ten and return to dummy to lead another heart.

If you play the queen of hearts, though, declarer is led to believe that your partner has the nine. When he wins with his king, he may lead toward dummy and finesse the eight; this would be the only way to make his contract if you had a singleton queen and partner ♡ A 9 5 2.

7.

	North		
	♠ K Q 9 7		
	♡ 8		
	◊ Q J 2		
	♣ A K Q J 4		

West		East	
♠ A		♠ J 8 6 5 4	
♡ 10 3 2		♡ Q 4	
◊ A K 10 7 6 5		◊ 9 3	
♣ 9 8 2		♣ 10 7 6 5	

	South		
	♠ 10 3 2		
	♡ A K J 9 7 6 5		
	◊ 8 4		
	♣ 3		

West	North	East	South
	1♣	Pass	1♡
2◊	2♠	Pass	4♡
Pass	Pass	Pass	

You win the first two tricks with the king and ace of diamonds; partner plays the nine and three, declarer the four and eight. Plan your defense.

Cash the ace of spades and then lead another diamond. The only chance to beat the contract is to win a trump trick. If partner has the king, queen or jack of hearts and ruffs your third diamond lead with his honor, it will promote your ten into a trick. In the actual layout, partner must ruff the third diamond lead with his queen of hearts; when declarer overruffs with the ace or king, your ten becomes a trick.

Note that declarer can make his contract if you lead a third diamond before cashing the ace of spades by overruffing partner's queen of hearts with his king, cashing the ace and jack of hearts, and then discarding his three spades on dummy's clubs. By the time you can ruff with your ten of hearts, he will have no more spades.

8.

	North		
	♠ Q 6 4		
	♡ K 8 5 3		
	◊ A K J 10		
	♣ 7 2		

West		East	
♠ 10 5		♠ A K J 7 3	
♡ Q 9 4		♡ 6	
◊ 8 7 3 2		◊ 9 5	
♣ K 6 5 3		♣ J 10 9 8 4	

	South		
	♠ 9 8 2		
	♡ A J 10 7 2		
	◊ Q 6 4		
	♣ A Q		

West	North	East	South
	1◊	1♠	2♡
Pass	3♡	Pass	4♡
Pass	Pass	Pass	

You lead the ten of spades, dummy plays the queen and partner wins the first three tricks with the king, ace and jack as declarer follows suit. What do you discard on the third spade lead.

Discard the three of clubs. Seeing your discouraging signal in clubs, partner should lead a fourth round of spades, hoping for a trump-promotion play; and you should know that that guarantees the contract will be set. If declarer ruffs with the two or seven of hearts or discards, you will ruff with the nine to drive out dummy's king; if declarer ruffs with the ten or jack (or ace), you will discard and your ♡ Q 9 4 becomes a natural trump trick.

If partner leads a club at trick four, declarer should win with the ace, planning to discard his queen of clubs on dummy's fourth diamond. The fate of the contract would depend on how he plays the heart suit. With nine hearts missing the queen, the percentage play is to cash the ace and king *if you have no information about the defenders' distribution*. But declarer knows West was dealt two spades to East's five, so West is a favorite to have the queen. A good declarer would most likely cash the ace of hearts and finesse West for the queen.

9.
North
♠ J 7
♡ A 9 6 4 3
♢ A Q J
♣ A K 10

West
♠ A 9 8 4 3
♡ J 7 5
♢ 10 5 4
♣ 9 2

East
♠ K 10 6 5
♡ K Q 8 2
♢ 6 3
♣ J 7 4

South
♠ Q 2
♡ 10
♢ K 9 8 7 2
♣ Q 8 6 5 3

West	North	East	South
	1♡	Pass	1NT
Pass	3NT	All Pass	

Your partner leads the four of spades and the seven is played from dummy. Which spade do you play?

Play the king of spades. Partner has obviously led his fourth-highest spade, so declarer has only one card higher than the four (Rule of Eleven). If he has either the ace or ♠ Q x x, he will win exactly one spade trick whether you play the king or the ten. The only holding that makes any difference is the one you see (♠ Q x), so going up with your king of spades is the right play.

Further, declarer's one higher spade cannot logically be the ace. If it were, his first play from dummy would have been the jack; the jack is a useless card unless it is played on the first trick and the opening lead was from the king-queen.

If you play the king of spades, your side can win the first five spade tricks. If you play the ten, declarer will win with the queen and make his contract with three overtricks. Quite a difference!

10.
North
♠ Q 7 6 5 4
♡ A J 9 2
♢ A 8
♣ K 3

West
♠ K 10 3
♡ Q 4
♢ 10 9 7 6 2
♣ Q 8 4

East
♠ A 9 8 2
♡ 10 7 6 3
♢ Q 5 4
♣ 10 5

South
♠ J
♡ K 8 5
♢ K J 3
♣ A J 9 7 6 2

West	North	East	South
	1♠	Pass	2♣
Pass	2♡	Pass	3NT
Pass	Pass	Pass	

You lead the ten of diamonds, dummy plays the eight, partner the queen and declarer the king. A club is led to dummy's king as partner follows with the ten. Another club is led, partner plays the five, declarer the jack and you win with the queen. What do you lead now?

Lead the king of spades. If declarer has the ace of spades, he has at least nine tricks; partner's high-low in clubs told you that declarer began with a six-card club suit. So the only chance to beat the contract is to find declarer with a singleton spade (other than the ace); in which case you can win the next four spade tricks. When you lead the king of spades, partner must play the two; you should be aware that he cannot afford to waste a higher card to signal. Then lead the ten of spades and declarer must lose three more tricks whether or not he covers your ten with the queen.

11.

	North		
	♠ Q 10 3		
	♡ Q 9		
	◇ A Q J 8 7		
	♣ K Q 5		

West		East
♠ A 6 5		♠ K J 9 8 7 4 2
♡ K 7		♡ 6 5
◇ 6 4 3		◇ 10 2
♣ J 10 9 8 2		♣ A 3

	South		
	♠ —		
	♡ A J 10 8 4 3 2		
	◇ K 9 5		
	♣ 7 6 4		

West	North	East	South
	1NT	2♠	4♡
4♠	Pass	Pass	5♡
Pass	Pass	Pass	

You lead the jack of clubs, dummy plays the king, partner the ace and declarer the four. Partner returns the three of clubs, declarer plays the six, you the eight and dummy the queen. The queen of hearts is led and finessed to your king. What do you lead now?

Cash the ten (or nine) of clubs. Unless partner has the king of diamonds, you must win a third trick right now to beat the contract. If declarer has a spade and only two clubs, the winning defense is to cash the ace of spades. How can you tell whether declarer has a spade or a club? After two rounds of clubs the only one missing is the seven. If partner clubs were A 7 3, *he would have led the seven at trick two, not the three;* so declarer has the seven of clubs.

12.

	North		
	♠ Q 6 4		
	♡ K J 4		
	◇ K Q 10 7		
	♣ 8 3 2		

West		East
♠ 8		♠ 2
♡ 9 7 5 2		♡ A Q 10 3
◇ 9 6 4 3		◇ A 8 5
♣ A J 10 7		♣ Q 9 6 5 4

	South		
	♠ A K J 10 9 7 5 3		
	♡ 8 6		
	◇ J 2		
	♣ K		

West	North	East	South
			4♠
Pass	Pass	Pass	

Partner leads the three of diamonds, dummy plays the king, you the ace and declarer the two. What do you lead now?

Lead the nine of clubs. If partner gets the lead with the ace of clubs, you want him to return a heart. Leading the nine of clubs implies you have nothing in the suit, and at the same time suggests that you want another suit led. When partner wins the second trick with the ace of clubs, he should return the two of hearts. Since partner would not lead the two if he had more than four hearts, declarer cannot have a singleton and you can set the contract by winning two heart tricks.

If you led a low club at trick two, your partner might try to cash a second club trick rather than lead a heart; declarer would make his contract with an overtrick.

Yes, it would have been easier if partner's opening lead had been a heart!

13.   North
            ♠ K J 7
            ♡ K J 3
            ◇ J 8 4
            ♣ 10 6 5 2
West   East
♠ 5 4 2   ♠ 9 6
♡ 10 9 8 7 4   ♡ 6 5 2
◇ Q 3   ◇ K 10 6 5
♣ A K 9   ♣ Q 7 4 3
            South
            ♠ A Q 10 8 3
            ♡ A Q
            ◇ A 9 7 2
            ♣ J 8

West	North	East	South
			1♠
Pass	2♠	Pass	4♠
Pass	Pass	Pass	

Your partner leads the king of clubs. Which club do you play?

Play the four of clubs. Although you want another club lead, you cannot spare the seven to signal. Suppose partner leads the king, ace and nine of clubs. Declarer will cover the nine with the ten and you will play the queen; the six will be high unless you still have the seven. Declarer can always discard one diamond loser on the third round of hearts, but must still lose two diamond tricks and go down one unless you signaled with the seven of clubs.

14.   North
            ♠ K 9 6 4
            ♡ Q 10 2
            ◇ Q J 8
            ♣ 8 5 3
West   East
♠ J 10   ♠ 7 3
♡ K 9 8 7   ♡ A J 5
◇ 9 5 2   ◇ A 10 6 4 3
♣ J 6 4 2   ♣ 10 9 7
            South
            ♠ A Q 8 5 2
            ♡ 6 4 3
            ◇ K 7
            ♣ A K Q

West	North	East	South
			1♠
Pass	2♠	Pass	4♠
Pass	Pass	Pass	

Your partner lead the jack of spades: four, three, ace. Declarer cashes the queen of spades: ten, six, seven. The king of diamonds is led, partner plays the two and you duck. Declarer leads another diamond, partner plays the nine and you win with the ace. What do you lead now?

Lead the five of hearts. The two of diamonds told you that your partner has an odd number, obviously three. The nine of diamonds is a suit-preference signal asking you to switch to the higher-ranking suit—in this case hearts. Since the only missing high heart is the king, partner must have it. If he wins with the king and returns a heart, the defense can win the three heart tricks needed to beat the contract.

15.
```
                North
                ♠ 8 5 4 2
                ♡ K 6 3
                ◇ A Q 6
                ♣ K 4 3
West                        East
♠ A                         ♠ J 10 9 3
♡ Q J 10 4                  ♡ 9 7 5
◇ K J 8 3                   ◇ 10 4 2
♣ 9 7 5 2                   ♣ 10 8 6
                South
                ♠ K Q 7 6
                ♡ A 8 2
                ◇ 9 7 5
                ♣ A Q J
```

West	North	East	South
			1NT
Pass	3NT	All Pass	

Your partner lead the queen of hearts, which is allowed to win the first trick. The jack of hearts is led and this trick is won with dummy's king. Then declarer leads the eight of spades from dummy. Which spade do you play?

Play the three of spades. Declarer intends to play an honor no matter which spade you play, so you cannot gain by covering the eight. In the actual layout, declarer will probably play the king or queen and you will win three spade tricks *if you play the three.*

If you cover the eight with the nine, ten or jack, declarer can save a trick by a safety play. Assuming he played the king on the first spade trick, he is left with ♠ Q 7 6 and you with ♠ J 10 3; by leading a low spade from his hand, or by finessing through you again, he can develop a second spade trick, which he needs to make his contract.

16.
```
                North
                ♠ A K Q
                ♡ 7 6 4
                ◇ J 10 3
                ♣ A K Q 5
West                        East
♠ 9 8 6 5                   ♠ 7 4 2
♡ 8 3                       ♡ A J 10 9 5
◇ A 7 6                     ◇ K 4 2
♣ J 10 9 7                  ♣ 8 6
                South
                ♠ J 10 3
                ♡ K Q 2
                ◇ Q 9 8 5
                ♣ 4 3 2
```

West	North	East	South
	1♣	1♡	1NT
Pass	3NT	All Pass	

You lead the eight of hearts, partner plays the nine and declarer the king. Declarer then leads the five of diamonds. Plan your defense.

Go up with your ace of diamonds at trick two and lead the three of hearts. Declarer would not play diamonds this way if he were missing the queen, so going up with the ace will not cost a diamond trick. And hopefully partner has the king. The purpose of going up with the ace is to save partner's entry. When declarer wins his second heart trick, he has only eight winners (three spades, two hearts and three clubs), so the contract is set.

Note that declarer will make his contract if you do not win the first diamond trick with your ace. If partner takes the king, he has no reentry; if partner also ducks, declarer has nine tricks.

```
17.              North
                ♠ 7 6 3
                ♡ A Q 10
                ♢ J 9 7 4
                ♣ J 8 5
West                          East
♠ K Q 10 4 2                  ♠ 9 8
♡ 9 8 3                       ♡ K 7 5 4
♢ 6 5 2                       ♢ A 10 3
♣ K 7                         ♣ 6 4 3 2
                South
                ♠ A J 5
                ♡ J 6 2
                ♢ K Q 8
                ♣ A Q 10 9

West     North    East    South
                          1NT
Pass     2NT      Pass    3NT
Pass     Pass     Pass
```

You lead the king of spades, partner plays the eight and declarer the five. What do you lead at trick two?

Lead a heart; do not lead another spade. If you look around the table, you can see all of the spades lower than the eight. So partner has played his lowest spade, *something he should not do if he has the jack.* Declarer is unlucky to find the king of hearts and king of clubs both offside, but the fate of the contract depends on what you lead at trick two. If you lead another spade, the contract cannot be set; if you lead a heart (or a diamond), the contract cannot be made.

```
18.              North
                ♠ Q 3
                ♡ A 4
                ♢ A Q 10 8 2
                ♣ 9 6 5 3
West                          East
♠ K 7 5                       ♠ 6 4
♡ J 10 9 6 5                  ♡ 8 7 2
♢ 7 3                         ♢ K J 9 5
♣ A Q 4                       ♣ J 10 8 2
                South
                ♠ A J 10 9 8 2
                ♡ K Q 3
                ♢ 6 4
                ♣ K 7

West     North    East    South
                          1♠
Pass     2♢       Pass    2♠
Pass     3♠       Pass    4♠
Pass     Pass     Pass
```

Your partner leads the jack of hearts and dummy plays the ace. Which heart do you play?

Play the eight of hearts. Since you have very good diamonds, there is no urgency to win tricks in the side suits—declarer will not be able to discard on the diamond suit. If your partner gets the lead with a high trump, the only damage he can do is to lead a club from a precarious holding. Seeing your encouraging heart, he will probably lead another heart. But if you play the two of hearts on the first trick, he may decide to lead a club, hoping that you have the king and fearing declarer can discard his club losers on dummy's diamond winners.

19.
```
                North
                ♠ A J
                ♡ K Q 10 8 7
                ◇ 10 8 5
                ♣ A K Q
West                          East
♠ 10 8 7 5 3                  ♠ K 6 2
♡ 6 4 2                       ♡ A 9 5
◇ A J 3                       ◇ Q 9 4
♣ 9 2                         ♣ 10 7 4 3
                South
                ♠ Q 9 4
                ♡ J 3
                ◇ K 7 6 2
                ♣ J 8 6 5
```

West	North	East	South
	1♡	Pass	1NT
Pass	3NT	All Pass	

Your partner leads the five of spades. You win the first trick with the king and return the six of spades; declarer follows with the nine and partner with the ten. A low heart is led to declarer's jack, then another heart to dummy's king and your ace. What do you lead now?

Lead the queen of diamonds. Partner's play of the ten of spades told you he does not have the queen. So declarer has nine tricks if he regains the lead (two spades, four hearts and three clubs). The only chance to beat the contract (unless your partner has the ace and king of diamonds) is if partner has the ace and jack of diamonds, declarer has the king and you can win the next three diamond tricks. If you lead a low diamond, declarer will play low from his hand, and it will be impossible to win more than two diamond tricks.

You must resort to subterfuge and lead the queen of diamonds. If declarer ducks, he will be set; but that would be his only way to make the contract if you had ◇ Q J 9. If he covers with the king, your partner can also see that declarer has nine tricks if he regains the lead. So he should take his ace and lead back the three of diamonds; then declarer must guess whether to play the eight or ten from the dummy.

20.
```
                North
                ♠ Q J 10
                ♡ A K 5
                ◇ J 10 9 8
                ♣ A K J
West                          East
♠ A 9 8 6 4                   ♠ 3 2
♡ 7 6 3                       ♡ Q 10 8 4
◇ A 2                         ◇ K 7 5
♣ 10 5 3                      ♣ 9 7 6 4
                South
                ♠ K 7 5
                ♡ J 9 2
                ◇ Q 6 4 3
                ♣ Q 8 2
```

West	North	East	South
	1◇	Pass	1NT
Pass	3NT	All Pass	

Your partner leads the six of spades and the first trick is won with dummy's ten. The jack of diamonds is led. Plan your defense.

Go up with the king of diamonds. There seems to be little hope to beat the contract unless partner has the ace of diamonds. By playing the king of diamonds and returning a spade, three spade winners can be established while partner still has the ace of diamonds for an entry.

21.   North
          ♠ J 4 2
          ♡ J 10 5
          ◇ 9 6 3
          ♣ K Q J 5

West   East
♠ A 3   ♠ 9 6 5
♡ A 7 6   ♡ 8 4 3 2
◇ Q J 10   ◇ 8 7 4
♣ 9 8 7 4 2   ♣ A 10 3

          South
          ♠ K Q 10 8 7
          ♡ K Q 9
          ◇ A K 5 2
          ♣ 6

West	North	East	South
			1♠
Pass	2♠	Pass	4♠
Pass	Pass	Pass	

Your partner leads the queen of diamonds, you play the four and the first trick is won by declarer with the ace. He leads the six of clubs, partner plays the two and dummy the king. Plan your defense.

Win the first club trick with the ace and lead the eight of diamonds. Partner signaled that he has an odd number of clubs. If he has three, so does declarer, and it does not matter whether you play the ace or hold up. But if partner has five, declarer has one, and you will lose your ace if you hold up.

If you win the first club trick and lead a diamond, declarer cannot get to dummy in time to discard his low diamonds; he must lose a trick in each suit and go down one.

22.   North
          ♠ A Q 8 2
          ♡ K 3
          ◇ K Q J
          ♣ J 7 6 4

West   East
♠ 5   ♠ 9 6
♡ Q 7 5 4 2   ♡ J 10 8
◇ 10 9 8 7 2   ◇ A 6 5 4
♣ K 8   ♣ A Q 9 3

          South
          ♠ K J 10 7 4 3
          ♡ A 9 6
          ◇ 3
          ♣ 10 5 2

West	North	East	South
	1NT	Pass	4♠
Pass	Pass	Pass	

Your partner leads the ten of diamonds, you play the ace and declarer the three. What do you lead now?

Lead the three of clubs. Declarer's four-spade bid marks him with at least six spades, so there appears to be no chance to beat the contract unless your partner has the king of clubs. If partner does have the king, you should get whatever club tricks are available before declarer has a chance to discard on dummy's diamonds. Just in case partner has a doubleton king of clubs, the best play is to underlead your ace-queen so you can win three club tricks.

23.

	North		
	♠ Q 9 7 6		
	♡ J 10 8		
	◇ K J 2		
	♣ J 10 5		

West		East	
♠ 10 8 3		♠ —	
♡ 9		♡ A Q 7 6 5 4 2	
◇ 10 7 6 5 3		◇ Q 8 4	
♣ K 8 4 2		♣ Q 9 3	

	South		
	♠ A K J 5 4 2		
	♡ K 3		
	◇ A 9		
	♣ A 7 6		

West	North	East	South
			1♠
Pass	2♠	3♡	4♠
Pass	Pass	Pass	

You lead the nine of hearts, partner plays the ace and declarer the three. Partner returns the five of hearts, declarer plays the king and you ruff. What do you lead at trick three?

Lead a trump. Partner's lead of the five of hearts is a suit-preference signal. With the Q 7 6 4 2 missing, you should recognize the five-spot as a middle card to discourage you from leading a diamond or a club from an unsafe holding. If partner wanted a diamond return, he would have led the seven of hearts; if he wanted a club return, he would have led the two.

It turns out that declarer will lose two tricks in the minor suits unless you lead either suit. So, after you ruff the heart lead, you must exit with a trump to beat the contract.

24.

	North		
	♠ A 9 7		
	♡ 8 5 4		
	◇ K 2		
	♣ Q 9 6 4 3		

West		East	
♠ K Q 10 6		♠ J 8 5 3 2	
♡ 10 7		♡ 9 6 3	
◇ Q J 9 5 4		◇ 6	
♣ 8 2		♣ K J 10 7	

	South		
	♠ 4		
	♡ A K Q J 2		
	◇ A 10 8 7 3		
	♣ A 5		

West	North	East	South
			1♡
Pass	2♡	Pass	4♡
Pass	Pass	Pass	

Your partner leads the king of spades. Declarer wins with dummy's ace, cashes the king of diamonds and leads the two of diamonds. Plan your defense.

Discard a spade; do not ruff the two of diamonds. Since declarer did not draw trumps before leading diamonds, he obviously has losing diamonds in his hand. If he tries to ruff in dummy, you will overruff. If he draws the trumps, your partner will win his diamond tricks. Due to the unlucky diamond break, declarer must lose three diamonds and one club *if you do not ruff the two of diamonds*.

If you do ruff the two of diamonds, declarer plays a low one from his hand and is left with ◇ A 10 8. When he regains the lead he will be able to draw all of the missing trumps in two rounds and ruff one of his diamond losers with dummy's third trump.

25.

	North	
	♠ K 8 6 3	
	♡ 6 5 4	
	◊ A K J	
	♣ Q 10 2	
West		East
♠ J 9 2		♠ A 10 7
♡ K Q 9		♡ A 8 3
◊ 8 7 3		◊ 6 5 4 2
♣ 7 6 5 4		♣ 9 8 3
	South	
	♠ Q 5 4	
	♡ J 10 7 2	
	◊ Q 10 9	
	♣ A K J	

West	North	East	South
			1♣
Pass	1♠	Pass	1NT
Pass	3NT	All Pass	

Your partner leads the king of hearts and you signal with the eight. He continues with the queen of hearts. Which heart do you play on the second trick?

Play the three of hearts. The ace would be the winning play (to unblock the suit) if partner had four or five hearts headed by the king-queen-jack, but then *his second lead should not be the queen* (this deal is the same as #14 in Chapter 2; see page 54 for a more complete explanation). If you overtake the queen in this deal, declarer can win two heart tricks and make his contract.

Partner's choice of an opening lead should not be criticized. Since the opponents bid clubs and spades, the king of hearts seems a better lead than a diamond. And you played a high heart to encourage him to continue the suit. As you might have four hearts to the ace, you cannot blame him for leading the queen of hearts at trick two.

26.

	North	
	♠ K 6	
	♡ K Q 8 3	
	◊ Q 8 7	
	♣ A 5 4 2	
West		East
♠ J 10 9 8 4		♠ 7 5 3 2
♡ A 10		♡ 4
◊ J 5 3		◊ A 9 6 2
♣ K 7 6		♣ J 10 9 3
	South	
	♠ A Q	
	♡ J 9 7 6 5 2	
	◊ K 10 4	
	♣ Q 8	

West	North	East	South
			1♡
Pass	3♡	Pass	4♡
Pass	Pass	Pass	

You lead the jack of spades. Declarer wins the first two tricks with the queen and ace of spades; then he leads the two of hearts. Plan your defense.

Go up with your ace of hearts and lead the ten of hearts. Cashing the ace of spades before leading a trump makes it obvious that declarer has no more spades and suggests that he is heading for an endplay. He wants you to lead a spade, which will give him a ruff-and-discard, or to lead a diamond or a club. If you duck the first heart lead and win the second, you will have to accommodate declarer; whichever suit you lead will give him a trick and his contract.

But if you defend correctly (win the first heart trick with your ace and return a heart), declarer will be set unless he chooses a strange line of play.

27.

	North	
	♠ Q J 3	
	♡ 8 7 5 2	
	◇ Q 10	
	♣ K 10 9 3	
West		East
♠ K 10 7 5		♠ A 9 6 4
♡ A 9 3		♡ 6
◇ 9 7 6 4 2		◇ 8 5 3
♣ 8		♣ Q J 7 4 2
	South	
	♠ 8 2	
	♡ K Q J 10 4	
	◇ A K J	
	♣ A 6 5	

West	North	East	South
			1♡
Pass	2♡	Pass	4♡
Pass	Pass	Pass	

You lead the eight of clubs, dummy plays the nine, partner the jack and declarer wins with the ace. The king of hearts is led. Plan your defense?

Duck the first heart trick. If you win the first heart trick, you won't know whether to lead a spade or a diamond to put partner on lead so he can give you a club ruff. Partner apparently has a singleton heart, so if you wait and win the second heart trick, he will play the nine of spades to encourage you to lead that suit. Then you can set the contract by winning the next three tricks: lead a spade to his ace, he gives you the club ruff and you cash the king of spades.

If you don't lead a spade when you get the lead with the ace of hearts, no club ruff is possible and declarer can make his contract by establishing a spade trick in dummy to discard his club loser.

28.

	North	
	♠ 8 2	
	♡ Q 6 4	
	◇ K Q J 9 3	
	♣ A 10 5	
West		East
♠ 6 4		♠ J 9 5
♡ J 10 9 7 5		♡ K 8 3 2
◇ 8 2		◇ A 10 6 5
♣ Q 9 6 3		♣ J 4
	South	
	♠ A K Q 10 7 3	
	♡ A	
	◇ 7 4	
	♣ K 8 7 2	

West	North	East	South
	1◇	Pass	1♠
Pass	1NT	Pass	4♣
Pass	4♡	Pass	6♠
Pass	Pass	Pass	

Your partner leads the jack of hearts: four, eight, ace. The four of diamonds is led, partner plays the eight and dummy the king. Plan your defense.

Hold up your ace of diamonds. Partner's eight is almost surely to show a doubleton (if he had a singleton, he would have led it), so declarer has two diamonds. By ducking the first diamond lead and winning the second, you deprive declarer of a crucial entry to dummy; he has two club losers and can discard one on the third high diamond—but that is all.

If you win the first diamond trick, he can discard both club losers. After regaining the lead and drawing the missing trumps, he leads his second diamond to dummy, discards a club on the third high diamond, ruffs the fourth diamond in his hand and crosses to dummy with the ace of clubs to discard his other club loser on the fifth diamond.

29.   North
                 ♠ K 7
                 ♡ Q 8 7 3
                 ◇ A J 5
                 ♣ K 9 6 4
West   East
♠ Q J 9 4   ♠ A 10 5 2
♡ 2   ♡ K 10 6
◇ 10 7 6 3   ◇ Q 8 4 2
♣ Q 8 7 5   ♣ J 3
                 South
                 ♠ 8 6 3
                 ♡ A J 9 5 4
                 ◇ K 9
                 ♣ A 10 2

West	North	East	South
	1♣	Pass	1♡
Pass	2♡	Pass	4♡
Pass	Pass	Pass	

You lead the queen of spades, dummy plays the king and partner wins with the ace. Partner returns the two of spades and you win this trick with the nine. What do you lead now?

Lead the jack of spades. There is no danger that this will give declarer a ruff-and-discard; partner returned the two of spades—an indication that he has four—so declarer must have another spade in his hand.

With the cards in this layout, any lead but a spade will help declarer. If you lead a heart, he will avoid a heart loser; which he will probably lose if he has to break the suit himself. If you lead a diamond, he will play low from dummy and establish dummy's third diamond to discard his club loser. If you lead a club, he cannot be prevented from winning a third trick with the ten or the nine.

Declarer can make his contract even if you do lead a spade at trick three, but there is a good chance he will fail.

30.   North
                 ♠ K 4
                 ♡ 10 7 2
                 ◇ J 9 5 2
                 ♣ Q J 10 9
West   East
♠ A 3 2   ♠ J 10 9 8 7 5
♡ 9 8 6 5   ♡ 3
◇ A K Q 10 3   ◇ 6 4
♣ 7   ♣ 8 6 5 2
                 South
                 ♠ Q 6
                 ♡ A K Q J 4
                 ◇ 8 7
                 ♣ A K 4 3

West	North	East	South
			1♡
2◇	2♡	Pass	4♡
Pass	Pass	Pass	

You win the first two tricks with the king and ace of diamonds as partner plays high-low and declarer follows suit. What do you lead now?

Lead the three (or the ten) of diamonds. You can see three defensive tricks, and there is virtually no chance of a fourth in the side suits since declarer surely has the ace of clubs.

You must try to develop a trump trick, which you can do if partner has a trump. If so, when you lead a low diamond and partner ruffs, declarer will be forced to overruff.

Now you have equal length with declarer in the trump suit, and he is left with a choice of evils. If he draws all of your trumps and cashes four club tricks, you will win the last two tricks with the ace of spades and queen of diamonds. If he leads a spade before drawing trumps, you win with your ace and establish a long trump by leading your high diamond to force declarer to ruff again. And if he leads clubs before drawing all of the trumps, you will ruff the second round.

With the cards as shown, the only way to defeat the contract is to underlead the queen of diamonds at trick three.

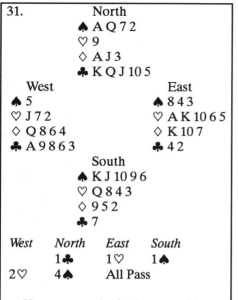

31.

	North		
	♠ A Q 7 2		
	♡ 9		
	◇ A J 3		
	♣ K Q J 10 5		
West		East	
♠ 5		♠ 8 4 3	
♡ J 7 2		♡ A K 10 6 5	
◇ Q 8 6 4		◇ K 10 7	
♣ A 9 8 6 3		♣ 4 2	
	South		
	♠ K J 10 9 6		
	♡ Q 8 4 3		
	◇ 9 5 2		
	♣ 7		

West	North	East	South
	1♣	1♡	1♠
2♡	4♠	All Pass	

Your partner leads the two of hearts and you win the first trick with the king. What do you lead now?

Lead the seven of diamonds. If declarer has any losing diamonds, he will discard them on dummy's clubs if given time. The only good chance to beat the contract is if partner has the queen of diamonds and the ace of clubs, and declarer has at least three diamonds. With the cards as shown, partner's queen of diamonds will knock out dummy's ace, and when he gets the lead with the ace of clubs he will lead a diamond so you can win two more tricks with your king and ten.

Note that if declarer has the queen of diamonds, you cannot beat the contract, but your seven-of-diamonds lead will not cost a trick.

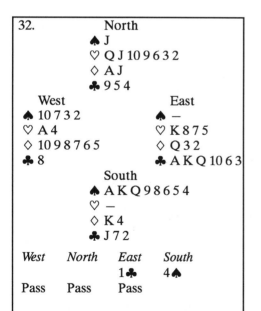

32.

	North		
	♠ J		
	♡ Q J 10 9 6 3 2		
	◇ A J		
	♣ 9 5 4		
West		East	
♠ 10 7 3 2		♠ —	
♡ A 4		♡ K 8 7 5	
◇ 10 9 8 7 6 5		◇ Q 3 2	
♣ 8		♣ A K Q 10 6 3	
	South		
	♠ A K Q 9 8 6 5 4		
	♡ —		
	◇ K 4		
	♣ J 7 2		

West	North	East	South
		1♣	4♠
Pass	Pass	Pass	

You lead the eight of clubs. Partner wins the first two tricks with the queen and ace of clubs while declarer plays the two and seven. Partner then cashes the king of clubs and declarer follows with the jack. What are your discards at tricks two and three?

Discard first the four and then the ace of hearts. When partner wins the first trick with the queen of clubs, you learn that he has the ace and king, but not the jack. When he wins the second club trick with the ace and declarer does not play the jack, you find out that partner can win a third club trick. So, catering to the possibility that declarer is void in hearts, the only sure way to beat the contract is to discard your two hearts; partner will lead a heart at trick four and your ten of spades is promoted into the setting trick.

Declarer would have been more deceptive if he had played the jack of clubs on the second trick; then you could not have been sure partner could win a third club trick. But discarding the four of hearts would still be best as it would lead to setting the contract if declarer has three clubs, or two clubs and one or more hearts.

33.   North
                 ♠ Q 9 8 3
                 ♡ 7 4
                 ◇ A Q 2
                 ♣ K Q 10 6
        West   East
   ♠ 7 4 2   ♠ K 5
   ♡ K 9 8 6 5   ♡ J 10 3 2
   ◇ K 10 5 4   ◇ J 7 6
   ♣ 3   ♣ A 9 8 2
                    South
                 ♠ A J 10 6
                 ♡ A Q
                 ◇ 9 8 3
                 ♣ J 7 5 4

West	North	East	South
	1♣	Pass	1♠
Pass	2♠	Pass	3♣
Pass	4♠	All Pass	

Your partner leads the three of clubs and you win with the ace. What do you lead at trick two?

Lead the two of clubs. It is apparent that partner has led a singleton, so the club you lead is a suit-preference signal. You might think the eight (the middle card) is the right lead because you have no high card in hearts or diamonds; but partner might read the eight as your highest and return a heart. Since a heart lead might give declarer an unearned trick, while a diamond lead will not jeopardize a trick whether partner has the king or not, you should lead the two of clubs.

As long as partner does not lead a heart at trick three, declarer must still lose two more tricks for down one.

34.   North
                 ♠ Q 8 4
                 ♡ J 9 3
                 ◇ K Q J 10 7
                 ♣ 5 2
        West   East
   ♠ 9 6 2   ♠ A 7 5 3
   ♡ 10 7 5   ♡ 8 6 4
   ◇ A 4   ◇ 9 3 2
   ♣ A Q 8 7 3   ♣ 10 6 4
                    South
                 ♠ K J 10
                 ♡ A K Q 2
                 ◇ 8 6 5
                 ♣ K J 9

West	North	East	South
			1NT
Pass	3NT	All Pass	

Your partner leads the seven of clubs and your ten is topped by declarer's jack. A diamond is led, partner plays the four and dummy the king. Which diamond do you play? The queen of diamonds is led at trick three. Which diamond do you play this time?

First *play the two of diamonds* as a count signal (to show an odd number of cards). Then *play the nine of diamonds* as a suit-preference signal—asking for partner to lead the higher-ranking major suit.

If your partner is paying attention, when he takes the ace of diamonds he will lead a spade to your ace, and you will lead a club through declarer's ♣ K 9 to beat the contract by two tricks. Without the spade lead, the contract cannot be set.

(For more information on count signals and suit-preference signals, see Chapter 7.)

35.   North
        ♠ A K Q J 9
        ♡ K 7
        ◇ 9 6 2
        ♣ 8 7 2

West   East
♠ 10 2   ♠ 7 5 4 3
♡ A J 8   ♡ 6 4 2
◇ A Q 5   ◇ K 10 8 3
♣ Q 10 6 4 3   ♣ 9 5

        South
        ♠ 8 6
        ♡ Q 10 9 5 3
        ◇ J 7 4
        ♣ A K J

West	North	East	South
	1♠	Pass	2♡
Pass	2♠	Pass	2NT
Pass	3NT	All Pass	

You open with the four of clubs to partner's nine and declarer's jack. Declarer leads the three of hearts. Plan your defense.

Go up with the ace of hearts and lead the ace of diamonds. Partner would not have played the nine of clubs on the first trick if he had the ace or king, so declarer is known to have three club tricks. You can see five spade tricks in dummy; so, if you duck the heart lead, the king is his ninth trick. The only chance to beat the contract is to find partner with four (or five) diamonds headed by the king. When you lead the ace of diamonds partner will give you an encouraging signal, and you will continue with the queen and five of diamonds.

36.   North
        ♠ J 6 5
        ♡ A K 10 3
        ◇ 7
        ♣ K Q J 9 8

West   East
♠ 8 7 4 3   ♠ A Q 10
♡ 9 5   ♡ 4 2
◇ 8 4 2   ◇ A K J 9 6 5
♣ A 6 3 2   ♣ 10 7

        South
        ♠ K 9 2
        ♡ Q J 8 7 6
        ◇ Q 10 3
        ♣ 5 4

West	North	East	South
	1♣	1◇	1♡
Pass	3♡	Pass	4♡
Pass	Pass	Pass	

Your partner leads the two of diamonds and you win the first trick with the king. What do you lead at trick two?

Lead the queen of spades. You need three more tricks to beat the contract, and the only good chance is to find partner with the king of spades or the ace of clubs, and declarer with at least three spades. Catering to the actual layout, you lead the queen of spades, which declarer wins with the king. When partner gets the lead with the ace of clubs, he will return a spade and you will win two more tricks with your ace and ten.

Conventional Leads and Signals

Here you will find several of the more popular conventions for leads and signals used by many duplicate bridge players, especially experts. Not all partnerships employ these conventions in exactly the same way—there are variations—so this is a subjective view. Before using any of these ideas, consider the following:

(1) You must inform your opponents in advance. In duplicate bridge, this is usually done by marking the convention card properly; however, some signals and discards (notably upside-down, odd-even and Lavinthal) require a special verbal announcement to your opponents prior to play.

(2) These non-standard procedures should be used only by partnership agreement in advance by two experienced players. A common mistake by eager players is to use too many "gadgets," often with little understanding. Before adopting any convention, in defense or bidding, study it thoroughly and discuss it with your partner; otherwise, it may lead to disastrous results. Further, even experts disagree on which of these conventions are good and which are not. The ones in bold type below are my personal preferences.

Lead Conventions	*Signaling Conventions*
Ace from Ace-King	**Upside-Down Signals**
Third from Even, Low from Odd	Lavinthal Discards
Zero or Two Higher	**Count Discards**
Jack Denies, Ten Implies	Odd-Even Discards
Queen from K Q 10 9 Versus Notrump	The Smith Echo
Attitude Leads Versus Notrump	**Present Count**
MUD	
Rusinow Leads	
Ace for Attitude, King for Count	

Ace from Ace-King

The standard procedure of leading the king from both ace-king and king-queen leaves third hand in doubt as to which the leader has unless he can see the ace or queen. The problem is solved by leading the ace from ace-king combinations. *This convention is recommended only when making an opening lead, and only against trump contracts (although the ace is led from ace-king at notrump in special cases, see #12, page 246).* Here is an example showing how this agreement enables third hand to give the right attitude signal.

#1

North
♠ Q J 7 2
♡ K Q J 7
♢ 6 5 3
♣ K 10

East
♠ 9 4
♡ A 10 4 3
♢ J 9 2
♣ J 8 6 5

West	North	East	South
			1♠
Pass	3♠	Pass	4♠
Pass	Pass	Pass	

Your partner leads the king of diamonds (which must be from king-queen), so you encourage him to lead the suit again by *playing the nine*. The four hands:

```
                    ♠ Q J 7 2
                    ♡ K Q J 7
                    ◇ 6 5 3
                    ♣ K 10
      ♠ 8 5                           ♠ 9 4
      ♡ 9 8 6                         ♡ A 10 4 3
      ◇ K Q 10 7                      ◇ J 9 2
      ♣ A 9 4 2                       ♣ J 8 6 5
                    ♠ A K 10 6 3
                    ♡ 5 2
                    ◇ A 8 4
                    ♣ Q 7 3
```

Partner is allowed to win the first trick with the king of diamonds and, seeing your encouraging signal, he leads another diamond to drive out declarer's ace. Declarer must now lose four tricks (two diamonds, one heart and one club), but if a diamond were not led at trick two, he would have time to establish dummy's heart suit and discard a losing diamond.

In the following layout your hand and dummy's are the same, but your partner's opening lead is the *ace* of diamonds. Since this shows the ace-king and declarer may have the queen, you should *play the two* to discourage partner from leading the suit again. (If partner holds ◇ A K Q or ◇ A K 10 x x, he will lead the suit again in spite of your discouraging signal.)

```
                    ♠ Q J 7 2
                    ♡ K Q J 7
                    ◇ 6 5 3
                    ♣ K 10
      ♠ 8 5                           ♠ 9 4
      ♡ 9 8 6                         ♡ A 10 4 3
      ◇ A K 10 7                      ◇ J 9 2
      ♣ Q 9 4 2                       ♣ J 8 6 5
                    ♠ A K 10 6 3
                    ♡ 5 2
                    ◇ Q 8 4
                    ♣ A 7 3
```

Seeing your two of diamonds, partner should realize the possibility that declarer has the ◇ Q x x and not lead the suit at trick two. In this case it does not matter which other suit partner leads. You will eventually get the lead with the ace of hearts and play a diamond through declarer's queen to set the contract one trick.

If your partner led the king of diamonds and you were playing the old-fashioned way—leading king from ace-king or from king-queen—you would not know whether or not to encourage another diamond lead.

A disadvantage of this convention is that the opening leader may lead the ace when he does not have the king (although it is usually a poor choice); third hand may think the lead is from ace-king and give a misleading signal. But the good outweighs the bad, and the proof of this is that a great number of good players are now leading ace from ace-king. I think this convention is good, and easy to play; all players should use it, but *only when making an opening lead, and only versus trump contracts (with the exception noted on the preceding page)*. Even then, there are four situations when it is better to lead the king from ace-king versus trump contracts:

(1) Lead the king from a doubleton ace-king.

(2) Lead the king from ace-king if it is in a suit that your partner bid first.

(3) Lead the king from ace-king if the contract is at the five-level or higher; further, in this situation third hand should signal count, not attitude.

(4) Lead the king from ace-king if the declarer made a preemptive bid at the three- or four-level.

Third from Even, Low from Odd

When defending against trump contracts, many experts lead their lowest card from an odd number (lead the two from K J 5 3 2, Q 9 8 6 2, K 8 2, 8 7 2, etc.) or their third-highest from an even number (the five from K J 5 3, J 9 5 2, K 10 5 4 3 2, etc.). These leads, sometimes called "Odd-Card Leads," are better than the standard fourth-highest, because third hand can read the leader's length in the suit more accurately after seeing just one card. For example:

#2

                                North
                                ♠ 9 5 2
                                ♡ A Q 10 4
                                ◇ J 3 2
                                ♣ Q 7 6
                                                                East
                                                                ♠ K J 10 7 4
                                                                ♡ 8 6 3
                                                                ◇ A
                                                                ♣ A 10 9 5

West	*North*	*East*	*South*
		1♠	2◇
2♠	3◇	3♠	5◇
Pass	Pass	Pass	

Partner leads the three of spades, you play the ten and declarer wins with the ace. A diamond is led to dummy's jack and your ace. You win the next trick with the ace of clubs and partner signals with the eight. What do you lead next?

Answer: *Cash your king of spades*. Seeing the two of spades in dummy, you know that partner led his lowest spade and has an odd number, so he started with three spades and declarer with two. The four hands:

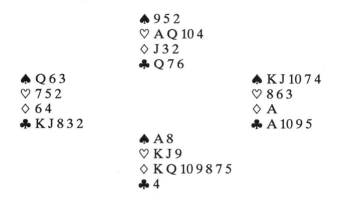

If you don't cash your high spade, declarer will make his contract by discarding his loser on the fourth round of hearts. If you play fourth-highest leads, partner would lead the two from ♠ Q 8 3 2 and from ♠ Q 3 2; not knowing which, you have a problem whether the third defensive trick can be won in spades or clubs.

Note that if the cards are changed so that North has ♠ 9 8 5 and South ♠ A 2, you cannot tell whether partner has three or four spades; he would lead the three from both ♠ Q 6 3 and ♠ Q 6 3 2. But if you are playing fourth-highest leads, you would know partner has three spades—he would not lead the three from ♠ Q 6 3 2. Although leading fourth-highest works out better if declarer has ♠ A 2, it does not if he has ♠ A 9, ♠ A 8 or ♠ A 5. So Third From Even, Low From Odd is *better* that fourth-highest; it is not infallible. Further proof of its merit: A vast number of experts use it.

Third From Even, Low From Odd should be used at trick two and later if your goal is to inform partner about your length. But if it is more important to tell partner about your strength in the suit, lead "top of nothing" and "low from strength" (see several illustrations beginning on page 83).

This convention is not recommended versus notrump contracts, mainly because the third-highest card from a four-card suit may be valuable. For example, leading the seven from K J 7 2 could later cost you a trick if declarer or dummy holds four cards; the right lead is the two—your fourth-highest.

Zero or Two Higher

In my view, this convention, along with Ace From Ace-King, should be used by all competent partnerships. You lead your *third-highest card* from inside sequences. For example, regardless of the length of the suit, lead the ten from K J 10, and lead the nine from K 10 9 or Q 10 9. *With the exception of when you are making the opening lead against a trump contract*, lead the jack from A-Q-J, the ten from A-J-10, and the nine from A-10-9. From a regular sequence headed by an honor card (such as J 10 9, 10 9 8) lead the highest card as you do using standard leads. Your partner always knows that you have zero or two higher cards in the suit.

Zero or Two Higher can be used in both notrump and trump contracts throughout the deal, but remember that you should not underlead an ace on the opening lead versus a trump contract. Consequently, *the opening lead of a jack denies a higher honor card unless you are leading from A Q J versus a notrump contract.*

The advantage of Zero or Two Higher is the card you lead makes it easier for your partner to figure out whether you are leading the top of a sequence or from an inside sequence. For example:

#3

North
♠ 5 2
♡ 9 7 4
◇ A K Q 10 9 3
♣ A 8

East
♠ Q J 10 9
♡ A 3
◇ 8 7 4
♣ 6 5 3 2

West	North	East	South
	1 ◇	Pass	2NT
Pass	3NT	All Pass	

Your partner leads the ten of hearts, you win the first trick with the ace and declarer plays the five. The strong diamond suit in dummy makes it apparent that declarer will be able to make his contract unless you win the first five tricks. Should you return a heart or lead the queen of spades?

Partner cannot be leading from a short suit, so with the nine in dummy you know he has ♡ K J 10. Another thought: Declarer's two-notrump bid implies that he has no four-card or longer major suits, so partner should have five hearts (and four spades); if so, you can win the first five tricks by *returning a heart*.

Even if you could not see the nine-spot, you should assume partner has K J 10 x x. If partner held 10 9 8 x, declarer's heart holding would be K Q J 5; predictably, his first bid would have been one heart. The four hands:

♠ 5 2
♡ 9 7 4
◇ A K Q 10 9 3
♣ A 8

♠ 7 6 4 3   ♠ Q J 10 9
♡ K J 10 8 2   ♡ A 3
◇ 5   ◇ 8 7 4
♣ Q 7 4   ♣ 6 5 3 2

♠ A K 8
♡ Q 6 5
◇ J 6 2
♣ K J 10 9

If you are thinking it would be routine to return a heart if your partnership agreement is to lead the jack from K J 10, suppose this were the layout and partner led the jack.

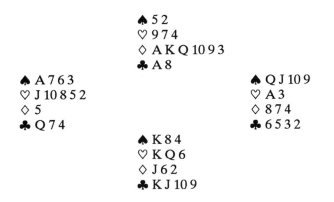

Playing Zero or Two Higher, you know partner has no heart higher than the jack; so declarer has the king-queen and returning a heart is futile. It is automatic to *lead the queen of spades* and hope that partner has the ace.

Using standard methods, the jack is led from both K J 10 x x and J 10 8 x x; you cannot tell whether to return a heart or switch to a spade.

Some experts prefer to play Zero or Two Higher from trick two onward, not on the opening lead. They contend that on the opening lead the convention is more helpful to declarer than to the defense because of deals like this:

#4
                         North
                         ♠ A Q 5
                         ♡ A Q 6
                         ◇ Q J 9 7 4
                         ♣ A 5

                         South
                         ♠ K 10 3
                         ♡ 5 3
                         ◇ K 10
                         ♣ J 9 8 6 3 2

West	North	East	South
	1◇	Pass	1NT
Pass	3NT	All Pass	

West leads the jack of hearts. As declarer, you win the first trick with dummy's ace and lead a diamond to your king. West wins with the ace of diamonds and leads the ten of hearts. If you knew that the lead of the jack denied a higher honor (East has the king), you would routinely play a low heart from dummy. But suppose you learn that your opponents are using the standard method of leading the jack from both K J 10 and J 10 9. When the ten of hearts is led you have a problem. Suppose this is the layout:

```
                          ♠ A Q 5
                          ♡ A Q 6
                          ◇ Q J 9 7 4
                          ♣ A 5
        ♠ 7 4 2                              ♠ J 9 8 6
        ♡ K J 10 7 2                         ♡ 9 8 4
        ◇ A 3                                ◇ 8 6 5 2
        ♣ Q 7 4                              ♣ K 10
                          ♠ K 10 3
                          ♡ 5 3
                          ◇ K 10
                          ♣ J 9 8 6 3 2
```

West made a good play by leading the ten of hearts, though it would be routine for an expert. Here, you must play the queen of hearts at trick three, or West will win four heart tricks. But if West has ♡ J 10 9 x x and East ♡ K x x, the winning play is a low heart from dummy to block the suit.

In this case, the defenders would regret playing Zero or Two Higher. But most players who use Zero or Two Higher consider it a good convention even on opening lead.

Here is an example of Zero or Two Higher being used *after* the opening lead:

#5   North
                          ♠ A Q 9 8
                          ♡ Q 7 6
                          ◇ K Q J 10
                          ♣ K Q
                                            East
                                            ♠ 4 3 2
                                            ♡ K J 10
                                            ◇ 9 7 5 2
                                            ♣ A 8 6

West	North	East	South
	1◇	Pass	1♠
Pass	4♠	All Pass	

Partner leads the jack of clubs and you win the first trick with your ace. It seems the best chance to beat the contract is to win some heart tricks before declarer can discard on dummy's diamonds. So, *lead the ten of hearts*. The four hands:

```
                          ♠ A Q 9 8
                          ♡ Q 7 6
                          ◇ K Q J 10
                          ♣ K Q
        ♠ 7 5                                ♠ 4 3 2
        ♡ A 8 5 3                            ♡ K J 10
        ◇ 6 3                                ◇ 9 7 5 2
        ♣ J 10 9 4 3                         ♣ A 8 6
                          ♠ K J 10 6
                          ♡ 9 4 2
                          ◇ A 8 4
                          ♣ 7 5 2
```

Your partner knows you have zero or two hearts higher than the ten, so either declarer has the king and jack, or you have them. He cannot lose by winning with his ace and returning a heart. Fortunately declarer has three hearts in his hand and you beat the contract. If you did not win the first four tricks, declarer would make his contract by drawing trumps and discarding one losing heart on the fourth round of diamonds.

Now suppose you held ♡ J 10 9 and led the jack of hearts at trick two:

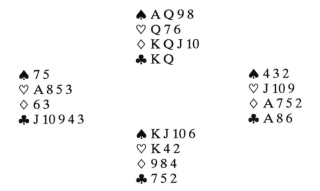

If you are playing Zero or Two Higher, your partner knows declarer has the king of hearts. So his only good chance to beat the contract is to allow the trick to be won by dummy's queen. With the cards as shown, you will eventually get the lead with the ace of diamonds and win two heart tricks by leading through declarer's king.

Jack Denies, Ten Implies

Another leading method is to agree that the jack *always* denies a higher card, and the ten is led from *all* of the following inside sequences: A Q 10 9, A J 10, K J 10, A 10 9, K 10 9 or Q 10 9. The queen is led from A Q J. It is also necessary to lead the nine from 10-9-8 or 10-9-7 to avoid conflict.

This method has an established following, but the fact that few experts use it suggests that Zero or Two Higher is better.

Queen from K Q 10 9 Versus Notrump

The customary lead from K Q 10 9, K Q 10 x and K Q x at notrump contracts is the king. If partner has J x, he may unblock—play the jack. This could cost a trick (and the contract) if the leader has K Q 10 x or K Q x. For example:

#6

		♠ 7 3 2	
		♡ A J 4	
		◇ K 9 5	
		♣ K 8 7 6	

♠ K Q 10 6   ♠ J 4
♡ 9 8 5   ♡ 7 6 3 2
◇ Q J 4 3   ◇ 10 8 2
♣ 10 3   ♣ Q J 9 5

		♠ A 9 8 5	
		♡ K Q 10	
		◇ A 7 6	
		♣ A 4 2	

West	North	East	South
			1NT
Pass	3NT	All Pass	

The king of spades is the normal choice for an opening lead, and if East drops the jack (the recommended play using standard leads), declarer can make his contract by establishing a second spade trick. If the partnership agreement is to lead the queen from K Q 10 9 and the king is led, East should realize the danger of losing a trick and play the four. West will not lead another spade for fear that declarer has the ace-jack. But in this case it makes no difference which other suit he leads, there is no way declarer can win more than eight tricks.

If third hand holds ♠ J x x and his partner leads the king, he should play the middle card, which is usually readable as an encouraging signal.

In the next deal, the queen is led from K Q 10 9 and third hand *must play the jack* if he has it; even if he has more than two cards in the suit.

#7

		♠ 7 3	
		♡ A 10 6	
		◇ Q J 9 2	
		♣ K 8 5 4	

♠ K Q 10 9 2   ♠ J 4
♡ 8 7 5   ♡ Q J 4 3
◇ A 6 4   ◇ 8 5
♣ 6 3   ♣ J 10 9 7 2

		♠ A 8 6 5	
		♡ K 9 2	
		◇ K 10 7 3	
		♣ A Q	

West	North	East	South
			1NT
Pass	3NT	All Pass	

West *leads the queen of spades*, East unblocks by playing the jack and declarer ducks. With the jack out of the way, West has no problem continuing spades and beating the contract. (Without the ace, king or jack, East should play his lowest card regardless of length.)

The queen is also the correct lead from K Q 10 x x x (no nine-spot); if third hand holds J x, it is unlikely that declarer or dummy will have more than three cards in the suit.

Should the queen be led from K Q 10 x x? This is a moot point. You must use your judgment based on the bidding, but in most cases leading the king is better.

Attitude Leads Versus Notrump

At notrump contracts only, the size of the card you lead indicates your "attitude" about the suit led (lead your lowest card from a strong suit, or a higher spot card from a weaker suit); the lead indicates nothing about your length. For example, lead the two from K J 9 2, K J 9 5 2 or K J 9 5 3 2; and lead the eight from 10 8 7 6, 10 8 7 6 4 or 10 8 7 6 4 3; etc. Not knowing the length in the suit makes it difficult for third hand to read the distribution, and this may be why Attitude Leads are not as popular as fourth-highest leads. But one good thing about the convention is that declarer does not know the length either. Experts hate to play against Attitude Leads because of length ambiguity and the inability to use the Rule of Eleven. The following deal shows a case where an Attitude Lead might influence the declarer to make a losing play; one that he would not make if the opponents were using standard fourth-highest leads.

#8

North
♠ 8 6 3
♡ A Q
♢ K Q J 10 7 2
♣ 10 9

South
♠ A J 2
♡ K J 10 6
♢ 8 3
♣ A 6 5 4

West	North	East	South
	1♢	Pass	1♡
Pass	2♢	Pass	3NT
Pass	Pass	Pass	

West leads the two of clubs and East plays the jack. If the opponents were playing normal opening leads, you would assume that West has at most a four-card club suit. Since the defense will not be able to win more than three club tricks, the contract is safe if you *win the first trick* and lead diamonds until the ace is driven out.

However, against an Attitude Lead you do not know how many clubs West has. If West has five clubs and East has the ace of diamonds, you can make your contract by ducking the first club lead unless East shifts to a spade at trick two. You might decide to take that chance and duck, intending to take your ace if a second club is led. The four hands:

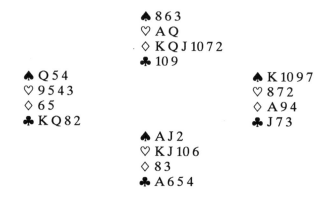

```
                          ♠ 8 6 3
                          ♡ A Q
                          ◇ K Q J 10 7 2
                          ♣ 10 9
      ♠ Q 5 4                                      ♠ K 10 9 7
      ♡ 9 5 4 3                                    ♡ 8 7 2
      ◇ 6 5                                        ◇ A 9 4
      ♣ K Q 8 2                                    ♣ J 7 3
                          ♠ A J 2
                          ♡ K J 10 6
                          ◇ 8 3
                          ♣ A 6 5 4
```

If you duck the first trick, it will be obvious that you have the ace of clubs. And if you have ♠ A Q and ♣ A x x (in which case West has five clubs) a good defender sitting East will realize that the contract cannot be set if he leads a club at trick two. You can exhaust his hand of clubs by holding up your ace until the third round. Therefore, East will shift to the ten of spades (or the nine using Zero or Two Higher), realizing that the best chance to beat the contract is if his partner has the queen of spades.

MUD

This convention applies to leads from three low cards versus trump contracts. Instead of leading the lowest card, as played by the majority of American experts, or leading the top card, which is considered obsolete among most good players, you lead the middle card, intending to play the highest card next and the lowest card last—from 8 5 2, lead the five, next play the eight and then play the two. From this order of play—middle, up, down—MUD gets its name. The trouble with MUD is that third hand cannot read his partner's lead until a second card is played; at trick two, he is usually in the dark. Of course, the declarer also has difficulty figuring out the lead, and this may account for MUD's popularity. Here is an example showing MUD in a good light:

#9   North
                                ♠ 10 6 3
                                ♡ K 8 7
                                ◇ K J 10 6 4
                                ♣ Q 5

                                South
                                ♠ Q 9
                                ♡ A Q J 5 4
                                ◇ A Q
                                ♣ K 10 8 3

West	North	East	South
			1♡
Pass	2♡	2♠	4♡
Pass	Pass	Pass	

West leads the five of spades. East wins with the king and cashes the ace of spades as West follows with the two. East then leads the jack of spades. If West did not play high-low, you should reason he has more than two spades and ruff with a low trump. But West did play high-low, so you ruff with the jack of hearts to prevent an overruff. The four hands:

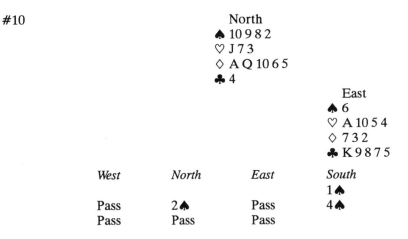

```
                    ♠ 10 6 3
                    ♡ K 8 7
                    ◇ K J 10 6 4
                    ♣ Q 5
      ♠ 8 5 2                        ♠ A K J 7 4
      ♡ 10 9 6 3                     ♡ 2
      ◇ 7 3 2                        ◇ 9 8 5
      ♣ J 7 4                        ♣ A 9 6 2
                    ♠ Q 9
                    ♡ A Q J 5 4
                    ◇ A Q
                    ♣ K 10 8 3
```

Once you ruff with the jack of hearts, West has a natural heart trick and you will be set in a contract you could make if you ruffed the third round of spades low. West made a good deceptive play by playing the two on the second spade lead; even an expert sitting South would likely fall into his trap and ruff the third spade with a high heart. (Yes, leading the eight of spades here—the top card—would work out equally well; but *it is not recommended*.)

Rusinow Leads

This convention was originated by Sydney Rusinow in the 1930s. He contended that the *second-highest card should be led from a sequence, except the higher card should be led from a doubleton*. For example, lead the king from A K x or A K Q; lead the queen from K Q x or K Q J; lead the jack from Q J x or Q J 10; lead the ten from J 10 x or J 10 9; and lead the nine from 10 9 x or 10 9 8. But you lead the higher card from a doubleton—A K, K Q, Q J, J 10, 10 9 or 9 x.

Rusinow recommended that his convention be used on opening lead versus trump contracts only, but not in a suit that partner has bid. At a notrump contract, or at a suit contract if partner has bid the suit, the highest card of the sequence is led.

In the following deal, a Rusinow lead provides a good result:

```
#10                          North
                             ♠ 10 9 8 2
                             ♡ J 7 3
                             ◇ A Q 10 6 5
                             ♣ 4
                                            East
                                            ♠ 6
                                            ♡ A 10 5 4
                                            ◇ 7 3 2
                                            ♣ K 9 8 7 5
```

West	North	East	South
			1♠
Pass	2♠	Pass	4♠
Pass	Pass	Pass	

Your partner leads the king of hearts and, after winning the first trick, continues with the queen of hearts. Since this shows a doubleton heart, *overtake with the ace and lead a heart to give your partner a ruff.* The four hands:

```
                              ♠ 10 9 8 2
                              ♡ J 7 3
                              ◇ A Q 10 6 5
                              ♣ 4
          ♠ A 5 3                                   ♠ 6
          ♡ K Q                                     ♡ A 10 5 4
          ◇ 9 8 4                                   ◇ 7 3 2
          ♣ J 10 6 3 2                              ♣ K 9 8 7 5
                              ♠ K Q J 7 4
                              ♡ 9 8 6 2
                              ◇ K J
                              ♣ A Q
```

If you do not overtake partner's queen of hearts with the ace and give him a ruff, the contract cannot be set. After driving out the ace of spades and drawing trumps, declarer will discard his heart losers on dummy's diamonds.

If not using Rusinow Leads, the usual play is to lead the king and then the queen from either K Q doubleton or K Q x (although in this case, leading low from Q x is better). But if partner does lead the queen, there is a problem whether to play low or overtake.

Ace for Attitude, King for Count

While Rusinow leads against suit contracts have few devotees today, an offspring of this convention has found popularity against notrump contracts. The following agreement is used by some of the world's best partnerships.

Defending at notrump contracts only, the opening leader has an option to lead the ace or king from ace-king combinations. If he wants his partner to signal attitude, he leads the ace; if he wants him to signal count, he leads the king. The king lead is generally made from very strong holdings such as A K J 10; third hand must play any missing honor card—king, queen or jack—if he has one, or else, assuming standard count signals, he must play his highest card from an even number, or his lowest card from an odd number.

Note that this convention reverses the meaning of the recommended opening leads from ace or king in Chapter 1; in which the ace requests an unblock or count, while the king requests attitude.

From sequence holdings not headed by the ace-king, Rusinow Leads are used; *but only at notrump contracts and only on opening lead.* Lead the second-highest card from sequences headed by the king, queen, jack or ten; except lead the higher honor from any doubleton. For example, lead the queen from K Q J x or K Q 10 x; lead the jack from either Q J 10 x or Q J 9 x; lead the ten from J 10 9 x or J 10 8 x; lead the nine from 10 9 8 x or 10 9 7 x. Also, lead the second-highest card from K Q x, Q J x, J 10 x or 10 9 x; but lead the fourth-highest from a four-card or longer suit headed by only a two-card sequence (such as K Q x x, Q J x x, J 10 x x or 10 9 x x). And from a doubleton A K, K Q, Q J, J 10, 10 9 or 9 x, lead the higher card.

Here are two examples showing when to lead the ace, and when to lead the king, from ace-king combinations.

#11

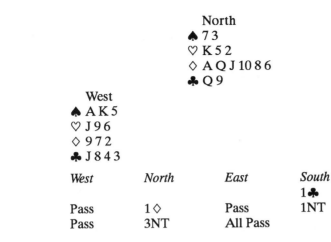

North
♠ 7 3
♡ K 5 2
◇ A Q J 10 8 6
♣ Q 9

West
♠ A K 5
♡ J 9 6
◇ 9 7 2
♣ J 8 4 3

West	North	East	South
			1♣
Pass	1◇	Pass	1NT
Pass	3NT	All Pass	

On this bidding, a spade lead seems the outstanding choice and, since we want to know whether or not partner wants the suit led again, *lead the ace*. The four hands:

♠ 7 3
♡ K 5 2
◇ A Q J 10 8 6
♣ Q 9

♠ A K 5   ♠ Q 10 9 6 4
♡ J 9 6   ♡ 10 8 4 3
◇ 9 7 2   ◇ 5
♣ J 8 4 3   ♣ K 7 2

♠ J 8 2
♡ A Q 7
◇ K 4 3
♣ A 10 6 5

Partner will give you an encouraging signal and you will win the first five spade tricks.

#12

North
♠ 6 5
♡ J 8 4
◇ A 2
♣ K Q 10 9 7 3

West
♠ A K Q 10 4
♡ 7 6 2
◇ 9 8 5 3
♣ 2

West	North	East	South
			1NT
Pass	3NT	All Pass	

This time you are interested in partner's length in the spade suit, so *lead the king of spades* to ask partner to give count. Using normal count signals, partner will play his lowest card from an odd number, or his highest card from an even number. Suppose he plays the two, which is almost surely from three (the only other possibility is a singleton). This means that the declarer has only three spades and you can win the first five spade tricks. The four hands:

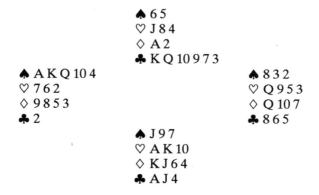

```
                    ♠ 6 5
                    ♡ J 8 4
                    ◇ A 2
                    ♣ K Q 10 9 7 3
   ♠ A K Q 10 4                        ♠ 8 3 2
   ♡ 7 6 2                             ♡ Q 9 5 3
   ◇ 9 8 5 3                           ◇ Q 10 7
   ♣ 2                                 ♣ 8 6 5
                    ♠ J 9 7
                    ♡ A K 10
                    ◇ K J 6 4
                    ♣ A J 4
```

Now suppose your partner signals with the eight of spades under your king and declarer plays the three. As you read earlier, partner is required to play the jack from J 9 8, or the nine from 9 8 x x, so he must have 8 x (except for the remote case of a singleton) and declarer J 9 x x. You cannot run the spade suit. Therefore, you should try to put partner on lead so he can play a spade through declarer. The best chance is to find partner with an ace, so *lead the seven of hearts*. The four hands:

```
                    ♠ 6 5
                    ♡ J 8 4
                    ◇ A 2
                    ♣ K Q 10 9 7 3
   ♠ A K Q 10 4                        ♠ 8 2
   ♡ 7 6 2                             ♡ A 9 5 3
   ◇ 9 8 5 3                           ◇ 10 7 6 4
   ♣ 2                                 ♣ 8 6 5
                    ♠ J 9 7 3
                    ♡ K Q 10
                    ◇ K Q J
                    ♣ A J 4
```

Luckily, partner has the ace of hearts. When he wins the second trick, he will return a spade to defeat the contract by two tricks. This defense would also beat the contract if partner had the ace of clubs instead of the ace of hearts. If you lead a spade at trick two, declarer will make his contract regardless.

Finally, note that if declarer false-cards on the first trick by playing the nine, you cannot be sure whether partner has ♠ 8 2 or ♠ 8 7 3 2—in both cases, he should signal with the eight. Then you have a problem whether to lead another spade or switch suits.

Upside-Down Signals

Upside-Down Signals are, as the title clearly says, the opposite of standard signals. They are generally used for:

(1) Upside-Down Attitude: a high card to discourage the lead and a low card to encourage.

(2) Upside-Down Count: a high card to show an odd number of cards and a low card to show an even number.

Note that the upside-down principle can also be extended to other signals, such as suit-preference, but there is no arguable advantage to this except to catch an unwary declarer.

Upside-down signals have been popular in many foreign countries for thirty years or more. Few Americans used them until recently, but the method is spreading like wildfire in duplicate-bridge circles, especially among expert partnerships. Some authorities contend they are far superior to standard signals and everyone should play them. Are they right? Should you play upside-down signals? Here are some of the pros and cons; you will have to decide for yourself. The first illustration shows no advantage either way; it is just the luck of the spot cards you are dealt.

#13

<pre>
                        North
                        ♠ J 10 4
                        ♡ A 5 2
                        ◇ A K Q J
                        ♣ K 7 6
                                        East
                                        ♠ K Q 2
                                        ♡ K 6
                                        ◇ 9 8 5 3
                                        ♣ Q 10 4 3
</pre>

West	North	East	South
			3♡
Pass	4♡	All Pass	

Your partner gets off to the inspired lead of the ace of spades and you *must play the two* regardless of your signaling agreement because playing the king or queen would give away a trick. The four hands:

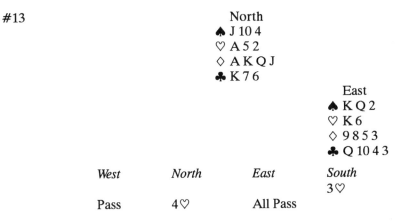

<pre>
                        ♠ J 10 4
                        ♡ A 5 2
                        ◇ A K Q J
                        ♣ K 7 6
        ♠ A 8 7 3   ♠ K Q 2
        ♡ 7   ♡ K 6
        ◇ 10 6 4 2   ◇ 9 8 5 3
        ♣ J 9 8 5   ♣ Q 10 4 3
                        ♠ 9 6 5
                        ♡ Q J 10 9 8 4 3
                        ◇ 7
                        ♣ A 2
</pre>

The only way to beat the contract is if the defense wins the first three spade tricks. This shows a gain for Upside-Down Attitude Signals; the two will encourage another spade lead. If you are playing standard signals, the two-spot may influence your partner to switch suits (in this case to a club).

Now suppose East hold ♠ K Q 9! Then you would be better off playing standard signals; the nine would encourage a spade continuation. But if playing upside-down attitude signals, the nine would be discouraging.

The next deal illustrates an important gain using upside-down attitude signals: The signaler does not have to play a high spot card—which might cost a trick—to give an encouraging signal. It is logical that you can more readily dispense with a higher spot card when you have nothing of value in the suit.

#14

                           North
                           ♠ K Q 8
                           ♡ 6 5 4 3
                           ◇ A K 9 5
                           ♣ Q 10

                                           East
                                       ♠ 7 2
                                     ♡ Q J 7 2
                                     ◇ Q 8 4
                                     ♣ A 9 5 3

West	North	East	South
			1♠
Pass	2◇	Pass	2NT
Pass	3♠	Pass	4♠
Pass	Pass	Pass	

Your partner leads the king of hearts. If you think he is leading from the ace-king, you are not considering the bidding. Declarer could not open without the ace of hearts, so partner predictably is leading from ♡ K x. Regardless of your signaling methods, you should *play the two*; the seven may be a valuable card. The four hands:

                             ♠ K Q 8
                             ♡ 6 5 4 3
                             ◇ A K 9 5
                             ♣ Q 10

♠ 9 6 3   ♠ 7 2
♡ K 9   ♡ Q J 7 2
◇ J 10 7   ◇ Q 8 4
♣ J 8 6 4 2   ♣ A 9 5 3

                             ♠ A J 10 5 4
                             ♡ A 10 8
                             ◇ 6 3 2
                             ♣ K 7

Declarer has four losers (two hearts, one diamond and one club). Assuming declarer ducks the first trick, another heart must be led to drive out the ace; otherwise declarer will have time to establish dummy's fourth diamond to discard his other losing heart. Using upside-down attitude signals, you will play the encouraging two of hearts and your partner will routinely lead another heart. If you are using standard signals, partner should *lead another heart even though you signaled with the discouraging two-spot.* He should realize that there are many holdings you could have where you cannot spare a higher card, such as ♡ Q J 2, ♡ Q J 10 2 or your actual holding.

Yet this is clearly a plus for upside-down signals because, using standard signals, some players would mistakenly signal with the seven; in which case the contract can no longer be set. Whether or not declarer wins the first trick with the ace of hearts, with the seven-spot gone, dummy's fourth heart can be established to provide a discard for his losing diamond.

It is interesting to note that the king of hearts is the best opening lead. If the opening lead were a club to your ace, the winning defense would be hard to imagine: You would have to *shift to the two of hearts*; then, if declarer plays his ace, your partner would have to *unblock by playing the king*.

Upside-down attitude signals may work out badly when third hand must unblock to beat the contract. For example:

#15

North
♠ K
♡ 8 7 2
◇ Q J 10 6 3
♣ A 9 5 4

East
♠ Q 10 2
♡ K J 6 4
◇ 9 8 5
♣ 10 7 3

West	North	East	South
			1NT
Pass	3NT	All Pass	

Your partner leads the six of spades and, using standard signals, you should *play the ten*. If you are playing upside-down attitude signals you have a problem. The four hands:

♠ K
♡ 8 7 2
◇ Q J 10 6 3
♣ A 9 5 4

♠ A 9 7 6 4
♡ 10 5 3
◇ A 4
♣ 8 6 2

♠ Q 10 2
♡ K J 6 4
◇ 9 8 5
♣ 10 7 3

♠ J 8 5 3
♡ A Q 9
◇ K 7 2
♣ K Q J

Suppose you are using upside-down attitude signals and play the two of spades on the first trick to encourage partner to lead the suit again. Declarer must drive out the ace of diamonds before he can win nine tricks. When partner gets the lead with the ace of diamonds, he will lead the four of spades to your queen. Then you lead the ten of spades and declarer ducks; the suit is blocked and declarer makes his contract. If you play the ten of spades on the first trick, you will be leading the two on the third round of spades; declarer would be left with ♠ J 8 and partner with ♠ A 9 7, so your partner will win the next three spade tricks and beat the contract by one trick.

As you read in earlier chapters, at notrump contracts, it may be necessary to save a low card in partner's long suit to play last to avoid blocking the suit. A good player sitting East might recognize the possibility of the spade suit's blocking and play the ten even if using upside-down signals. Since third hand might play the second-highest card from ♠ 10 x x x or ♠ 10 x x as a discouraging signal, his partner may read the ten as an unblocking play from Q-10-x and lead another spade. But this is an ugly situation when playing upside-down attitude signals and even an expert pair might go wrong.

Although there are rare situations where standard signals work out better, most experts agree that upside-down attitude signals are superior.

If you play upside-down attitude signals, should you also play upside-down count signals? People in the know say yes. They believe you can spare a relatively high spot card more readily from an odd number of cards than from an even number. Let's look:

#16

North
♠ K Q 5 2
♡ A 10 4
◇ A Q 3
♣ J 8 6

West
♠ J 9 3
♡ J 8 2
◇ 10 9 7
♣ A K Q 4

West	North	East	South
	1NT	Pass	3♡
Pass	4♡	All Pass	

You lead out your three top clubs, declarer ruffing the last. After drawing three rounds of trumps (partner follows twice, then discards a club), declarer leads the six of spades from his hand. Using standard count signals you would routinely play the three to show an odd number. Using upside-down count signals you should also *play the three*; it should be apparent that the nine of spades may be important. The common-sense rule that you should not signal with a card that may be worth a trick *applies to all forms of signals*. The four hands:

                    ♠ K Q 5 2
                    ♡ A 10 4
                    ◇ A Q 3
                    ♣ J 8 6
♠ J 9 3   ♠ A 7 4
♡ J 8 2   ♡ 7 5
◇ 10 9 7   ◇ 8 6 5 2
♣ A K Q 4   ♣ 10 9 5 3
                    ♠ 10 8 6
                    ♡ K Q 9 6 3
                    ◇ K J 4
                    ♣ 7 2

Declarer will lose two spade tricks if your first spade play is the three, but he can hold his spade losers to one if you play the nine—by finessing through you for the jack.

On the surface it appears that this deal favors the use of standard signals. But no good player would play the nine even if using upside-down count signals. When you play the two, your partner will realize that you might have three and could not spare a higher card to signal.

The next deal favors the use of upside-down count signals:

#17

                                    North
                                    ♠ K Q 5 2
                                    ♡ K J 4
                                    ◇ A 9 6
                                    ♣ K 8 7

West
♠ J 9 7 3
♡ 8 5 2
◇ K Q J
♣ 10 6 3

West	North	East	South
	1NT	Pass	3♡
Pass	4♡	All Pass	

Your king-of-diamonds lead is won with dummy's ace. Declarer draws two rounds of hearts with the king and ace as partner follows suit. The six of spades is led toward dummy. Using Upside- Down Count Signals, you routinely play the three to show an even number. Using standard count signals it is tempting to play the seven to show an even number; but you should *play the three because the seven might be important*. The four hands:

                              ♠ K Q 5 2
                              ♡ K J 4
                              ◇ A 9 6
                              ♣ K 8 7

♠ J 9 7 3   ♠ A 4
♡ 8 5 2   ♡ 7 6
◇ K Q J   ◇ 10 8 4 3 2
♣ 10 6 3   ♣ Q J 9 5

                              ♠ 10 8 6
                              ♡ A Q 10 9 3
                              ◇ 7 5
                              ♣ A 4 2

Declarer has four losers (two spades, one diamond and one club) and will lose them all if your first spade play is the three. (True, looking at all four hands declarer could make his contract by letting the six of spades ride, but this is farfetched; declarer intends to play the king or queen from the dummy.)

If you are playing standard count signals and make the mistake of signaling with the seven, declarer can establish the five of spades as a winner to discard his losing club. Here is how he does it: After your partner captures dummy's king of spades with his ace and you win a diamond trick, declarer will regain the lead and play the eight of spades:

(1) If you play the three of spades, he can play low from dummy and win the trick.

(2) If you cover the eight of spades with the nine, he will win with dummy's queen. Now the dummy has ♠ 5 2, declarer ♠ 10 and you ♠ J 3. You will win the next spade trick with your jack, but the dummy's five-spot is high and declarer can discard his club loser. Don't you wish you had the seven of spades back?

Earlier in the book are illustrations where you lead a king and it is hard to tell whether your partner's signal is for attitude or count. For those of you intending to play upside-down count signals, it is a good idea to bring it up again. When your partner leads the king from a suit in which dummy has length, it was recommended that you consistently play the higher card from a doubleton, and do it promptly (to hesitate before playing from a doubleton in this situation amounts to cheating). This may help your partner distinguish whether you have a singleton or a doubleton. For example:

#18

North
♠ Q 10 7 6 3
♡ 10 9 8 2
♢ K 5 4
♣ 7

West
♠ A K J 9 4
♡ A Q
♢ 9 7 3
♣ 6 5 2

West	North	East	South
			1♡
1♠	2♡	Pass	3♡
Pass	4♡	All Pass	

You lead the king of spades (or the ace if playing ace from ace-king), partner plays the five and declarer the two. If your agreement is to use standard count signals in this situation, you know declarer has the missing eight-spot and you can set the contract by leading another spade. The four hands:

♠ Q 10 7 6 3
♡ 10 9 8 2
♢ K 5 4
♣ 7

♠ A K J 9 4   ♠ 5
♡ A Q   ♡ 5 3
♢ 9 7 3   ♢ J 10 8 6 2
♣ 6 5 2   ♣ K Q 9 8 4

♠ 8 2
♡ K J 7 6 4
♢ A Q
♣ A J 10 3

If you do not lead a spade at trick two, declarer can make his contract by discarding his spade loser on the king of diamonds. Declarer missed a good chance to false-card. If he had played the eight of spades on the first trick, you would not have known whether partner began with ♠ 5 2 or ♠ 5.

Now suppose you are playing upside-down count signals, in which case partner should play the lower card from a doubleton. If your partner plays the five and declarer the eight, you know declarer has the two. But if partner plays the five and declarer the two, you cannot tell who has the eight; hence the right deceptive play by declarer from ♠ 8 2 is the two.

Note that the deceptive procedure for you, as declarer, in most cases is to signal with your spot cards the same way as your opponents. Versus standard signals, play a higher card than third hand if you would like the suit led again, or play your lowest card if you prefer a switch of suits. Versus upside-down signals, play your lowest card is you want the suit led again, or a higher card than third hand if you prefer a switch of suits.

Lavinthal Discards

Hy Lavinthal is credited with originating the Suit-Preference Signal in the 1930s, and using Lavinthal Discards a defender's first discard is suit-preference. This is a popular convention in duplicate bridge circles, and here is how it works: *Make your first discard in a suit you do not want led* and play the highest card you can spare to ask for the higher-ranking suit (other than the one being led and the one in which you are making the discard), or discard the lowest card to ask for the lower-ranking suit. To demonstrate, here is an example without actual cards:

#19

```
                          North
                        ♠ x x x
                        ♡ x x x
                        ◇ x x x x
                        ♣ x x x
                                          East
                                        ♠ x x x x
                                        ♡ x
                                        ◇ x x x x
                                        ♣ x x x x
```

West	*North*	*East*	*South*
			1♡
Pass	2♡	Pass	4♡
Pass	Pass	Pass	

Suppose partner leads a heart, and hearts are led again at trick two. You must make a discard: If you want a spade lead, discard a high diamond or a high club; if you want a diamond lead, discard a high spade or your lowest club; if you want a club lead, discard your lowest spade or your lowest diamond.

Now let's put some real cards in these hands:

```
                          North
                        ♠ Q 8 6
                        ♡ J 9 6
                        ◇ Q 4 3 2
                        ♣ K 7 5
                                          East
                                        ♠ A 10 5 2
                                        ♡ 4
                                        ◇ K 10 9 7
                                        ♣ 9 8 6 2
```

With the bidding as given above, the opponents reach a contract of four hearts and partner leads the two of hearts. Declarer wins the first trick and leads the king of hearts, which partner wins with the ace. It seems that a diamond lead from partner is best, so *discard the two of clubs*, which tells partner not to lead a club, and to lead the lower-ranking of the other two suits. The four hands:

```
                            ♠ Q 8 6
                            ♡ J 9 6
                            ◇ Q 4 3 2
                            ♣ K 7 5
            ♠ J 7 3                              ♠ A 10 5 2
            ♡ A 7 2                              ♡ 4
            ◇ J 8 5                              ◇ K 10 9 7
            ♣ Q 10 4 3                           ♣ 9 8 6 2
                            ♠ K 9 4
                            ♡ K Q 10 8 5 3
                            ◇ A 6
                            ♣ A J
```

Declarer has four losers (two spades, one heart and one diamond), and if partner shifts to a diamond, he will lose them all.

Count Discards

This convention is popular in duplicate-bridge circles and is relatively easy to play. It is used when making your first discard. You *discard from a suit you do not want led* and give count: Assuming you are playing standard count signals, play high-low with an even number, or play low-high with an odd number.[1] For example:

#20   North
                                           ♠ A 8 5
                                           ♡ K J 9 6 3
                                           ◇ Q 2
                                           ♣ Q 7 5

            West
            ♠ 10 9 6 4
            ♡ 10 4
            ◇ A J 9 5
            ♣ K 10 3

West	North	East	South
			1♡
Pass	3♡	Pass	4♡
Pass	Pass	Pass	

You lead the four of spades to partner's jack and declarer's king. Declarer cashes two high hearts and your partner discards the three of diamonds to *show an odd number* and discourage a diamond lead. Now declarer leads the four of diamonds and you should *play the ace*. If partner has three worthless diamonds, declarer has four to the king; there is no way to set the contract. But if partner has five diamonds, you might be endplayed if you do not go up with your ace. The four hands:

---

1. Count discards do not show suit-preference, but in most cases your partner can tell which of the other two suits to lead from an analysis of the bidding and/or from the appearance of the dummy.

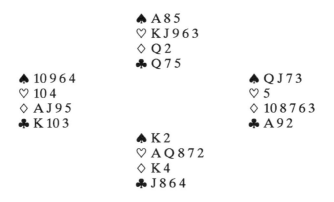

Declarer has four losers (one diamond and three clubs) and must lose three club tricks if he leads the suit first. If you win the first diamond trick and lead a spade or another diamond, declarer must break the clubs. But if you duck the first diamond lead, declarer will win the fourth trick with the queen of diamonds, cash the ace of spades, ruff a spade, then lead the king of diamonds. When you win with the ace, you are forced to break the club suit or give a ruff-and-discard. Declarer would have been more deceptive if he had led the four of diamonds at trick two, giving your partner no chance to give the count signal in diamonds. But that would risk suffering a club ruff if the suit divides four-two.

Here is a related deal to compare; your partner's hand and declarer's hand have been changed. Your partner discards the eight of diamonds on the second heart lead to indicate an even number, so you have nothing to lose (and a trick to gain) by ducking the four of diamonds.

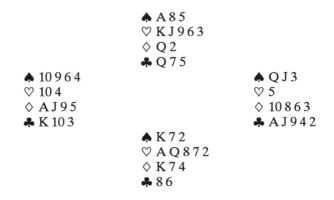

Your partner's eight-of-diamonds discard on the second heart lead shows an even number, which means declarer has an odd number of diamonds, almost surely three. With the cards as shown, if you duck the four-of-diamonds lead, declarer will lose four tricks (one spade, one diamond and two clubs). If you go up with the ace of diamonds when the four is led, declarer can discard a spade from dummy on his king of diamonds and make his contract.

Odd-Even Discards

This is a signaling method of increasing popularity used when *discarding*.[2] The discard of an odd-numbered card (9, 7, 5 or 3) encourages the lead of that suit. Whereas the discard of an even-numbered card (10, 8, 6, 4 or 2) discourages the lead, and may be a suit-preference signal if the discarder has two or more even cards. A high even card asks for a switch to the higher-ranking suit; a low even card asks for the lower-ranking suit. Here is one example:

#21

```
                              North
                              ♠ 7 4 3 2
                              ♡ K 4
                              ◇ A Q 10 8
                              ♣ 9 8 3
                                                  East
                                                  ♠ 6
                                                  ♡ 10 9 8 7 2
                                                  ◇ K J 9 3
                                                  ♣ 10 6 5
```

West	North	East	South
			1♠
Pass	2♠	Pass	4♠
Pass	Pass	Pass	

Partner leads the five of spades and declarer wins the first trick with the eight. The king of spades is led, partner wins with the ace and you are in a position to guide your partner's next lead by your discard. If you want a heart lead, discard the seven of hearts—encouraging—or the ten of clubs—discouraging clubs and suit preference for hearts. If you want a club lead, discard the five of clubs—encouraging—or the two of hearts—discouraging hearts and suit preference for clubs. But you desperately want a diamond lead, and since discarding a diamond may waste a trick, *discard the ten of hearts*—discouraging hearts and suit preference for diamonds. You could also ask for a diamond lead by discarding the six of clubs, but that would be foolish; partner may not recognize it as your lowest even club. The four hands:

```
                         ♠ 7 4 3 2
                         ♡ K 4
                         ◇ A Q 10 8
                         ♣ 9 8 3
    ♠ A 9 5                                    ♠ 6
    ♡ Q 6 3                                    ♡ 10 9 8 7 2
    ◇ 6 5 2                                    ◇ K J 9 3
    ♣ K J 7 4                                  ♣ 10 6 5
                         ♠ K Q J 10 8
                         ♡ A J 5
                         ◇ 7 4
                         ♣ A Q 2
```

---

2. Odd-Even Signals can also be used when following suit to partner's lead. However, these signals are disallowed in most American tournaments. One reason is that some practitioners tend to play out of tempo when they lack an appropriate odd or even card, thus conveying illegal information to partner.

Declarer has four losers (one spade, one diamond and two clubs). If your partner leads a heart or a club at trick three, declarer has an easy time making his contract. True, partner can lead a spade without jeopardizing a trick, but without guidance it would be tempting to lead a club: If you had the ace of clubs, or the queen of clubs and ◇ K x x x or ◇ K x x, it would be important to win club tricks before declarer can discard on dummy's diamonds. But your ten-of-hearts signal tells your partner to lead a diamond, and declarer will be set when all of his finesses fail.

The Smith Echo

Attributed to I. G. Smith of Great Britain, this signaling convention (especially popular in Europe) is used only at notrump contracts to reveal whether you have a good or poor holding in the suit led at trick one. The signal is given by the size of the card you play the first time declarer leads a suit: Assuming the card you play is not to win or promote a trick, or to give a vital count signal, *follow with the highest card you can spare if you have a good holding in the suit led at trick one, or follow with your lowest card from a poor holding*. The signal may be given by third hand to indicate whether he has any remaining strength in partner's suit, or by the opening leader to indicate whether he wants his partner to return his lead or switch suits.[3] For example:

#22

```
                North
                ♠ 7
                ♡ A K J 7
                ◇ 10 9 6 5
                ♣ Q 5 4 3
                                    East
                                    ♠ A Q 5
                                    ♡ Q 10 4 3
                                    ◇ 8 2
                                    ♣ 10 7 6 2
```

West	North	East	South
			1NT
Pass	2♣	Pass	2♠
Pass	3NT	All Pass	

Your partner leads the four of spades, you play the queen and declarer wins with the king. At trick two, the king of diamonds is led, your partner wins with the ace and you *play the eight* to signal partner to continue leading spades. The four hands:

---

3. Some, especially in Europe, play this signal *by the opening leader* in reverse. The opening leader plays a high card to discourage partner from returning his suit.

```
                          ♠ 7
                          ♡ A K J 7
                          ◇ 10 9 6 5
                          ♣ Q 5 4 3
        ♠ J 9 6 4 3                              ♠ A Q 5
        ♡ 8 2                                    ♡ Q 10 4 3
        ◇ A 7 4                                  ◇ 8 2
        ♣ J 9 8                                  ♣ 10 7 6 2
                          ♠ K 10 8 2
                          ♡ 9 6 5
                          ◇ K Q J 3
                          ♣ A K
```

Seeing your high diamond spot, partner leads another spade. The defense wins the next four spade tricks. Note that the contract cannot be set if your first spade play is the ace. See #5 on page 46 for another example showing the merits of third hand playing the queen from ace-queen.

You may be thinking: Suppose you held ◇ 3 2 and played the three. With the eight and the two missing, partner could not tell whether you had ◇ 8 3 or ◇ 3 2. This is one of the drawbacks of the Smith Echo—when your partner can see only one card, he cannot always read whether the card you have played is encouraging or discouraging. In this case, your partner should probably duck the first diamond lead and win the second. Then, he sees you play two diamonds and will know exactly what your signal means.

In the next deal, your partner's hand and dummy's hand are the same, the bidding and the opening lead are the same, but declarer's hand and yours have been changed so the winning defense is for your partner not to continue leading spades.

```
                          ♠ 7
                          ♡ A K J 7
                          ◇ 10 9 6 5
                          ♣ Q 5 4 3
        ♠ J 9 6 4 3                              ♠ Q 8 5
        ♡ 8 2                                    ♡ Q 10 4 3
        ◇ A 7 4                                  ◇ 8 3
        ♣ J 9 8                                  ♣ A 10 6 2
                          ♠ A K 10 2
                          ♡ 9 6 5
                          ◇ K Q J 2
                          ♣ K 7
```

After capturing your queen of spades with his king, the declarer leads the king of diamonds, partner ducks, and you play the three. Since you might have ◇ 3 2, partner cannot be sure which signal you are giving. But when declarer leads another diamond and partner wins with the ace, you play the eight to confirm that the three-spot was your lowest diamond. He should therefore switch suits, the attractive choice being to lead a heart. With normal play, declarer will win only eight tricks. But if partner leads another spade after he takes the ace of diamonds, declarer will score a ninth trick with the ten of spades.

Present Count

This convention is used when a defender has played a high card the first time a suit was led (to win or to help promote a trick), and wishes to advise partner about length the *second* time the suit is led.[4] The signal may be given by either defender; it doesn't matter whether he is leading the suit, following suit, or discarding. The highest non-useful card shows an even number, the lowest card shows an odd number. *Note that the count is for the number of cards held when the signal is given: present count.*

The most common usage is when returning partner's suit. For example, suppose your partner leads a spot card versus a notrump contract, you win with the ace and decide to return the suit: If your current holding is 7 3, return the seven; if your current holding is 7 6 3, return the three; if your current holding is J 7 6 3, return the seven (assuming you cannot spare the jack); if your current holding is J 7 6 5 3, return the three; if your current holding is J 10 9 5 3 2, return the jack.

Note that the standard procedure of returning fourth-highest from an original five-card or longer holding is not as easy for your partner to read as returning the highest or lowest card you can spare: From A 7 6 5 3, the seven is easier for partner to read than the five; and from A 7 6 5 3 2, the two is easier to read than the five. Of course, partner must determine whether you began with three or five (or four or six), but he knows it is not four (or five)—two apart is easier to read.

Here is one example where the signal is given by discarding on a suit led by the declarer:

#23

<pre>
                            North
                            ♠ 8 7 4
                            ♡ A K Q J
                            ◇ Q 5 2
                            ♣ A 6 4
        West
        ♠ 5
        ♡ 9 8 6 5 3
        ◇ K 7
        ♣ K Q 10 9 7
</pre>

West	North	East	South
	1NT	Pass	4♠
Pass	Pass	Pass	

You lead the king of clubs. Declarer wins with dummy's ace, plays a low spade to his king and continues with the queen of spades. You should *discard the ten of clubs* to show that you currently have an even number, which must be four—you could not afford to discard the ten if you had just the queen-ten left. Here are the four hands to show how this guides your partner into the winning defense:

---

4. Present Count can also be used after playing a spot card to give an attitude signal, but then there is a conflict with suit preference. Inexperienced partnerships should ignore this.

```
                         ♠ 8 7 4
                         ♡ A K Q J
                         ◇ Q 5 2
                         ♣ A 6 4
   ♠ 5                                        ♠ A 3 2
   ♡ 9 8 6 5 3                                ♡ 7 4
   ◇ K 7                                      ◇ A J 6 4
   ♣ K Q 10 9 7                               ♣ J 8 3 2
                         ♠ K Q J 10 9 6
                         ♡ 10 2
                         ◇ 10 9 8 3
                         ♣ 5
```

Your partner wins the third trick with the ace of spades. As stated, your ten-of-clubs discard revealed that you have four cards remaining in the suit (you began with five); consequently, declarer has a singleton club. Realizing that the only chance to beat the contract is to win three diamond tricks before declarer can discard on dummy's hearts, your partner *leads the four of diamonds*. By winning with your king and returning a diamond, you set the contract.